COLOURED RICE
Symbolic Structure in Hindu Family Festivals

STUDIES IN SOCIOLOGY AND SOCIAL ANTHROPOLOGY

Editor
M. N. Srinivas
Associate Editor
A. M. Shah
Editorial Advisers
T. Scarlett Epstein, Owen M. Lynch, T. K. Oommen

Other Titles in the Series

Biplab Dasgupta (ed.), *Village Studies in the Third World*
A. L. Epstein (ed.), *The Craft of Social Anthropology*
Prasanta S. Majumdar and Ila Majumdar, *Rural Migrants in an Urban Setting* (out-of-print)
Miriam Sharma, *The Politics of Inequality*
T. Scarlett Epstein, *Capitalism, Primitive and Modern*
M. N. Srinivas, *India : Social Structure*
Rhoda Lois Blumberg and Leela Dwaraki, *India's Educated Women* (out-of-print)
Raja Jayaraman, *Caste and Class*
Leela Gulati, *Profiles in Female Poverty*
N. R. Sheth, *The Social Framework of an Indian Factory*
Paul Hershman, *Punjabi Kinship and Marriage*
Barbara Joshi, *Democracy in Search of Equality*
J. S. Gandhi, *Lawyers and Touts*
Yvonne J. Arterburn, *The Loom of Interdependence*
Chitra Sivakumar, *Education, Social Inequality and Social Change in Karnataka*
A. R. Radcliffe-Brown, *Method in Social Anthropology* (edited by M. N. Srinivas)
Owen M. Lynch (ed.), *Culture and Community in Europe*
T. K. Oommen, *Social Structure and Politics*
M. A. S. Rajan, *Land Reforms in Karnataka*
Milton Singer, *Man's Glassy Essence*
Anthony R. Walker, *The Toda of South India : A New Look*
Dinesh Khosla, *Myth and Reality of the Protection of Civil Rights Law*
Bruce Elliot Tapper, *Rivalry and Tribute*
A. M. Shah and I. P. Desai, *Division and Hierarchy*

COLOURED RICE
Symbolic Structure in Hindu Family Festivals

SUZANNE HANCHETT

With contributions by
STANLEY REGELSON

HINDUSTAN PUBLISHING CORPORATION
DELHI   1988

COLOURED RICE
Symbolic Structure in Hindu Family Festivals

ISBN 81-7075-006-7

Printed in India by
Hindustan Publishing Corporation Press
C-74, Okhla Industrial Area, Phase-I
New Delhi-110 020

For Mimi Regelson
and
Dave and Kay French

CONTENTS

PREFACE

The original data on social structure and symbolic systems presented here are the product of 21 months of field study of two rural villages in India. In 1966-67 Dr. Stanley Regelson and I lived for sixteen months in the villages we came to call 'ours'. His work was financed by a grant from the National Science Foundation Dissertation Improvement Program and my own by a grant from the National Institute of Mental Health. A writing fellowship from the American Council of Learned Societies provided release time in 1975 for the conception and initial drafting of this manuscript. During subsequent summers I returned to India, re-checking data for this study while pursuing research on ethnobotany under grants from the American Institute of Indian Studies (in 1976) and the Fulbright Faculty Research Abroad Program (in 1977).

In the villages I call Chinnapura and Bandipur, the duration of our joint work and the great skill of our assistants enabled us to gather a wide range of cultural and social survey data. The villagers came to know us as friends and their patient good will has been our best guarantee of accuracy over the years. In order to respect the confidentiality we promised them and in gratitude for their extraordinary candour, we have used fictitious names for their villages.

We were sufficiently fluent in the Kannada language to converse and read simple materials but interviews were generally conducted with the aid of four able interpreters, our project assistants, Joyce George, A. G. George, K. Gurulingaiah, and (in 1976) H. Malathi. Though we were able to monitor our interpreters' translations of villagers' comments, we still relied on them for subtle and complex translations. In these modern villages many residents travelled and were educated; several spoke English.

Our survey interviewers, P. Jayamma, K. Rangaraju, Malla Setty, H. Bettaiah, Dakshina Murthy and Mr. Sivanna were all high school educated and spoke and wrote English. The first four of these were residents of Bandipur or Chinnapura. Not only did they provide us with excellent and conscientious assistance over our first research trip, but they also opened their homes and those of their neighbours to us, making sure that we had good friends and trustworthy informants in all the neighbourhoods of each village.

xii

Dr. Regelson and I maintained a house in each of the two villages. The first eight months of our stay were spent in Bandipur; thereafter Dr. Regelson shifted almost completely to Chinnapura for the remaining eight months. I commuted between the two villages, staying a few days of each week in each place until I had completed a full year in Bandipur; then I too shifted to Chinnapura as my primary base. This pattern of travel was similar to that of some of our village neighbours who had relatives in both places. The villages were only two miles apart; both news and people travelled easily between them.

The descriptions of Chinnapura are recorded in the ethnographic present tense, the timeless form in which anthropologists talk of vanished systems. In 1967 Chinnapura was in fact facing its own extinction, since engineers and contractors resident in Bandipur had already begun construction on a dam that was to flood the whole peninsula in which Chinnapura was settled. Many families had begun to plan new lives elsewhere, though facing such a possibility was easier for Brahmans and the landless labourers than for the vigorous non-Brahmans. Anxiety over the pending crisis was high during our period of residence there, but meanwhile the non-Brahmans and several others had made the choice to go on living as usual as long as they could.

My last view of Chinnapura as an intact community was in 1967. By the time I returned to the area in 1976 all that remained was one high roof forming a small island in a large lake.

A number of friends and colleagues have assisted me in preparing this manuscript. I gratefully acknowledge the help of the following individuals, most of whom have given much time to reviewing drafts and providing information and encouragement in many ways. Special thanks to Gorur Ramaswamy Iyengar, G. S. Gopala Setty, Smt. Shardamma, G. S. Sampath Iyengar, Smt. Rathnamma, the Garudachar family, Lawrence A. Babb, Susan Bean, Brenda E. F. Beck, Joerg Bose, Richard L. Brubaker, Leslie (Casale) Evechild, Barbara S. Clark, Doranne Jacobson, Owen M. Lynch, A. K. Ramanujan, Alan Roland, Rev. Fr. Cecil J. Saldanha, and Prof. A. M. Shah. Thanks also to Lisa Merrill for typing assistance, and to H. Malathi for both research and typing help. Hilda Fourman helped with major editing tasks. Carol Francis did the illustrations. Professors Conrad M. Arensberg, Abraham Rosman, and Robert Murphy inspired and supervised much of the research work on which this book is based.

In transliterating Kannada terms I tend to use local pronunciations rather than dictionary spellings when the two differ. Because of printing requirements, Kannada transliterations appear in the text without the diacritical marks that indicate correct pronunciation. Full transliterations, with diacritics, are only in the Glossary.

SUZANNE HANCHETT

New York
March, 1988

PLATES

ILLUSTRATIONS

TABLES

TEXTS

TRANSLITERATION OF KANNADA TERMS

ಅ	a	ಘ್	gh	ನ್	n	ಹ್	h
ಆ	ā	ಚ್	c	ಪ್	p	ಳ್	ḷ
ಇ	ı	ಛ್	ch	ಫ್	ph	ೞ್	ḻ
ಈ	ī	ಜ್	j	ಬ್	b		
ಉ	u	ಟ್	ṭ	ಭ್	bh		
ಊ	ū	ಠ್	ṭh	ಮ್	m		
ಎ	ę, (y)e-	ಡ್	ḍ	ಯ್	y		
ಏ	ē	ಢ್	ḍh	ರ್	r		
ಐ	ai	ಣ್	ṇ	ಲ್	l		
ಒ	o; (v)o-	ತ್	t	ವ್	v		
ಓ	ō	ಥ್	th	ಶ್	ś		
ಔ	au	ದ್	d	ಷ್	ṣ		
ಕ್	k	ಧ್	dh	ಸ್	s		
ಖ್	kh						
ಗ್	g						

INTRODUCTION

As the social anthropology of South Asia is coming into its own as a mature discipline, many questions still remain to be studied. An enduring folklorists' paradise—the field commonly called popular Hinduism—invites the anthropologists to revisit, to investigate the nature of ordinary Hindus' lives and views in the light of recent developments in anthropological theory and method.

What is the Hindu family as a cultural institution? What is the position of women in it? What can we learn from the popular myths and rituals?

It is the assumption of this study that village family festivals provide an insight into meanings beyond what their homespun contents might suggest. Thus, Hinduism studies have an important role to play in the development of research and theory on cultural symbolic systems. Each of the four festivals at the core of this book reflects (and reflects on) the family; together the four present an image of the family which is rarely, if ever, spelled out in words. Although most of the basic data used here represent one local, multi-caste tradition of Karnataka, south India, the symbolic themes and variations which they suggest are pan-Indian.

The folk festival is one of India's greatest arts. It ornaments the daily life of Hindu villagers with ritual and mythic designs. Festival activities, choreographed around vessels of water, give form to cultural concepts of men and women, of the family as a whole, of life and death.

The coloured foods offered in the festivals are intended to delight the gods and, therefore, reflect a Hindu sense of pleasing and appropriate form, symbolising the worshippers' profound beliefs. The festival combination of form, thought and feeling, studied as an art form, reveals socio-cultural meanings that dance through the patterns of mythic motifs and ritual offerings or actions.

The outward forms of Hindu festivals are everchanging. Each generation and every locality creates, destroys and recreates its cultural images through them. The ephemeral nature of festival practices has preoccupied several generations of scholars both in India and abroad. Though varying in details, they continue a vital and significant element of family life.

The central thesis of this book is that the myths and rites of Hindu family festivals are symbolic formulations which express and define the concept of family. In their very designs the festivals present ways of thinking and feeling about the family that supplement concepts available through language or day-to-day practice. In this function they represent a special development of the universal human effort to give meaning to daily life and social organisation. It is the Hindu art to use a wide variety of sense experiences (colours, tastes, physical images) and mythic motifs in building symbolic edifices. These non-verbal symbolic structures give form to otherwise nameless experiences and processes.

The nature, purposes and problems of the Hindu family, as highlighted in festival symbolism, may remain nameless but they do not therefore remain formless. These symbolic formulations-without-words have shapes which are richer and subtler than language can provide. While linguistic discourse can identify norms, values and other relatively conscious propositions, festival art can give a deeper and wider view.

Susanne Langer has called such representations "presentational symbolism." She coined the term to demonstrate that a picture, for example, or other artistic image presents itself as a whole rather than in a linear or discursive series as a spoken or written sentence must do. The simultaneous presentation of all the constituent parts of the whole enables the picture to represent or symbolise many ideas all at once. The concepts represented, made up of many small but connected parts, can incorporate relations-within-relations with great freedom, because their development is not limited by vocabulary or syntactic rules. (See Langer 1957 : 93-95 for further discussion of this concept)

The view of the family which emerges from festival symbolism is a picture of the Hindu family more complex than local statements of what a family is supposed to be. Local talk about the family emphasises its virtues and strengths and these are real qualities. The festival metaphors, however, convey a more complicated image of an institution which, like all man-made constructs, is vulnerable and embattled, a family whose members must work to ensure its continuity in the face of clear and present dangers.

What follows is based on a microscopic study of some family festivals of south India's Karnataka State. In the study Dr. Stanley Regelson and I used several scholarly approaches in our joint attempt to understand folk Hinduism and the way of life of which it is an integral part. Each approach, whether sociological, conceptual or structuralist, has plied the phenomenon with special questions or meaning. Hinduism has answered some of these questions while always raising others. Much still remains a cultural enigma.

In attempting to cast light on these mysteries, we collected and analysed much particular detail, but the goals are general and the conclusions applicable to similar practices in other areas. Part I introduces the communities of our ethnographic research, reviewing basic patterns of organisation among their families. Here I will also discuss some of the methods I have found useful in analysing folk festivals for their symbolic meaning. The use of colour and food pre-eminent in symbolic structure will be illustrated in such patterns as the offering ritual called *puja*, a configuration of elements whose totality expresses meaning for family life.

Part II will present a detailed view of the myths and rituals of some family festivals, offering conclusions about the ways in which they assist families in struggling with such fundamental issues as personal and family integrity, proper social obligations and roles, and the forces affecting a family's auspices for movement and growth.

Part I
THE CULTURAL SETTING

Chapter 1

THE VILLAGES

The villages we call Bandipur and Chinnapura[1] lie in different subdivisions of Hassan District, Karnataka State. Bandipur is in Hassan Taluk; Chinnapura, only two miles away, in Alur Taluk. Both are settlements with a long history.[2] An inscribed stone from the sixteenth century indicates that Bandipur had already been occupied for a long time before that period. Most of the permanent residents' families have occupied their existing homes for over 100 years.

Hassan, though one of the smaller districts of Karnataka, has been of central importance in the state's history. On the eastward slopes of the Western Ghat mountain range, the district lies in the path of many influences. Jains passed through, perhaps as early as the third century B.C., followed by at least seven major ruling Hindu dynasties, important religious philosophers including Sankara and Ramanuja, Muslim rulers and occasional Maratha invaders. A series of relatively tolerant kings left a tradition of friendly rivalry among several schools of Hindu thought, such as Saivism, Sri-Vaisnavism, Virasaivism and others—a heritage the present population continues to possess.

The district has maintained a reputation of political stability and conservatism through a history that has exposed it to several forms of rule. Hoysala monarchs of the eleventh to fourteenth centuries relied on the loyalty of the area's people. Palegars (feudal lords) of the fourteenth to seventeenth centuries lived in walled enclaves in both villages and paid tribute from their fiefdoms to the Vijayanagar emperors. As part of the Mysore Territory since 1694, Hassan District remained for some forty years under the hegemony of the autocratic Muslim rulers, Haidar Ali and his son Tipu Sultan. After Tipu Sultan was defeated in a valiant battle against the British in 1799, this region entered the

7

colonial period as the heartland of the princely state of Mysore and the home of several coffee plantation managers. Through Independence struggles and India's growth as a new, modern nation, this region has offered many sacrifices and contributions in the creation of new models for rural living.

For this study it is important to recognize that as early as 500-1000 A.D. south India was an integral part of the whole subcontinent. There was constant north-south traffic along this major route. Rapid diffusion of ideas marks the subcontinent as a whole, and Karnataka communities made their own contributions at key points in history. Therefore, it is not surprising if pan-Indian themes appear in the local folk culture.

Of importance in this region is the consistency and continuity of Hindu pre-eminence. Except for a brief period of Muslim rule at the end of the eighteenth century, Hassan District has been something of a sanctuary for indigenous religious groups, both Hindu and heterodox. The Vijayanagar empire literally fended off Muslim rule for over three centuries. Even after its capital city of Hampi was conquered and destroyed by Muslim sultans, this region still passed 150 years under the rule of the ardently Vaisnava Wodeyar dynasty before succumbing to the control of Haidar Ali.

BANDIPUR VILLAGE

Bandipur is a modern Indian village by any standards. It is electrified, has automobiles and one or two telephones; it is a center of transportation, shopping, crafts, services and entertainment for its immediate region. It has a relatively large indigenous population by local standards, with 1,510 permanent residents occupying 263 houses. 91.7% of these persons are Hindu; the Muslims are a minority (see Table 1).

As is typical of such south Indian Brahman villages, the Bandipur population includes a local land-holding elite, cosmopolitan Indians who have lived at times in large cities, together with educated mercantile groups. It also includes farmers and craftsmen or service castes who are most at home in rural settings. A more itinerant contingent, the landless labourers, includes many who alternate between rural and urban areas out of economic necessity.

CASTES

The thirteen Hindu castes (*jatis*) of Bandipur fall into three major groupings, two of which may be described as Mandelbaum (1970 : 19) termed them : *jati*-clusters. It is common for India's villagers to group into larger units of this sort on the basis of life-styles or other common features. The residents of Bandipur live in neighbourhoods according to their Brahman, non-Brahman or A.K. affiliations (though the first two are not entirely separated), with Muslims living among non-Brahman neighbours and socialising easily among them. A.K. is a shorthand name for the group also called Harijan, Holeya or the stagmatised

Table 1—Indigenous Population of Bandipur, 1966-67

Jati-cluster	Jati (Kannada Name)	No. of Households	Population	Percentages of Population	
				Jati	Jati-cluster
Brahman	Iyengar	45	220	14.6	16% Brahman
	Smartha	4	16	1.0	
	Sanketi	1	6	0.4	
Non-Brahman	Farmer (Okkaliga)	46	314	21.0	45.6% Non-Brahman
	Weaver (Devanga)	20	111	7.4	
	Oil Presser (Ganiga)	11	57	3.8	
	Fisherman (Besta)	11	53	3.5	
	Toddy Tapper (Idiga)	6	44	2.9	
	Washerman (Agasa)	7	42	2.9	
	Smith (Acari)	6	38	2.6	
	Barber (Hajama)	5	29	2.0	
A.K.	A. K. (Adikarnataka, Holeya)	79	446	29.6	29.6% A.K./A.D.
A.D.	(Adidravida, Madiga)	1	4		
Muslim		21	130	8.3	8.3% Muslim
	Totals	263	1,510	100%	100%

'untouchables'. A.K. stands for Adikarnataka, a Kannada name meaning 'original people of the Karnataka country'.

A *jati*-cluster is a group of different castes, or *jatis*, that are considered to be socially similar, though the *jati* continues to be the endogamous unit. Each *jati* remains associated with a particular occupation and is ranked in a purity-pollution, commensality hierarchy as it traditionally has been. For example, there are three distinct Brahman *jatis* in Bandipur, but to outsiders they are all Brahmans. They do not condone intermarriage and their orthodox members will not eat together with the other kinds of Brahmans. Still, they live in the same neighbourhood and they encourage their children to play together. They also see a common role for themselves as an educated and relatively affluent elite in the village community.

The middle-level non-Brahmans, on the other hand, are a diverse group, some of whom get on easily with Brahmans, while others are regularly invited to A.K. weddings as friends and guests. Because of their caste isolation, the A.K.s are somewhat homogenous, as the Brahmans are. In their free commensality and intermarriage, the A.K.s function more as one *jati* than as a *jati*-cluster, yet they may include more than one caste and thus can be defined as a *jati*-cluster for some purposes.

Within the first week of our arrival at Bandipur, we heard the following story. Long ago, in the days of the palegar village chieftains, a high stone fortification was to be built surrounding the central neighbourhood (now 'Brahman Streets'). A human sacrifice was required for the success of the project and a local A.K. man had been selected. (As we listened to the tale, we were standing on the same high mound where he had stood. From that high place we could see all the village and much of the surrounding agricultural land.) The sacrificial victim was then informed that his family was to receive all the dry crop land in his view (land irrigated only by rainfall) as compensation for losing him. Then he was put to death and the wall was built. That wall stood until the 1930s when it was removed by government order.

At present the local A.K.s do in fact own much of the village dry land. Though they are still living mainly on day labour and sharecropping incomes, they are eager to enter the modern world, sending more than 70% of their children to the village schools. The supposedly higher-ranking non-Brahmans send a lower percentage of their children to be educated.

The three-part division into Brahman, non-Brahman and A.K. somewhat oversimplifies the pattern of caste alignments, the actual affinities and alliances among castes in this village. Still it is a useful rough guide and reflects the political history of caste competition in south India over this century. Though villagers are vague about just how they came to divide their population in this way, there is little doubt that they have been influenced by the non-Brahman movements that have occurred in the south. Since the turn of the century mid-level groups have become more and more militant against the economic and social domination of Brahmans. (See Irschick 1969 and Hanchett 1971, 1972.)

LAND AND LIVELIHOOD

Most of the residents of Bandipur make their living directly or indirectly from the land. There are three types of land. The most lucrative is called garden land (*tota*) where the principal crop is areca nut, providing a high cash return from its heavily watered clusters of trees. Since Bandipur is on the border of the heavy and light rainfall zones of Karnataka, there are few groves of garden land in the village area. These are only occasional reminders of the lush countryside fifteen or twenty miles west in the foothills of the Western Ghat mountains, where one resident of Bandipur owns a coffee plantation. Of the 12.73 acres of garden land in Bandipur, 11.73 acres are owned by Brahman families and 1 acre by the village Narasimha temple.

The second best type of land is wet land (*gadde*) which is irrigated by a channel from the Yagachi River. Rice is the main crop, though the water supply allows only one crop per year, whereas other parts of the south produce two or even three crops with their more ample irrigation. Some Bandipur people grow peanuts as a cash crop rather than leave the rice land fallow for half the year. Most of the resident owners of wet land are Brahmans, owning 44% or 101.18 acres. Local Brahmans sometimes own wet lands in neighbouring villages as well.

Members of the 'Farmer' caste hold 10.1% of the village wet land; the Narasimha temple owns 4.5% or 10 acres. Despite the prohibitions of land reform, absentee landlords continue to hold at least 31.4% or 71.16 acres of this valuable land. The remainder is distributed in small owned or rented plots among other non-Brahman or A.K. households.

Least productive and least valuable is the dry land (*hwala*) where crops are limited by the amount of rainfall. Staple foods that thrive there include red millet, sorghum, pulses, beans and chili pepper, good cash crops. There is about as much dry land as wet land but it is more evenly distributed. Brahmans own 26%, non-Brahmans 18.5%, while 54.2% is owned by A.K.s.

Villagers who own no land, or not enough to support themselves, do several types of work. Most A.K.s and low-income non-Brahmans supplement their income by day labour or as servants in wealthier homes. Some have found work as construction labourers, carrying rocks and mud for the nearby irrigation dam, though here they are in competition with itinerant labourers who have come from other states to work on this project. The meager living provided by day-labour is only slightly better than the alternative of starvation which this category of villager has often faced in the past. Inflation continues; wages lag behind. A daily pay of Rs. 1.50-3.00 will no longer buy the kilogram of rice it bought ten years ago.

At a somewhat higher class level, some non-Brahmans have found opportunities as contractors recruiting day labourers. The contractor is an essential part of any rural construction project. The bridges, roads and channels built here have provided several non-Brahman families with good cash over the past fifty or sixty years. This process continues. The sudden appearance of a motorcycle, car or bright cement house is often a sign that a new labour recruitment contract has been awarded to some enterprising village man.

Other village jobs include the traditional crafts such as goldsmithing, carpentry or blacksmithing (all performed by the Smith caste). There are a number of tailors in Bandipur, some of whom are members of the 'Weaver' caste though they are an educated group who no longer do any weaving as manufactured cloth is readily available. The Smiths and Weavers are members of traditional 'left-hand' category of castes, as are the Oil-Pressers, some of whom still work at their caste occupation on a large, ox-driven oil press next to one village house.

There are small salaried jobs such as errand-bearers (*pyuns*) for local schools or shops, as well as various independent enterprises. The 'Fishermen' prepare limestone and do some fishing; the 'Toddy-Tappers' and some 'Farmers' operate illicit liquor stills; one ran a taxi service for a time. At least one non-Brahman woman has a roadside 'box shop' where she sells matches, soap and other such items. Another woman—an energetic and gregarious Brahman widow—runs a larger store next to her house in the 'Brahman Streets'.

Still in the middle- to low-income bracket, 'Washermen' and their women and 'Barbers' stay busy servicing the daily and ritual needs of the villagers. Along with the A.K.s, these 'service castes' continue the Hindu tradition of family contracts for ritual services, though barber shops and laundries are found among the village shops. Necessary for rites of passage, at times of birth and death (including the death of cattle), the ritual services continue to be available on the all-India 'jajmani' pattern, though people of these castes providing the services do not earn thereby enough to live without supplementary land and cash income. The village households feel obligated to donate small amounts of fruit, cloth and grain to their linked ritual-service families at several festivals throughout the year.

One family of 'Leatherworkers' are new residents in Bandipur. They represent the Madiga (A.D.) group, the other major Harijan *jati* besides A.K.s, who are Holeya. They do latrine cleaning for the village, work the other castes consider to be defiling.

A few village men depend on illicit sources of income, 'bootleg' liquor, banditry, burglary, theft of crops and cattle theft. As one or two go back and forth between home and jail, some jokingly call the jail 'their mother's house'. These, too, are occupations of sorts.

At the most well-paid employment level of the socio-economic hierarchy, a few villagers achieve the desirable status of civil service jobs, principally as teachers in village or taluk schools. These are Brahman men and women or educated non-Brahmans. They and their families mingle on equal terms with the government employees who live in the village on short-term appointments as doctors, postmasters, veterinarians and so on. In fact, several of the families have sent brothers, sons and daughters on similar assignments elsewhere in Karnataka.

Bandipur, then, is as much a part of the modern India as any present village can be. Cash incomes are at least as important as subsistence agriculture for most villagers, if not more so. Vulnerable to unemployment and inflation, they feel the impact of national events directly as well as through newspapers, radios and letters from relatives in cities and abroad.

Local people, whatever their occupation, are proud to describe Bandipur as an educated village. Even those who are illiterate feel the benefit of some reflected glory from this reputation. There is, furthermore, a great interest in sending children to the several schools. This tradition goes back at least to the 1930s when local Brahmans, inspired by the guidance of Gandhi, decided to reside in the village and improve conditions there. Though their motives were not entirely altruistic, they did succeed in building a hostel where A.K. high school students from other villages could live. That hostel still houses male students and maintains a full-time cook to feed them, though the building is in run-down condition.

LITERARY LEVELS

Statistics on literacy and education place the village right at the 44% average for the state as a whole (as of 1961) and far above the national figure of 24%. Considering that the average includes both rural and urban populations, Bandipur stands well for a village. The minimal literacy figures, however, are generous. According to our detailed survey, only 24.6% of the villagers over age 6 can in fact read and write acceptably. We may accept Bandipur's self-identification as an educated village, therefore, but with a few reservations.

CHINNAPURA

On first approaching Chinnapura, only two miles away along a dirt road and across a narrow river, we assumed it to be a miniature version of Bandipur. Both are Brahman villages including similar proportions of the various castes but in Chinnapura there are only 398 persons in 85 households (see Table 2).

Table 2—Population of Chinnapura, 1967

Jati-cluster	Jati (Kannada Name)	No. of Households	Population
Brahman	Iyengar	8	33
	Smartha	12	76
Non-Brahman	Farmer (Okkaliga)	14	70
	Fisherman (Besta)	2	6
	Washerman (Agasa)	12	53
	Smith (Acari)	2	11
	Barber (Hajama)	4	15
	Shepherd (Kuruba)	1	5
	Lingayat	2	2
A.K.	A.K. (Adikarnataka, Holeya)	28	127
	Totals	85	398

Many family ties link the two communities at all caste levels. The weekly market at Bandipur draws many of the farmers from Chinnapura and brings them into the same networks of gossip and exchange. The poorer residents of both villages share the benefits of a common environment providing herbs, small animals, fish, shrimp and crabs which they gather or hunt with a common knowledge that fends off starvation more reliably than unpredictable wages.

Nevertheless, the two villages turn out to be more different than it seems at first sight. Our experiences in the two and the types of villagers with whom we made friends are different. In Chinnapura we discover the old mythical and legendary south India. The dialect is the Kannada of Farmers and Washermen who are not so much influenced by their more urbane Brahman neighbours. Many villagers here are still proudly committed to the agricultural life and disdainful of service occupations that take wage earners out of the home and erode traditional ways of family security. Groups of women stay up together at night grinding millet on large granite wheels as they sing long, droning ballads in a call-and-response pattern.

These old fashions persist to some extent in the more modern setting of Bandipur as well, but as vestiges. There many women know the same ballads though few sing them any longer. A Bandipur Farmer family whose women still sing at rites of passage sing ritual songs for the interviewer but do so in a typically modern attitude of respectful distance from their own recent past. They even have a printed booklet with the words of their songs to ensure accuracy. The non-Brahman residents of Chinnapura are not yet so aware that their oral traditions are fading.

In Chinnapura are two sons of a man who once ruled that village and its hamlets as a petty king, a *jodidar*. He was long ago cremated on a seven-foot high pyre of pure sandalwood. Though his family's right to tax the peasants was withdrawn long back, his sons still sit on their verandahs at the village square, issuing orders to passers-by in an attitude of royal arrogance. Observing their role in Chinnapura sheds light on a little-recognised facet of Bandipur life.

During the colonial period Bandipur itself had a type of land-tenure system as a rayatwari village where landowners paid taxes directly to the government rather than to a jodidar (tax gatherer), but at least seven of the Bandipur Brahman families were at that time jodidars for other villages in the region. This position gave them widespread power and influence, vestiges of which still remain. Some Brahmans, though their ancestors came to rural Hassan 150 years ago as land-grantees and jodidars, still view themselves as city-dwellers by nature, only temporarily settled in the village. Now that their investments and power have declined significantly, Brahman families are gradually drifting back to the comfort and glamour of cities or large towns.

The real name of Chinnapura translates as 'golden village'. Though its central neighbourhood had at one time been a walled fort built by warring medieval village chieftains, its own legendary history is of an expansive kingdom with Chinnapura as the capital town. This legend has a fairy-tale quality, as does the old *nadu* region festival, a ritual exposing the skeleton of a larger system and elevating vestigial headmen to a position of local prominence for one week each year. Located on a peninsula within the sacred juncture of two rivers, Chinnapura's inner life puts it further from Bandipur than its physical distance. Periodically, its residents are inwardly oriented towards other peninsular villages where they find metaphors more satisfying than those of Bandipur's buses, trucks and busy roadside shops.

Despite the village's traditionalism, the modern world is making its imprint on Chinnapura almost as fast as on Bandipur. The range of occupations and businesses parallels that of the neighbouring village, though on a smaller scale. Villagers work the same kinds of garden, wet or dry land, with Brahmans still owning more of it. Basic educational levels are roughly equal, though minimal literacy is slightly lower in Chinnapura and reading ability slightly higher. A little under half the children attend school; comparative figures of women's and men's formal education are similar.

The future of Chinnapura is uncertain, as the dam now under construction will necessitate its removal at sometime in the years to come. This creates a good deal of anxiety among the population, yet life goes on more or less normally (see the Preface).

With all the differences between the two villages' sense of local identity, they are linked communities with a common cultural heritage. The family festivals of the two merge into a single series. As the basic patterns of family organisation and the inner dynamics of family life are approximately the same for the two villages, they will be treated as one Hindu system in the chapters to come.

NOTES

1. These are fictitious village names.
2. Historical sources consulted are Sreenivasa Murthy (1977), Nilakanta Sastri (1966), and Thapar (1966).

Chapter 2

THE KINSHIP SYSTEM AND WOMEN'S PLACE IN IT

Circles of relatives in Bandipur and Chinnapura are large and inclusive. As in other long-settled rural areas of India, village life here involves frequent contact among numerous relatives, links extending to the boundaries of the caste (*jati*) itself. Since each caste is endogamous, any caste-mate may be a distant relative. Through an implicit belief in shared fate among kin, events in one household are thought to affect many other households and, ultimately, the well-being of a whole caste.

Thirty-six genealogies place nearly all of Chinnapura's and Bandipur's Hindu households in their respective kin contexts. These genealogies start with the earliest known ancestors of each kin group and follow most families' histories back at least 150 years, defining links among hundreds of living relatives. The genealogies range from five to ten generations in depth, as indicated in Table 3, with a mean depth of eight generations. The seven Brahman genealogies have a mean depth of 8.28 generations (Table 4). Twenty genealogies for non-Brahmans have a mean depth of 7.3 generations; and nine A.K. genealogies have a mean depth of 7.44 generations.

Despite other differences in their life styles, Brahmans, non-Brahmans, and A. K.s use the same basic kinship system and struggle with the dilemmas it poses for individuals.

CATEGORIES OF KIN

THE LINEAGE

Descent is patrilineal in all castes, and every household is aware of relationships with a wide circle of agnatic kin. Within this circle certain subdivisions are recognised.

Table 3—Generational Depth of Bandipur and Chinnapura Genealogies,
Frequency Distribution

Number of Generations Included	Frequencies (All Jatis)
5	3
6	6
7	7
8	11
9	7
10	2
Total	36

Mode   : 8 Generations
Median : 8 Generations

Table 4—Generational Depth of Bandipur and Chinnapura Genealogies, by *Jati*-Cluster

Jati-cluster	No. of Genealogies in Sample	Range of Generational Depth	Mean Number of Generations Included
Brahman	7	7-10	8.28
Non-Brahman	20	5-10	7.3
A. K.	9	6-8	7.44
Total	36		

Brothers and first and second degree male cousins (i.e., those with common parents, grandparents, or great-grandparents) and their immediate families comprise intimate groups called *dayadi*. When women marry, they cease to be members of their fathers' and brothers' *dayadi* groups and join their husbands'. Another term for *dayadi* is 'brothers' (*anna-tammandiru*, lit. 'elder and younger brothers').

The *dayadi* is the minimal lineage unit and the most significant inheritance group within the kinship system. Its members share use and inheritance rights to property according to Hindu customary law which subdivides most property equally among male kin. When there is much property, the *dayadi* often serves as a corporate group that owns and manages it. *Dayadi* members share birth and death pollution (*purudu* or *sutaka*). When there is a birth or death within the group, no matter in what location, all member households must by custom refrain from giving food to outsiders for eleven days. The *dayadi* endures three or four generations at the most.

More distant agnates are less involved with each other than are *dayadi* members, in terms of property rights; and they do not share birth or death pollution. Aware of each other, they nonetheless share a sense of mutual responsibility and commitment, though obligations are not clearly defined.

Dayadi units are grouped into agnatic clans, called *kula* ('clan') or *tende* ('branch'). Such clans, which once had more important ritual (and social) functions than they do now, are themselves seen as segments of a very deep patriline called *vamsa*.

The *vamsa* is often compared to a tree, and, like a tree, may grow and thrive or not. A myth of one Chinnapura Brahman lineage actually creates a direct, magical link with a village tree. The lineage is said to have been on the verge of dying out several generations ago. Its one surviving member, a woman, asked a sage for help. The sage told her to plant a sacred fig (*pipal*) tree in the centre of the village, and since then the line is said to have prospered. In the image of a tree, the lineage's trunk is the *vamsa*; major branches, the clan (*kula* or *tende*); and further branches, the *dayadis*. The *vamsa* is, further, believed to be vulnerable to curses. There is an elaborate special vocabulary for such remarks as, 'May your whole line disappear and its name never be heard again', remarks considered to be powerful assaults.

The patrilineage at all levels is strictly exogamous. Certain other kinds of relatives can marry, but marriage within the *dayadi*, *kula*, or *vamsa* is considered incest.

MARRIAGE PATTERNS

Like other Dravidian language speakers, Bandipur and Chinnapura families favour marriage arrangements between certain specified types of relatives, as in Figure 1. From a man's point of view, female relatives eligible as spouses are : (1) his elder sister's daughter (*sose*); (2) his mother's brother's daughter (*nadani*); and (3) his father's sister's daughter (*nadani*). From a woman's point of view, eligible spouses are (i) her mother's younger brother (*mava*); (ii) her mother's brother's son (*bava/bhava*); and (iii) her father's sister's son (*bava/bhava*). Marriages between classificatory relatives included in these uncle-niece or cross-cousin categories are equally possible and preferred.

Parallel cousins, both immediate and classificatory, call each other 'brother' and 'sister', a usage that emphasises the fact that marriage between them is taboo, as shown in Figure 2.

Whenever a marriage is arranged, some family members are sure to trace relationships as carefully as possible to be sure that the proposed husband and wife are either in eligible categories, if kin, or are unrelated. Most villagers, however, are satisfied to ask whether the new spouses are 'old relations' (*halnentru*) or 'new relations' (*hosnentru*), that is, whether a pre-existing kin tie exists or not. Of the married couples heading households, 31.4% are 'old relations', linked either by common ancestry or by marriages previously contracted between their respective relatives. Table 5 shows that there are differences among the three *jati*-clusters in the proportions of marriages between 'old' or 'new relations', with non-Brahmans showing the strongest tendency toward the latter.

Dravidian marriage rules have important implications for the sister-brother relationship. In preferred marriages, between uncle and niece or cross-cousins,

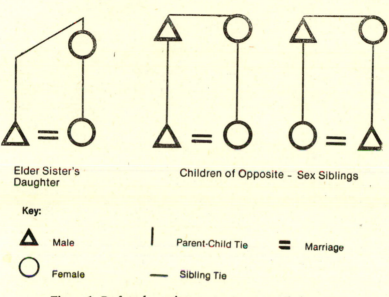

Elder Sister's Daughter   Children of Opposite – Sex Siblings

Key:

△ Male | Parent-Child Tie   ⹀ Marriage

○ Female   — Sibling Tie

Figure 1. Preferred marriage partners among relatives

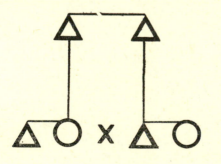
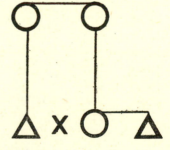

Taboo as spouses   Taboo as spouses

Figure 2. Prohibited marriage partners

Table 5—Marriage Patterns, Bandipur 1966-67†

Jati-cluster	Marriages to 'Old Relations' (O.R.)	Marriages to 'New Relations' (N.R.)	No Information	Group-by-Group Percentages O.R./N.R.
Brahman (N = 47)	17	28	2	36.2%/59.6%
Non-Brahman (N = 112)	23	88	1	20.8%/78.6%
A.K. & A.D. (N = 80)	36	42	2	45.0%/52.5%
Totals (N = 239)	76 (31.8%)	158 (66.1%)	5 (2.1%)	

†Household survey data on married or widowed Hindu household heads only.

links connecting eligible spouses always include a sister-brother pair. This marriage system therefore makes every sister and brother potential affines. Their children or grandchildren can marry each other; and an elder sister can also be her younger brother's mother-in-law. Such possibilities lend a uniquely south Indian twist to other features of the sister-brother tie, which is close and valued throughout the subcontinent.

HOUSEHOLD AND BIRTH GROUP (*Kutumba*)

At marriage a bride customarily moves into her husband's house, according to virilocal principles of residence among all castes.

The Kannada term 'house' (*mane*) means both house as building and home or household. It is the centre of life processes such as cooking and eating, sexual intercourse, and birth. Those who share a home are the most intimate of kin. Therefore, this family unit has a very creative role to play in determining the whole kin group's future and reputation.

The nuclear family, called *samsara*, is the most common type of residential unit in the two villages, as indicated in Table 6.[1] Of the 325 Hindu households, 45.2% are nuclear families. An additional 23.1% include at least one other adult member of the kin group as well. Some form of the more traditional joint family is found in 48 (14.8%) village homes. Despite the prevalence of virilocality, nearly 15 (4.6%) households have been established uxorilocally, i.e., by men moving in with their wives' families at marriage.

The house is the focus and source of the intimate group of kin who call themselves *kutumba*.[2] The meaning of *kutumba* tends to shift in different contexts, and there are differing personal views about who is or is not included (see Figures 4 and 5, below). Nonetheless, it is a common designation for those who do or once did share a home. Siblings of either sex, when grown and married, usually refer to each other as *kutumba*, for example. Nieces and nephews are usually also included. Closeness and day-to-day sharing, past or present, are the basis of *kutumba* sentiment. Along with shared food and shelter close birth ties bind *kutumba* groups together. For this reason I translate *kutumba* as 'birth group'.

Because of its intimate nature, the *kutumba*, or birth group, is the custodian of family purity according to the common view. As the house associated with it may be clean or dirty, so the birth group itself is judged to be of good quality or not. One hears comments about a 'good family' (*v*)*olle kutumba* in discussions of marriage arrangement or other serious family matters. The type of goodness expressed by the word (*v*)*olle* includes a concept of genuineness, as in a real pearl contrasted with an imitation. Similarly, a good person (*v*)*olle jana* is said to be sincere and straightforward in dealing with others. The reputation of a birth group is heavily dependent on the sexual chastity of its women and the presumed physiological purity of its offspring. The broader connotations of the term (*v*)*olle*, however, express a profound concept of family purity going beyond sex and mating to include general integrity, strength, and wholeness.

AFFINES, OR RELATIONS OF EXCHANGE

Within the total collection of all relatives there are many who are connected by marriage rather than by common ancestry. These are affines, or relations of exchange.

Distinctions between close and distant affines generally parallel segmentation patterns in the home or the lineage. For example, very close affines, such as a man's maternal aunt or uncle, his brother-in-law, or his daughter's husband, are called *nentru* 'close relations of exchange'.[3] Ties between *nentru* are considered to be as close, in affinal terms, as ties between *kutumba* members are close in their way. *Nentru* are invited regularly as guests on special occasions and share by custom and by choice in many of each other's home-centred festivals and rites of passage.[4]

More distant relations of exchange, called *bandugalu* or *bandavaru*, literally 'linked persons', are the affines of one's cousins or grandparents or others with even more remote marital connections. The affines of affines (a man and his sister's husband's sister's husband, for example) are called *bandhavya* and are usually acquainted.

Relationships among affines, unlike other kin ties, do not serve as a basis for the formation of kin groups in the way birth and descent relationships do. Affinal ties are said to create meetings (*kuta*) or gatherings (*samaja*), especially at weddings, but not to constitute enduring family units.

Table 6 – Organisation of Hindu Households According to Kolenda (1968) Typology

	Nuclear	Supplemented Nuclear	Sub-nuclear	Single Person	Supplemented Sub-nuclear	Collateral Joint	Supplemented Collateral Joint	Lineal Joint	Supplemented Lineal Joint	Lineal-Collateral Joint	Supplemented Lineal-Collat. Joint	Other	No Information	Totals	Cases of Uxori-local Residence
BANDIPUR															
Brahman	23	12	4	3	2	—	1	2	—	—	3	—	50	—
Non-Brahman															
Farmer	22	13	3	—	2	1	2	3	—	—	—	—	46	1
Weaver	10	3	4	—	—	—	3	—	—	—	—	—	20	2
Oil Presser	5	2	—	1	1	—	1	1	—	—	—	—	11	1
Fisherman	6	2	1	—	—	—	2	—	—	—	—	—	11	1
Toddy Tapper	2	1	1	—	—	—	1	1	—	—	—	—	6	1
Washerman	2	3	—	1	—	—	1	—	—	—	—	—	7	—
Smith	1	3	1	—	—	—	1	—	—	—	—	—	6	—
Barber	3	1	—	—	—	—	1	—	—	—	—	—	5	1
A.K./A.D.	28	25	7	1	3	1	10	4	1	—	—	—	80	8

CHINNAPURA

Brahman	5	6	3	1	2	1	—	1	—	1	—	1	1	20	—
Non-Brahman															
Farmer	7	2	—	—	1	1	1	1	—	1	1	—	1	14	—
Fisherman	—	—	—	—	1	—	—	—	—	—	—	1	—	2	—
Washerman	6	1	3	—	1	—	1	—	—	—	1	—	1	12	—
Smith	2	—	—	—	—	—	—	—	—	—	—	—	—	2	—
Barber	3	—	1	—	—	—	—	—	—	—	—	—	—	4	—
Shepherd	1	—	—	—	—	—	—	—	—	—	—	—	—	1	—
A.K.	21	1	2	—	1	1	3	3	—	—	3	—	1	28	—
Totals	147	75	30	8	12	3	3	28	11	2	1	4	1	325	15
Percentages	45.2	23.1	9.2	2.5	3.7	0.9	0.9	8.6	3.4	0.6	0.3	1.2	0.3	99.9	(4.6)

Affines are interdependent rivals. They are interdependent because they have exchanged members in marriage. Given the rule of patrilineal exogamy, no line can reproduce itself without taking in wives from other groups, of course. The presence of close relations of exchange (*nentru*), required by custom for certain festivals and rites of passage, reflects the deep interdependence between affines. This closeness has a problematic quality, however. Though having common family interests, affines see each other as outsiders and rivals. This is true even when 'old relations' marry. Tensions associated with marriage are said to create feelings of difference and competition even between relatives that might have been previously on friendly terms. Each marriage creates two sides where there originally may have been one.

Myths associated with some family festivals will be shown later to reflect feelings of both need and suspicion toward affines as outsiders to a lineage.

KINSHIP AS A PROCESS

Concepts of kin structure are essentially dynamic. Kinship is more like a fountain than a static framework. Continuously emerging, the parts of the structure unfold and flow into each other over time. Family members make every effort to promote auspicious growth and expansion by daily routines and by observing special occasions such as festivals or rites of passage. If they are successful, these efforts will cause every husband and wife in time to establish a home that will be the centre of a birth group they create. Every birth group will in turn become the heart of a new branch of the patrilineal tree and will involve the lineage in an ever-expanding series of affinal exchanges. Ultimately all are relatives, the circle of kin ties blending outward toward the limits of the endogamous caste as a whole. Boundaries distinguishing units of the kin group, seen in this way, are ephemeral.

Figure 3 depicts the auspicious flowing process involving all parts of the kin structure from the nuclear family and birth group outward.

THE AMBIGUOUS POSITION OF WOMEN

As those who give birth to children, women are charged with heavy responsibility for a family's survival and growth. Their sexual activity and birth-giving powers are topics of constant discussion and concern. Their auspicious role in the home, birth group, and lineage is greatly valued. They are so important that they are sincerely regarded as goddesses of wealth (Laksmi) in both their natal and marital homes.

Though marriage in reality can bring hardship to a bride, she ideally enters her husband's family as an agent of prosperity. One Farmer's description of the transfer of a token bridewealth payment (*tera*) during a wedding shows the strength of this ideal:

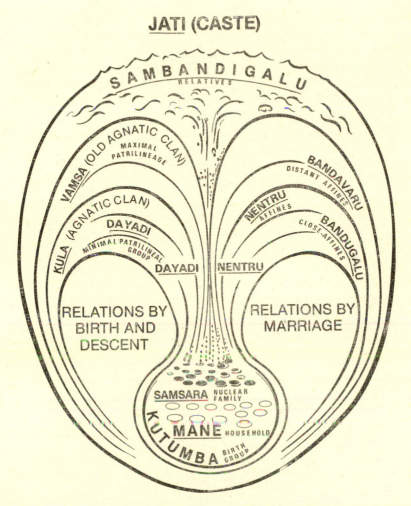

JATI (CASTE)

Figure 3. Relations of Karnataka kinship segments.

In front of the relatives they ask the bride's father, 'Will you take *tera*'? The bride has to buy something with this money, Rs. 26.50, something that will grow, perhaps a small animal. That is her father's gift to the prosperity of her husband's family. If we do this, our name will be honoured.

When that Rs. 26.50 grows to Rs. 1000, she will be able to say to her father-in-law, 'The family is prospering through me'. They then lose their voice and cannot have power over her.

As this statement demonstrates, a women's career in marriage reflects on the reputation of her natal family as well as affecting the future of her husband's family.

Women are also significant figures in family history. Although descent is patrilineal, uterine kin are prominent in all castes' genealogies, and many remembered ancestors are women. Our thirty-six Hindu genealogies begin either with a single male ancestor (25), or a husband-wife pair (10), or a brother-sister pair (1). More than half of the genealogies introduce daughters of the original ancestors and include some of their descendants, as indicated in Table 7.

Table 7—Appearance of Female Predecessors in Hindu Genealogies

Distance from Founding Ancestor(s)	Brahman Genealogies	Non-Brahman Genealogies	A.K. Genealogies	Totals (Percentages)
Founder	0	0	1	1 (3.0%)
2nd Generation	4	12	3	19 (52.7%)
3rd Generation	1	6	5	12 (33.0%)
4th Generation	1	2	0	3 (8.3%)
5th Generation	1	0	0	1 (3.0%)
Totals	7	20	9	36 (100.0%)

By the time the original ancestors' grandchildren are mentioned, nearly 90% of the genealogies are keeping track of relations through aunts who have married out. The importance of ties through women becomes even more notable when we realise that the original village of the founding ancestor's wife is known whenever (in 10 cases) the name of the wife herself is known. In the one case of a genealogy that begins with a brother-sister pair, an A.K. genealogy, the sister's husband's village is known (see Table 8).

Table 8—Founding Ancestor's Wife/Husband

Genealogies	Wife/Husband Known	Wife Not Known
Brahman Genealogies	0	7
Non-Brahman Genealogies	4	16
A.K. Genealogies	6	3
Totals	10 (28%)	26 (72%)

Beyond their importance as wives, mothers, and ancestors, women are credited with great spiritual powers. Hindu proverbs, myths and other lore endow women's blessings and curses with potency. Their kin, natal and marital, respect and fear these powers.[5] Even the unfortunate widow is said to have magical control over others' lives.[6] Such ideas reflect concepts of the spiritual side of family life and women's special position in the spiritual and ritual area. Discussing the Sanskritic Hindu concept of marriage, for example, Srinivas (1977) points out that the wife "is literally the moral and religious half of the husband." Furthermore, "feminine preoccupation with ritual provides [women] with power over men. Since much of a woman's ritual is concerned with the welfare of the household and its members, and the husband does not have the time for performing it, he is appreciative of the fact that his wife is looking after an important area of family life."

Some of the awesome powers attributed to women, however, can be related to their ambiguous position in the kinship system. Being ambiguous (compared to men), they are enigmatic; being enigmatic, difficult to control. Dumont (1975 : 213) commented on this ambiguity, stating that in relation to the patrilineage women are "Janus-faced persons." This results from the fact that women shift lineage membership at marriage, a key difference between women and men in this kinship system. Affines being considered as suspicious outsiders, the shift in membership creates structural ambiguities (especially in the early years of marriage) and makes women a common focus of ambivalent inter-group feelings.

Some local Hindu customs and beliefs highlight the ambiguities and dual affiliations inherent in women's kin status. At the time of marriage, for instance, all castes, to my knowledge, provide a woman with two pendants. These are small gold pieces, called *tali*, worn on a chain or string around the neck. One *tali* comes from a woman's natal family, and one from her husband's family. (Elsewhere in south India a girl may receive a *tali* from her natal family at her maturation, whether or not this is also the time of her marriage.) Each *tali* symbolises a lifelong kin attachment and commitment to one of two affinal groups that see each other as rivals.

Another, related custom is that of sending a married woman back to her natal home for her first two or three confinements, as practised among all castes. This practice symbolically confuses the young mother's two homes, natal and marital, and gives her natal home complete power to oversee the birth of a new member of an alien lineage. It is a comfort to the mother to be with her own mother during her confinement, of course, but the practice legitimises her bonds to her natal family and her continuing dependence on their support.

Even in death, the treatment of women indicates structural ambiguity. Among Iyengar Brahmans, if a woman dies without having borne sons, her husband's family does not perform a twelfth-day funerary ritual that endows her with status as an ancestor. Responsibility for this ritual, if it is done at all, reverts to her natal family. Since the ritual involves an expensive feast, the latter may be reluctant to perform it, thus preventing her from completing her social and spiritual evolution. This practice, or rather this lapse, shows that responsibilities of her husband's family are weak if she has failed to bear a son, but that her natal family may or may not come to assist her.[7]

Another type of lapse occurs in many non-Brahman and A.K. families. Since they believe that only after marriage is a mature person fulfilled and peaceful, they perform brief weddings for the spirits of mature sons who have died unmarried. Such a wedding is performed just before the wedding of another son. It consists in marrying the spirit of the deceased to an inanimate object such as a vessel, post, or *tali*. It is believed that this protects the living brother, as a groom, from the envy of his deceased sibling. I have asked members of most castes if the same wedding ritual is performed for mature, unmarried girls after death and have found none who do it. It is therefore not surprising that many villagers fear the ghosts of unmarried women. These ghosts, called '*mohinis*', are thought to roam about seducing and killing young men in a restless search for sexual satisfaction.

Direct study of the kinship categories reveals one area of structural ambiguity relating to women's status. In conducting interviews about categories of kin, I found evidence of disagreement, and possible confusion, about whether married women are affines (*nentru*) or birth group (*kutumba*) members vis-a-vis their natal kin. Figures 4 and 5 summarise the results of my limited set of interviews on this matter. Though everyone agrees that daughters leave their natal lineage at marriage, they do not agree about whether they continue to be members of their birth group. This is an important matter because of the intimacy of the birth group. If a woman retains her status as a member of her natal birth group after her marriage, she has a strong competing allegiance to a family other than her husband's. (She is always a member of her husband's birth group.) I assume that further inquiry on this subject would reveal that women do have dual birth group memberships for a period after marriage and that they shift to one or another depending on individual circumstances. For example, a woman who becomes well established in her husband's home may tend to become fully committed to her husband's birth group, whereas a woman (even with children) who leaves her husband and returns to live with her natal family would remain a member of her original birth group. For such ambiguities and alternatives to remain after marriage provides women with some insurance against complete loss of family protection. This possibility also, however, keeps women's kinship status much less clear than men's for much of their lives.

OTHER DILEMMAS IN WOMEN'S LIVES

As well as occupying an ambiguous position in the kin structure, Hindu women typically face certain practical problems. Though general differences in life style between classes or between *jati*-clusters make some more economic-

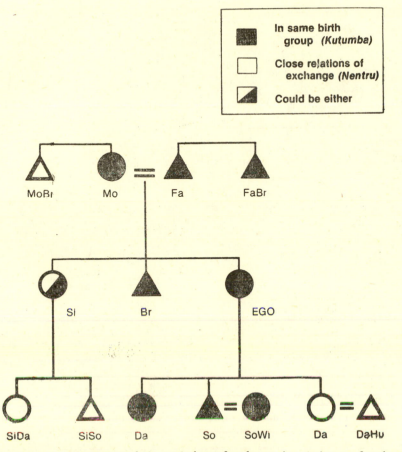

Figure 4. Birth group members and close relations of exchange, in relation to female ego.*
*Information from one A. K. female information.

ally secure than others, women of all groups are powerless relative to men. There is a sexual aspect to this. All women live with a stern double-standard of sexual conduct that tends to penalise any woman's extra-marital sexual activity while sanctioning men's. Women enhance their families' reputations primarily by their sexual discipline, while men maintain family honour in other ways. Sexual chastity is a supreme virtue for women—one elevating some legendary females to near-sainthood.[8] This value is, however, a burden to some and a cause of grief, or even death, for those who do not uphold it.

Brahman women live with special limitations not experienced by those of most other castes. For them, both divorce and widow remarriage are virtually impossible, though these are important options for other women. This make Brahman women more vulnerable to the whims of fate than others are. Since Muslim influence is historically weak in this area, women do not observe *parda,*

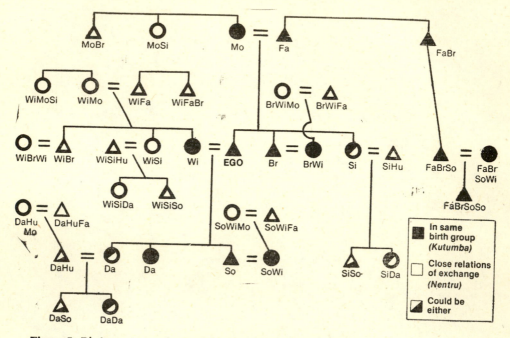

Figure 5. Birth group members and close relations of exchange, in relation to male ego.*
*Information from three Non-Brahman male informants.

seclusion; yet Brahman women's movements outside the home are quite restricted. Srinivas (1977) refers to them as "immured," since "women . . . find high
status inconsistent with even extra-mural movement . . . ."

The limitations affecting Brahman women can be explained in large part by
the economic position of Brahmans in rural areas such as Hassan District.
Brahmans are landed gentry in these areas. They live in peasant villages not
because of farming traditions but because they own much land, granted to many
Brahman families during the nineteenth century by Hindu kings and increased
by generally shrewd business activities. Rural Brahmans are generally literate,
urban and successful at exploiting rural areas for financial gain. Though par-
taking the benefits of this socio-economic pattern, Brahman women also can
suffer because of it. The lineage (*dayadi*), as the main economic unit among
affluent Brahmans, is a corporate entity playing for high stakes in the rural
economy. The needs of the lineage itself tightly control the lives of its members.
Its reputation and wealth, bases of its power, are carefully guarded. As a result,
tendencies to control women are exaggerated among Brahmans. The role of
Brahman women in maintaining the purity of the Brahman family line has an
additional, economic aspect that it does not have among most non-Brahman
and A.K. families; and regulating Brahman women's sexual conduct thus has an
extra measure of urgency.[9] Trying, as they often do, to live up to feminine ideals

of chastity and altruism, they are prone to depression and feelings of isolation.

Though Brahman women rarely work outside the home in the rural community, they do have a role in increasing their husbands' families' wealth. Long before dowry was as widespread in India as it now is, southern Brahman families were giving up large cash dowries to marry off their daughters. As Tambaiah (1973a) has observed, however, Brahman women's access to dowry is unusually limited. Little, if any, of it is controlled by brides themselves.[10] Some women's festivals, to be discussed below, show that Brahman women nonetheless insist on seeing their dowry contribution as a source of self-respect and glory. It entitles married women to stand up as virtual goddesses of wealth (Laksmis), although their real power is generally very limited. (Other castes tend to greater equality between a bride's and a groom's family in covering the costs of a wedding. The groom's family also makes a bridewealth payment (*tera*), a gift that moves in the opposite direction of dowry).

Because of large dowries and the prohibition of divorce, Brahman women's break with their natal families at marriage is more permanent than other women's; but the trauma of this separation is ameliorated to some extent by folk customs. One Iyengar group, for example, celebrates a festival in which they give food and gifts to young, unmarried daughters as the expression of a poignant message, that although they will leave the family one day, "We will never forget you."[11] There are several occasions on which a married daughter is the preferred guest of honour or the recipient of gifts. In the Gauri and Prati Festivals, discussed in Part II, Brahman families honour married daughters as visiting goddesses of wealth and glorify the vulnerable mother-daughter relationship. Other castes also express concern, symbolic and direct, about the painful separation of a married daughter from her natal home, but Brahmans are far more preoccupied with this problem than others.

SUMMARY

This chapter has reviewed the basic structure of the Karnataka Hindu kinship system by describing its component parts: nuclear family (*samsara*), household (*mane*), birth group (*kutumba*), and both lineal and affinal categories of kin. Within the exogamous patrilineage distinctions are made between the minimal lineage (*dayadi*), which is three or four generations in depth, and the more distantly related clan (*kula, tende*) and *vamsa*. Parallel distinctions grade affines as either close (*nentru*), moderately close (*bandugalu*), or distant (*bandavaru*). Though these segments and ties express themselves in differing ways and at different points in the growth of each family, they all add up to a concept of relatives (*sambandigalu*) or kin network, one of the most secure anchors available in Hindu society.

The contents of thirty-six Hindu genealogies show that although inheritance is patrilineal, uterine ties are socially significant. These genealogies reveal the importance of women in the system as a whole.

Marriage rules establish a preference for marriage between cross-cousins or between an uncle and a niece. These rules create a situation in which every brother and sister are potential affines.

A close look shows that despite their importance in both natal and marital families, women have an ambiguous position compared to men's. Rules of virilocality and patrilineal descent and certain ritual practices create dangers of uncertain status for all Hindu women that men do not have to face. As outsiders married into a lineage, for example, they can be the focus of ambivalent feelings between rivalrous affinal groups. Certain practices, such as the dowry system or prohibition of divorce and widow remarriage, reinforce and aggravate the powerlessness of Brahman women in their families; yet, they strive by various means to maintain their pride and their standing as goddesses of wealth in their homes.

The successful growth of a family is not taken for granted. Most families have members who perform numerous rituals to ensure the well-being of a kin group as a whole and to fend off danger. In Part II some of the most important calendrical festivals used for kin group protection will be discussed. Since these festivals are performed in a wider context of folk religion, the next chapter outlines essential features of local religious practice.

NOTES

1. Table 6 utilises the following residential typology, as defined by Kolenda (1968 : 346-347) :

A. *Nuclear family* : a couple with or without unmarried children.

B. *Supplemented nuclear family* : a nuclear family plus one or more unmarried, separated, or widowed relatives of the parents, other than their unmarried children.

C. *Subnuclear family* : a fragment of a former nuclear family. Typical examples are the widow with unmarried children, or the widower with unmarried children, or siblings—whether unmarried, or widowed, separated, or divorced—living together.

D. *Single-person household* [self-explanatory].

E. *Supplemented subnuclear* : a group of relatives, members of a formerly complete nuclear family, plus some other unmarried, divorced, or widowed relative who was not a member of the nuclear family. For example, a widow and her unmarried children plus her widowed mother-in-law.

F. *Collateral joint family* : two or more married couples between whom there is a sibling bond—usually a brother-brother relationship—plus unmarried children.

G. *Supplemented collateral joint family* : a collateral joint family plus unmarried, divorced, or widowed relatives. Typically, such supplemental relatives are the widowed mother of the married brothers, or the widower father, or an unmarried sibling.

H. *Lineal joint family* : two couples between whom there is a lineal link, usually between parents and married son, sometimes between parents and married daughter.

I. *Supplemented lineal joint family* : a lineal joint family plus unmarried, divorced, or widowed relatives who do not belong to either of the lineally linked nuclear families; for example, the father's widower brother or the son's wife's unmarried brother.

J. *Lineal-collateral joint family* : three or more couples linked lineally and collaterally. Typically, parents and their two or more married sons, plus the unmarried children of the three or more couples.

K. *Supplemented lineal-collateral joint family* : a lineal-collateral joint family plus unmarried, widowed, separated relatives who belong to none of the nuclear families lineally and collaterally linked; for example, the father's widowed sister or brother, or an unmarried nephew of the father.

L. *Other* : [a residual category, including, for example,] . . . a woman and unmarried grandchild plus her dead husband's brother; a woman living with her mother's brother's wife; and a woman living alone with a servant; and others.

2. Burrows and Emeneau (1960) derive the term *kutumba* from a Tamil or Dravidian root meaning 'house'. Like many other kinship category terms, this one is found outside of south India. It is used extensively in Bengal, for example, according to Inden and Nicholas (1977). The Bengali usage, however, has a less intimate connotation than that of the Dravidian regions. Beck (1972) also discusses the *kutumba* term and concept.

3. The term *balaga* is used instead by my one A.K. informant.

4. The term for parents of children married to each other is *bigaru*. It refers symmetrically only to the parents of one's child's spouse and is, to my knowledge, never extended to apply to anyone besides those specific persons.

5. Beck (1972 : 256) reports that in Konku, Tamilnadu, a man's sister is thought to have the power to bless her brother's family, "or, equally, to curse it if he does not do his utmost for her."

6. See Harper (1969) on this subject.

7. See Orenstein (1970 : 1366) for a discussion of this subject and further references. On the fourth day of an orthodox Hindu wedding, the *caturthi* day, a husband and wife are said to be 'united in all organs.'

8. See Hart (1973a, 1973b) for further discussion of this topic.

9. Several observers have written on the differing roles of Brahman or wealthy women and others. Some major contributions are those of Gough (1956), Srinivas (1977), Jacobson (1977), Wadley (1975), and Ullrich (1977). Kolenda's (1967) paper on regional variation in family organisation is also relevant to this discussion.

10. This applies to dowry wealth but not to other property of women. Srinivas's (1977) comments broaden and deepen this view. He argues that in general, "There is a sense of mine and thine between husband and wife, and only during a real crisis may a husband utilise her money or pawn her jewellry . . . In a great part of rural society, women stick up for their rights against their men, and public opinion supports them in this." Though these comments appear to contradict Tambaiah's (and my own) view, actually they do not, since the dowry system prevents women from gaining access to major portions of family wealth transferred at marriage.

11. The name of this festival is Ceredepandige. Because three *dose* cakes are served, it is also called 'Three Pancake Festival' (*Mur Dose Habba*). Because girls have a thread tied around their neck which some compare to men's sacred threads, it is also called 'Women's Thread Ceremony'. In the home where I observed the ritual on March 14, 1967, the festival is associated with the story, 'Satyavan Savitri.'

Chapter 3

GENERAL PATTERNS IN FOLK RELIGION

Thirty or forty festivals are regularly celebrated by the villagers of Bandipur and Chinnapura. Some are grand events including most of the village population plus hundreds or even thousands of guests from other places. Others are performed quietly by a mother and her children on a special afternoon or evening, hardly noticed even by her neighbours. There are also a number of intermediate types which bring together households, lineage units, subcastes, caste neighbourhoods or other groups for specific ritual occasions.

Most festivals include the two elements of ritual actions and the recitation of myths. Each distinctive complex of action and narrative creates a particular symbolic value for family or community life.

RITUAL

The term 'ritual' refers to a conventionalised set of performances which are believed to help "protect, purify or enrich the participants and their group" by mystical means beyond sensory observation and control (Gluckman 1965 : 285).[1] They are by definition heavily symbolic, making use of unusual objects and actions, or usual ones in unusual combinations or settings, in ways whose meanings are complex and only vaguely understood on a conscious level by the actors.

The conventions of a ritual include several basic components First, a ritual is set apart in time and space. Second, it has what might be termed choreography, i.e., a pattern of movement in that time and space, including actions which formally begin and end it. These acts are often performed by specifically defined personnel, e.g. men; married women; virgins; or specific relatives. An important third in the Hindu pattern is the inclusion of symbolic objects representing the offerings made to spirit or deity.

34

When a ritual is repeated in a regular cycle it becomes a festival,[2] usually including a group larger than the single household. Called *habba* in Kannada, the cyclical festival may be annual, biennial, twice in three years or on any regular time schedule. As a repeated event, the *habba* is distinguished from a rite of passage. *Sastra*, 'ritual requirement', or *samskara*, 'sanctifying rite or essential ceremony' (Sanskritic terms, the latter used mainly by Brahmans) occur only once in each person's development, producing a permanent change in social status.[3] Other non-cyclical rituals include short-term vows (*harake*), promises made to specific deities, e.g. an agreement that one will donate one's hair to the god if the god will cure a sick child. Once the child is cured, the devotee fulfills his or her promise, ending that ritual sequence.

Other vows, called *vrata*,[4] can become festivals if a person or group promises to continue a ritual for a long period, perhaps several years or in perpetuity. Other rituals, called either *sastra* or *puja*, (welcoming, and serving a deity/ spirit as an honoured guest) may be reserved for occasional use as need arises.

A family may develop an individual style of ritual activity over the years, using particular forms of worship for favoured deities, typical foods and other offerings to convey special feelings and meanings. For example, those foods a family customarily prepares for birth and marriage celebrations tend to be used on auspicious festival occasions, whereas foods usually served during funerary periods are avoided on such occasions because of their traditional connotations of sadness and misfortune.

The festival ritual is a religious event oriented toward a concept of a deity or spirit. This deity or spirit (god, goddess, ancestor or ghost) is thought to have some sort of personality and is nearly always given physical form for the occasion. This may mean that it is worshipped as a finely carved statue; or a crude stone or roughly carved wood may be the object of attention. A vessel of liquid, the *kalasa*, is another common way of incorporating a god/spirit.

Forms of worship follow the ancient Hindu practices of *puja* and *bali* (sacrifice). The procedure of *puja* suggests a simulation of traditional hospitality, welcoming the god/spirit into the space and image. In its simplest form it requires purification of place and worshipper (cf. Babb 1975; Sharma 1970) followed by presentation of offerings. After the offerings have been presented, they are left near the image for a time and then redistributed among the group of worshippers as *prasad*, a holy substance never to be rejected when offered as a gift.

Local Kannada terms for *puja* include *seve*, 'service', and *dhupa*, 'incense'. The rotation of fragrant incense sticks before the image of a spirit is so much a part of ritual that *dhupa* can be used as an abbreviated term for the whole procedure. In the same way, circling small oil lamps, *arati*, is another distinctive act of worship performed in both homes and temples.[5] For Brahman women this term has become a brief way of referring to a family celebration, especially one connected with an auspicious rite of passage. When a new bride returns home for the first time, at a child's first birthday and on numerous other happy occasions, Brahman women gather to sing songs and share sweets at an *arati*.

Mangal arati, waving burning camphor before the god-image, is part of some formal rituals. It punctuates the phases of the *puja* and finally marks its end. Beck (1969) has suggested that burning camphor offers to the deity/spirit a sequence of excitation and calming. As camphor is thought to be a cooling medication, it is believed to soothe a spiritual being, 'to cool the spirit's eyes', as villagers put it.

Animal sacrifice is still an important part of folk ritual in Karnataka and some of the festivals to be discussed include this element. Different types of *bali* are distinguished locally according to the method of killing; whether decapitation is partial or total; whether the animal is held still or allowed to run freely as it dies. The sacrificial offerings are selected to suit the nature of the deity and to manipulate that nature to the advantage of the worshipper(s) :

"If you sit for meals, some eat milky rice, some clarified butter, etc. Similarly, each god needs a certain type of offering" (comments of a Hassan District soothsayer).

For example, the goddess Bandamma is an irritable and powerful diety who resides permanently in three growths inside the trunk of a tree on the outskirts of Bandipur. She is believed to be available to perform destructive acts on behalf of those who apply to her through ritual sacrifice. Most of the *amma* or 'lady' goddesses of this type require as sacrifice fresh blood and a cooked meat meal. The kind of offering to Bandamma varies, however, with the purpose of the petitioner. If one wishes to have her kill someone, then one must give her an animal which is coloured black. This will presumably bring out the death-dealing capacity in her nature.

For less lethal intentions there are other types of offerings, sweets or bland foods, thought to bring out benign and protective tendencies. There are varying degrees of sacrificial offerings. When discussing sacrifice, villagers often mention the number of legs which are to be offered. Thus one goat with four legs can equal two chickens of two legs each. Vows sometimes promise offerings of two legs, four legs, eight legs, and so on, rather than specifying a particular animal.

In many festivals certain offerings are forbidden. These taboos are as important as the positive requirements in defining the structure of symbolic themes. For example, the serpent deity must not be offered food cooked with pungent seasoning such as chillies. It is said that such flavour will 'heat his eyes' and make him angry, bringing skin diseases and other misfortune to the performing family.

The selection of offerings is not made anew with each repetition of an established ritual. In fact, little thought goes into the routine assembling of *puja* items beyond remembering an exact list of requirements. Nevertheless, the designs vary sufficiently to express some individuality.

The layout of a *puja* offering of foods, flowers and other objects, spread across a floor or piled on a chair-pedestal, forms a sort of language of art. The design conveys a message, combining symbols in a simultaneous expression of many relationships. The presentation is seen as bringing together the spirit/ deity and the worshipper(s) in a process affecting both.

In accordance with the old Tantric principle that human beings (like deities) have "divine powers that could be activated and experienced by means of special ritual procedures" (Hopkins 1971 : 112), the villagers of Bandipur and Chinnapura enter into festival rituals with the feeling that they too are changed by the experience of the rites. The influences can be of various sorts. In married women's rituals for benign goddesses, for example, the women do everything they can to assimilate themselves to the goddesses they are honouring. They feel this makes them more goddess-like in status.

Other spirits, however, need to be kept distinct and separate from their devotees, who sense danger as rituals bring them into close contact with powerful spirits. For example, members of a close patrilincal group (*dayadi*) do not impersonate their ancestors in the death-anniversary ancestral feast. They bring in others, often close 'relations of exchange' (*nentru*) to perform the annual impersonation and eat food on behalf of the revered and feared dead members of the family. This restriction may reflect a deep belief that members of the same descent group are already so close that the actual impersonation of the dead could bring about their own deaths; the contagious action of ritual might destroy the living. By the use of comparative outsiders, a social barrier is erected between the spirits and their supplicants.

Participants in rituals are believed to be influenced not only by deities/spirits and by their own ritual actions, but also by each other. For example, one part of the Birth Group Festival (related to serpent worship) in Chinnapura is a blessing solicited from a mother of sons for one's own son. Both the donor and the mother-recipient of the blessing must be in an absolutely pure (*madi*) state. Both observe a total food and drink fast before they meet for the blessing. Though only one of their sons receives a blessing (from the outsider) they both are influenced by their exchange. It is as if a sort of reverse-pollution could insult the donor of the blessing if the recipient were not in an adequate state of 'purity'.

In some rituals, objects may also be in purity-pollution interaction. For example, many non-Brahmans cook two separate vessels of food on the occasion of their ancestor festival at the Mahalaya New Moon, one to serve the ancestors and close family, the other for the guests who may arrive in large numbers on that evening. This practice is at variance with ordinary Hindu food-exchange purity rules, according to which it is only the recipient who is affected by the purity state of the donor. In that case, one who is being cautious about one's purity will take food from very few others, but may give food to others without fear of being affected by the recipient's state of pollution or purity. The ritual of cooking two pots of food for the ancestor festival, however, suggests the possibility of a sort of reverse pollution. It is as if the ancestors and the descendants might be polluted by those to whom they give food; therefore, outsiders are prevented from taking food from the same vessel as close family members.

RITUAL SPACE

The location of a ritual site and the definition of the space are important ways of controlling the relation between the human and spirit domains. Rituals are celebrated in many different kinds of space—in homes ('inside' in the kitchen, or 'outside' in the front room); in village shrines and temples, in fields or other places (such as trees), in village lands and near village boundaries. Each ritual has its customary site and its typical housing for the god-image at that site. Housing can be permanent, as in a rock shrine or a small or large temple. The common village word for a small temple is, in fact, an old Kannada word for 'house', *gudi*. A large temple, *devastana*, 'god's place', houses gods and goddesses of the Hindu Sanskritic pantheon. Silver images of some of these deities are used for processions in Bandipur's wheeled 'temple cart' (*teru* or *ratha*), a temple on wheels. There are also palanquins for gods' processions; these are transportation vehicles rather than movable temples.

Shrines may be temporary, set up in homes or fields for the ritual and dismantled on its conclusion. The most common form is called *mantapa* and consists of an open structure with posts supporting a roof which is usually made of leaves. There are three *mantapas* in the Bandipur-Chinnapura area which are constructed of permanent stone, but they are considered temporary in the sense that they are not shrines when they do not actually shelter god-images. *Mantapas* cover any and all ritual zones, human or divine, serving, for example, as the place where a bride and groom first meet in a wedding and exchange garlands in front of the bride's home.

There seem to be social circumstances which determine whether a deity, ancestor, or house god will or will not have a temple or shrine built for it. A spirit regularly worshipped by a formally constituted group, such as a caste, a lineage, or a village, is generally housed in a permanent shelter. In Bandipur and Chinnapura, where ancestor worship is a household ritual, there are no permanent ancestral shrines that I know of. Ancestors are enshrined in areas of Tamilnadu (Beck 1972 : 206-208) and Kerala (Gough 1958), where the ritual is more communal in the traditional Nayar lineages. This difference reflects the attenuated role of the agnatic lineage in Hassan District and the resulting smaller numbers gathering annually for ancestor worship.

Shrine location may indicate the distance which the family maintains from the deity/spirit being honoured. Some benign spirits are welcomed into the house and much care is given to setting up a comfortable and honourable place for them. The violent lady goddesses (*amma*), on the other hand, are not enshrined in homes; such nearness, it seems, might court disaster. They are most likely to reside in fields and groves at a distance from residential neighbourhoods. An exception is the goddess Maramma. Though she is traditionally thought to bring plague, smallpox and other ills, she seems to be evolving out of the *amma* pattern into deity status, becoming a more neutral spirit. She has small temples in the central residential areas of both Bandipur and Chinnapura.

Funerary rituals are all performed outdoors, to orient the dead person's soul away from the home, until the final feast at the end of the ten-day mourning period. Some non-Brahman castes serve the funerary feast outside as well.

Deities and spirits are thought to be hungry for food. They can be bribed with food and are thought to be attracted to places where food can be found. Thus, one sub-caste of Farmers prepares pork only outside of the kitchen since pork is considered a favourite food of malevolent ghosts. These ghosts may be drawn to the cooking pork, it is said, but will not find the real stove in the 'inside' kitchen, and will remain on the verandah or in 'outside' rooms where they cannot do too much harm.

The house and its parts form a virtual metaphor for the family and its parts, as elsewhere in India (see Khare 1976b). In Karnataka the house receives ritual attention as representing a body or a family. It is thought, for example, to attract ghosts which may linger in the roof tiles until a magician can force them to leave. The purifying rituals for the space are comparable to those for the person. Whether the house rejects or welcomes a deity/spirit in a family festival is a measure of the appropriate distance that ought to be observed.

RITUAL TIME AND THE RELIGIOUS CALENDAR

In Hinduism, time is as important as space in locating ritual events. Heirs to the knowledge of four millenia of astronomers and astrologers, the people of Chinnapura and Bandipur are very careful to place their religious work correctly in time, as are other Hindus throughout the subcontinent. The basis for such caution is the belief that astronomical events influence human life, that auspicious or inauspicious configurations of the stars, planets, sun and moon can bring either good or ill fortune.

Some consequences of this belief may be localised or idiosyncratic. For instance, one Farmer family in Bandipur which had lost a daughter-in-law on the occasion of a certain festival felt that their home would always be defiled by death pollution at that festival time. They therefore had discontinued performing that festival ritual.

Cyclically recurring ritual times are thought to increase closeness among people and events. Thus it is common among the Brahmans and some other *jatis* to perform oblations for their dead on the lunar anniversaries of the deaths, as if the deceased would be most easily summoned back home for memorial services at the same time they originally departed.

The lunisolar calendar (*amanta*) used by the villagers to regulate their rituals is the one generally used throughout south India, different from that used in the north. It divides the year (*varsa*) into twelve lunar months of approximately 29.5 lunar days each. These months are named for lunar mansions or constellations (*naksatra*) recognised by ancient astronomers. Each month is divided into two halves (*paksa*), the first beginning with the new moon (*amavase*) and the second with the full moon (*purnima*). The waxing and waning periods are numbered separately. Each day (*tithi*) is divided into 24 hours and a seven-day week is recognised. In this local calendar system, the lunar year begins with the month of Chaitra, which comes in March or April. The solar new year, often a different time, is fixed at April 13th or 14th throughout India.

The cycle of lunar days and months is periodically adjusted to conform with the solar cycle, as both have been considered significant for several millenia. A lunar day, for example, may begin at any time during a solar day (*divasa*). When more than one lunar day falls on one solar day, or when there is no lunar day beginning on a solar day, lunar dates may be deleted, added or repeated. Lunar months are also added or deleted in order to bring the lunar year of 354 solar days into accord with the solar year of 365 days. Every two and one half to three years an extra month (*adhika* 'additional') is added to the calendar; deletions are made less frequently (see Freed and Freed 1964a : 77).

The year is also divided into two halves : *uttarayana*, the period after the winter solstice when the sun apparently moves northward through the skies, and *daksinayana*, the period after the summer solstice when the sun's apparent motion is southward. The spring time of lengthening days is considered by some villagers to be a lucky or auspicious period, while the shortening days after midsummer are unfavourable, in their view.

The winter solstice, fixed throughout India at January 14th, is a major holiday, marking the transition between the two phases of the year. It is a time for purification and special care of homes, children and cattle. It is not observed at the official solstice date but is timed with the passage of the sun into Capricorn (*makara sankranti, sankranti* being the term for any time the sun passes into a new zodiac sign).

Special attributes or deities are associated with particular dates, making them good or bad times for certain rituals. Two most important days of any month are new moon and full moon days. *Amavase* is considered to be dark and ominous and is the favoured time for communion with the dead. *Purnima* is a bright and lucky time when many auspicious celebrations are held. Depending on their family and *jati* traditions, villagers regard certain days of the week as of particular character : Weavers give their cattle a rest on Mondays; Brahmans consider Tuesdays and Fridays to be special to women and goddesses. These many considerations affect the scheduling of festival rituals.

The intricacies of the calendar are spelled out in almanacs called *pancanga*. Each village has literate residents who can read almanacs and advise families on the scheduling of religious activities. As an example, the lunisolar calendar of 1966-67 and associated festivals are outlined in Tables 9 and 10.

THE LIMITED ROLE OF RITUAL SPECIALISTS

There are several types of ritual specialists available to Karnataka villagers. Brahmans knowledgeable in the *Vedas*, *Puranas*, and *Agama* ritual texts often serve as priests (*purohits*) performing weddings and other home ceremonies for other Brahmans or non-Brahmans. There are some Smith *Mantravadi* or *Sastrahelavaru* (literally 'tellers') who are called on for divination from astrological tables, calculating by numerology, casting spells and removing them, and other magical assistance. One young Washerman of Bandipur is now starting a career as an oracle : he speaks with the voice of goddess Maramma on Tuesdays and Fridays. His father is a priest for the goddess. Another local specialist, the *Ainoru*, lives as a Farmer, calls himself a Brahman, and shows up at non-Brahmans' houses to remove the death pollution at the end of the initial mourning period. *Jajmani* types of interdependence produce other ritual services which can be done only by certain *jatis*, A.K.s replicating many of these service specialities within their own communities.

Festivals and pilgrimages bring other holy visitors from outside the villages, often providing special knowledge, wisdom and spiritual services, such as conveying a vow to far-off Tirupati. Even itinerant shadow-puppet players may be considered ritual specialists, as they make religious messages available to the public at large in their artful renditions of the Mahabharata and Ramayana.

Since many of these holy men (and a few women) have gone through arduous training, there is no lack of expert knowledge in the countryside. However, though each family respects the specialists and may consult them, their festival practices are not all the direct result of instruction. *Puranic* tales and *purohits'* formulas are woven into a fabric as embellishments to a family's own traditional design.

Festival ways are freely discussed in family and village. Because there is prestige associated with most of these rituals, people like to talk about how they do them and to muse over the fact that there are so many different customs in one small place. With this freedom of conversation it is easy to pick up ideas. In a case discussed in Part II, for instance, one women's festival appears to have been copied largely from another.[6]

In some well-established family or other group festivals, the details of procedures are transmitted within the patrilineal household. The usual line of

Table 9—Alternative Calendars: Correlations of Lunar and Solar Months, 1966-1967

Hindu Lunar Months	/Chaitra (1st mo.)	/Vaisakha	/Jyeshtha
Hindu Solar Months†	Panguni	/Chittirai (1st month)	/Vaiyashi
Gregorian Calendar	/March	/April	/May	/June

Hindu Lunar Months	/Ashadha	/Adikha Sravana††	/Nija (true) Sravana
Hindu Solar Months	/Ani	/Adi	/Avani
Gregorian Calendar	/July	/August	/September

Hindu Lunar Months	/Bhadrapada	/Asvija	/Kartika
Hindu Solar Months	/Peratasi	/Tula	/Karthikai
Gregorian Calendar	/October	/November	/December

Hindu Lunar Months	/Margasira	/Pushya	/Magha	/Phalguna
Hindu Solar Months	/ Margali	/Tai	/Masi	/
Gregorian Calendar	/January	/February	/March

† Only one set of names for the solar months is used here; each month has at least one other name.

†† This was an extra month, repeated twice in this year to adjust the lunar and solar calendars. Such adjustments are made every few years and can come at any point in the calendar.

Table 10—Festival Cycle and Agricultural Seasons, 1966-67

Lunar Months and Dates†	Gegorian/Solar Calendar, Ethnographic Observation Dates	Festival Names	Festival Descriptions	Seasons	Agricultural Work
Chaitra					
I : 1	10 April 1967	Chandramana Ugadi	Lunar New Year. All Hindus eat mixture of sweet and bitter items	Dry	Ploughing
I : 9	18-19 April 1967	Sri Rama Navami	Lord Rama's Birthday, celebrated by Brahmans		
I : 15	(not observed)	Maramma Jatra	Festival of Chinnapura A.K.s, to worship goddess Maramma		
Vaisakha					
I : 5	14 May 1967	Sri Sankaracharya Jayanthi	Birthday of Hindu philosopher	Dry, Hot	Preparation of fields and equipment
Vaisakha					
I : 6	15 May 1967	Sri Ramanuja-charya Jayanthi	Birthday of Hindu philosopher	Dry	
Jyeshtha					
	16 June 1967 (not observed)	Sankramana, Dakshinayana	Summer Solstice, of importance to some Brahman families as beginning of southward movement of the sun	Monsoon rains begin	Planting rice and millet

Table 10 (contd. on page 44)

Table 10 (contd. from page 43)

Lunar Months and Dates†	Gregorian/Solar Calendar, Ethnographic Observation Dates	Festival Names	Festival Descriptions	Seasons	Agricultural Work
Ashadha	June-July, 1966 / July-August, 1967			Wet	Planting continues / Replanting rice seedlings
Adikha Sravana (extra, added month)	July-August 1966			Wet	Replanting: Weeding
Sravana	August-September 1967				
	Solar month of Adi (July-August):		Iyengar Brahman Festival for Wife of Vishnu. Second Friday of Adi is especially important		
	Adi 1st-32nd 16 July-16 Aug. 1966 & Adi 1st-31st (17 July-16 Aug. 1967)	Prati Habba			
Sravana (1967) and Nija (true) Sravana (1966)	August-September				
I : 5	20 August 1966 / 10-11 August 1967	(V)odahuttidavara Habba, or Siri Yala Sristi, or Nagarapanchami	Sibling Group Festival of Smartha Brahmans, with cobra worship	Wet	Weeding
I : 11	26 August 1966	Vara Maha Lakshmi	Festival for Wife of Vishnu, celebrated by Smartha Brahmans		

Tithi	Festival name	Date(s)	Description	Agricultural note
I : 15 (full moon)	Upakarma	30 August 1966 19 August 1967	Men who wear sacred threads remove old ones and put on new ones as a purification ritual	
II : 7-9	Krishna Jayanthi	9 September 1966 28 August 1967	Birthday of the god Krishna	
Bhadrapada				
I : 3-4	Gauri Habba and Ganapati	17 September 1966 7 September 1967	Gauri Festival, for wife of Siva; Festival for Ganesha, son of Siva	Rains end this month
I : 10 I : 6 }	Kattarighatta Jatra	24 September 1966 9 September 1967 }	A fair on the outskirts of Bandipur, for individuals making vows to god Hanuman	Harvest some millet; Tend all other crops
	Kattarighatta or Doddaseve	9 September 1967	'Major Sacrifice' festival of 28-village region around Chinnapura, with a fair and a group procession	
I : 10	Gramadevate Puja	24 September 1966 (not observed)	Village worship for *amma* goddess enshrined near village boundary, Bandipur	
I : 10	Ganapati Utsava	24 September 1966	Send-off into river for Ganesha (day of event can vary), Bandipur	

Table 10 (*contd. on page* 46)

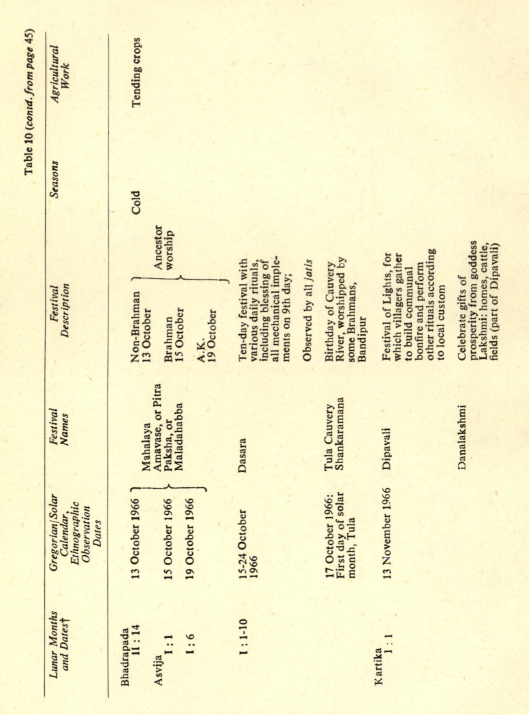

Table 10 (contd. from page 45)

Lunar Months and Dates†	Gregorian/Solar Calendar, Ethnographic Observation Dates	Festival Names	Festival Description	Seasons	Agricultural Work
Bhadrapada II : 14	13 October 1966		Non-Brahman 13 October	Cold	Tending crops
Asvija I : 1	15 October 1966	Mahalaya Amavase, or Pitra Paksha, or Maladahabba	Brahman 15 October } Ancestor worship		
I : 6	19 October 1966		A.K. 19 October		
I : 1-10	15-24 October 1966	Dasara	Ten-day festival with various daily rituals, including blessing of all mechanical implements on 9th day; Observed by all *jatis*		
	17 October 1966: First day of solar month, Tula	Tula Cauvery Shankaramana	Birthday of Cauvery River, worshipped by some Brahmans, Bandipur		
Kartika I : 1	13 November 1966	Dipavali	Festival of Lights, for which villagers gather to build communal bonfire and perform other rituals according to local custom		
		Danalakshmi	Celebrate gifts of prosperity from goddess Lakshmi: homes, cattle, fields (part of Dipavali)		

Festival	Lunar date	Date	Description	Season	Harvest
Mastiamma	I : 9	21 November 1966	Offering to a female spirit by one Farmer lineage		
Makkal Habba	I : 13 / (Full I : 15 moon)	25 November 1966 / 28 November 1966	Children's Festival, performed on different days by different families		
Sreshti Habba, or Subramanya Shashti	Margasira I : 5-6	17-18 December 1966	Festival dedicated to Subramanya, son of Siva; includes neighbourly exchange of vegetables, and some cobra worship	Cold	Begin harvest of rice and millet
Nagara Habba or Nagarapan-cami	(New moon) II : 15 / Pushya I : 4	10 January 1967 (Bandipur) / 14 January 1967 (Chinnapura)	Cobra Festival, worship for cobra spirit(s) at ant hill	Dry	Complete the harvest
Makara Sankranti, or Uttarayana		14 January 1967	Winter Solstice, celebrated by all villagers, with special attention to cattle and threshing floor		
Narasimha Jatra	II : 14 through Magha I : 10	8 February 1967 through 19 February 1967	Twelve-day festival for temple deity of Bandipur, including cattle fair and daily rituals	Dry	None

Table 10 (*contd. on page* 48)

Table 10 (contd. from page 47)

Lunar months and Dates†	Gregorian/Solar Calender, Ethnographic Observation Dates	Festival Names	Festival Descriptions	Seasons	Agricultural Work
Magha (contd.)					
I : 7	16 February 1967		Temple cart procession (climax of Narasimha Jatra)		None
II : 12	7 March 1967	Maramma Jatra	Communal worship of goddess Maramma and feast, Bandipur A.K. community		
II : 14	9-10 March 1967	Maha Sivaratri	All-night festival dedicated to god, Siva. Members of all Saivite jatis fast and go without sleep		
Phalguna					
I : 3	14 March 1967	Piriyapattanad-amma Habba	Worship of amma goddess, Piriyapattanad-amma, by Washerman family (on alternative dates, by others)	Dry	None
I : 3	14 March 1967	Ceredipandige Habba	Festival for daughters, in some Iyengar Brahman homes		

† I : Numbered days after the new moon, through full moon day.
   'Bright' half of the lunar month, called sukla or shuddha on calendars.
  II : Numbered days after full moon, through new moon day.
   'Dark' half of the lunar month, called krishna or bahula.
  Conventional English spellings in vogue in Karnataka State are used in this table. These spellings differ somewhat from those used in other states.

transmission is from mother-in-law to daughter-in-law, since nearly all of these rituals are performed for the welfare of the home and birth group.

Initiating a festival may be a personal decision, a group agreement or a suggestion from a ritual specialist. In the event that a problem should arise—say, a chronic rash on a child's skin or, more seriously, the deaths of too many family cattle—the members of the family will discuss it among themselves for a while. After some time they may decide to consult a soothsayer (probably a *Mantravadi* or *Sastra*-teller) about it. This does not mean that they will not also consult medical specialists or veterinarians. Most families use both medical and magical knowledge without any sense of contradiction between them.

The soothsayer will determine the source of their problem by calculations based on the time of their arrival at his place. He will divine that their child's rash is due, say, to the wrath of a serpent spirit, telling them that one of their predecessors once injured a serpent and that the ghost of that snake has returned to cause trouble for the family. He may suggest a ritual to propitiate the spirit. Or, suppose he divines that their cattle deaths are due to the anger of an *amma* goddess whose rituals they have discontinued. He advises resuming the ritual. Here his role ends.

I have asked several soothsayers and lay persons whether the ritual specialist ever spells out the methods of festival rituals; the answer has always been a clear negative. The most he will tell the family is one or two details: offer a golden item; wear white; give two chickens as sacrifice. The rest they work out themselves. It is therefore the inventiveness of common women, and a few men, which gives the festival its form as India's greatest folk art.

In the example cited, the family in discussion may remember that their grandfather had wounded a snake one time in the garden; or they agree that it was a mistake to stop performing the feast for that *amma*. Then they decide to make a festival for the serpent spirit, or recommence the festival for the *amma*, according to family traditions.

In these folk rituals each family faces the dangers and fears that confront it. This form of confrontation helps to identify the dangers. Though the concepts of danger may be unconscious, rituals aid in clarifying the problems by investing them with symbolic structures, just as dreams may do for an individual's mental processes.

In some of the festivals, such as those for troublesome ghosts or for cobra spirits, the object of worship is also the source of danger. Going through the rituals and telling the stories seem to produce a sense of rectification, safety, or order, which may be social, spiritual or cosmic. In other festivals, such as those for benign goddesses such as Gauri and Prati, families see themselves as securing the deities as friends and helpers. The outcome of the festival is a projective identification with the spirit, enhancing the woman's ability to shelter her husband and family by enlisting the aid of her supernatural ally.

MYTH

Most of the festival rituals described in Part II include myths (*kate*). These are stories which are told as part of the festivals. They are usually fantastic reports of miracles, females or male heroism, divine play, and the ordeals of the faithful.[7] Some might be called quasi-legends, tales of events which supposedly occurred in previous generations. These often seem to have been newly invented with the help of soothsayers approached to divine the causes of family misfortunes. Both myths and legends tend to be short, and I have found only one-per-family-per-festival. It is possible to trace some back to written *Puranas*, while others seem to be based entirely on oral tradition.

Myths and rituals form coordinated units, supplementing each other and partially overlapping in meanings. The myths' verbal content provides clues to the deeper meanings of ritual symbolism, and to the relationships implied by ritual actions and objects.[8] In some cases festival myths and rituals echo each other's meanings, but in others they have complementary roles in the total event. For example, rituals for the cobra deity stress benign theme of sweetness and purity, barely hinting at the ominous dangers which threaten the well-being of a growing family. On the other hand, the myths in this particular festival complex tend to be quite bloody and tragic. It appears that some myths speak of possibilities far too dangerous to enact in a physical way, and that rituals (being action) are used as powerful magic to prevent the dangers which lurk behind this festival. Though the power of the word is an old Sanskritic principle, the ancient power of the (ritual) act is greater in this Karnataka tradition.

Specific myths may or may not be connected with corresponding rituals in a given time and place. A few rituals seem to have no associated myths, or may have lost them. The two seem to be fairly easily separated and re-attached. In one case, for example, I found a festival ritual of importance to a few families of Bandipur, honouring the goddess Piriyapattanadamma, whose temple is about fifty miles south of the village. I was unable to find local mythic material on this goddess, though she was believed to have great power over the families who performed her rituals. A possible explanation for this loose attachment is that the myth and the ritual are equivalent as symbolic material and each can therefore stand alone. If myths were necessary as explanations (or exegesis), as some scholars have claimed, then they would be more firmly attached.

Myth is based on verbal material, but is not therefore discursive or didactic. Like poetry, the myth uses ellipsis and connotation, imagery that does not attempt to explain itself. Its elements may be symbols by metonymy or metaphor. Even the few which are self-consciously allegorical are still symbolically rich, capable of depths of non-conscious meaning unacknowledged by those who tell and enjoy them.

NOTES

1. Gluckman's definition of ritual is more narrow than some others, since it separates stylised performances based on 'mystical beliefs of effectiveness' from what he terms 'ceremonies', performances without a sense of magic or mystery. His definition fits precisely the festivals to be described in Part II of this book. These are serious and symbolic festivals, assumed to purify, protect, and enrich families.

2. It should be borne in mind that the English term 'festival' might be misleading : most *habbas* are not festive occasions but completely serious in intent even when lively in style.

3. A clear difference exists between festivals and rites of passage in that the latter are not primarily deity- or spirit-worship occasions. Rather, they are intended to magically protect and transform the person of concern, though religious worship may be part of the ritual for this person. It is, however, often said that a person is "like a god" when going through an auspicious (life-oriented) rite. This is generally said of brides and grooms. An Iyengar Brahman informant tells me that there is a special ritual by which a god can be brought into a bridegroom; and the same ritual brings ancestors into guests at a death-anniversary feast.

Visible differences separate treatment of persons from treatment of deities. In a rite of passage the ritually important person is seated on a low wooden stool called *mane* or *hase mane* (though this stool is not used in funerary rituals). A god-image is rarely if ever placed on a *mane*. When a deity is worshipped, it is always fed. Its food can be simple fruits, snacks, or a whole meal. (Terms for food offerings are *naivedya* or *(y)ede*.) This offered food is considered sacred and is distributed to the group in attendance as *prasad*, a term that can also apply to flowers or other offerings. When a person is honoured in a rite of passage, special foods—though always part of the event and often shared with guests—are not distributed as *prasad*.

4. Wadley explains *vrata* (Hindi, *vrat*) in her book : "The overall implication in *vrat* is a vow of worship given to the deity concerned" (1975 : 63). The gods honoured in *vrat* are ones with whom one has a "regular and auspicious relationship" (*Ibid.* : 136) on the same order as a relationship of intense *bhakti* devotion (*Ibid.* : 185).

5. See Beck (1969) and Clothey (1969) for further comments on *arati* in folk Hindu ritual. Lewis (1958) also discusses it for north India.

6. As I have discussed elsewhere (1972, 1975), it is common to imitate festivals of other groups or even of other regions. There is far more fluidity in regional festival systems than one might think on the basis of one year's observation and interviewing. Speaking in the language of permanence seems to make a festival legitimate. Long-term evidence, however, indicates that permanence is not necessarily a basic rule of festival behaviour.

7. I am using the term 'myth' in a broad, general sense. Any story which is connected with a festival is of mythic value here. Though more strict definitions of Thompson (1946) and others would require that a myth be sacred or considered true, the less rigid use is the one now customary in anthropology. The festival myth, therefore, need not be of sacred origin or considered true by all hearers.

8. This approach is based on Lévi-Strauss's (1955) distinction between myth and language as two entirely different modes of communication, and on Susanne Langer's (1957 : 195) view that, " . . . The myth-making consciousness knows only the appeal of ideas, and uses or forgets them without regard to their literal or logical value." The words of myths convey images, and it is the relations among those images or motifs which is the basis of myths' meanings, rather than sometimes disjointed or illogical series of sentences in which they are presented. Philosophical or normative statements, on the other hand, do have logical qualities typical of most discursive symbolism.

Chapter 4

UNDERSTANDING FESTIVAL SYMBOLISM

METHODS OF STUDY

Analysis of festivals in Part II of this book will rely primarily on structuralist techniques and concepts, supplemented by other approaches. The approach to meaning through structure is now familiar to many anthropologists. The key to festival symbolism is in the composition of elements in the rituals and myths. Interpretive techniques, first developed by structuralist Claude Lévi-Strauss, consist of identifying repeated patterns in relationships among elements. There are three basic steps to a structural analysis of any symbolic phenomenon.

(1) The first is to identify and sort the elements being used symbolically—colours, flowers, foods, tools, numbers and so on. For example: food forms a very significant part of many rituals and myths, but in the festival context it is clear that the preparation, offering, serving and eating are not done just because it is mealtime and people are hungry. Rather, food serves to suggest a condition, a process, or any number of analogous concepts.

(2) Once symbolic items are identified and classified, the next task is to consider how and why they may be interrelated in a particular festival. Unlike some other symbolic approaches, this sets no limit on how elements of a structure are to be considered related. That is, anything within the whole may be seen as related to anything else, whether or not the two items appear together. The method of assigning relationship is to discover contrast or opposition among features of ritual objects, and then to identify mediators combining features and providing symbolic transitions. For example, in the funeral-like Piriyapattanadamma ritual, the symbolic elements express a key problem or dilemma : the corporeal nature of the body housing a soul, the inevitability of death, and the necessity of mourning as a transition to peace. As seen in Tables 11 and 12 the opposition is symbolised by the condition of raw or cooked rice,

Table 11—Cooking as a Mediator in Piriyapattanadamma Ritual

(Major 'Meaning'/Dilemma:)	Living State	Deceased State	Peaceful Death
(Items:)	Raw rice	(is placed in) two pots	
(Mediator, cooking:)		(and) -boiled-	
			(to become) Cooked rice

Table 12—Symbolic Transition from Life to Death in Piriyapattanadamma Ritual

Living State	Deceased State	Peaceful Death
Vessel with water; Stove with coals:	Remove hot coals,	Pour water through stove

with cooking as the mediator. In a parallel way, pouring water mediates between the conditions of hot and cool at the conclusion of the same ritual.

(3) The final step in a structuralist interpretation is to present a general view of the meaning of a festival, expressed as an issue or dilemma, and to discuss the ways in which the festival handles the issue symbolically. In the example given, the ritual deals with matters of living and dying, and its structure indicates that funerals are necessary. This is an oversimplification. Though some rituals seem to come to neat conclusions about solving problems, not all do so, but leave matters unresolved instead.

The definition of meaning as a dilemma or cultural issue is central to structuralist method. The basis of this approach is a dialectical view of society or culture itself, defining any way of life as a struggle among contradictory or conflicting needs, forces and ideas, rather than a balanced and orderly system. It is through processes of contradiction that transformations occur and life—in society and in its symbolic products—continues and changes. In the author's view, this bold approach produces non-obvious and non-trivial insights into both festival rituals and the attendant myths, and is the best available empirical and interpretive technique for this material.

The festival analyses to be presented in Part II are not based entirely on structuralist theory, however. The comprehension of meaning has been augmented and expanded by incorporating some of the concepts of Susanne Langer. In her writings she develops ideas of art as presentational symbolism which seem particularly appropriate for the study of the materials displayed in folk festivals. Langer contrasts the aesthetics of works of visual art with what she terms the discursive symbolism of language.

Langer views symbolic meaning in art as a complex relationship between a symbol and some object or referent. A 'concept' is the basis of this relationship and also its product. The creative, constructive force of symbolic meaning depends on the complexity of the relationship rather than the pieces of which it is constructed. For any given concept there are many possible symbolic arrangements expressing specific 'conceptions' aspects or applications of a concept. The art of the *puja* offering is precisely such a presentation of material objects arranged in patterns that evoke symbolic meanings of a depth and subtlety beyond the reach of language. To quote Langer (1957 : 72),

"The power of understanding symbols . . . issues in an unconscious, spontaneous process of *abstraction*, which goes on all the time in the human mind: a process of recognizing the concept in any configuration given to experience, and forming a conception accordingly. That is the real sense of Aristotle's definition of man as "the rational animal." *Abstractive seeing* is the foundation of our rationality, and is its definite guarantee long before the dawn of any conscious generalization or syllogism." (Italics in text.)

When we come to the study of festival myths, the structuralist approach to meaning can be augmented fruitfully by reference to the formalist methods of Propp (1968) and Wadley (1975). The formalist attends closely to the actual sequence of a plot, while the structuralist is more concerned with the diverse qualities of motifs for information about the meanings of a myth. Despite differences, the two approaches are related both theoretically and historically. Propp's work made an early, if indirect, impact on that of Lévi-Strauss (cf. Lévi-Strauss 1976). Both complement each other in the analysis of specific myths. The common-sense logic of formalism is suited to the study of conscious ideals and role models in mythic narrative, while structuralism invites insights into the mixture of positive and negative found in every cultural system. The patterns (functions) of the formalist analysis perform at a macro-level a part of the work attributed to motifs at the micro-level in structuralism. The actions which are the object of formalist study are therefore referred to by Lévi-Strauss (1976 : 144) as "mythemes of the second power."

While an eclectic approach will serve until a comprehensive theory of cultural symbolism is developed, structuralism provides the most dynamic techniques to rise above immense detail and still produce semantic insights. Not always translatable into overt statements, structures transcend the limits of ordinary discourse and move us on to powerful, dialectical comprehension of festival practices.

As each myth is presented, its structure will be analysed, identifying the philosophical or social dilemma to which it addresses itself. The constituent motifs are isolated and their various possible relationships reviewed. In defining relationships, the interpreter studies the qualities of the elements under scrutiny, bearing in mind Hindu cultural definitions and striving for maximum objectivity while relying also on educated intuition.

The interpreter must decide the significance of each symbol or role. An ascetic holy man appears as a character in a myth. Does he represent celibacy in relation to another character's sexuality, or, alternatively, does he represent detachment from social rules in contrast to another's commitment to them? After organising each motif into at least one relationship, and some possibly into more than one according to their multiple qualities, the method requires alignment of sets into ordered groups. This is the step which produces insights into a given myth's structure.

As certain types of relationships among motifs begin to repeat themselves, the social or philosophical issue at the heart of the myth becomes more and more clear. There begins to emerge a sense of what a myth is about at a deep level. Studying overlapping relationships, one continues to refine or reshape hypotheses until redundancy appears to the eye. Once developed, structures are usually cultural contradictions or otherwise irreconcilable philosophical principles. They produce the tension which gives each myth its special force and appeal. One structure considered, for example, 'Cobra Festival Myth', is organised around the dilemma between incestuous desires and the social need for exogamous marriage.

The catalyst of movement or action in a given myth (as in ritual) is seen as mediator, a motif which seems not to fit neatly into either side of a relationship but rather straddles both sides of a basic dilemma. Such mediators are often readily evident, as they are usually the most interesting and exciting elements of myths. An example occurs in the 'Mangala Gauri' myth, when the power of a young bride's devotion transforms a deadly serpent trapped inside a vessel into a beautiful necklace. In this structure of opposition between death and vitality, the magically changed serpent incorporates both in one image, bridging the difference and revealing a basic feature of the myth's meaning.

In structural analyses of both myth and ritual, there is a method of verifying the interpretation. General criteria are the completeness with which the analysis incorporates all or most symbolic items or motifs within its framework; the logical relationship of a symbolic structure to the wider cultural system; and the demonstration of repeating patterns. In judging a structural analysis, the minimal questions to be asked are: Does the model account for a sufficient number of elements present? Does this analysis make sense in terms of the participants' way of life and other known practices? Are symbolic relationships within the structure repeated several times in analogous fashion? If these questions can be answered yes, then it can be demonstrated that the method of study has led to a valid interpretation.

GENERAL ELEMENTS OF FESTIVAL SYMBOLISM

Each festival is unique, but those of Chinnapura and Bandipur, as in many

other regions of Hindu India, are made up of certain elements which appear
both as objects of ritual attention and as motifs of myths. Myths and rituals
supplement each other in festival interpretations. For example, in one cobra
festival, called 'Sibling Group Festival', sisters and brothers offer each other
fruits and sweets and anoint each other with pandanus flowers dipped in a
special liquid. The sibling relationship also appears in a myth, in which a sister
saves her brother from death by snakebite in a pandanus tree. As in many
festivals, the myth is more dramatic and explores a more tragic idea than the
ritual, which serves as a positive gesture of healing unity and remediation.

Though widely varying, most festivals share many common features. A cobra
myth of one *jati*, for example, may illuminate the cobra worship rituals of another. In one case, Bandipur residents made regular offerings to a restless
amma female spirit called Piriyapattanadamma, unaware of a myth about this
spirit we heard only fifty miles away. Two festivals performed by and for Brahman married women (Iyengar and Smartha) are so nearly identical that they
may be merged and analysed together. Similar or identical customs of different
jatis may be presented and studied together, though taking place at different
times. Such methods, though out of the bounds of traditional, single-site ethno-
graphy, are justifiable in terms of the historical unity of the village community,
the region and the culture area.

As well as crossing social and geographic boundaries to gather symbolic information on festivals, it is sometimes necessary to cross from one aspect of life
to another. Families occasionally borrow from their own rites of passage, for
example. Interpreting the meanings of festival items which they also use in
birth, marriage, death or other personal rites therefore may require some study
of those rites, outside the usual focus of the more broadly-defined festivals. In
one case, a food preparation used in certain cobra rituals is also customary at
the time of a baby's birth. Such overlaps are significant in interpreting meanings of family festivals.

With all the differences and similarities, many festivals share certain specific
symbolic building blocks. The most important are colours, foods (especially
rice), numbers, plant items (flowers, leaves and so on), and particular utillita-
rian objects, such as cradles or winnowing fans. Social roles, such as the auspicious married women whose husband is still living, or acts of sharing and
exchange are also significant human components of meaningful festival structure. The cobra, an ancient and important animal in Hindu mythology, plays a
part in more than one festival, as does the sacred fig tree. Fire is omnipresent
in various kinds of lamps and stoves. There is pervasive use of vessels of water,
often as *kalasas*, with leaves and coconuts set on top.

CONDENSED SYMBOLS

Some parts of festival structure are summarised entities, virtual stories within the story. They enter the arena with a compact, meaningful history of their own and seem to stand as distinctive units almost without regard to a context. Such a complex element is the filled vessel called *kalasa*, often found at the center of a *puja*. It is used to represent a temporary embodiment of a deity, ancestor or other spirit receiving offerings. While discussing the significance of this type of vessel, Babb (1975 : 42-44) quotes a Chhattisgarhi priest as saying that it represents "the infinite in the finite."

The *kalasa* is a distinctive composition made up of several parts: the vessel itself, the liquid within it (usually water), some leaves (usually mango or betel) set around the mouth and a whole coconut set on the leaves sealing the mouth of the filled vessel (see Figure 9 appearing later, in Chapter 7). The coconut itself is like a brown vessel (the coir remains on it) with a white pulp and a liquid within, called coconut 'water'.

Viewed abstractly, it has a structure consisting of several implicit contrasts. An open-mouthed container, the vessel, is juxtaposed with a sealed container, the coconut; both contain water. The coconut temporarily closes the vessel, but with leaves placed between. The leaves commonly used are universally associated with ritual transitions and social exchanges; mango strands are hung over the door of a house celebrating a rite of passage or other festive occasion; betel exchange is a common method of confirming agreements, as in marriage arrangements. In the symbolic structure the leaves logically serve as mediators between sealed and open containers.

If water is parallel (as it often is in Hindu symbolism) to something like spirit, life, or *atman*, then the *kalasa* appears as a veritable conversation on the subject of mortality and immortality. Seen in itself as a set of interacting relationships, its condensed meanings speak volumes. More than an inert object, the *kalasa*, through its structure, suggests that spirit flows through many human vessels much as water flows in and out of this pot, water returning to a source once the usefulness of the *kalasa* ends. The coconut, the sealed item, represents a more permanent possibility, that of the gods with eternal life. These images, condensed in the *kalasa*, are found throughout Hindu theology and poetry alike, expressed in terms similar to these. Other ritual objects, for example the sacred fig tree (*pipal*), carry the weight of milennia of refinement and condensation of imagery into any local context they enter.

Metaphor

Festival acts and objects take on intellectual or cultural power chiefly through their capacity to establish metaphors. Derived from the human ability to conceive of logical analogy, the metaphor is ". . .the vital principle of. . .language, and perhaps of all symbolism. . . an image of the literal meaning [as a] symbol for the figurative meaning, the thing which has no name of its own" (Langer 1957 : 139). Whether an image is to be taken literally or metaphorically is understood by actors and observers in terms of the context. Thus, when villagers pound or winnow grain in the course of rituals (as they sometimes do) it is clear to all involved that they are not simply preparing necessary food, but are using the process as an analogy for some other process. They are borrowing everyday agricultural themes, transforming a literal feature to a metaphor for some aspect of the ritual experience.

In this way, festival metaphors create forceful parallels between social categories—the family in this case—as object or referent, and aesthetic constructs. The family may be compared to a growing tree, a pot of cooked rice, a vessel of water, to whiteness, or golden light, or gushing blood. In such images family relationships and processes of growth or decline are symbolised in a conceptual structure expressed in humble but profoundly understandable terms. This formulation process is no doubt one of the inspirations to performers, a basis of their faith in the efficacy of festivals to sustain the family.

South Asian folklore abounds in what Kongas-Maranda (1971) has called "productive metaphors," images used to stand for many different things. Ritual objects and mythic motifs—serpents, vessels, water, colours—are often used in varying ways, as analogies of many different objects and experiences. Some are exploited in literary traditions as well. In ancient Tamil poetry, for instance, the hood of a cobra is sometimes compared to a woman's pubis (Hart : 1973a). This is not the only role that the cobra plays in Hindu symbolism by any means, but knowing of this use helps locate clues to ritual and mythic metaphors.

Implicit in family rituals (both festivals and rites of passage) is a broad metaphor between the development of individuals and families and the growth and processing of grain, especially rice. The over-arching concept is the apparent guide to the multiple uses of paddy (unhusked rice) and husked rice in folk rituals, as well as the implements of pounding (husking) and sorting grain from chaff (winnowing). In this case the concept of metaphor is a guide to aid a student in explaining the appearances of specific items or sets in multiple ritual contexts.

The idea that different meaning contexts may influence each other was introduced into South Asian studies by Yalman (1969a), who defined the process as "operational meaning," a term borrowed from Ullman (1962). Operational meaning is identified by studying the various types of contexts in which a given symbol occurs, abstracting a sort of general meaning out of the common elements of its contexts of occurrence. For example, Yalman has distinguished some meanings of food offerings in Ceylon (Sri Lanka) by defining the ways various types of pure or polluted foods were offered to various categories of spiritual, demonic or human beings in a number of rituals.

The concept of operational meaning is useful in the study of folk Hinduism, so long as the student resists the temptation to give each cultural symbol a too-precise meaning, bearing in mind that the same symbol can perform multiple roles in different contexts. In village festivals, Hindus themselves try to assign symbols in as regular a pattern as possible, principally in the effort to isolate inauspicious (death-related) symbols from auspicious (life-enhancing)— with varying degrees of consistency or success. Villagers activate less self-conscious operational meanings when borrowing elements from birth, marriage, and other auspicious rites for use in festival structures.

SYMBOLIC USE OF COLOUR AND RICE

COLOURS

References to colour are woven throughout Hindu and other South Asian traditions, both literary and oral. In the *Bhagavad Gita* (Chatterji 1960 : xi, xiii) we find whiteness associated with light and purity; redness with passion and activity, blackness with darkness and heavy weight.[1] Beck (1969) discusses traditional associations of each *varna* with a particular colour.[2] Such relations combine physics, spiritual goals, moral values and emotions, marking contrasts in all of these domains simultaneously.

Oral traditions continue the heritage of colour symbolism. There is no collection of proverbs, songs or stories that does not get around to mentioning symbolic colours. In a local example from Bandipur non-Brahman lore it is stated: "Red and black are for grief." One festival occasion requires a yellow flower as hair ornament for young married women.

It is in the culturally variable and arbitrary nature of collective symbols that specifics take on their meanings relative to the systems in which they operate. "As the perceptual structure of colour has no meaning in itself, the content [emanates] rather from the culture than the colour," (Sahlins 1977 : 178). This cultural approach to colour symbolism has dominated American anthropological theory since Franz Boas taught his first students.

Humans naturally have physical and emotional reactions to colours but the symbolic meanings are arbitrary rather than natural. A given system of cultural symbols produces a range of semantic values for colours or combinations. The student is free to determine these meanings by observation with little reference to inherent qualities of perception. As Sahlins (1977 : 166) puts it, "each social group orders the objectivity of its experience, as the precipitate of a differential and meaningful logic, and so makes of human *perception* a historic *conception*" (emphasis added).

Hindu family festivals are colourful events, both literally and figuratively. Participants consciously produce a cheerful and varied setting creating a mood of optimism. This is in deliberate contrast to the severe simplicity of plain foods and lack of design in everyday life and solemn periods of mourning. Particular festival rituals include types of flowers and food and other offerings in specific colours linked to the supposed natures of the deities and the overall purpose of each festival. Within the profusion of objects at the typical *puja* ritual are to be found the required offerings, often buried in an auspicious pile but still indicating the dominant colour of the ritual. Close scrutiny of festival customs reveals the importance of colour in selection of many offerings.

During 1976 and 1977 field trips, the author conducted in-depth interviews on local colour concepts. Because colours are so much used in this cultural system it is necessary to view their *explicit* or conscious connotations, as well as their *implicit* or unconscious ones. Though most of the villagers interviewed were willing to make abstract associations of colours with feelings or with states of fortune, they were less likely to recognise colour as a structuring principle when thinking about their own ritual practices. Though they seemed to agree, for example, that red is a colour of danger and blood and violent emotions, they did not seem to see that the requirement of a red oleander flower for certain malevolent goddesses has those specific connotations. When asked, a village woman might respond: "Turmeric is just turmeric; we always use it," without seeming to realise the significance of its use in a ritual whose dominant colour is yellow with its connotations. It is the outside observer who must extract the implicit patterns in the use of colours in festival rituals.

Terms and Meanings

The Kannada colour vocabulary is evolving. Of the seven developmental stages identified by Berlin and Kay (1969), the villagers studied were all at least in the sixth stage with some evidence of advancement into the seventh and final stage. There are seven colour terms in local Kannada usage with generally accepted meanings. The colours are 'white' (*bili*), 'black' (*kappu* or *kari*), 'red' (*kempu*), 'green' (*hasiru* or *hasaru*), 'yellow' (*arasina*, lit., 'turmeric'), 'blue' (*nili*), and 'brown' (*kenda* or *kanda*, lit., 'scorched').

Only the first four of these terms are what Berlin and Kay call basic colour terms, or salient and indigenous monolexemic words (see Regelson 1972 : 200). The other three (yellow, blue and brown) are secondary terms, i.e., either borrowed from another language (blue) or names for other things (yellow, brown). In addition, there are other terms in use; the list is open and exploratory varying from person to person or group to group. In this additional set of colour terms we find the elements of the seventh stage of linguistic evolution, the use of 'purple', 'pink', 'orange' and 'gray', though they are not yet quite standardised.[3]

Four colours are of paramount importance in the set of family festivals, with a fifth providing further material: yellow (or gold), red, black, white and green. The benign goddesses of wealth and married woman status are adorned with golden flowers, and their rituals make much use of turmeric root and powder. Violent spirits, especially feminine ones, receive both red flowers and blood, expressing the wasted vitality that their stories and images represent for Karnataka villagers. Black, as the colour of difficulty and physical death, is an accent colour occurring in a few different contexts, both reminding us of danger and protecting us against it. White is, of course, the colour of cooked rice—ancestors' food—and of serpent-spirits' favourite milky offering. It is a colour of purity and continuity, the basic issues at stake in the last two festival studies. As the colour of new growth, green is a recurrent and benign symbolic element, but not a powerful one in the data of this study. Further information on specific colours is presented in Appendix A.

Colour Combinations

As life itself is said to be a combination of all contrasts, so also these festivals are combinations. That is, each uses more than one colour; thus the reader should not expect (this or any) great simplicity in uses of colour in family festivals. Nonetheless, the mood and spiritual vision of each festival still are reflected in its dominant colour. Some combinations are intentional, designed to produce a specific effect, possibly by combining forces which the colours symbolically represent. At other times, this is not deliberate but simply a consequence of the use of specific flowers or other items required by custom for a given rite.

Colours may be combined by overlay, by juxtaposition or by change in colour of one object or substance. In Hassan District it is common for married women to overlay vermillion (red) and turmeric (yellow) in the forehead dot, for example. Among the crops growing in a Karnataka field a clay pot, usually black, is painted with whitewash to avert the evil eye. In Madhya Pradesh, in central India, turmeric (yellow) is rubbed on the feet of a new mother at the Brahman-style *Chauk* ceremony, and red foot paint is put on over that.[4]

These examples appear without symbolic comment in ethnographic studies, but the prevalence of colour combinations in ritual practices is evidence of structural meaning-value. The black pot becomes a superficially white object (attractive to the sight) which is black on the inside and beneath the surface (capable of repelling malevolent forces). Beck (1969) mentions the potential associations of 'hot' and 'cold' forces with red and white colours, respectively. There seems to be a balancing principle in operation in many colour combinations.

One finds many juxtaposed colours required for popular South Asian rituals. In Gujarat the mother goddess of *Mata ni Pachedi* (Erikson 1968) can be depicted only in red, white and black on her typical cloth picture. In the *Neela Gauri* festival, as described by Dube (1955 : 100), a large earthenware pan is filled with several kinds of soil—black earth, red earth, earth from an ant-hill, and manure.[5] Thurston (1909, Vol. VII : 309) mentions a Valluvan ritual which requires cow urine in five different colours. There is also a red-white-yellow contrast implicit in the 'five kinds of rice' used for the Prati Festival of Bandipur and Chinnapura. Majumdar (1969 : 152) states that in Northern India red and yellow in combination are symbolic of fertility and are therefore typical marriage colours.

Distinctive colour combinations are also found in rituals of evil-eye removal and exorcism of malevolent spirits. Regelson (1966-67 notes) recorded a local ghost-exorcism rite that required three balls of cooked rice, one coloured red, one yellow and one black. To remove a spell or to divine the source of a problem red, yellow, black and white were used in combination. After removing the evil eye from a child, charcoal (black) and flowers were placed in the bottom of a broken clay pot at a crossroads (S. Hanchett, 1966 field notes).

Colour Transformations

Chemical and natural colour changes play a role in Karnataka folk rituals, which is at least as interesting and important as the role of fixed colour differences. Some of these are divinatory in purpose, such as the determination of whether or not a child has been hurt by 'evil eye' according to whether a dish of yellow liquid (water + turmeric + raw rice + a betel leaf punched with five holes) turns red or not when waved in front of the child's face. However they may be used magically, such possibilities are part of local awareness. They form a pool of images from which anyone may draw ritual or mythic material as needed.

In the regular cycle of local rituals some colour changes are part of the routine symbolic activity. A chemical colour change is used in removing the evil eye from anyone going through an auspicious rite of passage, such as birth, puberty or marriage. The candidate(s), seated on a little wooden platform (*mane*), is (are) presented with a plate of bright red liquid, which is waved before him/her (them) at several points along the course of a given ceremony. This liquid, of which Regelson (1966 notes) has heard it said that "Even blood itself is not so red," is the result of a chemical transformation. Its vivid colour is formed when turmeric and calcium carbonate (*sunna* 'lime') are mixed in water. The colour-symbol formula is : (yellow + white) → red. This metaphorical image of spoiling is perhaps presented to the initiate on the principle that 'it should happen to the liquid rather than to him or her (them)'.

A similar spoiling image appears in some of the family or community festivals for violent spirits, particularly the female *ammas* : a (white rice) → (red blood) transformation. The same occurs once in a myth for the goddess Bandamma, in which the parallel to family disaster is indicated by a simultaneous demise of young infants. It also appears—more as a combination than an actual change—in an offering typical of certain rituals for such spirits : cooked rice over which fresh blood has been poured. (White → red) is a vivid and ominous metaphor of destruction of a family line, the very danger which most of these festivals are designed to avoid.

A natural transformation, to be discussed more fully when discussing the ancestor worship festival in Chapter 7, is the possible basis for a significant festival food taboo. Whereas families tend to vary their customs, the nearly universal avoidance of one particular vegetable is conspicuous as a regular feature of such rituals. The vegetable is *Luffa acutangula*, called *hirekayi* in Kannada. The fact that its seeds, as they mature, turn from white to black, suggests a symbol of physical death which may be felt to be inappropriately inauspicious for a festival dedicated to the free movement of departed souls and cordial relationships between living and deceased family members.

As with many other symbolic elements of festivals, this natural phenomenon of colour change is part of a local pool of common botanical knowledge. Its use in ritual—or rather its consistent avoidance—is a good example of the way the practical and spiritual spheres come together in festival symbolism. The villagers know the natural facts but do not call into question the absolute wisdom of the festival tradition.

Appendix A includes some general views on specific colours, as elicited in village interviews, along with further comparative comments on colour symbolism in other regions of India.

RICE

In Hassan District the village fields produce a variety of grains and pulses (legumes) which form the basic diet of the village communities. For most of the labouring villagers these provide their chief nourishment. Rice is more expensive and less generally used, whether because of its cost or because of taste preference. Nonetheless, there is no family among them, rich or poor, which does not feel compelled to serve cooked rice to ancestors once a year. Though other foods are used in festivals, it is rice which is the major symbolic element in festival practices. Second only to colour, rice carries semantic value in all festivals and is a major key to understanding their meaning.

Bannagur, 'coloured rice', is an old word in Kannada (Bhat 1970: III: 1136). Though not in general use at present, it once suggested festivity and celebration in its very form. To metaphorically 'colour' cooked rice with spices and flavours is to affirm activity and movement. In the culinary metaphor such festival food is a condensed symbol for the auspicious nature of the festival in itself. A contemporary proverb refers to 'coloured rice' using the more specific colouring term, the word for turmeric. Best translated as 'Devoted to festival food, he wasted his year's supply', it expresses the sometimes-foolish fascination with the joys of a holiday feast.[6]

Just as 'coloured rice' is festival shorthand for 'auspiciousness', rice itself is shorthand for either 'food' or 'body'. Rice is the most plastic medium of all in the family-centred Hindu rituals. One finds it in wedding play of one *jati*—accompanied by four kinds of pulses, raw rice is in a pot of water in which a bride and groom dig for a gold ring. It is a flour base for delicate and intricate white line drawings made by Brahman women on their floors on festive occasions; or made into a paste they model into tiny oil lamps whose wicks extend from pools of *ghee* (clarified butter). Raw rice, covered with golden turmeric or red vermillion, is offered as an invitation to a wedding or a boy's religious initiation. A basket of unhusked paddy is the resting place for a bride-to-be, another of cleaned white grains, the platform for bride and groom at a later stage of their wedding.

Various foods prepared from rice—soaked, flattened, popped, puffed or boiled—identify the rituals with which they are associated, giving them popular titles such as 'three-pancake festival', 'five kinds of rice festival', or 'rice and green gram (mung bean) festival'. In the annual rituals dedicated to them, one 'puts rice' to one's ancestors in Hindu India as in Buddhist Japan or traditional China.

Whether as food, decorative item or object of play and medium of communication, rice has been a powerful symbolic medium throughout Asia from ancient times. Urbanites, peasants and tribal peoples alike endow rice with a magical equivalence to 'food' itself. More than life, 'food' is the very substance of a person, or even of a whole family line extending from ancestors to infants (cf. Khare 1976b : 178 and *Contributions* 1959 : 37). Describing some old Chinese rituals for gods of longevity and wealth, Williams refers (1941 : 373) to a half-filled measure of rice at the centre of the ritual display, and quotes a Chinese saying: "Rice is the stuff of life, so the rice measure is the measure of life."[7] In the Tibetan foothills:

> The upsetting of a basin of rice on the table or elsewhere is very unlucky, and to take away any person's rice-steamer and empty it on the ground is one of the greatest insults that can be given to a family (Williams 1941 : 341).

Venerated as the 'Rice Mother' of one tribe, the focus of rice sowing rituals of another, the seed's widespread importance throughout Asian cultures gives ample demonstration that India partakes of an ancient cultural pattern in using rice in folk rituals as an all-purpose symbol for 'food' or corporeality.

In her study of India's plant lore, Gupta quotes Danielou as saying, "Rice offering stands for the perception of Existence, Consciousness, and Experience in all things."[8] She herself explains (1971 : 83) in a more subdued tone:

> Rice being one of the earlier cereals that were known to man, it started being associated with food and is often considered to be the creator. . .Rice being held sacred, it is used for all religious ceremonies.

Although its symbolic value was no doubt originally related to the fact that it is an old staple crop, it retains its symbolic powers even in regions of South Asia where it is not economically important. Oscar Lewis has remarked (1958 : 242) that although wheat is more important than rice in the daily life of his Delhi State community, rice pudding is prevalent in nearly all ritual menus.

Khare proposes that all of the stages in the growth and processing of grains ought to be considered as a sort of cooking, this being close to his understanding of a Hindu cultural perspective, in which all transformations of edible substances are regarded as part of a single 'moral process' :

> Thus if cooking of food is the central purpose of a Hindu's domestic hearth . . .it is only a small, most visible segment of meaning that the Hindu has in mind. His extensions of this conception can mean or imply all those conditions and stages that help raise crops in the field, including "ripening," and those which help its actual procurement and handling up to the actual ingestion (Khare 1976b : 3).

Whether or not we all agree to use the word cooking in so broad a way, it makes sense insofar as all the stages of grain development, from germination to cooking (with fire) and seasoning indeed are used to symbolic effect in one or another Hindu ritual.[9] Some have been described above and others will appear in subsequent descriptions.

Rice functions as what Ortner (1973) would call a "key symbol" for Hindu culture as viewed through ritual. That is, its uses codify, clarify, and focus attention on basic life processes as defined in cultural terms. Furthermore, however, it is a key symbol only in "the elaborating mode." Like a scenario or favourite tale, the gradual development of rice and its various cooked forms provide aesthetic guides and models for the interpretation of life—birth, growth and maturation, interrelationships, even death and afterlife.

Only portions of this over-arching, elaborating metaphor reach conscious awareness in participants; most move situation-by-situation through their ritual transitions. Each of the four festival types presented next, in Part II, uses rice, other foods, and colour differently to highlight some aspect of family process.

NOTES

1. My former student, Adele Jacobson, brought this item to my attention.

2. Brahman (white), Ksatriya (red), Vaisya (yellow), and Sudra (blue/black). Her source of information is Ghosh's (1950).

3. In conversations about colour (*banna*) or about coloured things, additional distinctions emerge. *Roja*, rose, is an increasingly common term for 'pink'. One young woman mentioned 'snuff colour' (*nesada banna*) as a 'dark brown', 'close to black.' A second informant pointed to my maroon-coloured case and identified that as 'snuff colour', in 1976. Another such distinction is a 'yellowish white,' called 'spice colour' (*masala banna*).

An elderly man explained that there are certain 'natural colours' (*huttidabannagalu*, literally 'birth colours') as opposed to 'artificial colours' (*Kannubannagalu*, lit. 'visual colours'). An example of a 'natural colour' is 'wheat colour' (*godi banna*). This colour was used to identify one category of cobra, the *godinagaru*, by its colour.

There are also ways of distinguishing between 'true' or pure colours, (*purta* = 'complete' or *pura*) and 'off-colours', (*pura-irodilla*), such as the 'off-whiteness' of ashes. 'Ash colour' (*budi-banna*) is one of the most commonly used secondary terms.

In discussing the distinctions among flowers, a young woman expressed frustration at the limitations of her own language. She told me that there were three types of 'red' (*kempu*), but she had no way of labelling them, except to point to things of the same colours. (One of these was a dark purple.)

4. Doranne Jacobson, personal communication (1974).

5. According to Dube (1955), nine grains are planted in this mixture, and the sprouted plants are considered to be the goddess Gauri.

6. The proverb in Kannada is *Arasinada kulannu nambi varsada kulanne kaledu konda.* The first two words are 'turmeric rice', i.e., coloured rice.

7. As one of the Twelve Ornaments embroidered on vestements of state in imperial China, rice was the emblem of plenty (Williams 1941 : 410). Crooke (1896 : II : 292) mentions a rice-sowing ceremony for ancestors, who are thought by the Munda to have the power to stop rice from growing if not propitiated.

8. Yalman (1969a : 93) cites a Sri Lanka saying :" . . . About the Buddha : 'We offer him rice,' they say, 'to remind him of life.' "

9. In contrast to some tribal peoples, such as the Santal, who use rice beer, peasant Hindus of this region do not employ fermented grains as ritual symbols, to my knowledge. This is a visible gap in an otherwise complete inventory of grain processing stages used symbolically. It probably reflects an aesthetic aversion to the rotting and decay connotations of fermentation.

Part II
FAMILY FESTIVALS

INTRODUCTION TO PART II

The performance of festivals, central to the development of a Hindu family's self-concept, imposes numerous demands on each family throughout the year. Details of festival content constitute an imagery that works through that self-concept by comparing the family, for instance, to a pot of cooked rice, a wounded cobra, or a vine. By deploying familiar items in creative ways, families develop metaphors expressing their struggles to continue and grow.

Part II of this book consists of four studies of specific family festivals. Each is presented in an exploratory style intended to convey the intricate structure and the wealth of cultural meanings typical of such festivals throughout India. Table 13 identifies the specific festivals discussed and dates of their observance.

Table 13—Festivals Discussed in Part II

Lunar Dates	Gregorian/ Solar Dates	Festival Names
(Sravana)	Adi (July-August)	Prati Festival
Sravana I : 5	20 August 1966 & 10-11 August 1967 }	Sibling Group Festival
Bhadrapada I : 3-4	17 September 1966 7 September 1967 }	Gauri Festival
Bhadrapada II : 14 (non-Brahmans)	13 October 1966	
Asvija I : 1 (Brahmans) I : 6 (A.K.s)	15 October 1966 19 October 1966 }	Pitra Paksa
Kartika I : 1	13 November 1966	Mastiamma
Margasira I : 5-6	17-18 December 1966	Sresti (cobra worship)
II : 15	10 January 1967	Cobra Festival (Bandipur)
Pushya I : 4	14 January 1967	Cobra Festival (Chinnapura)
Phalguna I : 3	14 March 1967	Piriyapattanadamma

69

Chapter 5

GOLDEN OFFERINGS : TWO WOMEN'S FESTIVALS

Festivals celebrated in honuor of the goddesses Gauri and Prati (Laksmi) are of special importance to Hindu women. The married woman whose husband is alive, called *muttayide* in Kannada, enjoys a most fortunate and auspicious status in the ranks of village life. The myths and rituals pertaining to these goddesses express both the positive and negative aspects of this exalted position. The woman who is a wife today may be a widow tomorrow, her social status as degraded as that of the married woman is glorified. The festival symbolism expresses not only wealth but also fear of poverty, not only security but possibilities of conflict.[1]

TWO GODDESSES AND THEIR DEVOTEES

Gauri and Laksmi (called Prati in the local Iyengar dialect) are two benign goddesses very popular throughout Hindu India. Each in her own way represents all that is good in women, especially married women. They are beautiful and bring life and prosperity to all who become involved with them. Gauri is a form of Parvati, God Siva's wife. She is 'the golden one', having gold-coloured complexion as a boon from Brahma once when her husband chided her for being so dark (Wilkins 1975 : 289-290). She was also called Gauri when she directed her tremendous energy to winning the stubborn ascetic god for a mate. Siva had protested :

"Anyone bound with nooses of iron and timber can soon release but one bound with nooses of women never frees oneself." (Shastri 1970 : 570).

71

The chaste but determined lady Gauri thereafter uttered the five-syllable mantra of Siva for 3,000 years, so greatly had she hoped to 'make her beauty fruitful', and eventually she succeeded. Her myth compares her to a gold coin and mentions that the garden she planted during her penance bore flowers and fruits (Shastri 1970 : 553, 581-83).

Laksmi (Prati), as the mythological representation of prosperity, was the final product of the fabulous 'Churning of the Ocean of Milk'. She is, therefore, represented as the very essence of wealth and beauty in Puranic literature. Before her appearance, the churning produced the cow as fountain of milk and curds; the deity of wine; the celestial Parijata tree; nymphs; the moon; poison; and the Amrita elixir of vigour and immortality.

Then, seated on a full-blown lotus, and holding a water-lily in her hand, the goddess Sri, radiant with beauty, rose from the waves. . . . Ganga and other holy streams attended for her ablutions; and the elephants of the skies, taking up their pure waters in vases of gold, poured them over the goddess, the queen of the universal world. The sea of milk in person presented her with a wreath of never-fading flowers; and the artist of the gods (Visvakarma) decorated her person with heavenly ornaments. Thus bathed, attired, and adorned, the goddess . . . cast herself upon the breast of Hari (Vishnu); and there reclining, turned her eyes upon the deities, who were inspired with rapture by her gaze (Wilson 1961 : 65-66).

This fair goddess, who bears a lotus in her hand (Wilson 1961 : 67), is praised with many words which emphasise her bountiful nature; but loss of her favours can produce poverty and even greater tragedy :

"Abandoned by thee, the three worlds were on the brink of ruin; but they have been reanimated by thee. . . .
"They whom thou desertest are forsaken by truth, by purity, and goodness, by every amiable and excellent quality; whilst the base and worthless upon whom thou lookest favourably [are blessed] with families, and with power. . . .
"But all his merits and his advantages are converted into worthlessness from whom, beloved of Vishnu, mother of the world, thou avertest thy face. . . .
Be propitious to me, oh goddess, lotus-eyed, and never forsake me more."
(Wilson 1961 : 68).

In related folklore of Bandipur and Chinnapura, poverty-Laksmi (*daridra* Laksmi) is said to be as fearsome as the true Laksmi is benign (cf. Thurston 1909, Vol. 6 : 163).

Just as Gauri is the companion of Siva, Laksmi is the bride of Vishnu. Few images are spared in songs of their wondrous complementarity.

Vishnu is meaning; she is speech. Hari is polity . . . ; she is prudence. . . . He is righteousness; she is devotion. He is the creator; she is creation. Sri is the earth; Hari the support of it. . . . Sri is wealth; [Vishnu] is himself the god of riches. . . . Lakshmi, illustrious Brahman, is Gauri; and Kesava is the deity of ocean (Varuna). . . . She, the mother of the world, is the creeping vine; and Vishnu the tree round which she clings (Wilson 1961 : 52-53).

After further reciting a long list of experiences of light, warfare, emotion, moral qualities, geographical features, and so on, the singer sighs :

But why thus diffusely enumerate their presence?—it is enough to say, in a word, that of gods, animals, and men, Hari is all that is called male; Lakshmi is all that is termed female: there is nothing else than they (Wilson 1961: 53).

Tradition-minded women weave together classics and common sense notions in their views of the two goddesses. They envision greatness in them. The powers of goddess and woman alike are glorified in these images.

THE MARRIED WOMAN

There is no auspicious Hindu rite of passage—no birth, no feminine maturation, no boy's ritual initiation, and no wedding or other connubial function—which does not put the married woman to work. In pairs or in groups of three or five, she is required to bestow her blessings on all living and growing persons. Universally acknowledged to have magical power, Hindu wives are constantly engaged in regular ritual actions to protect the lives of children and husbands. Gauri and Prati are worshipped for this purpose, as well as Tulasi (a chaste feminine spirit incarnated as a sacred basil plant).

The high social status and almost magical significance of the wife involves her in both privileges and obligations. There are two primary sources of the married woman's life-sustaining power. One is within her; it is her own chastity, i.e., sexual discipline idealised as exclusive devotion to a single husband-partner. As George Hart (1973b : 197) has shown, chastity as the basis of magical-moral power is an old concept in India, appearing in the earliest extant literature of the south as well as in Sanskritic sources. It is her duty to preserve this discipline, and to so conduct her life as to preserve and enhance her husband's well-being.

It is her privilege and another basis of her power that she can create a special relation between herself and a benign goddess, with whom she becomes symbolically identified. This relation is based on a vow (vrata). She may enter into a vow as an individual, and is most likely to do so as a new bride; or she may be part of a family or community that has made a collective promise to a goddess during an emergency. The vow offerings may be promised for a limited period, say, for the first five years of her marriage; or forever, in which case they may be transformed into a 'festival' (*habba*), such as those to be discussed below. An important part of many married women's vows is the offering of gifts to other married women, who are thought to represent both auspiciousness and the protection of the benign goddess herself.

The married woman status is defined as much by its relation of opposition to widowhood as by positive criteria. Widowhood, i.e., avoiding widowhood, is as much the point of myths and rituals for benign goddesses as are the happy, beautiful concepts. Widowhood is ugliness, tragedy and poverty contrasted to the married woman's beauty, pleasure and wealth. In former times, for Brahmans, the status was marked by a plain red sari and a shaven head. For other castes the traditional marks, though present,[2] are not so disfiguring and the consequences not so restrictive, since re-marriage is generally permitted. The widow was traditionally feared, considered to be dangerous in supernatural or mystical ways, though utterly degraded in social status and without any real power.

Thanks to recent humanitarian social and legal changes, the situation of the widow is not as universally desperate as it once was. Still, in tradition-centred villages, one can often find a few pathetic old hags, shaven bald and hobbling around in their red saris as persons without homes.

The fear of widowhood can be so intense that it can lead women to wish for death. Brahman wives in the two villages have several times been heard to express this wish: they would rather die before their husbands than survive to become widows. Women's fears have been clearly articulated by Mrs. Subbalakshmi in Felton's book, *A Child Widow's Story* (1966), which depicts the typical fate of a Brahman widow in the early years of this century:

> The humiliation and sufferings which widows were expected to endure were divinely ordained. Punishment, bravely borne, was also a form of penance through which the soul could be absolved for past sins and acquire the merit which would entitle it to a more fortunate existence in its next birth (p. 37). . . . They lived like ghosts, under-nourished, hard-worked (p. 42). . . .
> Young widows crept along the streets, their saris pulled tightly over their (shaven) heads to hide their disfigurement, hardly daring to show themselves, yet unable to refuse to perform whatever domestic errand had brought them out into the glaring light of day (p. 48).

It is no wonder that the fortunate woman whose husband is still living does everything in her power to honour the goddesses whom she believes able to maintain her in that favoured state of existence.[3] Even in daily grooming, her style of decoration proclaims her high status and her value. Her oiled hair, never cut, is combed into a long, tight plait or chignon, adorned by a cluster of fragrant jasmine and other flowers. On a necklace of alternating gold and black beads hangs her marital pendant (*tali*), with perhaps another, from her mother's family, strung on the thread as well. A hint of yellow turmeric powder lightens the tone of the skin on her cheeks and the tops of her feet. There are bangles on her wrists—some bright yellow gold, others glossy black. On all good days there is the brilliant touch of vermillion on the forehead center, with a layer of turmeric powder underlying the red. The sight of her is beauty (*laksana*). As one young Brahman woman explains, "If one sees such beauty, one feels great pleasure and satisfaction. . . . It is a good view." Her special colour is yellow or gold, auspicious for the success of family aspirations. She embodies the ideal of order and fulfillment; the life of her two families will be one of satisfaction (*santosa*). As one girl summarised her aesthetic pleasure in English, "It suits."

Thus proudly groomed, the married woman takes her place in the community. She goes to her marriage; she enters her bridegroom's home wearing the jewels of her dowry; she returns as an honoured visitor to her natal home. Just as the daily toilet is an expression and affirmation of her power, so also the festivals for Gauri and Prati are annual expressions. Both daily and annual rituals maintain the projective identification between women and goddess.

Every year, in July-August or in September, the two castes of Brahman women in the two villages invite the goddesses by their festival rituals. Gauri and Prati, divine heroines of the Puranas, come into their homes as if they were married daughters returning for long-awaited visits. As each remains for a time in their homes, villagers hope that the goddess will bestow her grace on the women of the family and assist them in becoming more and more like her, the golden, never-to-be-widowed image of good fortune.

GAURI AND PRATI FESTIVALS

The women who celebrate the Gauri Festival, both Brahman and non-Brahman, do talk of her as a daughter. She comes to their village and their homes as a daughter who has married and is returning for a visit to her natal home, here, the home and village of the worshipper. The river from which she is summoned (in the form of a ball of sand) is described as her marital home.[4] Her husband, Lord Siva, is said to miss her after she leaves him. So he sends their son, the elephant-headed bachelor, Ganesa, to call for her. After Ganesa has been ritually installed in home and village shrines on the next day after his mother, the increasingly popular Ganapati festival begins its local three-to-nine-day celebration.

Unlike the Gauri Festival, which is popular throughout Hindu India, the festival for Laksmi, here called 'Prati', is a purely local affair, limited only to the two villages of Bandipur and Chinnapura, and in those villages done only by the Iyengar Brahmans of Hebbar sub-caste.[5] They have a belief that this goddess once helped them out of a tragic situation, and they continue the festival in gratitude to her, and in honour of their promise (ritual vow) to her. Over the years, however, they have come to disagree about the exact nature of the original situation.

The reason for the original decision to start this festival has been obscured by the branching of local oral traditions. One informant gave an account of two Iyengar brothers of this Hebbar Iyengar group who began to perform this vow more than one hundred and fifty years ago when they were otherwise unable to have children.[6] Another explanation of the origin mentions a big flood which receded when the villagers began this festival. The third one relates the two-village ritual to the miraculous revival of a dead child :

> In these two villages long ago, they say, there was a married couple, the wife from Bandipur and the husband from Chinnapura.
> Their baby died at 4 p.m. one Friday afternoon. So the people of the two villages got together and did this festival and promised the goddess that they would always do it, if only she would make the baby all right.
> When they went to bury the baby, they found their wish granted. The baby was alive. (Told by a woman of Chinnapura, 1967.)

Members of the group of Iyengar houses that do the Prati Festival explain to outsiders that this is the same as the widespread vow for Laksmi, the goddess of wealth. This vow, *Varamaha Laksmi,* is popular among Hindus of various sects, as is the *Mangala Gauri Vrata* associated with Gauri.

Whatever its origin was, the form of the Prati Festival ritual is so similar to that of Gauri, that there can be little doubt that it was modeled on the more widespread Gauri celebration. In concept and in action, the two festivals (done by two different groups of Brahmans) are as similar as any two Hindu festivals ever could be.

Both Gauri and Prati are spoken of with affection and joy. The women who worship them seem to delight in making small ornaments for their goddess-guests. This affection is co-mingled with their feelings for their own married-out daughters and sisters, who are urged to return to their natal homes for these occasions. If they cannot return, they receive appropriate married woman gifts by mail—gifts which women exchange among themselves on these festival occasions. The women of each neighbourhood use these festivals as an occasion to gather for singing and feasting as well. Brahman streets develop an atmosphere of pleasant activity for their beloved daughter-goddesses. Villagers tell each other several stories of the past achievements of the benign goddesses, some stories combining the affairs of the two. Parvati (Gauri) herself is said to have gotten back her wandering husband through performance of the Prati ritual. As her husband, returned, he said, "I am happy with you. I am under your power," one young woman relates enthusiastically.

Women's discussion of these goddesses is filled with allusions to their daily concerns and to the problems of barrenness, desertion, and poverty which are their views of potential disaster. They make repeated assertions of Gauri's or Prati's power to help with life's problems. "If you do this," says a member of one of the Prati ritual groups, "you will have children and grandchildren. If your husband has left you, he will come back." Another comments, "Women should do this Prati festival for the welfare of their hubands and families." "A good housewife," she adds, "is a blessing to the family". The virtues of the Prati ritual are further proclaimed, as kings' kingdoms expand through Laksmi's bountiful assistance and reverent paupers see their bad luck changing to good. "Mahalaksmi is the only one in the world to give good things," says one lady hopefully. "She and her consort Narayana will give us all that we need. They are the only gods who will do this."

There is, however, not much conversational reference to the culturally disastrous possibility of widowhood. But rituals and myths, especially myths, are expressive on this subject. In the 'Mangala Gauri' myth, for instance, a bride fends off a deadly snake about to bite her groom by praying to Gauri. And in the ritual symbolism, emphases and taboos in colours and flavours hint at the tragic possibility, though they do not weigh heavily on it.

Local visions of the goddesses Gauri and Prati themselves, of course, affirm the married state. They are with consorts in a mythical permanence which provides an illusion of stability in an unpredictable world, where Brahman women are particularly vulnerable. The goddesses named Gauri and Laksmi are never widows.

This is not to say that the goddesses are without their own problems. They have mythical quarrels with husbands and deity co-wives. They menstruate and purify themselves. And they can be mythically caught in nets of ambivalent sexual relations, as O'Flaherty (1973) has amply demonstrated. The following myth of Parvati (Gauri) and Ganga (the water-goddess), her co-wife, demonstrates one sort of predicament in which goddesses may find themselves. It was related to me by an Iyengar Brahman of Bandipur.

Parvati and Ganga were sisters, both married to Siva. Parvati was the senior co-wife. She told Siva that she would leave him unless he stopped seeing Ganga.

So Ganga ran away and hid herself. When Parvati had her menstrual period, she could not bathe afterward, however, because Ganga [water] was gone.

She asked Siva for advice on how to purify herself. He first suggested using milk. But that would not do. Then he suggested clarified butter. But that would not do either. "Then," he said, "you have to find Ganga."

So she searched the whole world. But there was not one green thing in it, for there was no water. Finally in a tree she saw a silver of green, and she knew that Ganga must be there.

Begging her sister's forgiveness, she accepted her back as a co-wife.

Envisioned so realistically vulnerable, the goddesses receive compassionate attention from their devotees. The women who worship them find in such myths dramatised renditions of their own, human experiences.[7] The chief conceptual difference is that the goddesses are structurally 'safer' from widowhood than women are.

Although both goddesses are addressed as 'mother of the world' in religious texts, the Gauri and Prati of these villages are not 'mother goddesses', in the maternal or nurturant sense in which we usually use that term. They are better seen as 'daughter goddesses' or 'married woman goddesses'. Though they are thought to give spiritual 'shelter' to their devotees, their powers do not seem to be discussed in maternal terms. Rather, as they bring their holy visitors out of their river-homes and send them off again, worshippers think of the goddesses as married daughters linking inter-marrying houses; and enshrined in each home, they are given all of the attentions due to a married woman. Their worshippers, of course, share in this honoured status with them. Links between natal family and married daughter are strongly evident in both myths and rituals of these festivals. But it is the natal family, especially the mother, as provider of jewels for dowry or as assistant in the effort to protect the husband, who is acknowledged here, more so than the mother as giver of birth.

Not a typical mother goddess, Laksmi or Gauri is also not seen as a fertility goddess. This became clear in a 1976 interview of a young Brahman woman who carefully defined the concept of 'wealth of the married woman' as centering on the present, on all the needs of a living, growing family, *rather than* on fertility itself. Sexual activity is accepted as part of this good life and of the marital experience, but the subsequent birth of children relates to another set of structural and symbolic arrangements. Birth is a question of the long-range future of the whole line, an eternity best symbolised in the colour white (as emphasised in ancestor or serpent festivals). The daily concerns relating to overall health and welfare, or prestige and success, of the family are best summarised in vital colours such as yellow-gold or an accent on red. With her goddess as her aide, the typical married woman, especially the Brahman, strives to be a dutiful guardian and magician-producer of all sorts of auspicious good news for her family.

In performing her ritual vows or her vow-based festivals, a married woman hears or recites myths. These myths provide encouragement to her, since they relate the successes of previous women who have taken the same vows. They provide textual authority and legitimisation for the ritual; but, at a cultural level, they also bring her into the very center of the exciting and dangerous process of her own family's development.

FESTIVAL MYTHS: 'VARAMAHA LAKSMI' AND 'MANGALA GAURI'

Myths for Gauri and Laksmi are associated with vows and vow-based festivals throughout Karnataka. Regional scholars have published some of them, local scholars have written out some of them for the use of villagers, and women themselves have written them for the use of their daughters and daughters-in-law. Though most of those who enjoy these myths are literate, the myths still have been changed in various ways from their original epic or Puranic sources in the process of transmission. There is nothing unusual in the fact of change, since from the earliest times the writers of epics and Puranic tales were themselves borrowing from each other and adapting specific myths to their purposes.

Though each woman herself recites the particular myth when it is associated with a private vow, the groups of women who do the two festivals call in men to tell the stories. Near the end of each group's rituals, there are neighbourhood gatherings of women, the main purpose of the gatherings being to hear the myths from the mouths of men, even though Brahman women of these two villages are almost universally literate and could therefore read the myths themselves if they wished to do so. (There are other roles, especially conducting elaborate *puja* offerings, for male caste-mates in these festivals also. In fact, in Chinnapura's Gauri festival, Brahman men not only volunteer to read to women, they also meet in a separate gathering of men to hear the Gauri myth among themselves.) In any event, whether they join with women in order to receive Brahman women's deference or to receive their blessings and the benefit of the holy tales, Brahman men are present during public recitations of these myths.

'VARAMAHA LAKSMI'

The 'Varamaha Laksmi' myth is widespread in the area and can be found in many different versions. Unlike 'Mangala Gauri', it is a loosely integrated collection of other stories drawn from a variety of classical sources and presented in abbreviated form in the amalgamated myth. The common narrative theme which binds all of the parts together is the strength of the female devotee, especially the virtuous married woman, to divert misfortune away from her own people.[8]

'Varamaha Laksmi' myths which are told in connection with the Prati Festival for Laksmi conform to the pattern of 'Danger-Rescue-Shelter' which has been defined by Wadley (1975). They are mostly stories of women in difficulty who find that by praying and offering *puja* to the goddess of wealth they can improve their luck. The short version related by village women of Chinnapura transforms poverty into wealth:

Version I

Long, long years ago one day all the holy men met in one place. They were very poor men. Therefore all the holy men went to heaven and saw Lord

Siva, and told him all their sorrow. And Siva said, "Listen. I will tell you a story." Siva began.

The story is this. In olden days there was a small village, and in that village was one poor woman. She was always praying to God. One day she was sleeping outside. At midnight the goddess Laksmi came near her and said, "Oh, poor woman, why do you [unfinished sentence]?" Hearing her story, Laksmi told her, "I will tell you one *puja*. When your *puja* is finished, you must take *prasad*. In a few days you will become rich, and also your name will become famous in the world."

And the woman asked, "How should I do that *puja*?" Goddess Laksmi said, "First you must take a bath, and then you must make *sajjappa*." *Sajjappa* was the favourite snack of the goddess. "And you must pray to Laksmi, and at the end of the *puja* you must take *prasad*. After some days you will become a rich and noble woman of the world."

(Written by K. S. Rangaraj, Chinnapura, 1967).

The problem of poverty in this myth is emphasised by a redundant motif. Both the holy men and the lady devotee were mentioned as poor.

The other versions also frame the Laksmi *puja*-solution with a similar consultation device. In the printed version (Sastri 1961) Parvati herself asks Siva to recommend a ritual that will provide 'all prosperity' to devotees. He recommends the Varamaha Laksmi ritual vow as a way of gaining 'prosperity, children, and grandchildren'. When she asks whether there were any previous devotees who had benefited from worshipping Laksmi in this way, he tells of a 'very big city called Kundina':

Version II

This city was one of many riches. All the big buildings were covered with golden ornaments. There was a Brahman lady [in that city]. Her name was Carumati. She was obedient to her husband and to all elders. She was a learned woman. She had a good nature, and spoke with mild words to all. She had a pure heart.

One day she had a dream. Maha Laksmi [Great Laksmi] came to her, saying, "To do all goodness I have come to you. If you do my *puja* sincerely on that particular Friday [the Friday preceding the full-moon day of the month of Sravana], I will certainly bless you."

The lady was immensely pleased to see the mother goddess. She prayed in this manner: "Oh mother. You are the mother of the world. You are the embodiment of all good qualities. You are the real mother who can bless your devotees. You are praised by all the people of three worlds. You are in the heart of the Great Vishnu, and sitting in the midst of the heart of Lord Vishnu [the same]. People who pray to you—they are truly worthy. I am very happy that I had the opportunity of seeing you in my dreams. Because [it means that] I must have done good things in my previous birth."

She was always thinking about this valuable dream, and telling most of her friends about it too. Then all of her friends met one day, wanting to perform the sacred vow or *puja*. They all bathed in pure river water, [put on] all jewels and good clothes.

The group got a golden pot. The pot was filled with rice and many flowers. They prayed to God in the form of this sacred golden vessel.

The story goes on to tell how they found a student (*brahmacarya*) who 'had knowledge of God and all religious thoughts'. Having performed their *puja* with sincere feeling, they gave this student rice, money, and grains and got his blessings.

Siva concludes his explanation by testifying, "After performing this *puja*, they had immediate change in their fortune. They had gotten the blessings of Varamaha Laksmi. That is how they were able to get these divine blessings."[9]

This version of the myth does not mention poverty, but it does use the motif of gold, a symbol of wealth, and raises hopes of achieving wealth and fame. It is more gentle in referring to the difficult and disastrous than the versions I have collected in the villages, and it represents a decision to play up the positive side of women's religious lives.

The final sample of this myth (Version III) in my collection was written out by a Brahman scholar, the noted folklorist Gorur Ramaswamy Iyengar, for the use of village women in the Prati festival. He adapted the story from Vedavyasa's *Mahabharata*, and read it annually to a gathering of women until he himself emigrated from the District. It is framed as the suggestion of the sage Visvacharya to the desperate Draupadi. She wants to help her Pandava husbands regain their kingdom from the Kauravas. The sage tells her that telling this story will be the best way to get back the kingdom and that the story also gives sons to those who read it.[10]

The story which Draupadi is to tell is a story about Parvati. In the story Parvati (Gauri) is performing her penance in hopes of marrying Siva. As she sits there, Siva tests her by becoming invisible, and Indra's wives come along to observe her and test her determination even further. Arundati asks her, "Why are you doing this *tapas* [discipline]? Even if it is a secret, confide in us." Impressed by her discrete and vague reply, Indra's wives suggest that she should perform a ritual vow to Laksmi. "If you do that," they say, "you will get what you desire." Before telling her how to do the ritual, they assure her that, "In the past many great ladies . . . have been relieved of difficulty by doing this vow." The list includes Sacidevi, one of Indra's wives; and also Draupadi (who asked the original question in this version). "Oh Parvati, by observing this, Sacidevi got her husband back. So, you also do it." After hearing these words from Arundati, Parvati did the ritual vow. And, the story concludes, "she gets Sri Esvara [Siva] as her husband," a boon from the goddess of wealth. When Siva came to her, in this rendition, he said the following words: "Oh, Parvati, I am very much satisfied with this ritual vow. And I am now your servant."

Other than providing assurance of the efficacy of the ritual vow, the myth offers little other symbolic material. In fact, I would be reluctant to call it a myth at all except that it refers to so many other richly symbolic stories of the classical Hindu literature. Perhaps its symbolism is best described as 'condensed', working through one's extensive knowledge of the figures mentioned (Arundati, Sacidevi, Draupadi) and evoking their stories by mentioning their names.

Like the other village version (Version I), however, this one does provide some sketchy instructions on how to perform the ritual:

[Arundati tells Parvati,] ". . . Have a bath in the rivers. Make a ball of sand. And put some water in a vessel, adorning the top of the vessel with mango leaves and a whole coconut. Put the vessel (*purnakumbha*) next to the sand ball."
"The ladies performing this vow must have on clean clothes."
"On the plate with these things," the narrator continues, "they must also have the newly sprouted leaves of the banyan and pipal trees. [Devotees] come with the tray to the house and keep it in a very good, decorated place. Afterwards they convert the one sand ball into three balls."

Also like Version I, this one mentions food. Worshippers are instructed to prepare the stuffed rice flour snack called *kolakatte*, which is a customary part of the feast menu.

After this generally it is the custom everywhere to give to a Brahman twenty-one of these delicacies, or at least two.
Then you must light the entire house, and you must hear this story from the guru. And you must give ritual gifts (coins and raw rice) to Brahmans and serve meals.
In addition, you yourself must eat the delicacies and take a meal.

Though these instructions are spoken in the voice of Arundati, they are obvious efforts on the part of a village scholar of the region to record and preserve village tradition. Arundati did not tell Parvati to do these foods. The scholar interviewed some village women, and returned their own customs to them each year during their festival.

Like the north Indian women of Karimpur, the Brahman women of Karnataka believe in the efficacy of these myths and these ritual vows as ways of getting out of trouble, or at least staying out of trouble. All versions conform to a Danger-Rescue-Shelter pattern, as outlined in Table 14. Wadley has described this pattern for vow-related myths elsewhere (Wadley 1975). This pattern applies equally well to the 'Mangala Gauri' myth, in which a woman devotee is shown rescuing her newly-wedded husband from death by her alliance with Gauri. But since this myth is more symbolically rich than the *Varamaha Laksmi* material, it provides detailed information about the dangers and the processes involved in rescue.

Table 14—Danger-Rescue-Shelter Pattern in Prati Festival Myths

Versions	Danger	-	Rescue	-	Shelter

I	Poverty
	Low prestige,
	  obscure life
			(Goddess comes in a
			  dream)
			Puja, prasad
					Wealth
					High prestige,
					  fame

II	[Implied :]
	Poverty
	No children
			(Goddess comes
			  in a dream)
			Ritual vow
			  by women's group
			Bathing, ornamentation;
			  use of golden pot. Offer-
			  ings to student
					Prosperity
					Children and
					  grandchildren
					Blessings of
					  goddess, for
					  'city of riches'
					  and its women

III	Loss of kingdom
	  (Draupadi)
	Loss of husband's
	  affection (Parvati)
	No sons
	[Others by innuendo]
			Ritual vow to goddess
			Bath, clean clothes
			Sanctified vessel and
			  sand balls
			Puja and *prasad*
			Offerings to Brahmans
					Kingdom re-
					  gained
					Husband
					  regained
					[Sons]

'MANGALA GAURI'

The myth for devotees of Gauri is an intact whole. Unlike 'Varamaha Laksmi', which is a listing of many stories, it tells the story of one young woman's danger-rescue-shelter as completely as possible. The basic myth (Variant I), which provides the framework, is one which I recorded in a Smartha home in 1977, as paraphrased by the singer. The other two (Variants II and III) are from Ullrich's research in Shimoga District (II) and from Sastri's printed collection (III). The variants collected from outside the villages provide valuable supplementary data on cultural principles at play in this myth. Given the easy movement of lore, these same outside variants could be known and used by other Bandipur or Chinnapura women beside the one I interviewed.[11]

Motifs or actions which are missing from one variant are still there by implication and often can be predicted to occur in other variants on the basis of a broad view of the cultural structure of the myth.

Like the 'Varamaha Laksmi' myth, 'Mangala Gauri' is framed by a consultation device. Krishna tells Draupadi to do the Mangala Gauri ritual vow for five years. Draupadi asks him, "What is it? Who else has done it?" He tells her the 'Mangala Gauri' story. Three variants are compared in Table 15.

The 'Mangala Gauri' myth relates to the continuation of a family line, with special emphasis on the complex social and personal process of marriage. Like other myths in family festivals, the structure of 'Mangala Gauri' expresses dilemmas relating to family and marriage. The two main dilemmas are : (1) the fragility of human life itself and the possibility that succeeding generations will not survive, or that couples will not reproduce; and (2) the need for the birth group to bring in outsiders for the perpetuation of the lineage.

As might be expected in a myth used mainly by women, 'Mangala Gauri' (especially Variants I and II) gives poignant expression to the transition of a bride from her natal family to that of her husband. It is easy to understand the heroine's pathos as she struggles to unite with her true husband despite the difficulties confronting her. Like her, the wandering groom goes through danger and confusion before resuming a normal social life in marriage. Their struggles in the myth have many parallels in ordinary, drawn-out Hindu marriage negotiations between families. The myth therefore gives us a picture of the inevitable tensions surrounding marriage and the effects of those tensions on individual brides and grooms.

The groom's parents also gain our sympathy in this myth. They are, after all, the couple with the initial problem of barrenness; and many episodes of the myth express typical anxieties about the well-being of future generations. Another theme relates to the difficulty of incorporating a new bride into a family. Many of the bride's struggles in the myth may therefore be seen as paralleling a human bride's efforts to gain acceptance in her marital home. It is significant in this light that the myth begins with the groom's parents and ends with the bride being welcomed by her husband's mother.

Various plays on the act of exchange identify this as a key aspect of the myth's structure. In the beginning of the myth the barren mother's offering to a holy man is rejected. In Variant I the beggar goes so far as to throw some jewels she gave him into a garbage pile : a dramatic gesture of wasted value. (It is interesting as a connection to festival rituals that in Variant I the woman offers these jewels on a winnowing fan, the container of ritual gifts in the Gauri Festival.) During the period when she is waiting for her husband to return, the wife, in Variants I and II, insists on presenting betel leaf and areca nut to all of her father's guests in hopes of meeting her husband. For her to do this, however, represents a disorderly and demeaning act of exchange because guests were invited without any concern for their social status.

As the bride and groom are about to be reunited, exchange actions begin to take on a normal aspect, and they measure the progress of the unification. It is necessary at this point for the reader to understand the Karnataka distinc-

Table 15—Three Variants of 'Mangala Gauri' Myth

I. *Bandipur Variant*	II. *Totagadde Variant* (Ullrich 1975)	III. *Printed Variant* (Sastri 1961, K. Gurulingaiah translation)
In our Karnataka there **was** a town called Swarnavati. The king of that town **was** a good ruler and just. He and his wife Manjule were devotees of Iswara (Siva). They were very **worried** because they had no children.	In ancient days there was a town called Suvarna. A king ruled that city. His wife's name was Manjuli. They did not have any children.	A famous kingdom called Kundanipura is the setting. The unhappy man's name was Dharmapala.
Iswara was attached to these devotees, and he began to come daily as a beggar to their door.	They worshipped Ishwar with much devotion. Ishwar appreciating their devotion came disguised as a beggar. He stood at the door and called, "Mother, give to a beggar."	A holy man (*sannyasin*) with sacred *rudraksi* beads, matted hair, and clothes made of bark used to come to their home daily. But he always left without taking any kind of alms.
When the beggar came to their door, Manjule brought offerings to him on a winnowing fan—jewels of the best quality. She said to herself, "If I make this offering to a poor man, maybe God will bring me a child." But the beggar always took all precious offerings and threw them into the garbage pile. This puzzled the lady, and she suspected a greater meaning in his acts. For he took even rice grains from others but threw out her jewels.	As soon as she saw the beggar, Manjuli, came to give food to him. Immediately on seeing that she had brought (something), the beggar left. The beggar did not take (anything).	The peculiar act of not taking any alms was very disrespectful to both husband and wife. One day the wife told her husband about how badly she felt that the sage was unwilling to accept her alms. He said to her, "Why are you worrying about this, my beloved? Be standing with golden coins in your hand.
Manjule told her husband all of this, asking him why it was happening. So he said, "Tomorrow do the same thing. I'll be hiding and watch it all." Then they agreed to ask him together after he had rejected their offering again.	Manjuli told her husband, "Listen, Lord, daily a beggar comes to me. As soon as I go to give the beggar (something), he won't take (it). He just goes."	
	Then what did the king say ? He said, "Manjuli, have your bath tomorrow, put on *madi* [pure] clothes, and (then) give (to the beggar)." According to these very instructions the next day Manjuli bathed, brought out the handout, put it aside, and waited.	

Table 15 (*contd. on page* 86)

Table 15 (contd. from page 85)

I. Bandipur Variant	II. Totagadde Variant	III. Printed Variant
Then the next day she gave him the offering again. As he was going to throw it away, the two approached him and asked him the meaning of his actions. He said, "Because you have no children, I throw out your offering."	That day the beggar came and said, "mother, serve a beggar." As soon as he spoke, Manjuli brought the handout. Then what did the beggar say? He said, "(I) don't want (anything). Mother, I won't take what you give as a handout. You don't have any children. You are barren : therefore, I won't accept your handout," and so saying he left.	When he comes for alms, slip the golden coins into his begging bowl."
They were very hurt by this comment, and sad. They asked him if there was anything they could do. He told them there was no chance of their ever having children. Then both of them touched his feet. He lifted them up and said that as a boon they would get a son, but only for sixteen years.	Then Manjuli was very depressed. She brought the handout inside and sat weeping and meditating on god. "O Parmatma, why haven't (you) given me children? O Lord, no matter what I undertake, it is ill-fated. Not even [beggar] will accept (gifts) from me. If I cook rice (as an offering) for god, it is rejected. No matter to whom I offer water (they say), 'I won't take any. You are barren. I won't drink the water you serve. It is unacceptable'. They say," Manjuli said in deep despair, "O God, whoever is barren doesn't desire it. if there are children, they play a lot. They cut flowers. If something is full of water, they play and spill it. They erase all the chalk drawings with their hands. They get into all kinds of mischief. It is not my fortune to see all this," she cries.	The next day she tried but was rejected again. The holy man said, "You are a barren woman. That is why I do not accept your offering. If I accepted it, I would go to hell. And in spite of my deliberate refusal to take alms, you cheated me by putting coins into my bowl without my permission. So be a barren woman throughout your life," he cursed her. He then turned around to leave the house. Then the woman prostrated to that sage, and holding his feet, she pleaded, "Oh, holy sage, I am an accursed woman because of my indiscretion. Do please tell me how to be liberated from this curse."

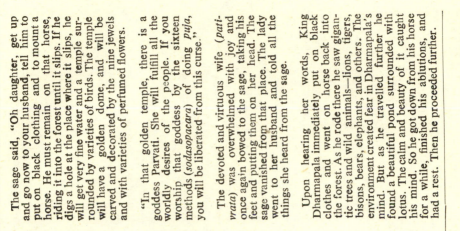

The sage said, "Oh daughter, get up and go now to your husband, tell him to put on black clothing and to mount a horse. He must remain on that horse, riding it into the forest until it slips. If he digs a hole at the place where it slips, he will get very fine water and a temple surrounded by varieties of birds. The temple will have a golden dome, and will be carved and decorated by the nine jewels and with varieties of perfumed flowers.

"In that golden temple, there is a goddess Parvati. She will fulfill all the worldly desires of the people. If you worship that goddess by the sixteen methods (*sodasopacara*) of doing *puja*, you will be liberated from this curse."

The devoted and virtuous wife (*pati-vrata*) was overwhelmed with joy and once again bowed to the sage, taking his feet and putting them on her head. The sage vanished from that place. The lady went to her husband and told all the things she heard from the sage.

Upon hearing her words, King Dharmapala immediately put on black clothes and went on horse back into the forest. As he rode there he saw gigantic trees and wild animals—lions, tigers, bisons, bears, elephants, and others. The environment created fear in Dharmapala's mind. But as he travelled further he found a beautiful pond surrounded with lotus. The calm and beauty of it caught his mind. So he got down from his horse for a while, finished his ablutions, and had a rest. Then he proceeded further.

At that time her husband arrived and asked, "Why are you crying? What happened?" So saying, he wiped away her tears.

Manjuli said, "Lord, not even today did that beggar take a handout. He just went. Therefore I am very depressed. I can't go on like this," she wept.

Then he said, "Manjuli, get up. You must not be even a little depressed. The one who came to beg is not a beggar. I know that it was Parameshwara himself who came. If one observes his walk, listens to his speech, his talk, (observes) his glow, one knows definitely he is not a beggar, but can be no one but Parameshwara. Just now I saw him. He said, 'Do *puja* to Kali Devi.' Therefore we must go to do *puja* to Devi. Let's bathe, put on *madi* clothes and go." Then the two together took the vestments for *puja* and went.

They went to the temple, worshipped Devi, finished offering the *nevedya* and doing *mangalarati*, and asked Devi for a boon. With exceptional piety, they said, "Mother, we have no children. Therefore give us one son."

Table 15 (*contd. on page 88*)

Table 15 (contd. from page 87)

I. Bandipur Variant	II. Totagadde Variant	III. Printed Variant
		His horse did slip at one place as he rode on. Recognising this sign, he got down and dug in the earth until he found the temple. It shone with golden dome and golden walls. It was decorated with precious gems. He worshipped the goddess there with golden coloured flowers, sandalwood powder, perfumed incense, raw rice mixed with turmeric (akṣate), and with a porridge (kṣira) prepared of sugar.
		The goddess was immensely pleased by Dharmapala's puja. She came to him in her real form and told him to ask for whatever he wanted. He said humbly, "I have much wealth, but I am worrying very much about the continuation of my family line. Without offspring my family cannot grow. So, oh Mother Goddess, Parvati, grant me and bless me with offspring. Let me be clear of this worldly worry." Dharmapala thus prayed for offspring. Then the goddess said, "Oh Dharmapala, you are unlucky. You do not have the luck to enjoy and play with children. So I grant you a babe, because you pleased me very much with your adoration."
	Devi appreciating their devotion appeared and said, "What is it? Do you want children? If that's the case, I will give you a son. He will be stupid and stubborn. Is that satisfactory?" Devi	"You make a choice between these three," she offered ; "a daughter who will become a widow very soon; or a very handsome son who will live a short life;

asked. "Except for that, he will live to be a hundred."

To that they said, "Mother, we don't want a stupid boy. It doesn't make any difference if he has a short life span. Give us a good boy," and so saying, with great piety they folded their hands.

Then Devi replied, "In that case, I will give you a handsome, lovely man. But he will have a short life span. He will live for sixteen years. Is that agreeable (to you)?" To that they assented. Then Devi said, "In that case, at a slight distance from here is a mango tree. Cut one fruit from it and return."

There was a Ganapati stone there. He (the husband) climbed on it and cut (the mango fruit). On that Ganapati stone there was a cobra hood. As a result of his (the husband's) stepping on it (the cobra hood), the cobra became angry. Ganapati realized this. Ganapati said, "You stepped repeatedly on it (the cobra). Therefore, when your son is sixteen years old, the serpent will bite him and your son will die." ...

According to instructions he went to the mango tree. There were many fruits on it. He climbed the tree and picked an infinite number of mangoes. After climbing down (from the tree) he looked. In his pocket there was only one fruit. Upon observing this, he was surprised. He said, "Oh, dear, although I picked a hundred fruits, there is only one in my pocket. God has not allowed my having more. So be it. This is the very fruit I

or a blinded son whose span of life will be very long." Dharmapala chose the second alternative, a very handsome son whose span of life would be short.

Then the goddess showed an image of Ganapati to the king, and told him to climb over its belly and go pluck a mango from a nearby tree for his wife. She said, "From that mango your desire will be fulfilled."

Dharmapala climbed over Ganapati and plucked several mangoes instead of one, so great was his ignorance and his desire. After he got down from Ganapati, all of his mangoes disappeared except one. Again he climbed and plucked several, and again he had only one in his hand when he climbed down. Again he climbed, but the same thing was repeated over and over, to a total of sixteen times. Then Ganapati got angry with him and cursed him, saying that his son would die by snakebite in his sixteenth year of life.

Table 15 (contd. on page 90)

Table 15 (contd. from page 89)

I. *Bandipur Variant*	II. *Totagadde Variant*	III. *Printed Variant*
	will give (to Devi)," and he took it and went. "Devi, I brought you the fruit," and so saying, he did *namaskara*.	
	Then Devi asked, "How much fruit did you pick?" He said, "Mother, I picked lots of fruit. But, Mother, I have only one fruit. This was a surprise. I disregarded your instructions and picked lots of fruit. That was completely wrong," he said, and bowed to her.	
	Then Devi (said), "It is all right. But from now on you do as you're told. Now give this mango to your wife. If she eats it, a handsome child will be born. (Now) go home." Both prostrated themselves and went home.	
	Manjuli ate the fruit. After a little while, a child was born. The parents happily announced, "We have a son." They reared him with much love. They sent for the astrologer, and had the horoscope read, and requested an interpretation of the horoscope.	After being cursed by Ganapati, he returned sadly with his one mango in his hand. He gave it to his wife. As she swallowed the mango, she became pregnant. They named the boy Siva.
Manjule got pregnant. After nine months a beautiful boy was born to them. They named him Candrasekar, and did all the proper rituals for him—his naming, his first haircut, and all of them. He grew up into a very clever boy.	"He will not have a long life. He only has sixteen years, but his fortune is very good. If you send him on a pilgrimage to Benares, he can escape this fate (of death at an early age)," (the astrologer) said. They gave him (the astrologer) presents and sent him on his way.	

When the boy attained his tenth year of age, Dharmapala's wife insisted that her husband arrange a marriage for their son. Dharmapala told his wife that he made up his mind to send him to Kashi Kshetra. He assured his wife that he would do the marriage after the son returned. So he sent his son with his brother-in-law.

They came to the town called Pratista Nagar, where they saw a group of girls swimming in a river.

. . . In the midst of those young virgins, the girl Sushila was very beautiful. She was glittering like gold. Another girl was abusing Sushila, calling her an unlucky, wretched vagrant, and a widow (rande). . . . Sushila said, ". . . I can escape the state of widowhood by the glorious Mangala Gauri Vrata, which has been performed by my mother before me. By that ritual vow I will always be a married woman."

As he finished his fifteenth year, they knew they would lose him. Manjule told her younger brother, "You take him to Kashi. We don't want him to die in front of our eyes."

Sometime later, they held the sacred thread ceremony for their son. He was being educated. In this way sixteen years passed. All were very worried. "Alas, this boy's death time has come. We have to escape it. O God," they prayed, and sent (him) on a pilgrimage to Benares with his uncle (mother's brother). As he was leaving, that boy prostrated himself before his parents. Their eyes filled with tears. Weeping, they said, "Return, son." They blessed him with "May god protect you. If Benares Visveswara has mercy, we will see this son again," so thinking, they sent him on his way.

Both uncle and nephew left. They did not have a vehicle. They walked. He (the boy) was accompanied by his uncle. On the way they reached Mandopura.

So the maternal uncle and the boy left for Kashi. On the way they came to Mandoraya's kingdom, and stopped in a garden.

The king's daughter had come there to gather flowers with her maids. As they did this, one of the maids began to quarrel with the princess, scolding her. The maid shouted out that the princess's horoscope had determined that she would lose her husband right after her marriage. The princess wouldn't be a married woman for long!

The princess was grief-stricken. But she answered, "Whatever my horoscope says, I have the blessings of Mangala Gauri. She won't let me down. So I am not afraid."

Table 15 (contd. on page 92)

Table 15 (contd. from page 91)

I. Bandipur Variant	II. Totagadde Variant	III. Printed Variant
The two travellers overheard these words. Candrasekar proposed to his uncle that if he married the girl, perhaps she could save his life. The uncle said, "If we pray to Iswara, they themselves will call us and offer her to us."		Siva's maternal uncle overheard the girls' words. He thought to himself that it would be very good to create a marriage between this girl and his nephew. So they followed the girl from the river and found out where she lived. They set themselves up in a house near there. . . .
		The boy's uncle hid behind an image of Parvati when the girl's father came to a temple to ask permission to arrange the marriage. The uncle spoke to them, telling them to give their daughter to the boy Siva who had come from a distant place. Thinking that this was the goddess speaking, [the girl's family gave their daughter to the boy after the boy's uncle made a proposal to them in a visit the next day.]
	That evening they stayed with Adugolaiji. On that very night was Mandoraya's daughter's wedding. The procession from Kollapura had arrived, but it was impossible for the bride to see the Kollapura groom because he had leprosy. Finally they (the Kollapura wedding party) had a plan. (They knew that) if she saw him, the girl would not agree (to the marriage). Therefore, they came to Adugolaiji's house and asked the boy whether he would consider coming (to the wedding). They asked the boy's uncle, "Lord, please do us a favour. My son has to get married. I have come with this wedding procession, but the boy has	
But they had already made arrangements for the princess's marriage. The groom's party arrived in town.

The boy who was to be the groom had leprosy and leucoderma.

When the groom's father saw Candrasekar, he asked him to stand in for his son at the wedding. He did not know that Candrasekar was a prince. Candrasekar's uncle laughed at this idea, saying that people would offer gifts, but no one would offer such a boy as his nephew. But then he thought again, realising that this was the last day of the boy's | | |

life, and the princess might be able to save him. So the uncle agreed to the proposition.

leprosy. Therefore, if that girl sees him before the marriage, she won't agree (to the marriage). Up until the wedding give (us) this boy as a stand-in." These two agreed.

The boy said, "I will be there until the wedding. Then I'll disappear. I will go to Benares at four in the morning. If you wish, I'll be around until then. Is that satisfactory?" he asked.

Then the in-laws said, "Younger brother, will you remain or not until the wedding?" "I will." "But if you are only around until four, it will be even better," he said. "Then in that case I'll make some plan," he said. Then they gave this boy clothes, decked him out, gave him a crown, and prepared him as a groom. They had the Kollapura boy sit at one side and they all went in the wedding procession to Mandoraya's house. Mandoraya rose, took the groom and in-laws inside, welcomed them and celebrated the marriage. They had the *mangalarati*. Everyone feasted.

By that time it was evening. All the ritual was finished and they sent the bride and groom into a room. Husband and wife lay down with happiness. That was the very day on which the groom became sixteen. His life span was over. However, this girl had made a vow to Mangalagawri. She had put the Mangalagawri *kalsha* near her.

So Sushila and Siva married.

On the same night the wedding took place. They prepared the snack called *ladduge*; and made popped rice, *aralu*, with brown sugar. They set out five of each snack in the bridal chamber—pressed rice (*avalakki*), puffed rice (*puri*), popped rice (*aralu*), white sesame, and roasted Bengal gram (*hurikadale*). The bride and groom ate these things and lay down together.

Table 15 (*contd. on page 94*)

Table 15 (contd. from page 93)

I. Bandipur Variant	II. Totagadde Variant	III. Printed Variant
As he was eating the snacks, the groom had slipped off his ring. Without the bride knowing it, he had dropped it into a cup of clarified butter that was sitting there. (Clarified butter is required, 'sastra'.) The ring had his name engraved on it.		
The bride had slept for only a short while when Mangala Gauri came to her in a dream. The goddess warned her that a snake (kalinga sarpa) would be coming to kill her husband. She should wake up and stay awake. She got up.		Taking the form of her mother, Mangala Gauri came to Sushila in her dream on the wedding night, saying, "Oh daughter, the snake is coming to bite your husband. Get up, and keep the milk for it. Set a clay pot, and the snake will go into it. Seal the pot with your blouse, and get up early in the morning. After your morning ablutions, give a presentation (bhagina) to your mother."
	Then a hissing serpent came to their room. He (the husband) had fallen asleep. She was awake. As soon as she saw this snake, she was afraid. She watched it. Suddenly that snake raised its hood and was coming toward him. It seemed, as if it would bite the boy.	After hearing these words, Sushila awoke in terror. As she saw the snake approaching, she put (a dish of) milk for it according to Devi's words, and set the pot nearby. The snake entered the pot, and she covered the hole with her blouse.
The princess immediately went to get the turmeric-coated raw rice (aksate) and water that she used for her puja. As the snake came, she sprinkled these two onto it, and it died. She took the dead snake and put it into the silver puja vessel (kalasa) that was there and covered the mouth of the vessel.	As soon as she saw this, that girl removed the lid of the Mangalagawri kalsha which was nearby (and said), "Mangalagawri, you alone can (allow my husband to) escape this fate. O Devi, save my husband's life. O Devi," and so saying she prostrated herself. Finally as	

a result of the Mangalagawri prayer, the snake went into the *kalsha*. Immediately that girl tied a silk blouse piece to the *kalsha*, put turmeric and *kumkum* (on it), roused her mother, and gave her the *kalsha bagina*. Accordingly this boy escaped his fate.

Then he awoke. He said to his wife, "I'm a little hungry. Give me a snack." She gave him some food and water and did *namaskara* and told him what had occurred. "Lord, by Devi's intervention your life was saved."

As he was eating, the ring which was on his finger fell off and she took it. Then he said, "Dear one, I will get up and go at four in the morning. I have to go to Benares."

Then she asked, "Lord, why do you have to go to Benares? When will you return? I am very depressed (at the thought of your leaving me)," she said. He said, "There I will study some, make the pilgrimage, and then return in a few days." Then the two lay down and slept.

A little later, he awoke and looked at his watch. It was four o'clock. At that moment his uncle came and according to the plan made earlier, he knocked at the door of the room. He told his wife that he had to go. He saw she had fallen into a deep sleep. "It would be a shame to disturb her," and so he

The boy woke up early the next morning and left for Kashi with his uncle. After he had left, the leper was brought in to complete the required rituals on the next day. But when they brought her to be seated on the low ritual platform (*hase mane*) next to him, the bride saw him from afar. She immediately said

At that time, Sushila's husband got up and said, "I am getting very hungry. Give me something to eat." Sushila brought him *laddu* and *jelebi* [sweets] in a golden plate. They ate them together, and slept after putting the groom's seal-ring in the golden plate.

Before sunrise Siva went out without telling his wife.

She awoke after sunrise and noticed her husband's absence. She felt sad, and she went to give *bagina* her mother.

Table 15 (*contd. on page 96*)

Table 15 (contd. from page 95)

I. Bandipur Variant	II. Totagadde Variant	III. Printed Variant
to her father, "He's not my husband. I've been tricked. I will not sit next to him on the platform." The father told the impostor and his group to leave : "We will not give our girl to you." They were ashamed and they left.	opened the door and went with his uncle. He had after all told her earlier. As soon as he left, they brought the Kollapura boy with leprosy and had him lie down beside her. She did not wake up. When the girl awoke in the morning, she saw that the man lying beside her was not her husband. She was very upset. "O dear, what is this? Who is this strange person? My husband must have set out for Benares. Then someone else came here and lay down. It isn't possible to look at him," and she was thinking of going upstairs to lie down. She didn't drink coffee. She didn't eat. She was weeping. The women all said, "Get up. You must have the turmeric and oil ceremony." She said, "I won't have it. He isn't my husband." "It was a night wedding. Therefore you have forgotten what he looks like," they all teased (her). Hearing all this ruckus, the Kollapura procession returned (home).	After sometime Lord Siva came in the form of Sushila's husband Siva. Not finding any difference between the God Siva and their son-in-law, her parents decided that this man was he. So Sushila's mother told her to play with this man. With one glance Sushila knew that he was not her husband, and told them so. She said she did not want to play with him. Even before she finished talking God Siva vanished from the place.
The princess then asked her father to feast anyone who came, no matter what their jati (caste). After dinner she herself would give betel leaf to the guests. She said that she would know her husband in that act. So the father began to do this.	She called for her father and said, "Father, from now on have dinner for all those who return from Benares." According to his daughter's wishes, Mandoraya provided dinner for all coming from Benares.	Sushila's parents became desperate to know the whereabouts of their daughter's real husband. So they made a plan, to arrange the 'giving of meals' (annadana, lit. 'the gift of cooked rice') to Brahmans, as a way of finding their son-in-law.

They began to do the ceremonial 'giving of meals', during which Sushila, keeping the seal-ring [on her finger], used to wash the feet of Brahman guests as her mother poured washing water for her. Her father presented the guests with betel and areca; and her brothers and sisters distributed sandalwood powder, perfumed water, and flowers among them. They did this ceremony for a long time, but still were unable to find Sushila's husband.

This uncle and nephew went to Benares and paid homage to Visveswara. While bathing in the Ganges, this boy slipped and floated a little distance. At that time Gangadevi lifted him up and putting him on her knee, said, "Son, you have a long life," and so saying she blessed him and sent him off. Then the two worshipped Iswara, Bhagirathi, Anapurna, and having completed the Benares pilgrimage, they returned to Mandopura.

Meanwhile Siva and his uncle went to Kashi-Kshetra (Benares), bathed in the holy Ganges, and worshipped Visveswara, [who is also called Kashi Visvanath]. . . . [They were] highly satisfied by the benefit of God's presence there. They visited all the sages of that place too and got their blessings. Then they visited all the Brahman houses in the vicinity, presenting gifts and money to all of them and having them bless the boy, Siva, for a long life. . . .

They resided in Kashi-Kshetra for a time, until there were only a few days more to Siva's 16th birthday. The uncle was preoccupied with thoughts of his nephew's coming death.

Siva had a dream. In that dream the God Siva came to him and blessed him for a long life. When he awoke, the boy told his uncle that in his dream he was fighting with the Yamadutas, messengers of the god of death. In the midst of the fight the God Siva had come and saved

Table 15 (contd. on page 98)

Table 15 (contd. from page 97)

I. Bandipur Variant	II. Totagadde Variant	III. Printed Variant
		his life. Both the boy and uncle felt happy about this dream, and they continued to reside happily in Kashi-Kshetra.
		One day they heard much about the 'giving of meals' being arranged by Sushila's parents; so they went to Sushila's house.
		Sushila recognised her husband there. She felt very happy, and she washed her husband's feet and put the washing water on her own head. Her parents also felt very happy and gave many precious gifts to [their son-in-law] Siva.
After finishing two or three years in Kashi, the boy and his uncle returned to the town. They stopped to rest in the same garden where they had first seen the princess. As they sat there, the king's priest came and invited them for food, but they refused his invitation. The king heard of this, and sent his messengers to tell them that the invitation was a king's command. They must come and eat. So they did.	As soon as he saw them, Mandoraya said, "Come to my house.", "We won't come now. We won't eat in anyone's house until we go home and have a feast for Ganga." No matter how much they protested, Mandoraya would not listen. He was obstinate in saying, "You must come." He would not let them continue. Then they realised, "All this must be Ishwara's desire," and came. He gave them a big welcome and provided them (with) dinner and all the trimmings. Mandoraya's daughter was very happy. She came to give them vilya. As soon as she saw her husband, she stood frozen with shyness.	
As she gave them betel leaf after dinner, the girl recognised her true husband. She told her father, and he summoned them to his presence. The uncle explained : "This is my elder sister's son. He was destined to live only sixteen years. Your in-laws (bigaru, son-in-law's parents) came and asked me to offer the boy as a substitute groom, and so I had him seated here for the one day dhare wedding ritual. And according to our agreement with them, we left after that day. What happened after that we do not know."		
The group of people gathered there asked the boy if he could prove that he		

was the real husband. He told them about the ring he had dropped into the cup of clarified butter. Since the girl had kept everything as it was, they found the ring with his name on it.

Then they asked the girl if she had any proof. So she told them about the snake in the ritual vessel. She brought it forward, and they opened it up. Inside they found a beautiful necklace. They were all very happy.

Her father was very pleased with the girl. "A good girl like this, so pious and intelligent, overcoming all the problems that come to her, is a credit to her father," he said.

They kept the couple there, but the boy wanted to go back to his parents. After they had been there for four days he said to his uncle, "My father and mother must be worried about me after all this time. My mother would be very happy to see me. Let's go home."

So her parents seated her in a new sari and put the good luck offerings (*sogalakki*) into her lap—five kilograms of raw rice, two coconuts, five sets of betel and areca, one large cube of brown sugar, and the tip of a turmeric root. The girl's parents cried at losing their only daughter, but they soon sent her off in a chariot.

Then everybody teased (her). "This very one must be your husband, but give us some proof," they said. So she brought the wedding night *kalsha* to the group. They took it and looked at it. The snake inside it had become a gold chain. As soon as they saw it, everybody was surprised. As a result of the snake's having become a gold chain, they said, "Mangalagawri is a powerful spirit." They said, "Now show (us) proof of (your) acquaintance (with) this boy." She showed the ring which he had given his wife that day. Then everybody believed. "I bless you both and the favor of god is on both the girl who is a devoted wife and the boy who has religious merit. To you both," they said. "May you have good fortune." Then Mandoraya again hosted a marriage, gave his daughter presents, and sent the couple home.

Table 15 (*contd. on page 100*)

Table 15 (*contd. from page 99*)

I. *Bandipur Variant*	II. *Toiagadde Variant*	III. *Printed Variant*
The journey was a long one. The month of Sravana came, and on Tuesday she had to do her Mangala Gauri *puja*. She told her husband this, but he said, "No one has to do it on the road." She should wait, he said, until they got to his town. She insisted, "Whatever facilities I have, I will do the *puja* here. There's a river nearby. I will take a bath and do worship with my things." So she did.	Along their route they came to a river. The girl said, "There today, Tuesday, I must perform the Mangalagawri *puja*." The husband said, "(If you wait until) tomorrow, we may, do it at home." To that she replied, "This vow must be done on this very day.", "If that is the case, do it," said the husband. She did the Mangalagawri *puja*. They finally gathered all their things and went on. No matter how far they went, they did not see a village. The reason was that by this river, in this very place, they had forgotten the Mangalagawri *kalsha* and had gone on. Therefore, they didn't find a (single) village or house. They turned around in the forest. Then she remembered. She said, "O, I forgot the Mangalagawri *kalsha*. Therefore, I will go back," and so saying she went and brought it. Then the village appeared. The villagers told Manjuli, "Your son is coming. A daughter-in-law is also coming." "Go" they said. "Meet them and bring them (here)." Hearing their words, Manjuli responds, "You all are teasing (me). My son has not come. Let it be as god wishes," she said. Finally, the villagers said, "Why is this doubt, Manjuli? It is the truth, your son has really come." They said, "It is not a lie." Then Manjuli went and welcomed her son and daughter-in-law.	This side, the parents of Siva, Dharmapala and his wife, were worried about the whereabouts of their son. After a while they got news from a messenger about him. So they gladly welcomed their son and daughter-in-law to their house. They heard about the Mangala Gauri vow, and they asked their daughter-in-law to perform it.
As they came to the town, the people saw them and ran to tell the king and queen that their son had come. Everyone gave the proper honourable greetings to each other. The boy's mother asked her younger brother, "What happened? How did you save my son?!" He replied, "I do not know. I did not do anything. Ask your daughter-in-law." The lady embraced the girl, told her she was a good woman, and that she had brought honour to the		

O! Dharmanandana, son of Yama, one must perform this vow on the Tuesdays of the month of Sravana. Get up early in the morning, take a bath, and install the image of Mangala Gauri. Perform the 'sixteen ways of worship' for it with sixteen lamps, which you must give to sixteen virtuous women whose husbands are alive (*suvasini*).

On the day this vow is performed, eat saltless rice.

This story was told by Sri Krishna to Dharmaraya, [the eldest brother of the Pandavas], and it comes to an end in the *Bhavisyottara Purana*.

family. "But," the boy's uncle reminded his sister, "this is also your own birth-fortune (*hwatepunya*)."

Both prostrated themselves. The father-in-law and mother-in-law of Manjuli were very happy. She asked her daughter-in-law, "Younger sister, what vow did you make? You saved my son's life," she said.

The daughter-in-law replied, "I don't know anything at all (about this). I only made the Mangalagawri vow. This is all your merited good fortune (*punya*)," and so saying she prostrated herself. From that day on she continued to do the Mangalagawri *puja* and they lived happily.

"So," Krishna concludes his story with some advice to Draupadi, "you should all do this *puja*."

tion between 'snacks' (*tindi*) and 'meals' (*uta*). Snacks include many kinds of food, even rice, made from flour or from soaked and processed grains; but not boiled rice. Meals, which are considered to be genuine nourishment, inc' .de boiled rice. Most families of this area are far more careful about eating 'meals' than they are about snacks. That is, although they may eat snacks at restaurants or at casual acquaintances' homes, they prefer to take meals only from the hands of caste-mates or from castes they consider superior to themselves.

It had been mentioned earlier that the groom ate snacks in the bridal chamber on his wedding night. Variant I lists the snacks by name, and some of them appear in festival menus. Variants II and III make a point of mentioning that the groom was hungry during the night, and that the bride fed him snacks.

When the boy and his uncle come back from Kashi, they are invited to eat meals in the bride's home. They are reluctant to do so: a reference to the awkward status of the impostor-groom in the story, but also a reference to the dangers involved in sharing meals with outsiders. The *denoument* of the story (and the beginning of full family life) begins when the boy and his uncle do eat a full meal as guests of the girl's father and take betel-areca from the girl herself. This narrative device parallels an actual Hindu wedding sequence. All of the castes of this region celebrate the first commensality of bride and groom in a ritual called *buvve sastra* towards the conclusion of the wedding (though before consummation of the marriage). Regelson has described the various ways in which this is done in his dissertation (1972).

Though the girl and boy get married, they maintain their separate attachments during the story, as he continues to travel with his uncle and she, to stay with her parents for a few years. Even after they are re-united, he soon misses his own family and succeeds in pulling her away from her kin. On the road she defies him and remains steady to her commitment to her goddess: a repetition of the theme of their separate interests. At the reunion with his family, an interesting concluding sequence first has the couple greet his parents (a patrilineal contract), after which the maternal uncle greets his married sister (an 'exchange relation'). At the very end of Variant I the mother-in-law and daughter-in-law begin their relationship in the newly viable birth group. It is worth noting that the husband-wife pair is a more egalitarian and cooperative team in the variants written down by village women than in the published variant, which is supposedly closer to the original *Purana* than the village tales are, but which may reflect the views of its publisher to some extent.

The myth suggests certain sources of support to a family and its members. As bad luck changes to good, both deities and people intervene to make sure that the family survives. Some of the human helpers are insiders to the boy's or girl's family—mothers and fathers helping their children in whatever ways they can. Some of them are outsiders. The boy's maternal uncle, who accom-

panies him on the long journey that saves his life, is the closest outsider mentioned as a source of assistance. He is considered to be a 'relation of exchange'
(*nentru*) to the boy's birth group. It is common for a woman to ask her brother
for help with problems in her marital home, as the boy's mother did in
'Mangala Gauri'. A point of contrast between this myth and festival rituals
for Gauri, however, is that while the myth indicates multiple sources of human
support for women, rituals stress same-sex ties, to other women.

Other outsiders included in the myth represent greater power and greater
danger than the maternal uncle does. The holy man, for example, is a figure
who has rejected membership in human society altogether. His strength is "the
potency of the non-structured flux, chaos, disorder, the irrational substratum
. . .; the unknown, the strange, the remote, the alien, the hostile, or simply
the 'other'" (Lannoy 1971 : 174). In Hindu culture, the holy man, or *sannyasin*,
"is dead to ordinary society and is bound only by the extraordinary goal of
. . . seeking spiritual release and enlightenment" (Tyler 1973 : 91).

The wildness, or asocial orientation, of the holy man contrasts with the
strictly proper, social concerns of most of the other characters in the myth. The
relationship of contrast between wild and tame recurs throughout the myth's
structure. It is repeated, for example, when the boy's father (Variant III) tra-
vels from his hometown into a forest, and when the boy and his uncle venture
into foreign regions, occupied by complete strangers. This aspect of the structure of 'Mangala Gauri' suggests that although some outsiders are necessary
to the survival of a birth group, contact with outsiders is dangerous and has
unpredictable results.

MEDIATORS

There are several critical images and incidents in the myth which propel the
story forward by representing a transformation from bad luck and disorder into good luck and order. It is typical of such 'mediators' that they embody
contradictory or opposed structural elements in single images. They provide
valuable clues to the dilemmas with which the myth, in various ways through
all of its variants, attempts to deal.

An important mediator in all vow-related myths is the partnership the vow
establishes between a god(dess) and a person. Such partnerships repeatedly
rescue the boy from death and the girl from widowhood in this myth.

The episode which solves the couple's barrenness problem in Variant III presents a more down-to-earth transformation-juxtaposition which is colour-cod-
ed in black + gold. On the instructions of the holy man, the childless man
dresses in black and rides a horse into a forest until his horse falters. At that
spot he digs a hole, in which he finds a gold-domed temple of goddess Parvati
(Gauri). The man in black offers her a *puja* that includes yellow-coloured
flowers and (yellow) turmeric-coloured raw rice. The black-gold juxtaposition,

which we also find in women's ritual gifts as in their daily ornaments, is directly keyed to the barrenness-fertility problem in this myth.

An important mediator image is the switching of grooms that enabled the
boy to marry the girl-devotee of Gauri. The difference between the two
grooms, one diseased and disintegrating and the other natural and whole,
neatly expresses the basic problem of the hero's family which is in danger of
disintegrating without a viable son to carry it on. Not only does the intended
groom have leprosy, in Variant I; he also has leucoderma, a skin condition
which gives a mixed, partly-bleached colouration to the skin.

Through the negotiations of the maternal uncle, the boy saves himself, and
his own family, by pretending to be the son of another ('outsider') family for
the day of the wedding. As a literary anticipation of the later working-out of
the story, the boy with the good body and the protective wife replaces the
boy who is not viable. That is, he and his family both survive partly as a result
of this deception.

Another mediator episode is the snake in the vessel changing into a necklace. The many relationships involved here summarise the themes of danger
and the woman's power to save her husband's life. As the second and crucial
event which changes the boy's bad luck to good, this mediator deserves close
attention. I will re-write this passage of Variant I, bracketing my interpretations of the meanings of its elements. The bride kills the snake [death itself]
with the combined powers of her *puja* water [birth], her raw rice [pure body]
with turmeric powder [marital tie and vow to golden goddess] on it. The snake
[the husband's life *and* death] is enclosed [controlled] in the vessel [her body],
which is covered by a piece of cloth [her modesty]. Eventually the serpent
[life-death tension] is transformed into a necklace [beautiful feminine ornament]
after some years of vigilant waiting [discipline], in which she kept all the wedding things exactly as they had originally been set out on the night he left
[indicating her respect for order].

Lore from another region also relates woman and vessel and relates discipline and power. Whitehead (1921 : 116) describes a legendary woman (Mari-
amma, later to be a goddess) as being "so chaste in mind that she could carry
water in a mass without any vessel. . . ."[12]

Tables 16 and 17 outline the structure of the 'Mangala Gauri' myth. In
Table 17, which includes the story line, the narrative events and motifs move
several times across the columns of the structure, rather than progressing
evenly from one point in the structure to the next. This is because the myth's
structure is implicit in relationships between motifs, rather than being directly
evident in the narrative sequence.

The motifs of the 'Mangala Gauri' myth overlap with elements of Gauri
Festival and Prati Festival structure. The repeated appearance of gold objects
and the idea that gold is somehow related to both women and goddesses is clear
in both myth and ritual.

Table 16—'Mangala Gauri' Structure : Summary

DANGER	CHAOS	DISORDERLY OR DISRUPTED EXCHANGE	PARTIAL SUCCESS
Possibility of disintegration of birth group and patrilineal line	Interaction with strangers or outsiders; Contact with wild and foreign places		Success combined with risks to the well-being of the family (present and future)
———→	———————→	– – – – – – →	– – – – – – →
	MEDIATORS Juxtaposition of extreme opposites, to signify the transformation from danger and failure to safety and success for the birth group and its members		
	———— – ——→		
NATAL FAMILY SUPPORTS THE WELL-BEING OF CHILDREN	RELATIONS OF EXCHANGE SUPPORT THE WELL-BEING OF CHILDREN	NORMAL AND ORDERLY EXCHANGE	FULL SUCCESS
		Productive exchange between representatives of different birth groups	Birth group is whole and promising to continue the family line
– – – – – →	– – – – – →	– – – – – →	– – – – – →

The promised son is cursed to die at the age of 16 years in Variant III as a result of 16 repetitions of an ominous numerological shift. Told to climb over the fat belly of the elephant-headed god Ganapati and pluck a fertilizing mango for his wife, the would-be father plucks several instead. As he returns from the mango tree, however, his several fruits are repeatedly changed into one solitary mango until the curse finishes the sequence. Numbers are very important elements of ritual structure in these festivals, though rituals avoid the number one as an inauspicious number.

Beauty and the visual capacity to see it appear like a steady drumbeat in all variants of this myth, and rituals are intended to be beautiful also. In Variant I the would-be mother offers colourful jewels of the best quality to the

Table 17—'Mangala Gauri' Organization of Content

Structure	Danger	Chaos	Disorderly or Disrupted Exchange	Partial Success	Mediators	Natal Family Supports the Well-being of Children	Relations of Exchange Support the Well-being of Children	Normal and Orderly Exchange	Full Success
Story Line:	Married couple has wealth but no child	Holy man/God Siva comes as a beggar	Beggar refuses barren woman's alms						[II:] Woman thinks about what it would be like to have a lively, mischievous baby
	[I:] Beggar throws away jewels offered as alms				[I, II:] Husband and wife worship god(dess) and gain boon of a child	[III:] Husband and wife make a plan to determine the meaning of the beggar's rejection of their alms			
	Holy man curses woman to be barren because she tricks him into accepting alms [III]	Husband goes into the forest [III]			[III:] Husband, dressed in black, digs ground for golden dome of temple; makes puja to goddess				

[II, III:] Husband cuts many mangoes, but they change into only one mango	[III:] Husband returns sadly to wife, to give her the one mango	
	Couple is granted a child, with the curse that he is doomed to die at the age of 16	[II, III:] Husband gives mango to wife, who becomes pregnant
		Birth of a beautiful, [II:] intelligent son
	Son grows up, goes through required rites of passage, reaches age 16	Boy's [I, II:] mother or [III:] father seeks help of ... boy's maternal uncle, who agrees to accompany boy to Benares (Kashi)

Table 17 (contd. on page 108)

Table 17 (contd. from page 107)

Structure	Danger	Chaos	Disorderly or Disrupted Exchange	Partial Success	Mediators	Natal Family Supports the Well-being of Children	Relations of Exchange Support the Well-being of Children	Normal and Orderly Exchange	Full Success
	Son leaves his anxious parents	Boy and uncle set out on journey and stop in girl's town along the way							Boy and uncle observe beautiful virgin [I:] playing in a garden [III:] swimming in a river
	[I, III:] Girl's friends mock her as a future widow				[I, III] Girl affirms her vow to Gauri, as protection against widowhood		Uncle arranges for the boy to marry the girl		
	[I, II:] Proposed groom has leprosy		Deceit of affines in marriage arrangement		[I, II:] Agreement between two families to substitute healthy boy for diseased groom				Girl marries healthy boy [I,II:]; Marriage occurs [III]

Wedding night of bride and groom: couple share food (snacks) and boy's ring is left with girl

Boy's life has been saved, [I,II:] removing the curse under which he was born

Goddess Gauri comes to girl in form of her mother, to warn her of danger to her husband [III]

Boy has wedding, but as impostor [I, II]

Girl's effort (vow) saves boy from death. [I:] Girl kills snake; [II, III:] Snake enters *kalasa* vessel. Girl covers vessel opening

Girl gives *bhagina* gifts to her mother after her husband's life is saved

Snake comes to kill boy

Table 17 (*contd. on page* 110)

Table 17 (contd. from page 109)

Structure	Danger	Chaos	Disorderly or Disrupted Exchange	Partial Success	Mediators	Natal Family Supports the Well-being of Children	Relations of Exchange Support the Well-being of Children	Normal and Orderly Exchange	Full Success
	Groom leaves bride	Bride put together with wrong groom	Bride rejects substitute groom; humiliates affines; refuses to complete wedding rituals			Father agrees to help daughter find her lost husband	Uncle escorts nephew on pilgrimage to Kashi		
	[II:] Boy almost dies by drowning in Kashi	Meals served to strangers [I: regardless of caste] while groom is absent	[I, III:] Girl offers gestures of intimacy to guests at meals		[II:] Drowning boy is saved by goddess Ganga in Kashi				
					[I, II:] Snake in vessel changes into a necklace	[I, II:] Girl's family give her presents and blessings	[III:] Girl's family give gifts to boy	Boy and uncle take meal from (affines) girl's father	Bride and groom are re-united
		Journey from girl's town to boy's	[II:] Girl forgets to bring along her Gauri kalasa after performing pūja		[I, II:] Bride maintains her obligation to perform Gauri vow even while travelling			Bride leaves her parents for her husband's home	

[II :] Villages appear again

[II :] Girl gets back her Gauri *kalsa*

Bride and groom arrive back in groom's town

Boy's father and mother welcome their son and new daughter-in-law

[I :] Uncle greets his sister, the boy's mother, upon returning to boy's home town

[II :] Bride and groom prostrate themselves before groom's parents

[I :] Uncle reminds his sister that the success is a result of . . .

. . . the good fortune with which she herself was born

Mother-in-law agree that her son is alive because of the daughter-in-law's commitment to the Mangala Gauri vow

[II :] Whole villages disappear when the girl lacks her Gauri *kalasa*

wandering sage. These are thrown into the garbage pile. In Variant III the would-be father has three choices offered to him, all of which play on the motif of vision and beauty:

(i)   a [beautiful] daughter, doomed to early widowhood,
(ii) a handsome son, doomed to early death, or
(iii) a blind son [without the capacity to see beauty] who will live a long life.

In taking the second choice, the man chooses short-life-plus-a-view-of-beauty over long-life-plus-no-view-possible. When we first meet the girl that the boy will marry, her beauty is compared to gold. But soon she is singled out by the 'Widow!' curse, and the saga of her marriage arrangement and marriage begins.

These startling combinations of beauty and danger give the story tension and movement. Viewed in abstract terms, they are part of the general problem of family frustration and incompleteness which the myth-maker has to solve by the end of the story. The symbolic use of eyes and vision is common to other festivals besides Gauri and Prati, and will appear again in those relating to *amma* goddesses and cobra worship.

FESTIVAL RITUALS

The principles which structure the two myths, especially 'Mangala Gauri', are also implicit in associated rituals. The medium of their expression in ritual is physical—the objects of worship and offering. In the relationships among required objects for each ritual we can again discern the image of the valiant married woman who appeared in person in the myths. Her context of relatives, natal and marital; her goddesses; her mother, her sisters, and her dowry—most of these figure in the non-verbal choreography of the long annual *pujas*. The dangers of widowhood or poverty with which she struggles also figure there, though they have a subdued role, appearing mainly as taboos or with minor emphasis.

The two annual festival rituals are celebrated by Iyengar Brahmans (for Laksmi/Prati) and by Smartha Brahmans (for Gauri).[13] We observed each of them twice, once in 1966 and then in 1967; and we saw each festival done in each of the two villages. Some years after eliciting information about preferred and prescribed actions, ritual paraphernalia, foods, and so on, I became aware of patterns in colour use as I reviewed my own colour slides. The 'discovery' produced this chapter and eventually the rest of this book as well, as I came to wonder about colour-patterning of festivals with other types of spirits and purposes.

The festival rituals are typical of Brahmanical rites, though they are done on a relatively simple scale with homespun elements. Contrasted with the rituals of some of the other castes, they are relatively intricate and have an abundance of detailed requirements. Another Brahmanical element, as pointed out by the Freeds (1962), is their having justification by reference to texts of the classical traditions, i.e., the myths just discussed. The fathers of the Brahman families, or interested and knowledgeable Brahman neighbours, therefore have a role to play in performing the more intricate parts of the *puja* offerings. The overall construction of the festivals, however, must still remain a woman's and non-specialist creation, since it is they who cook special foods and plan out most of the things to do in welcoming their goddesses out of the river, feeding them while they visit, and sending them off again.

Laksmi/Prati Festival Rituals

The local festival for Laksmi, as Prati, is performed according to the ancient Indian solar calendar, Saoramana, rather than the lunar calendar. It occurs in the month called Adi (also Kataka), extending for a total of five Fridays of that month. Adi lasted for 32 days in 1966, going from July 16 through August 16, and coinciding with two lunar months. The Second Friday is the most important ritual day, since it is on that day that groups of women go to the river to summon their goddess guest.

The goddess Prati is worshipped in two different forms: as a *kalasa* vessel which is kept in the house for worship on all of the five Fridays, and also as a ball of wet sand which is taken out of the river on the Second Friday and sent off again on the following Saturday after an elaborate feast meal.

The following is a summary outline of the Prati rituals of the Second Friday and following Saturday, as we observed them in 1966 and 1967. A basic requirement is for at least two households to do the festival together. A single house cannot do it apart from others.

In anticipation of the Second Friday installation of the sand-ball goddess image, some members of the household are expected to be 'pure' and to fast. That means that they will have bathed, and will not take cooked rice 'meals' before the goddess is brought to the house and installed on her temporary pedestal there with appropriate *puja* offerings. The persons who fast take responsibility for bringing her out of the riverbed, for making the Sanskrit prayers to her, and for preparing food offerings that will be served to her, and later to all as *prasad*, 'sanctified offerings'. The fasting parties, then, are most likely to be the male head of the household or other Brahman man called to perform rituals; his wife, if he has one (the Chinnapura head is a widower); any other woman who either takes the sand-balls from the river to the home, such as a daughter-in-law or daughter who accompanies her when she does this fetching journey (in Chinnapura in 1967, the wife of the head's wife's brother).

Bringing the Goddess Out of the River

On the afternoon or evening of the Second Friday a group of women, representing at least two households, goes merrily to the river to summon the goddess for her worship. They believe that the goddess lives (with her husband) in the 'very deep place' in the river. They are accompanied by traditional village musicians, pipers and drummers of the Barber caste, and their path is lighted

Plate 1. Summoning goddess Prati out of the River, Bandipur 1966.

by a cloth torch, held by a member of the Washerman caste. They bring with them silver trays piled with ornamental and ritual objects. The trays will be the resting places for the goddess as she enters each home. On each silver tray are the following items:

   (i)   *kalasa* (water and betel leaf) vessel from the house
  (ii)   3 small cotton necklaces (*gejjestra*)
 (iii)   1 large cotton necklace
 (iv)   6 balls of turmeric paste
  (v)   6 yellow cloths (coloured with turmeric)
 (vi)   balls of cotton with turmeric and vermillion spots on them
(vii)   silver cup with flowers in it: pandanus spike, champak, jasmine
(viii)   newly sprouted leaves: sacred fig (*pipal*), country fig, and
 (ix)   bunch of bananas ('plantains') for distribution as *prasad*.

Singing devotional songs, each woman reaches into the river, takes a large ball of wet sand from the bottom, and divides it into three parts. (In Bandipur, 1966, a male temple functionary reached into the river bottom to retrieve the sand-ball, Plate 1). She puts the *kalasa* vessel next to the sand-ball goddess and decorates the vessel with flowers, cotton necklaces, and spots of turmeric and vermillion. A brief series of worship and blessing acts follows :

> Women offer betel-areca sets to the goddess on each of their trays and rotate incense before her.
> A pair of women from each house then waves a tray of bright red liquid before the tray with the goddess on it, to remove the evil eye. (This rotation is called *arati*.)
> Women distribute *prasad* to all those present. *Prasad* consists of bananas, betel leaves, 2-paise coins, and either turmeric + vermillion (for married women) or vermillion alone (for dotting the foreheads of others present).

The group of hostesses then proceeds homeward, accompanied by the tooting and whining of village musicians' horns. In Chinnapura, a lady of the Washerman caste holds a cloth torch to light the path.

Installing the Goddess in the Home Shrine

As each pair of women reaches home, the one carrying the goddess tray stands on a special low wooden platform (*mane*), her companion next to her. Both get their feet washed by a member of the household who comes out to greet them, and who then puts vermillion on their foreheads (Plate 2). They enter the house, where a decorated shrine has been prepared for the goddess-visitor.

Once inside the house the carrier of the tray hands it to the male household head, who places it on a decorated platform inside the shrine (Plate 3). Under the decorative shelter of hanging mango leaves, flowers, and some vegetables he arranges the tray and its sacred contents, draping more jewellery and other ornaments over the goddess at the top of the pedestal, including a long cotton necklace and some other jewellery kept in the home for this festival.[14] The sari which drapes the pedestal beneath the tray may be kept especially for the goddess's visit also.[15] And a couple of opened lotus blossoms establish a symbolic reference to the goddess's birth out of the 'Ocean of Milk', as one member of the family explains to me. Other items placed next to goddess Prati also include:

> pearls,
> a small statue of Laksmi,
> palm-leaf earrings (*biccole*), and
> *tali* pendant and turmeric roots (4), with other items from welcoming tray.

In Chinnapura, 1967, the youngest daughter of the family, an unmarried

Plate 2.   Arriving home with Goddess Prati on a tray, Chinnapura 1967.

woman in her early 20's, quietly puts some vermillion to the frame of the back door, walks into the backyard, where she performs a *puja* for the sacred Tulasi (basil plant) growing in a concrete planter.

The worship is done differently in the two Iyengar houses observed, though both rituals are guided by Brahman fathers of the families, and both follow a roughly similar pattern of development, as described in Table 18.

For the performance of the summoning and *puja*, two women or more per household are required, in addition to at least two houses in each village being required for the festival to occur at all. The order of preference as to which women bring the goddess from the river to the home is : (i) wife of household head, (ii) daughter-in-law of the house, or (iii) daughter of the house.

The welcoming ritual for the goddess is done preferably by women who live at the home which she visits.

Table 18—Welcoming Ritual for Prati : Two Households Compared

Bandipur, 1966	Chinnapura, 1967
Household head makes worship for Visnu *aradane puja*, with Sanskrit formulae.	Guided by the household head, women chant 108 names of the goddess, offering a differently-named flower for each name (actually the same flower called by various flower names).
	Lighting of oil lamps.
	Presentation of tray with lighted lamps on it, waving tray before the goddess; someone beats a loud gong for accompaniment.
	Male head chants long Sanskrit prayer, while women stand and listen.
	Worshippers circle a tray with 21 rice-dough lamps before the goddess.
Household head offers foods (*naivedya*) to refresh the goddess after her journey : milk, fruit salad (*rasayana*), sweet *pongal* rice, *iddali* and other 'snacks', *tambittu* and *kolakatte*.	A pair of women offer a plate of delicacies to the goddess : *obbattu, tambittu,* or *kolakatte* (list not clear or complete) 'snacks'.
All present do *puja* for the goddess, sprinkling her with turmeric-coloured raw rice, setting flowers before her, and waving lamps before her on a tray.	Worshippers present goddess with two trays at once, waving them before her; A sequence of three pairs of women do another tray-waving *arati*, now holding a single tray between them. There are two oil lamps shining on the tray.
Sequence of pairs (listed below) of worshippers present her with a tray that has 5 lamps on it.	A child sprinkles rice onto the goddess and prostrates before her.
Household head waves an ornate spoon with burning camphor on it, a soothing *mangala arati*, in front of the goddess.	
Pairs of women come forward to present waving trays, held between them, that each have two lamps on them.	
Household head, with all others following in sequence after him, does the waving presentation of a tray with 21 rice-dough lamps on it (Plate 4).	

Table 18 (*contd. on page* 118)

Table 18 (*contd. from page* 117)

Bandipur (cont'd)	Chinnapura (cont'd)
	Male head of household reads a myth selected from the epic *Mahabharata* poem.
	All present, family members, bow down to the male head of household.

Male head of household gives sacred, offered water and 'five elixirs' into the out-stretched palms of (in order) :
   his wife
   his eldest son (unmarried)
   his married daughter
   3 unmarried daughters
   a 'married woman' guest
   (no relation to family)
   3 small sons.
	Male head of household distributes sanctified *prasad*: 'snacks'; passes spoon full of sacred water (*tirta*)—actually mixture of river water and coconut water that has been offered to goddess—into the outreaching palms of those present. He also gives a liquid mixture called 'five elixirs' (*pancamrita*) into their hands. They drink quickly from their right palms, wiping their hands on their hair.

Offered 'snacks' and other foods and distributed to all present as *prasad*.	
Family and guests sit down on the floor in a few perpendicular lines to eat dinner.	Family and guests sit down on the floor to eat dinner.

There are other parts of the ritual, however, where the married daughter takes precedence. In the Chinnapura home, for example, she leads the first greeting bows done by women after the goddess is installed on the home pedestal with Sanskritic chants. Her worship precedes that of her mother's brother's wife, and her younger, unmarried sister, even though the last is a resident of the host home. A second instance in which the married daughter takes precedence is in the Bandipur home at the conclusion of the ritual, when the male head of the household gives sacred water and 'five elixirs' to those assembled there. She receives the items after her mother and brother, but before her unmarried sisters.

The married daughter leads off the earlier five-lamp *arati* as well, in the Bandipur ritual. She pairs up with her eldest unmarried sister for this worship act. After these two come the two younger, unmarried sisters; the mother (a married woman still) and the eldest unmarried girl;[16] and two pairs of brothers.

All of the elements of the ritual, even this far, are special and symbolic. Each item and action is placed carefully in the overall scheme of welcoming the goddess and honouring her as the glorious patron of married women. Although I was hardly aware of it when I first saw the ritual in July, 1966, hardly a month into my fieldwork, these few hours presented me with a microcosm of distinctions that only several years of further work could define.

Plate 3. Prati shrine in a home, with pandanus spikes, Chinnapura 1967.

One feature of significance in this event is rice. On the Second Friday, even the floor decorations are made with a mixture of water and rice-flour. Each house makes further use of rice by molding 21 tiny oil lamps (burning clarified butter) for part of the worship. Raw rice covered with turmeric powder, the widely used *aksate*, is thrown onto the little sand-ball goddess as soon as she arrives home; and, later on, she is sprinkled with plain raw rice by a (Chinnapura) child. In its edible forms, rice dominates the feast of 'snacks' as well, all of them being made with rice grits or rice flour for this occasion. The most important preparation for the Second Friday is the 'snack' *iddali*, which is a steamed cake made from rice grits and black gram paste.

There are special uses for certain flowers as well. The most firmly required flower, surprisingly enough, is not the mythic lotus out of which the goddess is said to have been born, but rather an obscure and unusual flower called *tala*

Plate 4.   Five sisters perform *arati* with twenty-one rice dough lamps, Bandipur 1966.

Plate 5.   *Kolakatte* snacks, Prati Festival.

or *tale* in Kannada. This flower is difficult to find, and becomes available in its distant field growths only at this specific time of year. It is the pandanus flower (also called 'screw pine' or 'calders bush').[17] The whole flower is a long, whitish staminate inflorescence with fragrant yellow staminate spikes jutting out from it. It is the yellow spikes which serve as the 'flower' in rituals, not the whole thing (Saldanha 1976 : 779-780).

Though villagers offer no symbolic explanations for using this flower beyond claiming that "Prati likes it," there may be historical and structural reasons for its use in her festival. Sri K. K. A. Venkatachari, a renowned Iyengar philosopher and religious community leader, informs me that the Iyengars traditionally consider this flower to be special because of the tightness of its bud (see Plate 6). This yellow bud, he points out, is closed up so tightly that

Plate 6. Pandanus buds.

not even a honey bee could enter it. It is, therefore, a model for chaste women to follow. Though they use the flower at a more mature stage, after it has opened up, village Iyengar women claim that its strong scent attracts cobras because it is so good. (In fact, one Smartha Brahman myth associated with a serpent festival to be discussed later has a young man killed by a cobra that is resting inside a pandanus flower.) The one other ritual in which they require this flower, as one of five, is when they send off a married daughter to her new home.

In the context of the Prati festival, it is important to recognise the yellow colour of the required pandanus spikes as fully appropriate in an offering to the goddess of (gold) wealth. Yellow colour is found in the sweet-smelling champak flower, Kannada *sampige, Michelia champaca* L., placed alongside the pandanus and jasmine on the welcoming silver tray brought to carry the goddess away from her river home. Jasmine, which is white, and champak are not requirements like the pandanus is; they merely add their perfume and their whiteness or yellow colour to enhance the pleasurable and auspicious connotations of the welcoming event.

I shall discuss the presence of new country fig and sacred fig leaves below, in connection with operational meanings of elements of ritual symbolism.

Certain numbers have become visible in this portion of the festival, particularly 5, 2, 3, and 21. A number of widespread relevance to married women rituals throughout India, 5, is an all-purpose good number; thus its use in preparations such as the 'five elixirs' by the trained Brahman of the two families observed. Apart from the fact that the whole festival is organised as a series of 5 Fridays, however, the number is not yet prominent in the festival ritual. Though it makes a brief appearance as the number of lamps on the waving *arati* tray, 5 will only take a central place on the next afternoon, when a 2 p.m. meal of 'five kinds of rice' is served.

Regarding 2, the welcoming is taking place on the *Second* Friday in the festival series; it is performed by no fewer than 2 houses, with a pair of women representing each house. In the ritual distribution after the sand-balls have been removed from the river, coins worth 2 paise (np) are distributed as part of the *prasad*; and in the rituals at home there is frequent need for pairs of worshippers to act together. Trays and lamps also appear in pairs during the *puja*.

Number 3 is another crucial number in this phase of the festival ritual. The goddess's silver tray has on it three small cotton necklaces, $6 (= 2 \times 3)$ balls of turmeric and $6 (= 2 \times 3)$ yellow cloths. She herself is quickly divided into three sand-balls out of the handful of wet sand first taken out of the river.

The number 21 is a fixed part of the village ritual, as in the offering of 21 rice-dough lamps; but I do not have any data on other instances in which it is used, or even any mythic references to this number.

With these insights behind us, let us now proceed to the events of the send-off day, the Saturday after Prati was welcomed into the home. After a *puja*, done by the priestly head of the household, there is a camphor-burning offering called *mangala arati*, witnessed by everyone in the group. After that the afternoon is filled with several activities:

Outline of Send-Off Rituals for Prati

1. Women invite friends to the house.
2. At 2 p.m., serve a special meal centering on 'five kinds of rice'.
3. Host a gathering (called *arati*) of friends who are 'married women', to pay respect to the goddess on her pedestal.
4. Putting on a traditional-style Iyengar sari, one that is especially 'pure' (*madi*), performs farewell worship for the goddess.

5. Take the goddess back to the river, and perform worship and send-off there.
6. Go to village temple (Chinnapura case), and attend worship there.
7. Return home.

I shall discuss the feast of 'five kinds of rice' further below.

As Prati is about to be taken out of the house, at stage 4 above, there is a ceremonious departure ritual done for her by the women of the family. The male household head brings the silver tray out of the room with the draped pedestal and sets the tray onto a small, low platform (*mane*) of the sort used in auspicious rites of passage. The platform has a woolen shawl (wool is always 'pure') folded on top of it. Her silver tray rests on that shawl.

Set next to the small platform are two identical plates. One is for the goddess, and the other is for a friend—a woman of a different household who will receive the plate as a gift later on. The two plates have on them cubes of brown sugar, betel leaves with areca nut on top of them, pandanus spikes, some raw rice, and pieces of turmeric root.

Spread around the platform and plates are some other items :

Small oil lamps and some large brass lamps
A two-cup holder for turmeric and vermillion
A small bowl with raw rice coloured with turmeric (*aksate*)
A basket or plate holding a coconut, five cubes of brown sugar, and some
    clusters of flowers: nearly identical to the presentation for a married
    daughter leaving her natal home.

As women gather together in front of the goddess's platform and display, they pair off and begin to perform an abbreviated version of the ritual they do for their own daughters when they send them to their husbands' homes. Approaching the little sand-ball goddess in pairs, they sprinkle raw rice onto her with three quick pinch-and-flick motions they also use in auspicious rites of passage. After each pair finishes sprinkling rice, they present flowers to the goddess, put dots of turmeric and vermillion onto her, and give betel-areca, brown sugar cubes, and other items in the manner of the fruitful good wishes expressed to married daughters on the occasion of their departure.

When all have finished this farewell offering, someone waves a red liquid *arati* tray before her, and all throw rice on her and put water on their own eyes (to 'cool' them, or to prevent their giving her the evil eye ?). All of the women present then circumambulate her little platform three times and make deep prostration bows (*pradaksana*) to her.

The woman who is to take the goddess back to the river then goes around the group falling on the feet of all those present, the male household head first. After leaving the house, she walks around her neighbourhood carrying the goddess on a tray, in order to form a group to go to the river with her. As she passes neighbours' houses, other Brahmans come out to make quick gestures of worship for the sand-ball goddess.

As the collection of women with their goddesses congregates to go to the river, a few Barber musicians join in and begin to play.

At the river there is a brief *puja* for each goddess, and trays from all the households are set next to each other for the final red liquid *arati*-waving, after which all present take some gram-salad as *prasad*.

Each woman then begins the departure by taking a betel leaf piled with a piece of banana ('plantain'), some gram-salad (*kosambari*, of which more will be said later), and some coins. After passing her hands around the group and having everyone touch the betel leaf gently, as if to express their collective approval of the gift, she throws it into the river.

Each woman then sets about sorting out the items on her house's tray, removing the objects of financial value and keeping a half-share of all the items for the benefit of the house itself. As she sorts the items, one Chinnapura woman comments to me, "A 'married woman' should always be with Laksmi."

The jewels (pearl and *tali*) are removed from the tray and put into a wooden box. As items on a tray are sorted, two pieces of turmeric root are left with the goddess and two removed for the house; similarly, two palm-leaf earrings are kept, and two sent; the *kalasa* vessel is removed. And pieces of cotton necklace, some plantains, and a small Laksmi statue are removed. After sorting items, each woman gives her tray to a boy of her house. He wades into the river and dumps its contents, including the sand-ball goddess, into the river.

Leaving behind their daughter-goddess, the gathering of women saunters to the village temple, where they sing devotional songs as the priest or temple cook prepares a sweet fruit dish for distribution as *prasad* after his temple ritual. The dish is called *rasayana*, and is made of fresh banana, honey, sugar, clarified butter, coconut, and cardamom powder. The priest makes the burning camphor offering, *mangala arati*, said to soothe the spirit; and the women share the sweet *prasad* that follows.

Prati Festival Elements and 'Operational' Meanings

In a Brahman wedding there is a Sanskrit formula uttered at the crucial bonding moment, called *dhare*, when the bride and groom's joined hands are anointed with some holy water. It reads :

I brought my daughter up to this stage. From this time onwards she will serve the continuity and prosperous growth of your family. I give her to you with my heart at peace, before Agni, the witnessing god of fire. I hand her over to you. (K. Gurulingaiah notes, Smartha Brahman informant, 9 October 1967).

Many of the elements of the Prati and Gauri festival rituals dwell symbolically on the implications of this promise. Not only do they optimistically move their daughter-goddess back and forth in a parallel with their human daughters; but also they fill the festivals with foods and objects also used in birth and wedding rituals they celebrate for their children.

On the silver tray used to welcome the goddess out of the river, we saw two kinds of leaves. These are new shoots, called *cigaru*, of the 'country fig' (*Ficus glomerata*, Kannada *atti*) and 'sacred fig' (*Ficus religiosa*, Kannada *arali*, also called pipal) trees. Other families substitute banyan leaves (*Ficus indica*, also *F. benghalensis*) for those of the 'country fig'.

The new leaves (*cigaru*) placed on the welcoming tray for Prati are also found in a pregnancy ritual done by the Iyengar Brahmans. In the sixth month of an Iyengar woman's first pregnancy, her husband's family performs a *Srimanta* ritual for her and her unborn child. This is done soon before she is sent to her mother's house for her eventual confinement. In the ritual her husband squeezes the juice of a special paste into her nostrils while her mother-in-law holds her head. This juice, which supposedly enters her baby's mouth and shows him that 'he is going to be born a Brahman', is the juice of a paste. The paste is a well-ground mixture (ground up by virgins) of newly sprouted leaves of three special trees, namely, pipal (*arali*), country fig (*atti*), and banyan (*ala*). It is moistened with a little milk. At the same ritual the pregnant woman is fitted with new glass bangles that are coloured green—affirming the growth imagery of the whole ritual.

At least two of the same newly-sprouted leaves appear in the Prati-welcoming trays of local Iyengars. In the observed ritual at Bandipur there were country fig leaves and sacred fig leaves. But as I mentioned, in some other Iyengar families' rituals a combination of banyan and pipal is used instead. Even if the leaves were not exactly those used in pregnancy ritual, the mere use of new green leaves would be enough to convey birth imagery.[18]

This ritual is commonly referred to as the 'green bangle ceremony'.[19] This name comes from the fact that the pregnant woman puts on green glass bangles for the occasion. She wears these bangles to her mother's house, and keeps them on through her confinement. The colour green, as a repeated motif in this ritual, thus gives emphasis to the concept of pregnancy, birth, and the growth of a baby.

Another item on the silver welcoming tray provides a diectic reference to wedding rituals: it is the turmeric root. Though turmeric root has several other uses in rites of passage, it is arranged in a similar fashion, on a tray of offerings, in Iyengar (and some others') weddings. The groom's party places a turmeric root onto an important tray presented to the bride. The tray contains a number of small items around a central cube of brown sugar. The items include a blouse piece, some salt, some pressed soaked rice (*avalakki*), fresh whole Bengal gram, roasted Bengal gram, raisins, nuts, and sugar candy. The sugar cube (*bella*) is sprinkled with cumin seeds, and serves as a pedestal for the most important object on the plate: the new bride's gold marital *tali* pendant.

Other items on the silver tray present more indirect references to the birth or fates of daughters. For instance, the six balls of turmeric paste, factored into a pair of threes, may relate to birth through their very arithmetic. As I shall discuss below, the number three is important in birth rituals of all castes. In this case the meaning of the balls might be translated something like, 'Our wealthy and fortunate [turmeric-paste bodied] daughter is born [#3] from our marriages [#2]'.

The special, required 'snack' for Prati's Second Friday is the steamed delicacy called *iddali*, as mentioned above. This preparation is also a part of the last meal served before an Iyengar girl is married. The meal, shared by both parties to a wedding, is served by the bride's family. Though it is as lavish as possible, the menu has only one compulsory item: *iddali*.

The other snacks served on the Second Friday have ritual uses by other castes in connection with birth (especially the soaked, pounded *tambittu* balls), but not by this caste. Being sweet and festive, however, such 'snacks' as the fried and stuffed (v)*obbattu*, the steamed *kolakatte* (Plate 5) and *tambittu* balls are generally found at most joyous family occasions.[20]

The soaked-gram salad, *kosambari*, served at the end of the send-off ritual, also appears in rites of passage. Our interviews with local Brahmans, both Iyengar and Smartha, determined that it is a standard part of the menu at both baby-naming feasts and meals shared by prospective affines. It is also served at dinners for a bride or groom just before a wedding: at the bride's natal home, such a dinner marks the occasion on which her natal family puts a *tali* of their own on her, the *huttidamane*, 'birth house', *tali*. In these cases, however, two types of *kosambari* appear: one made from green gram (*hesaru*) and the other from Bengal gram (*kadale*). My data are not clear, however, on whether this is a strict requirement or not.

The most dramatic food served in Prati's festival is the 'five kinds of rice'. The assortment of preparations served at the Saturday 2 p.m. feast is varied in a way that condenses a maximum of symbolic 'food power', as it were, into one meal.[21]

As the basic cooked rice of the festival—i.e., boiled rice, as opposed to the ingredients of 'snacks'—the 'five kinds of rice' can be expected to carry strong bodily imagery. That is, the ways in which they are seasoned (and coloured) will 'present' the strongest imagery of tension, contrast, or family dilemma of concern in this festival.

The list of 'five kinds' varies around a fixed set. At least four preparations are standard: plain, boiled white rice; sweet *pongal*, a yellow-coloured mixture of boiled rice and boiled green gram; pungent-sour-and-sweet *puliyogare*, which is red in colour and strongly flavoured; and white rice with yoghurt mixed into it (*mosaranna*), which is sour-flavoured. A fifth item seems to vary: my informants choose either a salty, pungent dish called *kadamba*, which is yellowish in colour, or a common ritual dish called *citranna*, which is also yellow and sour-flavoured. The characteristics of 'five kinds of rice' are best seen in the form of Table 19, which distinguishes them according to colour and flavour.

Table 19—Qualities of 'Five Kinds of Rice', Prati Festival

Colours: Flavours	Yellow	Red	White
Bland (*sappe*)			1. boiled rice
Sweet (*sihi*)	2. *pangal*		
Pungent (*kara*)	5. *kadamba*	↑ 3. *puliyogare* ↓	
Sour (*huli*)	(alternate 5. *citranna*)		4. yoghurt rice

In this context they combine to an effect of tension-plus-balance, covering the wide range of potential meaning that they do. In this set, and in the festival as a whole, the most problematic colour is red. Red, as the minor but persistent accent colour accompanying the many benign yellows and whites of this festival, seems to represent both feminine 'energy' and 'danger'. In the Puranic tradition of which these festivals are clearly a part, both of these connotations take a uniquely feminine form in menstrual blood. This blood, widely thought to play a necessary part of the procreation of children, is the feminine contribution to the process. And, being that, possibly also a symbol of wasted, wild energy, it is widely feared as a polluting agent when it flows each month. Rather than specifically alluding to menstrual blood, however, the colour red in this festival must have a wider, and more diffuse meaning-relationship to ambiguous femininity as the key to family growth and the source of many family problems. It is also the colour of special Prati saris in many households.

It is appropriate, then, that the red-coloured festival dish should also be the one with the strongest, sharpest flavour. Pungent with many chillies, sweetened with sugar, and heavy with sour tamarind, the dark red *puliyogare* is a strong 'mediatory' force in itself, equal to the mythic serpent in the 'Mangala Gauri' vessel or any other transformative symbol presented here.

Like colours, flavours have traditional connotations expressed in proverbs and elsewhere throughout Hindu folklore. These expressions relate flavours to feelings and life aspirations in many ways that would agree with the Western views of them. Strong, pungent flavour is strength and passion. Bland flavour is a calm, peaceful state of mind. Sweetness is happiness, good luck, sometimes immortality, and commonly associated with little children's birthday parties. The one flavour whose connotations may not be obvious to a Western student is sour.[22] This flavour is associated with women, as supposedly their favourite flavour. Green mangoes, for instance, are considered to be a frequent craving of pregnant women. Green mangoes are extremely sour. Another association sometimes made with sourness is wealth.[23] Sour flavour, then, is a good flavour; and its intersection with white and gold in a festival for 'married women'-as-Laksmi is appropriate in Hindu culture. (See also Regelson 1972.)

Missing or tabooed elements are usually as important as included ones, if we want the whole cultural view involved in a festival of this sort. The reader should note, therefore, that there is no black-coloured food or other object used in these rituals;[24] and that two important flavours of local cuisine are also missing. The flavours not in the 'five kinds of rice' or other preparations are bitterness (kay or kahi) and astringent or acridity ((v)ogaru). These last two flavours are normal, named parts of daily meals; but given their generally inauspicious connotations, their omission from this feast may be a conscious removal of reference to true disasters such as death (of either the women or their husbands). Though these omissions do not result from any spoken taboos I have heard, Gauri does have such a taboo (of which, of course, more later).

A final inventory of symbolic objects and other elements for the Prati festival, stressing 'folk' elements rather than 'great tradition' details, is as in Table 20.

GAURI FESTIVAL RITUALS

The Gauri Festival, which brings out gatherings of Smartha Brahman women in their most radiant silks, is widely celebrated throughout south India. It occurs on the third day after the new moon which begins the lunar month of Bhadrapada (I : 3) : a good time, of the waxing moon. As the model on which the Prati Festival was probably designed, Gauri ritual summons the goddess Gauri out of the river, either as a ball of sand or as some water in a kalasa vessel. After having been welcomed into the home as a returning married daughter and having been worshipped and feasted by villagers, she, like Prati, returns again to the river.

Preparations for Gauri's arrival and puja are generally similar to those for Prati. Brahman women fast on that day, taking only milk and fruit. An additional restriction appears here, in that they also avoid pungent (kara) foods.

Women begin the formal preparations at 5 a.m. They wash their faces,

Table 20—Elements of Prati Festival Rituals

Colours:

Yellow   — turmeric paste balls
                turmeric root
                turmeric powder
                pandanus flower (spike)
                champak flower
                special *tali* pendant
                pangal and others of the 'five kinds of rice'

White †   — pearl
                jasmine flowers
                lotus flowers
                cotton necklaces
                cotton balls
                silver tray (considered to be 'white')
                floor decorations (*rangoli*)
                rice-paste lamps
                rice flour, as ingredient of all 'snacks'
                iddali 'snack' required on Second Friday
                plain boiled rice, in 'five kinds of rice'
                yoghurt rice, in 'five kinds'

Green   — new leaves on silver welcoming tray
                decorative leaves, mango leaves, on home shrine canopy (*mantapa*)
                betel leaves

Red   — liquid in tray to remove evil eye
                puliyogare as one of 'five kinds of rice'
                special sari for the goddess, in some homes (but not in all homes)
                vermillion powder
                areca nut

Rice: — liquid paint for floor designs
                grits, as ingredient in *iddali*
                flour, as ingredient in other 'snacks' cooked, plain or seasoned
                in 'five kinds of rice'
                turmeric-coloured rice (*aksate*)

Numbers: 2, 3, 5, 6, 21

Flowers and
Plants: — pandanus staminate spikes
                champak flowers
                lotus
                jasmine
                leaf sprouts of
                    country fig
                    sacred fig
                    (possible—banyan)

Table 20 (*contd. on page* 130)

Table 20 (*contd. from page* 129)

                    mango leaves decorating shrine
                    vegetables hanging in some home shrines††

Snacks: — *iddali* (only requirement), steamed bland cakes
                    tambittu, sweet balls
                    obbattu, stuffed balls flattened out
                    kolakatte, steamed in two shapes, ball or crescent
                    kosambari, soaked-gram salad
                    rasayana, very sweet fruit salad

Miscellaneous
Special
Items: — turmeric-vermillion blessing spot
                    6 yellow cloths
                    cotton balls
                    cotton necklaces
                    sweet fruits (bananas)
                    4 turmeric roots
                    tali pendant
                    2 pairs palm-leaf earrings
                    pearls
                    cubes of brown sugar (5, at send-off)
                    betel-areca sets

Identical Trays for Exchange-Partner and Goddess, at send-off

†Though they are light or dark brown to the sight, the cubes of brown sugar (*bella*) used in this region are referred to either as 'white' (the light brown ones) or 'black' (the dark brown ones). I had originally speculated that they might be either black or red, but found local colour classification to differ from anything I might have guessed. I do not have information regarding whether the 'white' or 'black' cubes are preferred for Prati.

Palm-leaf earrings (*biccole*) are either 'red' or 'white'. The 'white' type, used by most houses, is actually light greenish-white to the sight.

†† The Bandipur Iyengar home shrine had a large assortment of vegetables hanging among the mango leaves above the goddess's pedestal.

purify their house floors with a light adhesive coat of moist cow dung, and decorate the floors with elaborate line drawings in white liquid that dries soon after being applied. Adding another festive touch to the home decorations for the occasion, they hang strings of mango leaves at the tops of their front doors.

They then rub their children and themselves with oil and douse with pots of hot water, the 'oil bath' ensuring everyone's ritual purity (*madi*). Dressing their children in bright new clothes, they put on their own ritually pure saris, and get ready to summon their beloved Gauri from the river.

Meanwhile, a group of men (their temple priest and a Brahman assistant in Bandipur; others in Chinnapura), also bathed and fasting, is bringing Gauri too. The men go to the river with a large wooden cradle that hangs down from a long pole. At the river they rest a sand-ball in the cradle, and they take their Gauri in this form into the village for everyone to worship together in public.

The women, however, take neither cradle nor sandball. They carry a tray with a vessel on it and fill the vessel in the name of the goddess. While worshipping the Gauri vessel at the river, the women also pay respects to her co-wife, Ganga, deity of waters. They then take Gauri to a home shrine.

We observed different aspects of this festival in our two different villages. But the Smartha Brahmans of the two villages are so closely related that some of the 'Bandipur' women celebrating the festival were actually married to Chinnapura families and returning home to their 'mothers' houses' in Bandipur for the occasion. So we can safely assume that the details of home rituals, at least, are generally similar in the two villages.

Bringing the Goddess Out of the River

My data are not clear as to whether all Smartha Brahman houses send representatives to the river to gather a fresh vessel of water (or a sand-ball), or whether one escorted vessel (or sand-ball) per village is the only one used for communal worship by gatherings of Brahman women. In Bandipur we heard of at least two trips to the river, one by the priest (for a sand-ball) and one by a group of five women (for a vessel). In Chinnapura the notes mention only one trip to the river, by a priest—actually the same priest who performed the river summoning the previous year in Bandipur; but each Smartha Brahman house hosts a special gathering for its own goddess after the communal worship. Tables 21 and 22 summarise ritual actions.

As the women gather for the communal ceremony, they bring offerings for the goddess and for each other. In the Prati Festival we saw each household set aside a tray of offerings for a neighbourly exchange with a married woman of a diffreent house. In the Gauri Festival there is much fanfare around the exchanges among women. Each married woman participating in the festival selects a partner; and the two agree to exchange ritual gifts back and forth evenly. The gifts they exchange are contained in winnowing fans, called 'wealth-producing fans' (bhagina mara). Each woman prepares a set of two fans filled with special items and covered over with two more fans. She gives one to her goddess and one to her partner. A pair of doubled winnowing fans also rests in the cradle with the goddess in her sand-ball form.

This festival, for Gauri, is more important to some non-Brahmans than to others. It is my impression that the mercantile 'left-hand' castes, such as Oil-Presser, Weaver, or Smith, are more interested in Gauri than are other non-Brahmans. The A.K.s show very little interest in the festival. It is difficult to determine the level of interest in Gauri among non-Brahmans, since many of them make a great celebration for the Ganapathi Festival, which is celebrated for Gauri's son right after her festival. Since the household shrines are built

Table 21—Bringing the Goddess Out of the River

Bandipur, 1966†	Chinnapura, 1967††
(Priest of Esvara temple gets Gauri from the river as a mud ball. Not observed.)	At 5:30 a.m., a group of men congregates at the village Laksminarasimha temple : Brahman man of the village; visiting priest from Bandipur; a man and boy of the Fisherman caste, to carry the cradle; a villager of the Washerman caste, to carry a cloth torch. Barber caste musicians join them.
	After circumambulating the temple once, and going around the village once, the group goes down the road to the river. They carry a large wooden cradle.
	At the river, the Brahman takes up a ball of mud and puts it into a cloth; sets the ball onto a tray; sprinkles some purifying water onto the floor of the cradle and sets the tray into the cradle for the return to the village.
	Returning to the village, the group of men meet a group of women at the entrance to the village hall for religious meetings (Rama Mandira). Someone throws down a whole coconut, smashing it in front of the hall's door; and the group of men enters the hall with the cradle.
	The cluster of women, carrying trays of family offerings, enters eagerly into the hall behind the cradle.
	While an old Brahman villager reads aloud, women decorate the cradle with many pink dahlias.
	All leave the hall, for the throwing-down of another coconut.
Five Brahman women go in procession to the river with musicians of the Barber caste. (Two are married women, and three are unmarried.)	
Arriving at the river with their vessel and decorative items, the women put some water into the vessel. Building it into a *kalasa,* they insert two betel leaves into its mouth and set a whole coconut over them into the mouth.	

Table 21 (*contd. on page* 133)

Table 21 (*contd. from page* 132)

Bandipur	*Chinnapura*
They call it 'Gauri' now, and they do *puja* for Gauri with dots of turmeric and vermillion, applied to the vessel; decorations of flowers; and rotating an incense stick before it. The women then perform worship for Ganga, goddess of water: first setting some pinches of turmeric and vermillion into the river, then putting some flowers into the water. The *puja* concludes with the breaking of a coconut and the waving of burning camphor (*mangalarati*) before the vessel. The women and their musicians return home; the women enter the house and set the goddess-vessel into the makeshift shrine that has been decorated for her with an arch of bright yellow and red flowers. Neighbours come with trays of offerings to offer respects to the goddess.	

†As described by village women to Mr. Dakshina Murthy, research assistant.
††As observed by Stanley Regelson, 7 September.

up anyway, most non-Brahman houses seem to pay a token respect to Gauri as Ganesha's mother but not as a pre-eminent sponsor of married women.

Interest in Gauri is enhanced, at least in some 'left-hand' households, for the first three years after a daughter's marriage. During that period, one Oil-Presser household (that of Mr. G) sends winnowing fans with gifts in them to the married daughter at the time of this festival, for example.

In another, Weaver household I observed a pair of doubled winnowing fan gifts at the time of this festival. They had come from the natal home of the wife, a woman in her mid-to-late-30's with several children The list of contents of her *bhagina mara* differed slightly from that of Brahmans' gifts. Her list included several items, most notable among them being a special cotton thread ('Gauri thread'), which is customarily tied onto the wrists of daughters *by their mothers* at this festival.[25] The Brahmans also tie a thread to their wrists, but they have a man do it.

Patterns of exchange partnership among Brahmans follow lines of friendship and convenience. In Bandipur, which has a relatively small Smartha Brahman contingent, there are only a few women who can exchange ritual gifts.

When the women gather for the group worship of Gauri, they bring along trays filled with offerings; and they bring pairs of doubled winnowing fans, the *bhagina mara*. Their trays of offerings include the following items (see also Plate 7) :

Plate 7. Feminine items used for Gauri worship : turmeric, vermillion, red and white *biccole*, comb, mirror, miniature black bangles.

Turmeric powder
Vermillion powder
Flowers (mostly chrysanthemums, Bandipur; dahlias, Chinnapura)
Camphor (for *mangalarati*)
Cotton wicks soaked in clarified butter, for lamps called *jyoti*
Coconut
Bananas
Betel leaves + areca
Cotton garland (*gejjestra*)
Cotton thread with 14 knots in it (Gauri thread)
Turmeric-coloured raw rice (*aksate*)
Small mirror
Miniature black bangles
Black beads
Palm-leaf earrings (*biccole*)
Comb

Ritual Gatherings

Rituals for Gauri are community projects, more so than rituals for Prati. In each village Smartha Brahman households keep representations of goddess

Table 22—Celebrating the Arrival of Gauri in the Villages

Bandipur	Chinnapura
Day I : Women go to river and obtain Gauri by making a *kalasa* at river.	Day I : Priest and assistants take Gauri from the river. Goddess is in form of a mud ball. Take her to community hall.
Temple priest obtains a separate Gauri at river. He and assistants take this Gauri, in a cradle, through the Brahman streets of the village, so that women can make individual offerings.	Women gather in community hall to perform group *puja* for Gauri. Ritual includes exchange of winnowing fan gifts, as in Table 23, but also includes the reading of a story by a priest.
After bringing their *kalasa* to the house where they will perform group worship, women perform welcoming ritual for Gauri. (Described in Table 23.)	Goddess is circulated around the village in a cradle. At each house women come out to make offerings and then go inside. Then men, household heads, perform *idakayi*, lit. 'dropping the coconut' : each man throws a coconut down on the house stairs so forcefully that it shatters into pieces. Youngsters scramble to pick up the pieces.
Women continue their day-long fast, ending the day with a light meal of fruit and milk.	Men and women circulate among each other's homes, as in Bandipur. Men's gatherings include story-reading. (Men invite each other separately from women's exchanges of invitations.) Men perform *mangalarati* with burning camphor.

Arati Gatherings in Homes
(both villages)

Puja for Gauri
Offering of special foods
Distribution of *prasad* :
   kosambari (soaked-gram salad)
   (*y*)*ellu* (mixture of Bengal gram,
      dried coconut, and white
      sesame seeds)
Give guests perfume, betel-areca,
flowers, and turmeric-vermillion
(Men's gatherings include reading
of stories and *mangalarati*

Day II : Feast Meals
(both villages)

Ritual meals in homes,
together with invited guests.

Gauri separately in their homes; but they gather together for the principal welcoming rituals. In Chinnapura the gathering is in the village religious hall, the Rama Mandira. In Bandipur it is in a private home, the home from which the above description of bringing the goddess from the river is taken.

Gift Exchange

As the women gather for the communal ceremony, they bring offerings for the goddess and for each other. In the Prati Festival we saw each household set aside a tray of offerings for a neighbourly exchange with a married woman of a different house. In the Gauri Festival there is much fanfare around the exchanges among women. Each married woman participating in the festival selects a partner; and the two agree to exchange ritual gifts back and forth evenly. Each woman's gifts are contained in a winnowing fan with another inverted over it. The top of each doubled winnowing fan has a large X-mark across it, drawn in turmeric-water, with a red dot at the intersection of the two lines. Lifting the inverted fan which is the top of each ritual gift, some women of Bandipur show us the following items :

Raw rice (husked)
Split pulses (*bele*), four kinds :
    togari (*Cajanus cajan*, pigeon pea)
    kadale (*Cicer arietinum*, Bengal gram)
    hesaru (*Phaseolus aureus*, green gram)
    uddu (*Phaseolus mungo*, black gram)
Semolina
Salt
(Taboo : neither coriander seeds nor chilli peppers can be included)
Cube of brown sugar (jaggery)
Bananas
Coconut
Betel-areca sets
Pair of miniature black bangles
Black beads (optional)
Turmeric root piece (optional)
Turmeric powder in folded paper packet
Tiny mirror
Comb
Dried palm-leaf earrings (*biccole*), either 'white' or 'red' in colour
Other items which may be included at the choice of the donor, such as a
    blouse piece[25]
(From S. Hanchett and S. Regelson notes, 1966.)

With their winnowing fan gifts piled in a corner, women proceed to make their collective offerings to Gauri, with the guidance of a local Brahman man, who is home priest (*purohit*) for the occasion. Subsequent actions, in summary, are as in Table 23. After welcoming the goddess by dressing and

Table 23—Welcoming Ritual for Gauri, Bandipur 1966

A group of nine women, all with strongly coloured silk saris and bright yellow chrysanthemums in their hair, performs a welcoming and installation ritual for the goddess, under the guidance of a village man serving as priest (*purohit*).

Seven or eight young girls watch.

Sequence of women's *puja*:

Pray to Ganesha (in the form of a cattle-dung cone with *garike* grass in its top) to give them the power of doing the ritual without any obstruction.

Begin Gauri *puja* by sprinkling some water on all the ritual paraphernalia while the priest chants *mantras*.

Put perfume on the silver vessel so that, "*kalasa* will have a real life, and be converted into the real Gauri."

Bathe Gauri (vessel) with *pancamrita*, a mixture of honey, milk, clarified butter, yoghurt, and sugar.

Dress the goddess and ornament her with new clothes, gold jewellery, flowers, and cotton garlands.

Set other *puja* items on and around the goddess.

Offer special food items (*naivedya*) to Gauri, by placing them in front of her together with a broken coconut: (*v)obbattu* 'snack', *iddali* 'snack', cooked rice, *payasa* (a sweet, milky liquid), and fruits (banana).

Women come forward to the shrine in pairs and rotate incense sticks before their goddess. This is called *arati* or *mangalarati*.

After this initial greeting to the goddess, the women offer a token payment (*daksina*) to the priest, together with an offering of betel-areca and one coconut. The priest accepts their gift/payment and then ties cotton threads to each woman's wrist. After this, each woman bows and touches the priest's foot in the *namaskara* gesture. Women then return to worship the goddess:

They rotate cotton-wick lamps that burn clarified butter in front of the shrine. These lamps are called *jyoti*, and the rotation of them is *arati*.

Women bow to the goddess after *arati*. Each woman takes a piece of offered flowers and puts it in her hair at the top of her braid.

The next act is to exchange winnowing fan gifts with partners.

The *puja* concludes with a presentation of burning camphor before the goddess. This is *mangalarati*. After concluding the ritual, the women give ritual payment to the priest. This payment consists of raw rice, brown sugar, betel-areca, banana, and coconut (whole). This is called *phala-tambula*, lit. 'fruits and betel-areca'.

feeding her, the gathered women of each village turn toward their Brahman man religious guide. In Bandipur they offer the priest a token payment of a few coins set onto betel-areca sets; he ties a 'Gauri thread' to each woman's right wrist after taking her *daksina* payment. She touches his feet in gratitude for his benediction and his help with her ritual. In Chinnapura, though the women probably also get threads tied to their wrists, I do not have information on when or who does it. But, following a style of gratitude slightly different from their Bandipur relatives and caste-mates, the Chinnapura women approach their neighbour-priest in small groups and throw rice on his head. After doing this they distribute turmeric powder, flowers, and soaked-gram salad (wrapped in a small leaf) to those all around, getting their children to help them. The *prasad* also includes a few coins, though not when given to members of the same *dayadi* (patrilineage), since lineage mates should not pay each other in this way, even by token coins of thanks.

Bandipur women disperse at the end of their ritual, but in Chinnapura the gathered women remain together in the religious hall for further celebration. As they sit quietly, their priest reads them a story. (I assume that this is 'Mangala Gauri' but my notes do not indicate which story.) After the story is over, shortly before 9 a.m., the scene becomes a merry confusion of activity; as some women sing, the priest chants sacred verses, and other groups of women wave several trays full of little cotton lamps before the goddess in unison. They present rice and coconuts to their priest at this time, but also make the same offerings to a young man who has been initiated into the Hindu 'student' (*brahmacarya*) phase of life. (These offerings are called *upayadana* when presented to a 'student'.)

They also present their soaked-gram salad *prasad* to the ritual service caste members who lighted the path to the river with cloth torch, who played music, and who carried the goddess's cradle. A woman of a service caste may also receive a pair of winnowing fans with ritual gifts from one of the Brahman houses on this occasion. The manner of offering gifts to outsiders delicately ensures that the Brahman women maintain their 'ritual purity' : they set a cup of vermillion before the lady anthropologist from America, rather than handing it to her directly. They drop a large packet of soaked-gram salad with half a coconut into the long skirt (*pance*) of one of the cradle-carriers for all the ritual servants to share among themselves.

Chinnapura women follow these actions with a noisy procession of the goddess in her cradle around the 'Brahman Streets' of the village, while Bandipur women rest.

In Bandipur the women are preparing for a 'sleep fast' (*jagarne*), to be conducted through this night. They will not sleep all night. While sitting up awake, they will sing devotional songs. It is possible that they also will tell each other the 'Mangala Gauri' story at this time as well, although my notes do not tell whether they do or not.

The menu at the feast meal in honour of the goddess, on the day after her arrival in the village, has two required elements. These are yoghurt rice and sour yellow rice, called *mosaranna* and *hulianna*, respectively. These are eaten together with side dishes.

After these welcoming and merging celebrations are over, there is a lull in the Gauri Festival. This is a period when the goddess's son, elephant-headed Ganesha, is said to arrive in the village. The reason given for his appearance is that his father and her consort, Siva, is lonely. After celebrating Ganesha's arrival and visit (as the Ganapathi Festival), villagers send off the mother and son into the river. The send-offs for the goddess and her co-wife Ganga conclude the Gauri Festival.

Sending the Goddess Back to the River

The send-off ritual for Gauri is performed on the third or the fifth day of the festival (i.e., on the fifth or seventh of the lunar month, or three or five days from the day she was first brought from the river). There is a taboo on sending the goddess at the second or fourth day, these being each evenly numbered days with correspondingly unlucky connotations. An outline of send-off events for Gauri is presented in Table 24.

Table 24—Sending the Goddess Back to the River

Invite a group of married women to the house (or hall).
Women bring with them to the house (or hall), for each to offer to Gauri:

> one blouse piece
> rice
> betel-areca
> turmeric-vermillion
> brown sugar (jaggery)
> comb with turmeric on it

Puja for Gauri and Ganesha :

Put turmeric-vermillion on Gauri.
Pour rice on Gauri.

Women present their plates with *puja* things (as listed) to Gauri.

Mangalarati for Ganesha.

Arati for Gauri : brass plate of turmeric-coloured water, with a cotton-wick lamp (*jyoti*) on it is circulated before the goddess (for removal of evil eye).

Give offering to married women guests :

> turmeric-vermillion
> *kosambari* soaked gram salad
> betel-areca
> bananas

Table 24 (*contd. on page* 140)

Table 24 (*contd. from page* 139)

Put Gauri (vessel) and Ganesha image on a brass plate, together with some flowers.

(Bandipur :) Group of women who had performed earlier *puja* for Gauri in a group go together to the river with the brass plate. They are accompanied by the male head of the household where the large *puja* was done, the village priest, and some village children (Brahman and non-Brahman).

Male household head does *mangala arati at* riverside shrine.

At edge of river,
   Male household head does Ganga *puja,* offering the following :
      Puts turmeric-vermillion in river.
      Puts flowers in river.
      Puts a plate full of 'married women items into the river for Ganga :

        black bangles,
        palm-leaf earrings,
        mirror,
        comb,
        turmeric-vermillion.
      Offers worship with incense sticks.
      Offers betel-areca.
      Breaks coconut.

Women make *arati* and *mangalarati* for Gauri.
Put Ganesha image into river.
Collect items, to be sent off with Gauri :

      mirror,
      turmeric-vermillion,
      betel-areca,
      flowers : including one *Pandanus* spike comb,
      'some food for the journey' (snacks and rice dishes).

The send-off :

Arati for Gauri.

Release water out of vessel by submerging it.

Drop clay image of Gauri into the water, if there is one, and

Drop ball of sand into water.*

Put collected items into water.

*One participant's comment at this point was, "Gauri is nothing but a small amount of sand."

As in the summoning ritual, Gauri's co-wife, Ganga, receives special gestures of respect at the conclusion of the Gauri Festival. Just after the married woman

Table 25—Brief Worship of Ganga at Conclusion of Gauri Festival

---

Bring Ganga devi out of the river for a short visit :

Put fresh water into *kalasa* vessel.†

Place the same betel leaves and the same coconut on the top of the filled vessel (these were not sent off with Gauri).

Serve *prasad* : *hulianna* (sour-flavour, yellow rice); *mosaranna* (yoghurt rice, white).††

Bring Ganga devi back to village :

Bandipur, stop in front of house, make *arati* for Ganga. Women of the house formally invite Ganga to enter.
Chinnapura, bring Ganga to community hall. Perform *mangalarati* for her in the evening.

Send off Ganga, back to river, next day.

Distribute good quality remaining flowers from *pujas* to neighbours as *prasad*.

†Explanation : "We won't bring back an empty vessel from the river. We shouldn't come back from the river empty-handed."
††Household head warns Regelson to throw a small amount of *prasad* on the ground, in order to determine whether or not it is poisonous to animals who eat it.

---

goddess has departed into the water, villagers refill their vessels for another, brief round of rituals (as in Table 25) for Ganga.

GAURI FESTIVAL ELEMENTS

Like the Prati Festival, the Gauri Festival requires the use of a number of special items. These are mostly common objects easily available to village women, but are objects used in non-ordinary ways. In the rituals they become symbolic elements, things with semantic value beyond their everyday uses. The most interesting and important of all ritual items appearing in this festival is the pair of doubled winnowing fans which contain ritual gifts for the goddess and for married women partners. In exploring the possible semantic role of the winnowing fan in this ritual, I have investigated its wider use and significance.

The Winnowing Fan and its Edible Contents

I have come to think of the winnowing fan as a particularly suitable container for ritual offerings, especially those related to married children. As the device by which pounded grains are actually separated from their useless husks (pounding has removed the husks, and winnowing separates grain from chaff), it is a logical symbol of separation and purification. Specifically in relation to children, in this case daughters, its separating function is particularly analogous to the separation of the child out of the family at marriage. If her child-bearing services are seen as providing physical growth for her marital family, and if the family's physical growth is (as Khare (1976b) suggests) analogous to the 'cooking' or processing of grains in general, we can say that it is at marriage that a girl separates from her family of birth and provides 'food'—or a source of physical vitality—for the society. Some rites of passage also connect winnowing fans with emergence and transformation of children.

The winnowing fan appears as a customary element in Hindu folk rituals of many other parts of India besides Karnataka. For example, Luschinsky's study of a village near Benares describes a ceremony performed in both bride's and groom's homes one week before a marriage consummation ritual (*gauna*). Each of five women guests receives a winnowing fan after having vermillion placed in the part of her hair. Then, "assembled women begin to sing and when their song ends, the five women touch their winnowing baskets or shake them . . ."[26]

The winnowing fan appears in Karnataka at the time when children are born, as well as on other occasions of ritual transition. In Hassan District it is the custom of most castes to set a newborn child into a winnowing fan immediately after it is cleansed of the membranes and fluids adhering to it. The winnowing fan is its first bed. It stays there for a few days, until it is ritually transferred to its cradle for the first time. This procedure is similar for all castes, whether Brahman, non-Brahman, or A.K. As the child's first bed, the winnowing fan also plays a role in most castes' baby-naming rituals.[27]

A few other local customs relating to the winnowing fan guarantee its universally auspicious value. First, one is never allowed to purchase a single winnowing fan in the market. As I shall discuss below, the number 1 is an inauspicious, death-related number. We stumbled over this rule ourselves in 1977, when my friend, Mr. George, attempted to buy a single winnowing fan for me in the Bandipur weekly market. He was scolded by the peasant businessmen with the disparaging question, "Who taught *you*?!" Subsequent inquiries around the village affirmed that no one ever buys a single winnowing fan. Furthermore, our Oil Presser friend added, in his *jati* even a single pair is not good enough for Gauri offerings to new brides. It must be a pair of pairs.

A second local custom also deserves mention, for it connects women and their ornamentation with the winnowing fan. Among all *jatis* except Brahmans it is required traditionally that women be tatooed around the time that they mature, or sometimes earlier. These tatoos are interesting in themselves, since women receive them as gifts from friends and relatives. They are considered to be essential decoration for a woman's body and decorate the arms and hands of the old-fashioned ladies of the area. More than one woman told me, in 1976, that the tatoo is necessary embellishment for a woman's naked body when she is buried. In the course of doing interviews on the subject of these tatoos, I was surprised to find that the winnowing process is connected to them:

> "A women must not winnow grain
> if she has no tatoos."

This is a universal rule for traditional women of all *jatis* except Brahmans, and does not apply to men, who may also winnow grain at times. There is no other agricultural process that is restricted in this way. The old Fisherman women quoted here connected women, their tatoos, and family prosperity with a further terse comment : "We put tatoos for Laksmi."

Considering that the winnowing fan produces clean, husked raw rice, the usable grain, the absence of any paddy (rice with husk) is notable in the Gauri Festival. Many rites of passage, and a few festivals also, do use paddy as a ritual object. This is especially true of wedding rituals. But Gauri and Prati festivals do not. This may be due to the fact that they are structurally connected with the matured, married woman, even though they make ritual allusions to the fact that she has been born and raised in her 'mother's home'. Raw rice, as one of the grains contained in the pair of gifted winnowing fans, is a suitable element for this occasion.

The rice, farina, and pulses included with the winnowing fan gift are the type of foods referred to by the Kannada term *danya-davsa* 'grains, grams, and pulses' (Regelson 1972 : 57). This is a popular category which includes those foods dried and preserved for basic nutrition, except for oil seeds or spices. In short, it is the sum of most things considered staple food; and especially much so for these vegetarian Brahmans. (Fruits, vegetables, and greens are in another category, considered to be side accompaniments to 'grains, grams, and pulses' in the diet.) Together with the banana, coconut, salt, and cube of brown sugar, this assortment represents a full range of foodstuffs, i.e., could symbolically substitute for a totality of all the foods (and nourishment, and growth) that could be seen as a sort of good luck wish. (Cf. Eichinger Ferro-Luzzi 1977.)

As in the send-off rituals for Prati, these foodstuffs bear a strong resemblance to the things sent along with a married daughter as she returns to her husband's house after visiting her natal home. (Cf. Regelson 1972 : 134, on (*y*)*ecca*.) When families of any caste send a girl, especially the first time, they fill her lap (actually her *madilu*, the diagonally draped portion of her sari that goes across the front of her body) with 'good things' like these, as a gesture of hope that 'she will be happy and have all good things in her life, especially prosperity'. This presentation is called *madilakki* in ordinary village language, and *sogilakki* in the Smartha Brahman dialect. For them, it includes, at least, some raw rice, a piece of turmeric root, a large piece of brown sugar (*bella*), betel-areca, and a coconut.

On a more abstract interpretive scale, the Gauri winnowing fan foodstuffs themselves could possibly be analysed for numerical, colour, or other structuring principles inherent in their variety. But beyond noting that there are two sets of two (=total of four) commonly used pulses; three white substances (rice, semolina and salt); and three flavour distinctions (bland, sweet, and salty), I find this assortment of edibles yieding little symbolic structure to my view. (Colours white, brown, yellow, and green cover most items, with the cube of brown sugar being labelled as 'white'. But colour does not seem to be an effective organising principle in these items.)

Festival Foods

Like the foods used as offerings and *prasad* in the Prati Festival, those for Gauri also have wide uses throughout the village system of folk rituals. In fact, some of them are even the same ones served for Prati.

Like Prati, Gauri receives the steamed 'snack' called *iddali* as she enters the village as if it were her natal hometown. Though this presentation does appear in auspicious rites of passage done by Smartha Brahmans (they calling it by an older Kannada name, *kadabu*), it is not the strong allusion to wedding ritual that it was for the other festival. Its companion offering, (*v*)*obbattu*, is, however.

The snack called (*v*)*obbattu* has a special association to wedding ritual for the Smartha Brahmans, who also use it in their Gauri Festival. After the daughter's *tali* has been tied onto her throat and she is officially a 'married woman', there is a custom of sending her formally over to the place where the groom's party is staying. This will be a temporary 'residence', since the wedding is held at the bride's home, but women speak of this short journey as the time 'when we send a daughter to her husband for the first time'. As she walks to her husband's place, the bride takes along some foods. There are two 'snacks' required for this occasion, and one of them is the 'brown-coloured' stuffed sweet, (*v*)*obbattu*.

One other sweet preparation, called (*y*)*ellu*, which is served at the home gatherings after the community worship for the goddess, also appears in rites of passage. This tasty combination of white sesame, Bengal gram, and dried coconut chips is served in connection with a variety of auspicious rites of passage, especially in some wedding gatherings, as a small tribute to joy.

The sweet, milky liquid, *payasa*, served to the goddess upon her arrival and also at more complex festival feasts, is similarly 'auspicious' in its connotations. Villagers serve it so regularly at holiday meals as a sort of dessert, that it could be used as the identifying marker indicating in its very presence that a meal is special.

Soaked-gram salad, *kosambari*, also found in Prati Festival, was the subject of some folk exegesis when I observed Gauri Festival rituals in Chinnapura. Since it is so rarely that women comment on the possible significance of their actions, the remarks are worth including here. "If we wanted to," one woman explained, "we could make 21 'snacks' for this festival. Or we could make 9 or 5." "Not being able to do this because of 'our poverty'," she went on, "and since in *kosambari* there are 5 ingredients—Bengal gram, cucumber, coconut, chillies, and salt, we find that *kosambari* alone satisfies the requirement." Disregarding consistency, she has mentioned a taboo element (chillies); but she considers the power of numerology sufficient to explain the choice of *prasad*.

There are two special cooked rice preparations served in the Gauri Festival, more or less at the point where Prati's 'five kinds of rice' appear, at the common meals of gathered 'married women'. This pair of two—sour-flavoured yellow-coloured *hulianna* (lit. 'sour cooked rice') and sour, white yoghurt rice (*mosaranna*)—appears so commonly in festivals and rites of passage that it is almost synonymous with 'married women' in the Smartha system of folk rituals. For example, the pair is compulsory at the meal served (by a bride's family) on the day when the groom first arrives, the *vara puja* 'groom welcoming' day. *Hulianna*, with or without yoghurt rice, is considered essential for several other festivals as celebrated in Smartha Brahman homes, including the lunar new year, the Festival of Lights, Sibling Group Festival (cf. Chapter 8, below), and Durga *puja* day in Dassara. It is also essential at the first sacred thread ceremony for a boy of the family (*munji*, also called *upanayana*).

Like the Prati rice dishes, this pair represents a structural paradigm, but a less complex and 'dramatic' one than the 'five kinds of rice'. The only structural opposition in the pair is that between yellow and white, since they are both sour in flavour.

Unlike those of the Prati Festival, foods for Gauri are structured by taboos. Where the Prati Festival rules simply omit black or bitter things, for instance, Gauri Festival rules include overt taboos. The taboos are on coriander seeds, forbidden in the winnowing fan assortment, and on chillies, in fan or in the first day's diet of 'married women'. Though Prati Festival includes the pungent flavour of chillies at a crucial juncture in ritual practice while Gauri Festival generally forbids it, this difference need not prevent translation between the two ritual structures. Both festival rituals magically confront and organise danger, though in different forms and in different ways. Note, for example, that there are black items (black bangles and sometimes black beads) in the ritual gifts for Gauri, while there are no black items in Prati rituals.

Colours

The predominant colours of the Gauri Festival are red, yellow, white, and black. One required 'snack' is brown in addition. In Chinnapura nearly all the flowers used to decorate the cradled goddess are red and pink (also called 'red') dahlias. In Bandipur there is an arch of yellow chrysanthemums over the makeshift shrine, with a red flower at its highest point.

Red is a stronger colour in this festival, especially as done in Chinnapura, than in the Prati Festival. I shall discuss the ideological implications of this further below.

The presence of black bangles and beads distinguishes this festival from the one for Prati; but it also makes it a well-balanced structure, closer to the daily ornamentation of married women, as I shall discuss shortly.

The Cradle

In concluding the review of ritual items used in association with Gauri, I wish to draw the reader's attention back to the beginning of the festival, when she is brought into the village in a cradle. The use of a cradle intensifies and clarifies the emphasis on a woman's birth-growth-marriage career which is implicit in so many of the other elements of festival. In this festival, as in Prati, the poignant feelings for daughter-as-goddess are heightened and intensified through worship of the goddess-as-daughter.

Table 26 provides a listing of the elements of the Gauri rituals.

Table 26—Gauri Festival Rituals : Inventory of Items and Features

Colours

Red — dahlias for decoration (Chinnapura, Bandipur)
†vermillion powder
†liquid in tray to remove evil eye
†palm-leaf earrings (or may be white)
†areca nut
(taboo—chillies)

Yellow — chrysanthemums (Bandipur)
††turmeric powder
††turmeric root (optional)
†gold ornaments used to decorate goddess
†bananas
  pulses : *togari* (pigeon pea)
       kadale (Bengal gram)
†clarified butter, for lamps
††turmeric-coloured raw rice (*aksate*)
†*hulianna*, sour-flavoured cooked rice dish
†(one pandanus spike, used by Bandipur priest in send-off
  ritual, not a requirement of folk rituals)

White — †silver vessel for *kalasa*
†some flowers
†(*rangolli* line drawings ?)
cotton lamps

Table 26 (*contd. on page* 147)

Table 26 (*contd. from page* 146)

		†cotton necklaces
		'Gauri thread'
		†palm-leaf earrings (or may be red)
		pulse : *uddu* (shelled black gram)
		farina
		salt
		†yoghurt rice, cooked dish
		†*iddali* 'snack'
		(*y*)*ellu* sweet combination
	Black —	miniature bangles
		beads (optional)
	Green —	betel leaf
		pulse : *hesaru* (green gram)
		soaked-gram salad (*kosambari*)
Rice	—	†turmeric-coloured raw rice (*aksate*)
		†yoghurt rice
		sour-flavoured yellow rIce (*hulianna*)
		†grits, ingredient in *iddali* 'snack'
Numbers	—	2, 4 (types of pulses, 2 x 2?), 5, 7, 14 (2 x 7?)
		(9, 21 mentioned but not used)
Flowers	—	red dahlias (*bettadavarehuvu*)—Chinnapura and Bandipur
		yellow chrysanthemums—Bandipur
		others, white—not identified
		†pandanus spike—one, in priest's send-off, Bandipur
Snacks	—	†(*v*)*obbattu* (stuffed ball, pounded flat, made with wheat flour brown in colour)
		†*iddali*
		(*y*)*ellu* (mixture of white sesame, dried coconut chips, Bengal gram)
		payasa (sweet liquid, dessert)
		†(possibly also served for Prati feast?)
		†*kosambari* soaked-gram salad
Miscellaneous Special Items	—	turmeric-vermillion blessing spot
		winnowing fans, pairs of doubled sets
		cradle
		cotton necklaces
		jewellery for decorating goddess
		palm-leaf earrings
		cube of brown sugar
		betel-areca
Taboos	—	Eating pungent flavour; offering chillies or coriander seeds

†Also in Prati Festival rituals.

NUMBER SYMBOLISM

Most of the numbers which are part of these ceremonies are odd (*besa*) numbers—3, 5, 7, 9, 21—with a connotation of auspicious imbalance. Except for the numbers 2 and 4 (2 × 2), which also play a role here, even (*sama*) numbers are generally considered to have an inauspicious connotation of finality. Since an even amount of money, for example, suggests finality and 'no future', in the words of one Kerala friend, people of south India sometimes pay Rs. 101 for an item officially priced at Rs. 100.

Only two numbers, namely, 2 and 1, regularly contradict the even-odd/inauspicious-auspicious cultural rule. Although it is an even number, 2 often has benign connotations, as it does in the Prati and Gauri festivals. Gifts and offerings are frequently made in pairs. The auspicious married couple, a pair, is required at many rituals, especially Hindu weddings. Thus, if one or another of the bride's or groom's parents are widowed, an aunt-uncle or some other married couple will fill in for them at the places in the wedding where a set of parents is required. The number 2 thus has acquired a connotation of fruitful partnership. But it also may derive some of its positive symbolic value from the fact that it is 1 + 1, i.e., more than 1, the number 1—odd number though it is— being the most inauspicious number in Hindu folk religion.[28] I shall discuss the extensive use of 1 in funerary ritual in the following chapter, and its allusion to existential solitude. A pair, on the other hand, is symbolic non-solitude, two 1's keeping each other company, so to speak. Thus, as the reader will recall, winnowing fans are never for sale as single items, but rather only in pairs.

With the usual even-odd/inauspicious-auspicious dichotomy as background, one finds that other specific numbers have also come to acquire general meaning-values that influence their symbolic usage in folk rituals. (Cf. Eichinger Ferro-Luzzi 1974.) The Gauri and Prati festivals emphasise auspicious numbers. The most prevalent of these in relation to married women and their auspiciousness perpetuating strengths is the number 5. This is so throughout Hindu folk ritual of many South Asian regions (though, like all seemingly firm rules, it is not without its contradictions even in Bandipur). In contrast to the number 3, also a generally good, activity inducing number, 5 is considered very powerful in its ability to induce fertility and vigorous growth. Thus, for example, one finds a Chinnapura Brahman bride's parents sending five small silver cups along with their daughter as she enters her new, marital family.[29] Another newly wed Smartha Brahman couple worships five coconuts. Other *jatis* have parallel number-structured wedding customs. Even in funerals, which are considered to be the most dangerous of all personal transitions, the fifth day after death produces special efforts among most castes to get a dead family member moving along his or her path to the world of ancestors. This ritual is supposed to be financed by a married-out daughter and her husband among non-Brahmans. Thus, even at funerals, we see 5 associated with married women and their powers.

The number 3 is especially important in birth rituals. As an all purpose growth-producing number, its uses are more widespread than those of 5, but it is also less specific and powerful an agent than 5 is. For example, the third day after birth is the usual time for a new baby to 'graduate' from winnowing fan to cradle (though not universally so for all *jatis*). Another tripling of particular interest here is found in the Iyengar sixth-month pregnancy ritual, described above, in which the husband of a pregnant woman squeezes the juice of three new plants into her nostrils before sending her to her mother's house for her confinement. (Cf. Diehl 1956 : 331, on 3 and multiples of 3.)

Other specific numbers (7, 9, and 21) which figure in Gauri and Prati rituals are less easy to interpret than are 2, 3, and 5. It is possible to note, however, that 9 and 21—in addition to being auspicious as odd numbers—are products of 3. They are, of course, 3×3 and 3×7, respectively. This fact may well have contributed to their acquiring symbolic importance in local traditions, as multiples of sacred numbers often do. Specific mythological referents may also be involved, though these are less evident than they might be. (Wadley, for example, notes that the number 16 is important in Gauri festival rituals of Karimpur—a possible reference to a motif in the 'Mangala Gauri' myth.) The number 7, mentioned by Eichinger Ferro-Luzzi (1974) as a favourite number of Tamilnadu women, may be such a case. The number of stars in the Pleiades constellation (*krattike* in Kannada), number 7 has figured in the development of many south Indian stories about groups of seven sisters.

When put into terms of auspicious imbalance, the positive value of odd numbers can be seen to have a sociological parallel. A universal principle of social reciprocity, the desirability of imbalance applies to the relations between 'exchange relations' as to other Hindu cultural experiences. Depending as they do on a linking action (marriage) to connect them, 'exchange relations' are more and more enhanced in value, the more that they follow the universal cultural rule that out-of-balance exchanges continue a bond. If they wish to strengthen their ties, they keep a steady flow of gifts moving between them. The gift that moves between them is the third member, transforming their paired evenness into productive activity. An official member of both 'birth group' (*kutumba*) and 'close relations of exchange' (*nentru*), the powerfully ambiguous married-out daughter is herself often spoken of as just such a 'gift'. In the magical sum of $(2 + 1 + 2 = 5)$, she is the one moving between pairs.

STRUCTURAL PRINCIPLES OF GAURI AND PRATI RITUALS

Gauri and Prati festival rituals—welcoming, worship, and send-off—each make up a series that reflects the typical and ideal experience of a woman in her natal family. A daughter is born into her family, and a goddess is brought out of a river. A daughter lives in her parents' home until shortly after her marriage, and a goddess rests as a *kalasa* on a temporary family shrine where she receives offerings including married women's special ornaments. Finally, "a woman given in marriage leaves the family (*kula*) forever," as a local proverb says; and a goddess is sent off into a river again, to join her husband in his home. Just as each daughter's legal ties to her family are temporary in the eyes of customary law, Gauri or Prati is only a visitor.

The operational meanings of several ritual items used in the two festivals make these parallels between daughter and goddess very clear. Winnowing fan, cradle, and leaf shoots associated with pregnancy ritual all have been discussed in connection with the festival rituals where they appear. *Puja* items such as turmeric root, *tali*, black bangles, and plates of send-off offerings create further obvious connections between festival rituals and the maturation, marriage, and departure of daughters.

Along with these life-cycle allusions, festival rituals offer images of what women themselves are, and what they aspire to be to their natal and marital families. The structure of symbolic relationships among *puja* items—foods, flowers, lamps, and so on—extends concepts of womanhood beyond what words alone can express.

Women's wealth, for example, is a subtle concept interwoven with other themes of festival meaning. This concept has a wide range of applications. At its most literal, it includes the dowry itself as the money or property brought into each family estate by daughters-in-law. At its most general, it refers to the auspicious role of married women in increasing family prosperity.

It is significant in this connection that married women exchange symbols of wealth (turmeric root, for example) with partners of different households as part of festival rituals. Such exchange acts are meaningful in more than one way. They express interdependence among women. They express an idea that each woman's wealth comes from another woman. It comes directly in the form of gifts from mothers to daughters. It also comes through the passing along of dowries. That is, each woman who marries and brings in dowry increases a family's wealth and makes it possible, directly or indirectly, for the family to pay dowries for her sisters-in-law and her daughters. In the 'Mangala Gauri' myth it is the bride's mother who provides her with the material she needs to worship the goddess; the bride also gives her mother a gift after her vow has succeeded in preserving her husband's life. This is a mythic reference to the interdependence between women expressed also in rituals.

As festival myths show, however, the ties between women, especially mothers and their marriageable daughters, are problematic. Although there is interdependence, there is also a need to separate upon a daughter's marriage. This is a universal problem created by Hindu customary family law, discussed earlier in Chapter 2. Specific family practices of southern Brahman groups further intensify this problem by restraining and isolating women socially at marriage. Women's actual control over the disposition of their dowries, for example, is minimal. Other restrictions, such as forbidding sisters to marry into the same immediate families among the Haviks (Harper 1969), often thrust brides into alien, and sometimes hostile, environments. In this social context exchanges of symbols of wealth among women can have a strong restorative effect reducing isolating forces in women's lives.

Beauty, as *laksana*, is another basic concept in these festivals, as discussed at the beginning of this chapter. This concept includes both visual delight and order. It is a concept of the well-groomed married woman whose presence inspires pleasure and satisfaction (*santosa*) in those near her.

Relationships among colours are the most important semantic dimension of festival structure. Ritual colours define the basic forces with which the married woman contends in Gauri and Prati festivals. Her unique strength is in her woman's wealth and her alliance with her goddess. This quality is represented by yellow/gold, the predominant colour in both festivals. Her strength is mobilised, through her disciplined attitude (whiteness), to enable her to control biological energies (red), fend off danger (black, some red), and thereby protect the continuity (white) and prosperity (yellow/gold) of her husband's family line. Concepts symbolised by specific colours are given in Table 27.

Table 27—Concepts Symbolised by Colours

White	Red	Black	Yellow/Gold
Chastity, as sexual discipline	Vitality	Death or the deceased	Prosperity
Duty to family line	Sexuality	Poverty	Beauty (*laksana*)
Continuity of family	Generative life forces	Obstacles	Married woman

Birth and growth are symbolised in these festivals by a minor colour, green. Though this colour appears in leaves, and once in the Ganga-Gauri myth as well, the colour does not perform major functions in ritual structure.

As much as the individual colours themselves, ritual combinations of colours express several ways in which life forces interact. In fact, ritual combinations of colours may be said to control the possibly destructive force of any one colour standing alone. Table 28 depicts alternate meanings of isolated and combined colours.

The two festivals present somewhat different concepts of the married woman in their symbolic uses of colours. In Prati there is much use of the white-yellow colour pair, emphasising women's wealth and discipline. Comparatively less use of red coloured ritual items serves to de-emphasise references to such strong life forces as sexuality. The Gauri Festival, on the other hand, high-

Table 28—Symbolism of Colours, Isolated or Combined

Isolated Colours	Combined Colours
White : Withdrawal from sexuality Extreme spirituality, purity	White + Yellow/Gold : Power of chastity to produce wealth, beauty, or family continuity
Red : Uncontrolled energy (Colour of Brahman widow's sari)	Red + Yellow/Gold : Sexuality in marriage
Black : Physical death Poverty Widowhood†	Black + Yellow/Gold : Power of the married women to protect against death
Gold : Wealth not exchanged Daughter not married (dowry retained)	Struggle between poverty and prosperity in family life—emphasis on the opposition or dilemma Overcoming obstacles

†Omvedt and Zelliot (1978 : 5) cite the following Marathi riddle, which associates widowhood with the colour black : 'Red carriage with green handles, widowed prostitutes sit inside', is the riddle. The answer is, 'Watermelon', as something with red flesh, green skin, and black seeds inside.

lights the colours red and yellow. This brings in sexuality and other strong passions to a greater degree than in Prati. The presence of white items, as in Prati, refers to duty and discipiline, but as a less prominent theme. Also minor is the colour black, whose presence represents the problems challenging the married woman, the obstacles she wishes to overcome.

Discipline is essential to the ideal married woman's role. This concept includes sexual chastity but goes beyond it to produce a quasi-ascetic power in all endeavours. The presence of a comb among the winnowing fan gifts of the Gauri Festival is significant in this connection. The grooming of hair has widespread symbolic value throughout south Asia, and it is considered to be important by the people of Bandipur and Chinnapura. As Hallpike (1969), Leach (1958), and Hershman (1974) have shown in a series of reports, the combing, brushing, washing, and oiling of hair relates strongly to concepts of sexuality and sexual discipline in south Asia. The comb's symbolic function among ritual gifts is thus clear.

Additional qualities of festival items reiterate themes set by colour relationships. Flowers, foods, and other objects express dilemmas of discipline versus sexuality and the dangers that the married woman overcomes in these rituals. Oppositions between flowers, foods, flavours, and numbers, parallel each other and echo this theme in several aspects of each festival.

The existential significance of these festival themes is confirmed daily in the customary ornamentation of Hindu married women. The items used for daily grooming are included in the *bhagina-mara* : black beads, black glass bangles, turmeric and vermillion. (In the Prati Festival there are no winnowing fan gifts, but similar items are used and exchanged among married women who are neighbours or relatives.) These items are, of course, red, black, and yellow, signifying an auspicious and controlled combination of the processes symbolised by these colours. Daily grooming combines black and yellow/gold on the wrist and neck, and red and yellow/gold on the forehead.

DISCUSSION

The myths and rituals discussed in this chapter relate to many social and cultural issues which also figure in the subsequent three festival studies. The problem of family continuity depending on marriage to outsiders will come up again and again in other festivals. As family-oriented festivals, Gauri and Prati highlight the marital pair and the problematic situation of married women—themes found in other festivals' myths and rituals also. Whereas Gauri and Prati rituals and myths affirm women's importance and their links to both natal and marital kin, other festivals include these themes as minor ones. Matters such as the long-range survival of a family as a whole, on the other hand, are in background in Gauri and Prati but take precedence in other festivals.

These two festivals also have introduced several symbolic elements used to structure other festivals. Most of the colours used in family festivals have appeared, with yellow predominant. The black, red, and white with which yellow is combined in Gauri and Prati rituals will now move forward to emphasise other symbolic themes in other festivals. Festival foods and menus, like colours, display contrasts among symbolic values through their different flavours and forms, these contrasts paralleling those among colours and other elements. Number symbolism, an element appearing throughout the next three festival studies, is important in Gauri and Prati structure. The uses made of the winnowing fan in festival rituals give a clear indication of the ways in which festival symbolism, rites of passage, and the process of growing and preparing food grains intersect in this culture.

Some minor motifs in Gauri and Prati symbolism play more significant roles in the following studies. For instance, some of the tragedies—distinctly feminine tragedies in this culture—which these two festivals are intended to prevent receive more direct attention in festivals described in the next chapter and in widespread concepts of the violent, restless *amma* goddesses. The serpent, centre of attention in another chapter, has made a brief but dramatic appearance already in the 'Mangala Gauri' myth.

Both the presence and the absence of certain symbolic elements become important to note from now on. For example, foods and flowers which appear in auspicious festivals such as Gauri and Prati may not appear in less cheerful ones. Though there are caste variations in customary food and so on, each family, regardless of caste membership, has a system of alternative customs expressing the moods and meanings of various ritual times.

The concept of auspiciousness, of central value in Gauri and Prati worship, defines the goal of most family festivals. In Gauri and Prati auspicious influence is embodied in the married women who maintain a lively, active state of being for their husbands and families. In other festivals the contributions of women to family well-being are supplemented by contributions of others, including ancestors. In the next chapter, we shall observe offorts to counteract inauspicious forces of destruction and stagnation threatening family vitality.

NOTES

1. An earlier version of this chapter was presented in 1974 to a meeting of the Conference on Religion in South India, in Chicago. The title of that paper was "Two Women's Ceremonies."

2. Non-Brahman or A.K. widows are identifiable by their plain metal bangles, usually silver, and by their loss of rights to wear flowers in their hair, glass bangles, or the forehead vermillion spot (except when the spot is put on as part of temple worship).

3. The only human females who are guaranteed to remain non-widows are those who do not marry human husbands. In a culture where marriage is supposed to be universal these are women who have been married to a god. In northern Karnataka, these women are called *basavi*. Elsewhere temple dancers, *devadasis*, maintained auspicious states of non-widowhood by marrying their god (see Marglin 1980).

4. The Durga Festival of Bengal is celebrated in a similar concept, i.e., that the married daughter, Durga, another form of Siva's consort, returns home for a visit. This is shown clearly in an excelent film, "Panchthupi," by Hiri Dasgupta (produced by Burmah-Shell).

5. The Tamil Lexicon gives the term *piratti*, feminine form of *piran* 'lord', as 'lady, mistress'. The local name for the goddess Prati is a form of that word. Bandipur and Chinnapura Iyengars' home language is a dialect of Tamil heavily influenced by Kannada.

6. The people of the two villages do not join to do the festival. Each village group does it in its own place.

7. Dube (1955 : 113) describes a local Gauri festival, the Baktamma Festival of Andhra State, in which the goddess is said to be "piqued by her husband."

8. A printed version (Sastri 1961), discussed as Version II, is from the *Bhavisyottara Purana*. Another, handwritten version, Version III here, was adapted by Gorur Ramaswamy Iyengar from the *Mahabharata*'s 52nd Chapter; it is kept in a village home. Version I was told by village women to K. Rangaraj, one of our assistants. It seems to be an abridged and altered version of the puranic tale.

9. I am grateful to S. Srinivasan of Mysore City, who provided me with this translation out of his own devotion from Sastri's (1961) Kannada version in 1977.

10. In this rendition of the myth, Gorur Ramaswamy Iyengar mentions that men can keep wives through performing the ritual vow, just as wives can keep their husbands. However, I am not aware of any case of men performing such vows for the sake of keeping their wives alive.

11. I recorded one version of the 'Mangala Gauri' myth in Bandipur in 1977. A Smartha woman of the village had written it out in 1965 or 1966 at the time of her marriage. She told

me that both her mother and mother-in-law had dictated it to her, and that she had been instructed to recite it each year for the first five years of her marriage. She had done this in order to protect her husband. Now the busy mother of four small children, she was pleased to retrieve a little notebook from her cupboard and sit for an hour or so reading and chanting the myth. After singing the written version, she went over it section by section to clarify the story line. As she summarised the original text for us, my translator and I watched it change slightly. She added her own emphases and omitted written details that no longer interested her. Version I is her paraphrased telling of the myth, which was done with her notebook before her.

Version III was translated from Sastri (1961) by K. Gurulingaiah in 1967.

12. This is a local version of the more widespread 'Renuka' story (cf. Brubaker 1977). Whitehead heard it from a Christian, who heard it from his Hindu father.

Vessels are used to many different purposes in Hindu symbolism. The purposes vary with each context of their occurrence, though most uses center around the concept of the mortal body in some way or another. Its characteristics—corporeality, round shape, hollowness, opening at the top—define the vessel's eligibility for such symbolic use; but they do not control its meaning the same way in every symbolic structure where it appears.

13. Only members of the Hebbar sub-caste of Iyengars celebrate the festival. The Hebbars have tended to be an endogamous unit in the past but are now intermarrying with other Iyengars.

14. One family mentioned that it is customary at a wedding for the groom's father to present a nose ornament to the bride for her use in Prati *puja*.

15. The sari this family uses for the Prati Festival was purchased "from Benares 62 years ago for Rs. 150." It is ten yards long and is kept carefully just for this purpose. Other families also may have such saris kept specially in their homes, or they may purchase new ones each year for the *puja*.

16. The Bandipur family was in the process of arranging a marriage for their daughter, and they succeeded in finding a groom after this festival. They may have hoped that pairing her up with her married sister and again with her mother would somehow help the process of marriage arrangement.

17. Villagers weave durable floor mats out of the palm-like leaves of this plant.

18. Mark Nichter (personal communication, 1977) informs me that the same plants that are important in these festival rituals are also ingredients of native medicines used for pregnancy and birth-related disorders (cf. Nichter 1977).

19. There is a movie of this pregnancy rite available. It is produced and distributed by Dr. Daniel Smith of Syracuse University in New York State.

20. The cookbook writer, E. P. Veeraswamy (1936) says that *kolakatte* snacks serve as "christening cakes" in Tamilnadu. This is not true, to my knowledge, for the Iyengars of Bandipur or Chinnapura, though, being of Tamil descent, some may share such a naming ritual custom, or at least know of it. They also call the snack *modaka* or *molaka*. Another recipe is in Meenakshi Ammal (1980 : 202-207) under the spelling of *kozhukkattai*.

21. When Smartha families send their daughters-in-law back to natal homes for confinement, they send along 'five kinds of rice' with them. (Iyengars, however, do not seem to observe this pregnancy custom.) Smarthas also prepare the 'five kinds of rice' for *prasta*, nuptial rituals preliminary to the consummation of a daughter's marriage (see Regelson 1972 : 134).

22. These colour and flavour classifications are based on interviews with village Brahman women and detailed recipes collected in 1976 with the assistance of Miss H. Malathi. They are the women's own classifications.

23. When I presented an earlier version of this chapter as a paper in 1974, Professor Kees Bolle brought a Karnataka saying about a popular fool, Tinnevelly Rama, to my attention;

the saying includes a reference to his taking yoghurt as 'curds of wealth' and 'sweet milk for immortality'.

In her study of plant symbols, Shakti M. Gupta (1971 : 102-104) relates a folk story which is the basis of a north Indian festival, Chet, during which women avoid salt and replace it with sour tamarind. The story is that Usha, daughter of Parvati, hid in a barrel of salt when Siva went on a rampage and cut off his son Ganesha's head. The substitution of tamarind for salt is said to have been a directive from Parvati.

24. The black gram of which *iddali* is made is a pulse whose husk is black, but which has a white bean used for cooking. It is an important ingredient for some ancestor ritual snacks. I discuss its symbolic role in these ritual snacks elsewhere.

25. A Weaver house winnowing fan contained the following items :

Raw rice	Two bananas
Bengal gram	One coconut
Green gram	Betel-areca set
White sesame seeds	Blouse piece
Tambittu balls, sweet	Five cotton wicks for lamps
One piece of cucumber	Gauri thread
Cube of brown sugar	Packet containing : two miniature black bangles, one pair earrings, turmeric powder, and vermillion powder

26. Luschinsky (1969 : 296). On the subject of ritual uses of winnowing fans in other regions, see also, Crooke (1896 : II : 189, 308) and Khare (1976b : 196, 212). Wadley (1975 : 171) mentions a Divali event when mothers go through the village at night waving winnowing fans, "to chase away poverty, illness, and evil spirits." In the *Visnu Purana*, Vyasa says to Arjuna at one point, "Has the wind of a winnowing basket lighted upon you? or has an evil eye gazed upon you, Arjuna? that you look thus miserable" (H. H. Wilson translation, 1961 : 483).

27. As one might expect, the winnowing fan also plays a role in maturation and wedding rituals. It is, however, little used in death rituals. One use in mourning ritual that I know of is in the Smith *jati*, who use it to deliver ancestral *pinda* balls to a river at the end of mourning. As an offering to a soul that has made the transition out of life toward pure spirituality, this *pinda* offering has a somewhat auspicious quality to it.

I once saw another use of a winnowing fan in a funeral, for a Fisherman in 1966, at the point when the party had returned from the burial ground and was about to re-enter the deceased person's house. One of the mourners picked up a winnowing fan full of raw rice which had been set on the place (verandah) where the corpse had received honours. Turning his back to the house, the mourner threw three handfulls of the rice backwards onto the roof.

28. The number 2 is the only even prime number. In fact, it is possible that what is commonly regarded for symbolism purposes as the odd-number category may actually be the set of prime numbers, which are the irreducible factors of all other numbers. Number symbols are as old as arithemetic/mathematics itself; and India, as a culture that made significant contributions to mathematics in ancient times, has a long and sophisticated numerology tradition, both folk and literary.

29. Actually they send five small silver cups and one large one. The large one, rather than being a solitary item, should probably be considered a symbol of the summation of the power of the five smaller ones.

Chapter 6

RED OFFERINGS TO DEATH'S BLACKNESS : MYTHS AND RITUALS FOR SOME RESTLESS SPIRITS

Tragedy, frustration and anger are the nature of the ghostly spirits known as *amma* goddesses. If the married woman and her Gauri are successes, these spirits are failures. Some are the ghosts of murder victims or frantic suicides; the queen of them all, Mari, was once a virtuous wife betrayed. Others are furious for no apparent reason. In their raging they direct wild powers to waste and destruction. Their victims—including whole towns, herds of cattle, or families—are stricken with terrifying diseases and disorder, deserved or not. Once stricken, the human community finds its guilt and rapidly mobilises to appease the *amma* (lit. 'mother' or 'lady') in whatever way they feel they can. They create myths which establish problems, and then then they solve those problems.

They provide her with flattering ornaments and ritual compliments. They satisfy her desire for blood and destruction within a safe ritual zone. They feast her in village groves and fields, hoping that she will stay away from their homes. They control their own fear while doing these things; for they often comment that such spirits can kill simply by provoking fear.[1]

Most of the rituals for such spirits are done on an emergency basis. That is, they are only done when something is wrong. But once in awhile a village or a family gets into a regular relationship with one of them and starts doing a festival. The annual festival for Mari, known for its dramatic buffalo sacrifice, has been a popular village festival throughout the south. Though it has ceased to be so dramatic, it continues in an abbreviated version in Bandipur's A.K. Colony. In this chapter we will consider two more private festivals, which are performed by families for less well-known *ammas*, Piriyapattanadamma and Mastiamma. Though started in times of family crisis, these festivals have evolved into continuing obligations.

The contrast between these *ammas* and the benign Laksmi (Prati) is visible in a simple detail of their pujas: the flower which is offered to each of them. While the goddess of prosperity receives a yellow flower, the *amma* receives a red one. Her well-known need for blood and violence is given form as a red oleander in every *puja* for her. This is not a conscious symbolic choice on the part of those I have asked about it. But its meaning is clearer and clearer, the more bright red items one sees associated with village *pujas* for such spirits. (Villagers are universally unaware that the oleander is poisonous. I have asked at least six informants, representing each *jati*-cluster, about this.)

Representing even more than blood, the red flower sums up feelings of anger and experiences of wasted energy. In contrast to the visions of benign goddesses, some possible meanings of redness come into focus as in Table 29.

Table 29—Contrasts Between Rituals for *Ammas* and Festivals for Benign Goddesses

	Amma Rituals	*Gauri or Prati Festivals*
Offering :	Red flower	Yellow flower
Emotion :	Auger (*kopa*)	Satisfaction, pleasure (*santosa*)
Associated Life Experience :	Spilled blood, waste	Prosperity, safety, growth

A little story from Bandipur illustrates the close connection between *amma* spirits' anger and blood. It is a legend about the discovery of a shrine. There is a striking destructive transformation in it, as pots of cooked white rice turn into pots of fresh blood. The symbolism of this transformation is so obviously related to the welfare of the family that the simultaneous decline of children which occurs seems almost superfluous. The story goes as follows:

Many years ago some saints (*rsis*) were here meditating beneath a nearby tree. People often came to be near the saints and cook their food. One day a group was preparing rice and sauce (*saru*) near the tree where we (they) now keep the Bandamma shrine. They had no stone to grind their spices. So they took a stone they found at hand and ground their spices with that. They finished their cooking and left the rice and sauce in pots.
But when they went to eat their meal, they found the pots full of blood—only blood. And their babies in cradles had lost consciousness.
They wondered what had happened. Then the goddess possessed a member

of the group. She said, "You have ground me (the stone) and I am bleeding. That is why these things have happend."

So they came near the god, and apologised (*tappaytu helli*), and made *puja* to her. The blood again became rice, and the children revived. Then they ate their food.

The juxtaposition of fresh blood with cooked white rice is not limited to village conversation or stories. It is in fact done regularly in emergency rituals for the *ammas*, especially for Mari. The mixture is called *kulu*, which is an old word for both cooked rice and food. For example, in an emergency ritual (*Midicilu*) done for Mari as a way of fending off cattle disease, villagers sacrifice a pig and pour its blood into a brass vessel which contains cooked rice. Pig blood, like pig meat, is considered to be physiologically 'cooling' and a favourite food for all ghosts. But other animals, such as goats or buffaloes, may also be used in the same way.[2] The mixture is sprinkled onto the cattle. An A.K. places the vessel on his head and may go into trance.

This combination of blood and rice is symbolically a human sacrifice and philosophically a mixture of two irreconcilable opposites. They are, on the one hand, eternal destruction, waste and anger, in the form of pure flowing blood; and, on the other hand, eternal fulfillment, continuity and peace, in the form of cooked rice. The difficulty/near-impossibility of combining these two, or rather changing the former into the latter, is another basic struggle implicit in the *amma* complex. In some villagers' conversations about the two family festivals to be discussed below, the problem takes a slightly different, though parallel, symbolic form: the transformation of their cows' milk into blood. I shall return to this theme further below.

The *amma* shoots and kills from her eyes. It is through her glance that her destructive anger is most able to turn all to blood and waste. I first realised this while observing a procession for Mari in Chinnapura. As a gaggle of marching villagers returned from the river, where the goddess had been bathed, it stopped in the middle of a dusty hill. Someone had placed a small banana tree, cut from its base, in the path before them. Everyone waited. What were they waiting for? I asked. They explained in hushed tones that the tree, instead of they themselves, was now getting the angry stare of the goddess.

That goddess, however, was a featureless wooden doll. It had no face or eyes at all, unless someone happened to put its silver mask over its crudely carved head. In fact, most of the *ammas* are without faces. Whether in wood or stone, whether man-made or naturally 'born' out of a sacred spot in the ground, most (though not all) *ammas* are crude lumps and slabs, while other deities are beautifully carved. It began to occur to me that this may be a significant fact in itself, rather than being a failure of folk iconography. So I asked a local member of the Smith *jati* about it in 1976.

Sri Nagalingachari is in the Smith *jati*, whose members traditionally sculpt temple images. He is also a soothsayer (*mantravadi*), the most active one in Bandipur at this time. He knows a lot about *ammas* and has a technical term for this type of violent female spirit: *ksudradevaru*. After hearing about their anger and their potential for violence from him, I asked why they are so rarely represented with faces or eyes. He dodged the question at first with a distracted comment that people who make Mari images, for instance, probably do not know how to sculpt faces. But within a minute he confirmed my hunch. In fact, he said, "You can tell from the eyes that it is that type of god," since "the *ksudradevaru* shows its anger through the eyes." He solved the riddle once and for all with a final comment: The sight of a *ksudradevaru* must not fall on people. That is why they don't make eyes on those images (Plate 8).

Plate 8.   Maramma icons lacking anthropomorphic features, Bandipur A.K. Colony

This being village Hinduism, no such comment will ever apply universally. But a vital concern with eyes is general, and is significant throughout this book. In the previous chapter it appeared as a love of beauty, accented with a myth-ical emphasis on the eyes and vision. In this chapter it is the dangerous poten-tial in an angry glance as a background theme, even though one of the *ammas* (Mastiamma) is given anthropomorphic representation in her shrine in the fields. And in the final study, on serpent worship, villagers tell us that they avoid pungent spices in order to avoid 'heating' the serpent deity's eyes. "Chillies" they say, "would heat the serpent's temper, which he would show through a look. And that look would harm us,[3] producing severe skin diseases and barrenness."

The stare of an *amma* goddess makes blood flow. The blood she craves fills her own dark emptiness with a stolen vitality. Though she is a goddess, she is also a ghost (*gali*). Not quite finished with life, she, like all ghosts, is frustrated and paralysed. Her eyes are the instruments of the envy she feels toward those who are satisfied, active and living. And with them she can draw the living into her vacuum of death and gain energy (*miridu*) for her own temporary release from paralysis.

Since she was once a living woman, she remembers the experience of having blood flow through her body. But since she most probably quit life too abruptly, she constantly wishes to recapture the feeling of being alive. Perhaps she needs to marry, or to give birth to her child. Perhaps she regrets killing herself, or wishes to avenge her own murder. Whatever her original tragedy was, she never has been able to pass satisfied beyond life's concerns.

As a woman she was more likely to become a restless spirit after death than a man was, although there are plenty of male ghosts (of murder victims or suicides) travelling with her on the country roads in the Hindu night-time. Her implication in life-giving processes had been greater than men's. And she had always been more vulnerable to neglect and violent abuse than most men.[4] As a spirit she is more likely to harm her relatives (natal or marital) than to harm outsiders or strangers. But in passing to the goddess status she will have acquired a new name merging her with many other such women. When her family decides to placate her, they use her new, category title—Mari, Mastiamma, or some other. (Appendix B includes a local Mari myth.)

In colour-symbolism language, her problem, and that of her victims, is that she stays in the transitional phase of 'black' death itself, continually robbing the living of the 'red' blood she once felt inside of her, and unable ('black' = frustration) to move onward to 'white' peace and the freedom of her spirit, which is also called her subtle body.

The corresponding goal of rituals done for her is to overcome the 'black' inertia of her state, and thereby enable her to exit fully into the state of 'white', peaceful indifference to the living and their 'red' blood. For this transition to occur, a periodic offering of 'red' blood (and flower) is required.

Death is an obstacle in the popular Hindu view. A barrier between the living and spirit worlds, it receives elaborate attention in the folk ritual system. Getting over the obstacle in the first place, i.e., enduring ten days of rituals, is seen as the only way to spiritual freedom that is open to most ordinary people. But once they have traversed the mountain of funerary transformations, death remains as the barrier which now prevents their return. The living are protected by the barrier of funerals. Once certain that the dead have crossed it, the living maintain that barrier with friendly messages that are sent to the ancestors without fail every year. They hope that the ancestors will put in a word for them in the spirit world in appreciation of their good will.

Amma rituals often use the black colour. Mr. G. believes that if one sacrifices a black animal to an *amma*, especially to Bandamma, she will be inspired to kill on one's behalf. Perhaps the blackness of the animal is a reminder of one's murderous goal according to rules of sympathetic magic. He uses the black colour to a different conscious end in his Piriyapattanadamma ritual, to be described below. It is the colour of the mud which he builds up in two mounds for the *puja*. There is a funerary (death) allusion here, as in other details of this ritual.

The second cultural key to popular Hindu notions of death is separation. The deceased person must be ritually separated from the living and the corpse must be separated from the spirit. Separation of the living from the dead is symbolised by certain even numbers, especially 4; and by the number 1. Thus, for example, one finds that four people are always used to carry a dead body to its grave or funeral pyre. There is no exception to this rule in this part of India, as far as I can tell. Four, as an even number, symbolises stasis and finality. And the number 1 appears throughout the funeral ceremonies in such forms as a single coin or a single betel-areca. This is a symbolic allusion to the existential solitude of death, and of course to the inevitable separation of the dead person out from his family context.

The liberating separation of the physical body from the 'subtle body' or spirit is a subject that receives extended comment in Hindu religious discussions about death and the passage from 'ghostly' (*preta*) to 'ancestral' (*pitri*) status. The common folk representation of this separation or passage is the colour white, as the colour of the pure, unadulterated (by physical pollution) soul. One white substance, a perfumed powder called *bukki hittu*, is used in non-Brahman funerals for children. It is smeared on their little corpse faces, perhaps as a representation of the easy transition to spiritual freedom which they are expected to have.[5]

When an adult corpse is buried, it is always covered with a white cloth, whether it is a male or a female.[6] Thus we will see white stones placed on top of the black platforms in Mr. G.'s ritual for his *amma* goddess. And white, as the colour of plain, cooked rice, is the basic colour of the *puja* for the other *amma*, Mastiamma, who receives a consciously abbreviated ancestor ritual in her outdoor shrine.

Like funerary rituals (but unlike ancestor worship), rituals for the *amma* goddess are performed out-of-doors. The basis of this practice is the same as that of the practice of setting a dying person out of the house to quit his or her life on the verandah. Restless ghosts, as any ghosts, are not welcome in a house where people still live. This is also the reason why some families cook pork only in their front room or in makeshift stoves set onto the verandah. Since they consider pork the favourite food of ghosts, they fear that cooking it in the kitchen would attract them into the home's hearth and center. Ordinary ancestors, in contrast, are usually considered peaceful enough to be temporary house guests. But *ammas*, whether or not they were once members of the family, are not welcomed inside.

Like non-Brahman or A. K. funerals and ancestor ceremonies, *puja* offerings to the *ammas* include cooked meat. There is a hope that the cooked meat will satisfy the envy and restlessness of the deceased, whether ghost or goddess. I first understood this meat-need, and the general concern about frustrated spirits, when an old lady of Bandipur was dying on her verandah. Very old and weak, she was maintaining a tight grasp on her life until her foster son arrived to bid her farewell. As a week of waiting passed, she asked constantly for meat. Her family provided her with regular meat meals, but they still worried about her craving and reminded each other often, "Although we are giving her meat now, we also must be sure to offer it to her after she dies."

One final requirement for an *amma puja* is a feminine, married woman orna- mental gift. This is a packet of objects which is bought at the weekly market for a small amount of money. It is a combination of one pair of miniature black glass bangles; a strip of 'white' palm-leaf for rolled ear-rings (*biccole*); and, of course, small packets of turmeric and vermillion[7] (Plates 9A, 9B). It is called *ammanavara(y)ecca*, 'the woman's ritual gift'.[8] These are the traditional married woman things, an inherently desirable offering, to which all of the *amma* spirits are entitled.[9]

The same packet of things is included in Gauri offerings to married women, by both Brahmans and non-Brahmans. But when it is given to *amma* spirits, the style of its offering is different from that associated with the benign Gauri and Prati/Laksmi. Though the *amma* takes the gift from her propitiants, she is not welcomed into the house in the way that the benign goddesses are. Nor does she receive her gift on a winnowing fan. Nor do the propitiants share in her 'married woman' status by simultaneously exchanging the same gifts among themselves. The ornaments of the married woman status are granted to the *amma* as part of the effort to get her help or protection. But this gesture has a specific, fearful meaning in *amma* rituals: flatter the disturbed feminine spirit, but keep her at a symbolic distance from you. *Amma* rituals thus develop a pattern which I think of as 'pseudo-auspicious'.

Just as much as the Gauri and Laksmi festivals merge and identify worship- pers and their gods, the *amma* festivals separate them.

PIRIYAPATTANADAMMA

One day in 1967 I was strolling through Bandipur. Since it was a warm March afternoon, I naturally drifted toward the pleasant mango grove at the edge of the village. Noticing smoke from a cooking fire, I went over to query a small group of local picnickers who were gathered beneath a country fig tree. I knew them to be of the Washerman *jati*. My interest increased when I saw that they had set out a neat arrangement of stones and decorated them with bright red flowers and the tiny black glass bangles which are sold in the weekly market.

Plate 9-A. *Ammanavara(y)ecca* gift, packed with palm leaf earrings on outside

They, however, were not interested in answering my questions. I coaxed them into a short interview anyway, finding out that they do the ritual twice in each three-year period. And they agreed to let me photograph their stone-pebble 'house god', Piriyapattanadamma.

The photograph I took that day was soon filed and forgotten. But eight years later, as I 'toured' through my own notes and photographs on village festivals, I made a second stop at the Washerman ritual. It had acquired new meaning to me in the interim, since I was beginning to recognise the powerful significance of those red flowers and tiny black bangles.

Plate 9-B. *Ammanavara(y)ecca* gift, contents (white palm leaf earring, black bangle, turmeric, vermillion)

Gathering further information on this goddess, her festival rites, and her myths turned out to be one of the great adventures of my Karnataka fieldwork. In 1976, when I made a return visit to Bandipur, I found the Washerman family as uncommunicative as ever. But, determined to understand these *ammas*, I continued to ask other villagers about Piriyapattanadamma. The town of Piriyapattana, where her temple is located, is the backdrop of several epic ballads sung by local bards. Having heard of its central importance in the history of the region, I knew that romance and legend infuse the hilly, little town of Piriyapattana with glory.

I finally found some village friends who also do a family festival for the goddess Piriyapattanadamma. They also perform the ritual twice in each three-year period, and always on a Thursday.[10] Though they are of a different *jati* than the original group, and the Piriyapattanadamma is not their 'house god', Mrs. S. and Mr. G. were willing to tell me about their festival. They are of the Oil-Presser *jati*, but they make their living from agriculture. My interview of them extended over the summers of 1976 and 1977, as more and more questions occurred to me about the goddess. Though I was never able to observe their ritual, they satisfied my curiosity on all ritual points with diagrams and clear information. I had observed some of their other rituals first-hand; so they were practiced informants. They told me that, "She is a cruel god, like Maramma."

I found out from Mrs. S. and her husband that there was a good reason why I was having such a hard time finding out about rituals for Piriyapattanadamma. This festival is private and oriented only to family.[11] As an outsider, I would not be welcome at such an event, as clearly I was not welcome at the Washerman's picnic in 1967. No one but close relatives can share food with the family that does this ritual. The guests of choice are close exchange relations (*nentru*) This fitted in with my scanty information on the Washerman family's festival, to which the old mother of the family had invited her two brothers.

Despite their eagerness to help me, my search did not end with my Oil-Presser friends, because they did not know any stories about the goddess and were unable to track down anyone who did. An accidental gathering of neighbours in their home in 1977 produced one loose fragment of a story. Mrs. M., the mother of one of my assistants, performs rituals for Piriyapattanadamma, though only on an emergency basis. She is a resident of another village. Though interesting, her story was not satisfying. (It is included in Appendix B.) Nor could I locate any better ones in the collections of Karnataka folklorists.

So at last the Georges and I decided to go to Piriyapattana town itself in search of the missing myth. We found satisfaction there, in the voice of Sri Malagaiah, son of Puttaiah, who is the priest (*pujari*) of the goddess' temple.[12] A descendant of twelve generations of Piriyapattanadamma priests, he knew his goddess well. He kindly agreed to spend two hours with us on that sultry evening, rather than going to tend his fields (Plates 10 and 11).

The missing myth was worth the search.

PIRIYAPATTANADAMMA MYTH : 'THE SOOT-BLACK LADY' WHO NEVER DIED

When we arrived at the Piriyapattana temple on the evening of 17 August 1977, one of the first things we found out about our goddess was that she had another name. As we viewed the bright metal face and clothes adorning the stone before us, her priest told us that her name was really Masanikamma, which translates as 'Soot-Black Lady'. The names of her sisters, the six stone images lined up behind her in her sanctuary, also had associations with cook-

Plate 10. Piriyapattanadamma in temple, dressed and decorated

ing or foods, at least most of them did. They were introduced to us as (1) Elder Lady (Doddamma), (2) Younger Lady (Cikkamma), (3) Fruit and Betel Lady (Hannu Viladeleamma), (4) Stove Soot Lady (Volemasniyamma), (5) Dry Land Crop Lady (Bele Hwaladamma), and (6) Garden Land Lady (Totadamma). Malagaiah, the priest, did not know how they had all come together in his temple. "They [my predecessors] never told me," he said apologetically. He kindly allowed us to inspect the stones as closely as possible, even to the point of having his son undress the central figure.

As our heroine sat naked before our eyes, we saw that she was formless, as *ammas* tend to be. She was no more than a mound of solid stone, well rubbed with turmeric and vermillion. Particularly important, of course, was that she did not have any facial features—which meant that she did not have eyes. Quickly ending our inspection of the images, we asked for the myth which was the object of our quest. "Who is Masanikamma?" asked Mrs. George. Priest Malagaiah answered,

Plate 11. Piriyayattanamma, partly uncovered, showing featureless stone underneath
(turmeric and vermillion rubbed on)

Long ago all of these lands were funeral grounds, graveyards. A little **girl**, a
Brahman couple's daughter, used to play here in the cemetery with the other
children. All of the Brahman children used to come here and play. There
was also a brick oven here.
One day the little Brahman girl climbed into the hole in the brick oven. After
that she didn't go home.

"Why?" we asked. "Was it impossible for her to go that way?" "Wait," the
priest replied. "I'll tell you." He continued,

When the girl did not return home, her parents got worried and came looking for her. They called out her name.

"What was her name then?" He didn't know.

As the parents searched for their daughter, she called to them from within the brick house : "I am here." "Come on, let's go. Let's go home," they yelled to her.

"I'm going to be born as Masanikamma here. You go home. I'm not going to come with you," she replied. At that moment she became a statue.

Soon after that the *amma* appeared before King Virajasu in a dream and told him, "I am Masanikamma. I have been reborn in that place. You must have a house-temple built for me there."

"I will be your house god." she offered, "and I will protect you." So the king built this temple, and ever since then she's been famous."

Priest Malagaiah had finished the story, but we had more questions to ask him. We pressed on, "Didn't they give her a funeral when she died?" Little suspecting that he was on the verge of commenting on the funerary quality of Bandipur rituals for her, he said, "She didn't die. She was reborn alive. So there were no funeral ceremonies for her." I decided at that point that the Oil-Presser ritual compensated for that omission, since it bears some resemblance to a funeral.

Happy with the way that one had come out, we tried another hypothesis with less success. "They say that there is a lot of anger in the spirit of this *amma*, right?" we asked. "Yes," he confirmed. "What is the reason for that?" our line reached further. "Well," he replied, "if anyone goes against her, then she gets angry." I probed, coaching Mrs. George : "Is there anything he thinks, maybe something in her life, that made her especially angry?" "Did she run into any difficulty in her lifetime?" Mrs. George translated, addressing the priest. "No," he disappointed us, "none at all."

But he then added a further incident from the story which we found somewhat consoling, since it elaborated on a familiar theme—the separation of girls from their natal families:

When her mother came to call her out of the brick oven, she said, "I am not your daughter. It was just to be reborn as Masanikamma in this place that I was born of your womb [lit. 'stomach']. So leave off your affection for me. Forget me. I am no longer your daughter."

The remaining hour was filled with tales of the goddess's adventures in the region : intrigues with the patron deity of her king's rival, and an argument with her sister (whose temple is nearby)—also a period spent as a demon (*raksasa*). These are of folkloric interest and are included in Appendix B. Malagaiah attributes her well known thirst for blood and meat to the fact that she was a demon for a while.

We asked him how old the child had been when she became a goddess. "Five years old," he responded with the traditionally auspicious feminine number.

Our final question was. "Do you give *ammanavara* (*y*)*ecca* to this goddess?",

"People bring (y)ecca to her," he replied. "But we don't ordinarily give the red oleander to her ourselves. We give her the white oleander most of the time." That concluded the interview.

Sri Malagaiah runs a quiet temple. The offerings are mild and civil, considering that the goddess was once a demon. He does not even indulge in spirit possession, though his grandfather used to get the spirit of the goddess upon him. He gives white flowers to the *amma*, and he covers the dark, featureless face of the Soot-Black Lady with a carved silver mask.[13]

The priest's eldest son is in college and probably would not take over after him. As we left, we felt that the Piriyapattana temple center may have been in the process of graduating into obscurity. But in spite of all this, the myth that we heard that evening still has plenty of vigour.

The Soot-Black Lady's myth is one which disavows life and death. It faces the natural process of growth and degeneration and then abruptly turns away from it. The rejection of any transitional phase between human and spirit worlds is the most distinctive fact of this myth. It is reminiscent of neurotic 'pathological mourning' in the way that it denies the very existence of the mourning experience. The myth rejects pain rather than living with it and recovering from it. It is unlike some of the other myths here which make great symbolic use of pain or violence.

The structure of the myth is established in the first scene. A young, growing girl child is playing in a cemetery. She is actively jumping around the place as a symbol of the essence of life and growth. Meanwhile, we know, the black earth beneath her feet is filled with inert, dead, rotting corpses. These are the antithesis of her every quality. The fact that she is a Brahman girl further accentuates the contrast, for she has never had any contact with animal death, not even for food.

There is a minor agricultural theme here too. The lands of the neighbourhood were *not* planted with crops then, our priest implied. Rather they were 'planted' with dead human bodies, whose growth had ceased. The girl's youth is a reminder of the new plant shoots that would have been sprouting from the earth if it were not being used for a cemetery.[14]

The brick oven, actually a huge red pile of shaped bricks which has fires in its hollow spaces, is the place where she goes through her abrupt transition. There is a suggested parallel between those bricks and the girl. The red bricks were once soft, pliable clay; but they are now hardened and solid. The living girl had been born of a human womb and cared for in a natural home; but her soft body will now turn into a hard, stone statue. This transformation will take place inside a space that usually has hot coals in it.

Just as the Washerman family's festival has a peculiar method of roasting chickens whole, the Soot Black Lady also was 'roasted', i.e., abruptly transformed without the intervention of any further physical processing, when she turned into a statue.

The events which comprise the girl's mythic transition to goddess deserve close attention. They turn on the swift cleavage of the living child into two parts : subtle body (like spirit) and physical body. The narrative sequence proceeds as follows, with possible symbolic interpretations bracketed. To begin with, we know that:

(1) The living girl has left her house and parents to play;
(2) She enters into a cavity in the brick oven, never to return to her human home. [Substitute womb and house.]

Next we see the phase of separation—both her separation from her human family and her subtle body's separation from her physical body:

(3) There is an exchange of calls between her and her parents. [Only sound goes between them, no more physical contact.]
(4) She establishes the severity of the separation, and its abruptness with her words, "I am not your daughter," and "Forget me." [I.e., We are separate and, do not mourn for me.]
(5) She also says, "I am going to be reborn here as Masanikamma," further, doubled emphasis of her separateness. [This brick oven is my new mother's-womb; my new name is *masi* = 'soot-black'/'impurity' = separateness.]

Her new name has a double connotation. It not only means 'soot-black', but also means 'impurity'. Impurity, in turn, always indicates separateness. The name itself is an emphasis of the separation theme.

Having effected the separation from her human parents, she completes the separation of her physical body from her subtle body :

(6) She turns into a statue.

The new body is of stone, which means that it cannot decay as a biological body can. Nor does blood and feeling (*rasa*) flow through it. It is a physical permanence to the highest known degree.

Meanwhile her subtle body, which has already communicated a farewell to the human parents, continues to travel and make arrangements for a new home:

(7) The goddess appears in a king's dream, and offers to be his house god and protector. [Her subtle body enters the king's mind. She becomes the caretaker rather than being cared for herself any longer.]
(8) She is the king's house god, and is established in a temple of her own also. [Her new combination of subtle and physical bodies now lives in a temple home, and will never experience death. She has a protective contract with a human home, that of the king, but she does not live in it.]

The priest's final comment, that "ever since then she's been famous," completes the full turn away from natural, kin-based ties into power, conquest, and issues of glory. Subsequent comments on her career played out these political themes in various intrigues against the goddess of Mysore City, Chamundeswari.

Questions of fertility and growth are mostly ignored in this version of the myth. But they are introduced with negative emphasis in the first part of it. That is, the cemetery setting is so non-agricultural that it makes crop cultivation conspicuous by its absence. The lost portions of this myth, which explain the appearance of the sisters whose names reflect growth and cooking processes, would work out this agriculture/ferlility theme. The best evidence of the existence of the lost portion is in those other goddesses' names, which are, incidentally, very funny, even in Kannada: Fruit and Betel Lady, Stove Soot Lady, Dry Land Crop Lady, and Garden Land Lady.

The ritual that Mrs. S. and Mr. G. do for this goddess is best seen as a realistic appraisal of one aspect of the myth. The person(s) who invented this ritual struck at the heart of the myth and reversed the disavowal process which is basic to its structure. The myth is caught in a paralysing trap which some neurotics invent for themselves: the need to mourn a loss combined with the intense wish to deny it. While the myth, like the neurosis, tries to cope with death, decay, and loss by ignoring them, the ritual faces them directly. The ritual provides the funeral that is missing in the myth.[15]

Both the Farmers' Mastiamma ritual and the Oil Presser family's festival for Piriyapattanadamma, which follows, are designed to soothe a troubled *amma* spirit. They do so with a series of transitional actions. Whatever their original relationship with the goddess was supposed to be, the inventors of these rituals clearly felt obligated to appease anger. Mrs. S. tells me, for example, that this is the meaning of pouring water in the mouth of either a person or a sacrificial animal as it dies : "There should be no bad feelings between you and us," as she translates the act into words.

The bad feelings of Piriyapattanadamma have a striking effect on Mrs. S.'s home. Before they started up the ritual again, too many cattle were dying.[16] She summed up the problem in a highly symbolic (and familiar) image : "If we do not worship this goddess, our cows' milk won't come. Only bloood comes."

FESTIVAL RITUALS

Like most *amma* rituals, the Piriyapattanadamma ceremony takes place out-of-doors. The Washerman group worships, cooks, and eats in the Bandipur mango grove, setting their icon beneath a country fig tree. Mrs. S. and her husband might do the ritual beneath any tree except the toddy palm.[17] Each group cleans the site of its ritual with cow dung, a necessary purificatory action before any ritual. But whereas on auspicious occasions the next step would be to put *rangolli*, the pleasing white powder line designs, this step is omitted by Mrs. S.[18]

Even before the images have been placed, the omission of *rangolli* introduces a funerary-style motif into this ritual. For at the time of death pollution also, *rangolli* is omitted from the daily house-cleaning and ritual routine.[19]

Unlike some other family rituals, this one does not require a high degree of family purity. Only the principal performer(s) (platform-builder, cook, and giver of offerings) must bathe before doing this ritual. And there is no requirement for anyone to fast. Mrs. S. mentioned that the woman or man who is to cook the food must, of course, bathe before cooking. Others may bathe or not, as they like.

The next stage of the ritual, after purification of the site, is the construction of the image to receive worship. The Washerman and Oil-Presser groups do this differently, as is to be expected. Washerman group sets a group of six small stones (collectively named 'Eating Goddess', Utadamma) around the larger single one they call Piriyapattanadamma (Plate 12).

Plate 12. Offering to Piriyapattanadamma, meals (covered) and other items, including oleander flowers and leaves, Bandipur Washerman family

Features of the Washerman ritual show that it has a more direct, reflective relationship to the Piriyapattana temple than the Oil-Presser ritual does. For example, the arrangement of six sister-stones around the central goddess stone is a feature directly parallel to the images in the main temple. A second feature, the method of roasting sacrificial chickens whole and uneviscerated, has an abstruse but interesting parallel with the myth, as I have mentioned above. The Oil-Presser group constructs a paired arrangement of two platforms. In Mrs. S.'s ritual, a man is required to set up the two platforms; a woman cannot do it.[20] He gets some mud out of the fields, with which he will construct them. The mud must be black in colour. He will then set eight clean, white-coloured stones taken out of the river on top of these platforms. Mrs. S. emphasises that there must be an 'even number' of stones taken out of the river. The two platforms are of a standard type, called *gaddige*, which appear in many non-Brahman rituals, both auspicious and inauspicious. In this case, they are about 9 inches long, 3 inches wide, and 2 inches in height. One is called 'north', and the other, 'south'. In this ritual, an inauspicious connotation is conveyed by the black colour of the required mud. The 'north-south' orientation is a borrowed funerary motif here, a body being customarily buried with its head at the north and its feet at the south.

The eight white stones are then lined up on the two platforms, five on one and three on the other, to produce a setting of the type in Figure 6. The reader should note that an even number has been transformed or subdivided into two more dynamic odd numbers. The stones are all about the same size, perhaps 1½ inches across.

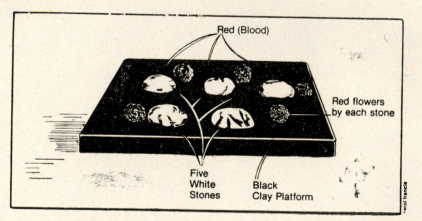

Figure 6. Mrs. S.'s offering to Piriyapattanadamma

After constructing the arrangement of stones, they set the ornamental 'woman's ritual gift' next to each of the eight stones, together with a red oleander flower (and the Washerman group's 7 stones received an identical decoration, with the addition of oleander leaves).

The next phase is what Mrs. S. calls '*puja*' :

(1) one broken coconut is offered to each platform together with a pair of
     bananas; and betel-areca is set in pairs or sets of four ("must be an even
     number") at both ends;
(2) incense-rotation is performed; and
(3) camphor-burning concludes the '*puja*'.

After the *puja* comes the blood offering. Both groups sacrifice chickens,
identifying them customarily by the total number of animal legs involved. In
the Oil-Presser rite, 'four legs' (two chickens); and in the Washerman rite,
'eight legs' (four chickens) are dedicated to the hungry goddess. The Oil-Presser
group does its sacrifice near the platforms, using the method of half-cutting
the neck, leaving the head partly on the body.[21] One holds the chicken, while
another uses a scythe (*kudlu*) to cut its neck. As it is slowly dying, they sprinkle the chicken's blood on the stones and platform to which it has been sacri-
ficed. They then remove each head completely and set it between the two platforms, facing it back-to-back with the head of the other chicken. When the
head is set down, they say, its mouth will be slightly open. They pour some
water into its mouth.

The *puja* and sacrifice require even numbers and the number 1 at key points.
Both families, Oil-Presser and Washerman, use an even number of chickens—
one uses 2, and the other 4. (Counting the legs of sacrificial animals, as villagers always do, makes the numbers into 4 and 8, respectively.) The number 4
dominates here, as itself and as its doubled product, presenting us with a
funerary association. The element of four is repeated when Mrs. S. and her
husband offer four betel-arecas, one each at the ends of their two 'north' and
'south' platforms. Offering betel in this way is also reminiscent of local funeral
ritual. Most groups of this region have a custom of putting a combination of
small items—one betel-areca, one coin (and, for Brahmans, one *dharbe* grass)
at each of the four corners of a corpse to be cremated or buried. The corners
where they set these things are identified in terms of the cardinal points, and
they correspond precisely to the points at which the Oil Presser family sets its
solitary betel-areca. They are 'east (the right), north (the head), west (the left),
and south (the feet).'[22]

After they make their sacrifices, worshippers cook, offer, and eat meals. The
Washerman group prepares two separate pots of rice (one for the main goddess,
Piriyapattanadamma, and the other for her six companions). The Oil-Pressers
prepare a single meal.

The Washerman family cook their four sacrificial chickens in a bizarre fashion.
They roast them whole, only later eviscerating them and cutting them up for
the meal. I have never seen this done before in the village, where meat is
thoroughly processed before cooking and usually boiled in water for a long
time, but animals are never roasted whole.

Roasting is, of course, the simplest, most direct method of transforming food from raw to cooked. In this context its symbolic value is in its directness, its lack of any intermediary processing acts (such as evisceration, cutting-up, or boiling would have been). At first I was tempted to interpret this ritual cooking act as similar to cremation of the dead. But the non-Brahmans do not cremate their dead; they bury them. When I finally learned the myth of Piriyapattanad-amma, I decided that the roasting of chickens in this peculiar manner was a direct allusion to the myth, as I mentioned above. Like the myth, the Washer-man family's ritual avoids transitions.

After cooking boiled rice and chickens, the Washerman family offers them on two plantain leaves to their set of goddesses. They then return home to eat their offered ((y)ede) meal themselves. They hope that their 'house god', will have been pleased with their ritual, and that she will bless them. Not so the Oil Pressers. She is not their 'house god', and they finish a long series of other, concluding rituals before they eat inside their house again.

Mrs. S. and Mr. G. never use a plantain leaf when they offer meals to Piriyapattanadamma. They place their rice and chicken offering on an ordinary leaf-plate, the type used in daily meals. (I assume that a plantain leaf would not fit in with the overall 'inauspicious' tone of their ritual for the ghostly goddess.) They set a single leaf-plate, piled with food, in between the two plat-forms.

The way in which the Oil-Pressers set out their offered meal has at least two possible, non-contradictory meanings. First, it is a solitary plate of food, a number 1, an isolation of the spirit. They also offer a plate of food to a recently-deceased relative on the eleventh day after his or her death, placing it over the center of the grave ('over the body'), before they take their own meals at home. On that eleventh day the women of the house will have cooked 'chicken and meat (whatever was the favourite of the dead person),' together with four eggs, two for the house and two for the grave. Though there are no eggs in the Piriyapattanadamma ritual meal, the parallel to the funeral meals is quite clear by now.

The second possible meaning of the Oil-Presser family's food offering is in its unification of opposites, a common symbol of 'totality'. They have killed two chickens for this occasion, one male and one female, but they have cooked them together in one pot. The use of a sexual distinction here seems, therefore, less a reference to sexuality as intercourse than to the unification of sexual opposites into a whole family. (In the Cobra Festival as done by A.K.s, a sexuality distinction is also used in ritual symbolism. But there we shall see it deployed in reference to sexual differences and sexual intercourse per se.)

After they have cooked, offered, and eaten food at the outdoor ritual site, Mr. G. and Mrs. S. conduct a final ritual for the stove on which the food has been cooked. The little stove is made up of three large stones in the shape of an open-ended rectangle. Unlike the stoves set on kitchen floors of village houses, this one is crude. It lacks the familiar cover of polished mud plaster, perhaps a reminder of its (hopefully) remote and ephemeral status vis-a-vis the family. (Cf. outdoor stoves discussed in Chapter 8 in connection with Cobra Festival rituals.)

They remove the red-hot coals from the stove, and then pour an odd number of vessels of water into it.[23] They look to be sure that the water flows a good two or three full arm-spans outward along the ground in front of the little stove. This would amount to at least twelve or fifteen feet.

After the water-flow has finished, they set an eating-leaf inside the little stove and arrange a group of offerings on it. The offerings are all numbered in 1—a single piece of coconut, a single banana, a single betel-areca, and a small portion of the offered rice and chicken curry. Without further distributing these offerings to the stove, the Oil-Presser family returns home.[24]

This concluding ritual is reminiscent of a funeral ritual which also requires that water should flow. Either right after interment or on the fifth day after death, the chief mourner stands at the burial site, holding a clay pot full of water. Someone else hits it with a scythe, causing the water to flow out. The funerary rite has further possible elaborations which can include the extinguishing of a red-hot firebrand in the spilled water.[25] The parallels between life flowing away and water flowing away—between the extinguishing of hot coals and the pacification of the soul—are extremely clear in the funerary rite. And in my view, there is an allusion to these same ritual images in the Piriyapattanadamma stove ritual. For, of course, the stove had held red-hot coals just as a ghost might have held angrily onto its worldly cares. And removing those coals from the stove was a sort of ritual removal of anger, backed up by a ritual encouragement to the soul to move onward away from life concerns.

Whether it was originally supposed to be for a separate stove spirit or for Piriyapattanadamma herself, the stove ritual sums up the meanings of this festival quite well.

RITUAL STRUCTURE

The ritual for Piriyapattanadamma is a re-enactment of a transition from angry, new death into peaceful death. As with funerals themselves, funerary motifs are appropriately used in this festival ritual. The basic oppositions of the ritual are in colours (black and white), in numbers (even and odd), and in the stages of processing from raw (blood, meat) to cooked (meat, meat and white rice). An additional opposition, in the stove ritual at the conclusion, is between the water contained in the vessel and the water flowing through the open stove. These oppositions and ritual transformations can be diagramatically expressed as in Table 30.

Table 30—Structure of Piriyapattanadamma Festival Ritual

Life and Social Status	—(mediation)—	Deceased State (recent death, burial)	—(mediation)—	Peaceful Death
		Setting up platforms on north-south axis. Even numbers : 2 platforms; 8 stones.		White stones for platforms.
			—Odd #'s : 5 + 3 arrangement of stones.—	
'Women's ritual gift' as decoration.	—red flower—	Even number, 4 : betel-areca sets; bananas. One coconut (#1).		
Living chickens, male-female. Water into mouths of dying chickens.	—prolonged death of chickens— —chicken blood, 'hot'—		—Squirting blood onto white stones (red + white)—	Chicken heads (mind, spirituality?) set facing platforms.
		Washerman : two whole chickens, uneviscerated,—	—Cooking—	
			—are roasted directly over fire [quick transition to cooked state]—	
Raw rice.		Two pots of rice.	—boiled—	Cooked. Cooked.

Raw rice	Oil-Presser : —single pot for both chickens—	—boiling—	Cooked chickens. Cooked rice.
Living people		—offer a meal—	Goodess eats cooked food.
Vessel with water in it; Stove with coals in it.	—coals removed from stove— —water poured.	Oil-Pressers : —people eat food outdoors.	
—water runs out of front of stove—	onto stove, empty of coals.		Long stream of water runs forward from stove.
—People do not eat stove's food (separation)—	Placing one — each of items for stove.		No exchange between life and death of physical food.
Meal at home with family. (Washermen and Oil-Pressers alike)			

THE ANCESTRAL OFFERING TO MASTIAMMA

One Farmer lineage of Bandipur performs its Mastiamma ritual during the Festival of Lights, *Dipavali*. One of the most important Hindu holidays, the Festival of Lights begins at midnight in the new moon time which starts the lunar month of Kartika. In the darkness there are two community bonfires, fueled only with stolen firewood. Village men—non-Brahmans at one fire, and A.K.s at another—spend the night sending boys to steal firewood from their rivals, drinking a bit, and tending the fires.

The early morning hours are taken up with numerous festival activities. Among the non-Brahmans, household members bathe by turns. And on each of the decorated Bandipur thresholds two or four bright orange-coloured marigolds are set out in honour of the goddess of wealth, a special deity on this day. The m⋯ e occupied with carrying mixtures of bonfire ash in small clay pots to thei⋯ spective fields, leaving powdery ash designs along their paths as they call softly, "*Ku, Ku, Ku.*" General fasting is for the sake of 'purity'. So families eat only special 'snacks', *dose* rice-flour pancakes or steamed *iddali* cakes, in the morning. During the afternoon, young sons bathe family cows and bullocks and decorate their horns with red clay and white lime powder, blessing them with a touch of turmeric and vermillion, and garlanding them with branches of the milky-sapped *motuli* plant.[26] Daughters perform a ritual offering to the goddess of the compost heap in family house gardens, as their fathers do an elaborate version of the same ritual for a built-up platform in their ash-marked fields.

Grateful for their rented share in the agricultural life, most A. K.s have convinced their Brahman landlords and employers to share in the festivities of the day. So they busily perform the ash-marking and cattle decoration for others' properties, while the Brahmans quietly amuse themselves in pondering this imitation of what was known to be mainly a Farmer caste custom.

For a few families of Bandipur and Chinnapura, however, the Festival of Lights is also an occasion to perform the annual ancestral offering. In such houses stringent bathing and fasting rules are observed, and the special offerings are prepared. A full lunar month later than the more popular Mahalaya New Moon Festival, this ancestral new moon day is observed in its stead either for reasons of expense or by caste or family custom.

Early in the afternoon our group of Farmer households gathers at a square-shaped granite shrine at the boundary between Bandipur Village and a neighbouring hamlet. Inside the Mastiamma shrine is a simple stone pair, male and female images, holding hands.

Men, women, and children alike from each of the Farmer houses—virtually all are present. Each house has brought a basket of food which they have prepared as an intentional abbreviation of the ancestral formula. The menu includes white rice, red millet balls, chicken curry, a seasoned vegetable dish (*palya*) made with a mixture of the bitter *Momordica*; bottle gourd; and egg-plant.[27] With these things are included the snacks and some butter; and the sweet, milky *payasa* found on all auspicious 'festival' menus (including the ancestral feast).

We arrive late, at 4 p.m. or so, because a cow has died in Swamy Gauda's house that day. Our friends' desultory preparations have been made in an atmosphere of overwhelming sorrow. Invited by the people of that house, we too are sharing the somber mood, and have stayed at home with them while the others have gathered at the shrine.

We first see that a sister-brother pair who live in their natal home, neighbours and relatives of Swamy Gauda's house, are performing the Mastiamma ritual. They have cleaned the floor of the shrine and decorated it with line drawings, *rangolli*. A sari and a towel for the goddess and her consort and two plantain leaves of food are set in front of the husband-wife god pair. The brother, a grown man without the ability to speak, and his sister, a widow residing in her natal home, lead some nieces and nephews (the children of another, divorced sister) in the incense-rotation, each one standing to do it individually. The incense-rotation is performed four times as each person stands and turns: first facing the shrine, secondly facing to the west, then to the east, and finally again to the shrine. After they conclude with the speechless brother's camphor-burning, this group gathers together their food and clothing and puts them back into the basket which they had brought. We are curious to see a widow doing *puja*. and find out that this goddess does accept widows' offerings. Their old father, mother, and younger sisters and brothers then prepare the shrine and make a simpler offering of their own, omitting the presentation of clothing.

After that house has finished, Swamy Gauda comes forward to do the preparations and begin his household's offering. Adopted into this house as a child when his widowed mother was outcasted many years ago, he had married one of their daughters and joined the lineage of his wife. Although his widowed mother-in-law lives with them, she has not come here today because of her grief at the loss of their cow. Pleased at being photographed and studied, he is especially careful as he sweeps the shrine and sets out a plantain leaf with a full complement of ancestral offerings on it; an arrangement of peeled cucumber slices placed vertically in a row along the wall of the shrine forms the background for the setting. On the plantain leaf he lays the feminine palm-leaf earrings, a packet of vermillion, a comb with vermillion on it, two betel-arecas, some white lime and the resinous *kacu* which women chew with their betel-areca, a bit of tobacco, some sacred basil leaves, and some marigolds and yellow chrysanthemums. He then sets out clothing for each of the holy couple: one sari and one pair of short pants. To these things he adds a set of offerings from his house on a second plantain leaf: another set of clothing, vermillion and betel-areca things, two bunches of plantains, and more cucumber slices

around the back of the shrine. Swamy Gauda decorates the goddess and consort images with turmeric and vermillion and then breaks a coconut into two
halves, setting one half before each image. A second coconut, however, goes
into the feminine side of the piled offerings after being broken. After doing the
four-fold incense rotation, he puts two baskets of food near the Mastiamma-
consort pair: one basket had come from his house, and one from his kinsman's.
After that, another man performs the incense rotation, followed by his own
little daughter. Swamy Gauda concludes this phase of the offering with a burn-
ing-camphor presentation and a deep bow on his knees.

Then come the children of the house, the immature ones, these being followed by Swamy Gauda's wife and their eighteen year-old daughter, Chinnamma
(who was my local Kannada-teacher and guide). These are followed by the
women of another household.

Thus each of the twelve related Farmer houses made their offerings. When
they had all finished, they returned to their separate homes. After some general
visiting to exchange 'snacks'—now sanctified as *prasad* after having been offered, they ate their separate offered meals (called (*y*)*ede* or 'sanctified-offered
meal') as distinct household units. Swamy Gauda invited his wife's sister's
husband to share their meal, and gave some food to two Moslem houses—
neighbours with whom they are friendly.

Since the ancestral style of this festival ritual is so clear, we needed to find
out as much as we could about the ancestor(s) who had become Mastiamma.
Our search produced some interesting stories. Gauramma, an old woman of the
Fisherman *jati*, told us her family's myth[28]:

> A hunter once killed a pregnant woman. After she died, she used to come
> into every house, giving fever to people and cows. All of them would die
> suddenly. She also used to cause people and things to fly from one room to
> another. Someone made a vow to her, promising to 'put rice' [as for
> ancestor] every year. So the trouble stopped.

This story is interesting because Mastiamma is said to be the ghost of a woman
who died in pregnancy. That is, she had had some important unfinished business
at the time of her death. But it was not from a Farmer *jati* informant.

Finally, we were able to hear stories about Mastiamma from the Farmers.
We heard a few different ones, all short. The one from Swamy Gauda's group
said that she had been a member of the Hunter *jati* herself originally, and that
she had converted to their, Farmer, *jati*. The story mentioned that she had been
kidnapped, but was unclear about the details of her death or exactly who had
kidnapped her. Others of neighbouring houses were more complete and more
interesting. One from Bandipur came through a local teacher who befriended
us. He was a native of the village, and of the Farmer *jati*, though not in Swamy
Gauda's family circle.

The story he told us went as follows:

In our *vamsa* [largest possible patrilineal group] there was once a woman named Chennajjamma. She was the eldest daughter-in-law. She was pregnant. Her husband did something wrong, and was taken to court. She became frightened about him and panicked. Before they could settle the case, she jumped into the village tank and drowned.

When she was jumping, a man named Iranna—a servant (*pyun*) had been watching. He had jumped into the tank also, in hopes of saving her life. But he had failed and was also drowned.

Later on Chennajjamma was reborn as a goddes on the same spot where she had jumped into the tank. And Iranna became a god. There is a Mastiamma stone at that spot.

We have to make offerings to that stone on special occasions. So when we want to make a marriage, we set all the clothing and jewels there.[29] You see, she was a daughter-in-law of our house.

Or if a calf is born into the house, we give the first milk there, pouring it over the stone. If we don't do that, the cow will produce blood instead of milk.

The possibility of cow's milk running as blood was becoming a familiar theme in local ghost stories. This was the second time we had heard it in one day. Mrs. S. had given the same explanation for her Piriyapattanadamma festival just that afternoon in her house, across the street.

Our teacher friend also told another Mastiamma story, about a girl of his *jati* who was 'taken by' [married to] a man of a different *jati*. Several years later some problems came to the 'house' of the girl : cattle diseases and other problems. The family went to a *sastra*-teller to get a diagnosis. He traced the misfortune back to this girl and advised them to make a figure of a boy and girl together, a joined pair of small dolls. They should do *puja* for it, he said.[30] (It could be of any material they could afford, whether gold, silver, copper, or stone.) In his home there is a gold marital pendant (*tali*) with a picture of the mixed-caste pair, holding hands, on it. In 1977 he told us that each year, when they do their ancestor ceremony, they still set the pendant near the ritual vessel and make the offering of clothes and other items to the pair along with the other ancestors.

A final Mastiamma report showed that the goddess may sometimes be the ghost of a woman cursing a family which is not her own. In a hamlet of the region we heard about an old Farmer who had constructed a Mastiamma shrine near the river. The ghost who inhabited the shrine was that of an A.K. woman whom he had murdered some years earlier. He had caught her stealing some of his crop and killed her. As a result of this sin, he thought, all of his four wives had proved barren. He was trying fervently to remedy the situation with an annual ritual at the scene of his crime. In that ritual he offered and ate a beef meal to the Mastiamma spirit. This meat would ordinarily be taboo to him, but he knew that A.K.s must offer beef to their ancestors. Though the lady had cursed a family that was not her own, her murderer tried to 'solve' the problem by emulating acts that only her own kin should have performed for her spirit.

Myths of this goddess are myths of frustration: a woman dead before bringing a pregnancy to term; a woman who has been murdered before her time of natural death: a suicide; a woman who married out of caste. But rather than symbolically completing her unfinished task with a ritual in the style of birth or naming ceremonies, Swamy Gauda's family somehow settled on an ancestor-propitiation rite instead. Rather than symbolically avenging her murder in a violent ritual, the old Farmer soothes her with the ritual for pacific souls. The culturally guided 'reasoning' of the inventors and perpetuators of this tradition is relatively clear: some woman of a lineage—perhaps a married-in wife, or more likely a married-out sister (see below)—was murdered or died in pregnancy. (This must have happened at least three generations ago, in Swamy Gauda's family, judging from the genealogical ties among the Farmer households which perform the ritual for Mastiamma.) The people of the lineage fell on hard times, perhaps finding themselves without sons and/or cattle. Their problems were attributed, after the fact, to the anger of the deceased woman in much the same way that Mrs. S. decided that her two cows died because she had neglected Piriyapattanadamma. So the forefathers of the lineal group instituted this ritual.

As to its form as an ancestral rite, it is culturally logical in view of (a) ritual neglect of some women spirits, and (b) the common belief that neglected ancestors will cause hardship, disease, and infertility to their descendants.

Uses of cooked rice to appease restless spirits, even in ancestral style, may not be unique to this region. In her review of Hindu plant lore, Shakti M. Gupta relates pan-Indian concepts of fertility and rice offering to 'demons': "Rice is believed to scare demons," she states, "particularly those that check the fertility of the union (1971 : 201)." Oscar Lewis also notes that a rice offering can be used to avert the various threats of 'demons'. Citing the *Arthasastra* of Kautilya (ca. 300 B.C.), he quotes (1958 : 201) : "In all kinds of dangers from demons, the incantation 'we offer thee cooked rice' shall be performed." This general view has transformed into an ancestor-style ritual in local traditions. (Plate 13.)

While it expresses a common past tragedy and a common present danger, the Mastiamma festival ritual of Bandipur also makes statements about the organisation of the group which performs it. The group is actor and symbol. Its parts and their relationships are features of the ritual as much as a *puja* itself is. The kinship dimension is defined in the physical movements, gatherings, and exchanges characteristic of the festival event. It is also defined in the cook-

Plate 13. Ancestor style *puja* arrangement, Bandipur Mastiamma shrine

ing, sharing, and eating of the two categories of foods: 'snacks' and 'meals'.

Beginning at home, the family cooks foods to be used in the *puja*. In 1966 there were twelve or possibly thirteen families involved in the ritual.[31] Then, as all the families gather at their common shrine, the larger patrilineal group takes form out-of-doors. This larger group calls itself either 'brothers' (*annatammandru*) or 'agnatic ritual and inheritance group' (*dayadi*). But it is also a local branch of the larger *vamsa*, and it is the *vamsa* that is the symbolic group harmed by the curses of such spirits as Mastiamma. Thus the gathering of twelve houses of 'brothers' serves as a social-symbolic shorthand expression for the larger spiritual unity of the endangered patrilineal family. The role of the separate families (birth groups) in providing offerings is parallel to their role of providing members and good fortune to the larger group.

The fact that this group gathers out-of-doors is in itself a telling fact. On ordinary ancestor-worship occasions, the same group gathers inside homes and shares common meals. The Mastiamma festival ritual keeps the dangerous goddess at a safe distance by worshipping her out-of-doors and apart from the other ancestors.[32] The location of the ritual is one of its most important structural features.

The member families also keep each other at a distance in this ritual, perhaps another cautious gesture. As a group they are as close as any non-Brahman patrilineage in this region. They not only share the common birth and death pollution experiences and witness each other's rites of passage, but they also manage a common temple for their common 'house god' (who is Laksmi). Representatives of the different houses rotate the responsibility of the temple priesthood. They are also a loosely-defined political interest group in local factional conflict. (In Hanchett (1970), these are discussed as the Das Vokkaligas of the 'Fort Area'.) Though they are a unified group by any definition, their unity is only sketchily expressed in their Mastiamma festival, for they do not take meals together on this occasion. They visit each other and share 'snack' foods which have been offered. But they take their full 'meals' in their separate homes, sharing them only with neighbours and 'close exchange relations' (nentru). ('Meals' indicates the presence of boiled rice, as I have mentioned previously on page 102). Not to share 'meals' is not to express the strength of their unity. This non-expression is as symbolically important as is the positive expression of patrilineal unity on other occasions. Non-expression of unity here can only mean one thing: danger. This danger is unique to the lineal group, and not shared by those who finally share the 'meals' of each house. Not being in danger themselves, perhaps these outsider guests represent safety.[33]

The member houses of the lineage do share 'snacks'. This fact must not be ignored. After returning home from the puja, the members of each house begin a round of visits to the other houses. They take 'snacks' from those other households and eat them. It is only after this round of visiting that each house eats its own 'meals'. The eating of each other's 'snacks' is a gesture of support, but not of intense unity. Translated into a social message, it means that each family (birth group) is on its own in defending itself against Mastiamma's curse, but that it has the sympathy of those who are similarly vulnerable.

Facts of the festival and myth connect the social and cultural features of Mastiamma belief and practice into a system which clarifies both local concepts of women's position, particularly with the descent-group standing of women of ambiguous personal and cultural-social careers—i.e. dead in the first pregnancy, murdered, dead without sons, and so on. These ammas emit the angry power of thwarted women.

Being an ancestral ritual, the Mastiamma puja also sheds light on non-conscious cultural notions of ambiguous feminine spirits and their powers to affect the fates of whole lineages. Moreover, the pacifying, soothing ancestral rite suggests that Mastiamma's presumed problems (and their corresponding solutions) are of a very different nature than, say, those of Piriyapattanadamma who receives a funerary-style ritual, or of others (such as Bandamma) who receive magical-manipulative offerings.

Mastiama's rituals describe her as the least 'ghost-like' of the ammas. While they usually take blood sacrifice directly before their meat meal, she takes only cooked meat. Nonetheless, the rituals and myths agree that some thing is wrong with 'her'. Actually as the collective spirit of pregnant-dead or other such unfortunate females, 'she' seems to be endowed with the power to inflict disaster on a whole line, which rallies to protect itself by giving her a personalised ancestral offering apart from other ancestors, and thus using 'her' to represent the tragic cases in their own family history.

Piriyapattanadamma, on the other hand, appears ritually as a feminine spirit to whom a funerary-style offering is more appropriate. The destructive power of this restless spirit is less widely respected in Hassan District than it is in her home town; and the one family for which we have detailed information does not link her explicitly to progeny and continuity of the lineage. Rituals for this soul replicate elements of funerary rites, which are consciously intended to move the spirit through the physical and spiritual transitions into peaceful ancestral status. Like the Mastiamma rituals, those for Piriyapattanadamma fill in a lack in her myth—the need for a funeral, in this case. But unlike the Mastiamma complex, both myths and rituals for Piriyapattanadamma focus on abstract, philosophical dilemmas of the soul more than on urgent questions of family survival. That is not to say that the only expressed concern of Mrs. S. does not have great indirect, symbolic implications; it does. If the cow's milk runs as blood, the family—by analogy—is not doing well at all.

DISCUSSION

Both the presence of 'the woman's ritual gift' and the myths and rituals presented above define the violent *ammas* in a new light, qualifying a scholarly view presented by Babb. In his (1970b), he argues from a view that the violent female Hindu deity is presented chiefly without consort, and her benign counterpart (Gauri) with consort. Therefore, he concludes, there is a general Hindu view that the marital union serves to control the potentially dangerous power inherent in the female: or, conversely, that the lack of a consort is the violent goddess's biggest problem. But of the spirits discussed here, this generalisation applies only to *Mari* (the murderer of her husband), and not to the others, who receive 'the woman's ritual gift' and who may be represented with consort (as Mastiamma is), angry though they are.

As I see it, the concept of the violent goddess is more complex than Babb has presented it. In the first place, there is a cultural notion of feminine chastity (discipline) as a source of power. I have discussed this at length above, in connection with festivals for benign goddesses. Secondly, the comments and stories of these *ammas* and other feminine ghosts demonstrate a belief that frustration and incompleteness in life pursuits produce great anger, directing women's stored-up power to destructive end. To focus on the presence or absence of male consort is to detract from the view of goddess (or woman) as disciplined, angry, and capable of violence—very much the mistress of her own feelings and actions, even if not the creator of her own fate.

Unlike the Gauri or Prati festivals' emphasis on married women and ties among mother, daughters, and sisters—albeit to thc ends of preserving husbands' lives—the emphasis of these two *amma* festivals is on the virilocal home and the patrilineage. Officiants of these *amma* rituals, though sometimes female, are representatives of patrilineal interests and are expressing concern and fear in the presence of some dead women's frustration and anger. (The *amma* ritual format covers even Piriyapattanadamma with this concern, merging her with other, local restless feminine spirits, even though she has already graduated to another, supposedly more peaceful state in her main temple.) Gauri and Prati festivals stress the positive values of chaste women's strength. *Amma* festivals dwell on the destructive powers of women thwarted. It is the birth group and the lineage that suffer from their curses and angry stares. And the kin groups enact the tragedy and waste that they represent by blood sacrifices and mythic transformations. They seem to be lamenting that the otherwise creative and constructive energies of some women have been drained out of the family line rather than contributing to its development.

Aside from the fact that the two festivals of this chapter are dedicated to malevolent goddesses, their symbolism is concerned with the boundary between life and death and with related cosmic tensions. In the Piriyapattanadamma myth, the boundary is 'denied' as a little girl instantaneoulsy changes into a goddess. In the Oil-Pressers' ritual for this goddess, the missing transitions are provided through manipulations of funerary oppositions, such as north-south, and funerary symbols, black mud mounds and the numbers 1 and 4. The Farmer lineage's Mastiamma Festival picks up on coneepts of after-life by providing an abbreviated ancestor ceremony for a restless and troublesome predecessor.

A major symbolic issue in both of these festivals is meeting the challenge of stagnation, frustration, or immobility—of which physical death is the most vivid example—with activity, movement, or process. This is the indigenous contrast usually spoken of as 'inauspicious-auspicious' but its ramifications are extended beyond the usual death-life explanations in these two festivals, much more so than in festivals for benign goddesses. Ritual symbols overlay cosmic or spiritual tensions between darkness and light with immediate personal and family problems of waste (white milk→red blood; or white rice→red blood), destruction (black), or lack of growth (even numbers) vs. integrity or 'purity' (white) and growth (odd numbers). Auspicious or inauspicious states are characteristic of whole families in this context.

NOTES

1. One Farmer of Bandipur, a teacher in a local school, hesitated to tell us about a family ghost named Alavaradamma during an interview in 1977. "You'll be too frightened", he warned my interpreter and me, "if I do." After we urged him, he did tell us a short myth

about the *amma*, which he called a *caudi*. The myth did not seem very frightening to us, so we asked him why he thought it was. He said that it showed that there are still spirits like this at work, and they can do destructive work.

2. Villagers say that ghosts get *miridu* 'strength' from blood, and that the rice-blood mixture is "food for ghosts and demons (*raksasa*)."

3. Concern with the power of eyes is old and widespread in Hinduism. It is important in both temple iconography and folk religion. Except for a universal fear of the evil eye, however, it takes different forms in the folk religion of different regions of south Asia. Kali, the most important goddess of Bengal and other regions, is represented with bright eyes shining on a black face. Sitala, important in northern, eastern, and western regions as a smallpox goddess, is covered with a disease-like rash of eyes.

4. Our research in Bandipur and Chinnapura uncovered several stories about the wrath of female ghosts. Unfortunately, it is not possible to include them here.

5. Bandipur Muslims smear the powder over the full bodies of dead children. Mrs. S., Mr. G's wife, includes this powder in her packet of feminine offerings to another *amma*—the offerings called *ammanavara* (*y*)*ecca*. The sweet smell and white colour of this powder relates symbolically to the good, peaceful transition which is the hoped-for outcome of funerals.

5. Among non-Brahmans and A.K.s, who bury their dead, women may be carried to their graves in coloured saris, but they are buried naked, covered by a white cloth as men are.

7. 'White' earrings are the only kind ever used for goddesses, according to Mrs. S. Human women use *biccole* too, but only ones dyed red. In the preceding chapter, however, Brahman women offered Gauri either red or white earrings; this indicates a Brahman—non-Brahman difference in ritual practice.

8. The only other context where I know the (*y*)*ecca* term to be used is in gifts to a newly menstruating girl from her mother's brother's house. These gifts are called (*y*)*ecca*, but the contents—mostly foods—are different. (See Regelson 1972.)

9. Maramma does not receive *ammanavara* (*y*)*ecca* as a rule, perhaps because she is a husband-killer in her myth. Some villagers still say, nonetheless, that they will give her this offering if they feel she has responded to a vow.

10. Neither the lunar month nor the phase of the moon is important to them. They say it must be done on a Thursday in summer, so that they can cook and eat out-of-doors.

11. Mrs. S., who directs her family's ritual, learned how to do it from her mother-in-law. It had been discontinued when the older woman died, but Mrs. S., who is the mother of thirteen children, decided to start doing it again several years ago when her cattle were ill and she lost two cows. Her own mother, who lives in another town, had consulted a soothsayer there about the problem. He told her that a female spirit was being neglected by the family and was angry. When she told Mrs. S. about this, Mrs. S. knew right away that the problem was due to neglect of the Piriyapattanadamma ritual.

12. He is a member of a non-vegetarian *jati* called Paravaradavaru, or Nayak. They had originally come from a place near the town of Srirangapattana. This goddess has a younger-sister goddess named *Kannambadiamma*, who is tended by a Brahman priest. A myth about these two goddesses is presented in Appendix B.

13. Silver is considered to be white in colour.

14. New plant shoots (*cigaru*) are a favourite ritual item, as discussed above in connection with the Prati Festival. The goddess's human age being five years further reinforces emphasis on her growth and the auspiciousness of her nature.

15. Cf. Laplanche and Pontalis (1973 : 261-263), who argue that 'disavowal' is better than 'denial' as a translation of Freud's original German term *verleugnung*.

16. Cattle do not participate in any way in this ritual. This is unusual, for in most rituals intended to fend off cattle disease the animals themselves receive a portion of the offerings. The cattle's symbolic role, therefore, is to represent family well-being in general.

17. When forced to speculate about this, informants guessed that the goddess might be offended by the smell of fermented sap, the toddy palm being a favourite source of country liquor. In view of the fact that one goal of the ritual is to symbolically prevent physical rotting, this guess had a sort of cultural logic to it.

18. I do not have corresponding information on the details of the Washerman ritual. From here on descriptions are of the Oil-Presser ritual unless specified otherwise.

19. *Rangolli* also disappears at the time of birth pollution. It is used at times of ancestor worship.

20. A person of either sex can do other aspects of the ritual.

21. This method of chicken sacrifice is called *harbali*. On a different occasion, an A. K. informant told me that it is not always necessary to offer cooked food, (*y*)*ede*, when giving this type of sacrifice. In this ritual, however, (*y*)*ede* is offered.

22. The source of this information is a Smith soothsayer, a relative of the Bandipur soothsayer. Though our data on Oil-Pressers' burial customs is limited, the numbers 4 and 1 have the same connotations of death and dying to Oil-Pressers as to others.

23. The number must be 3, 5, or 7, according to Mrs. S.

24. The Oil-Presser family, Mrs. S. and Mr. G., make a *puja* for their kitchen stove before they cook rice on the eleventh day after a death in the family. They also perform *puja* for the pot full of rice after they have cooked it. Although some residents of this region believe in a Stove Goddess and worship her, this Oil-Presser family does not mention such a spirit when performing these stove/pot *pujas*.

25. Specific data on this rite came from two Farmer informants (K. Gurulingaiah notes, October 1967). I am not certain that all castes do it.

26. *Sarcostemma brevistigma* [now] *acidum* (Roxb.) Voigt.

27. See Pitra Paksa ancestor propitiation discussion in Chapter 7.

28. Her husband and his brother alternate responsibiliry for an annual *puja* to Mastiamma, whom they call by the name Baedaramma 'Hunter Lady'.

29. Another, A. K. family also makes an offering to Mastiamma before each wedding.

30. His family does not do a special festival for this goddess. They only do a full *puja* for her when there is a crisis they think she might have caused.

31. In one of the offerings described above, note that an adult brother-sister pair did their *puja* separately from their parents and younger siblings, even though all of them shared a single household. The separation indicates that they were defining themselves apart from their natal family.

32. An alternative explanation for the outside *puja* was made by Farmer of Bandipur (mentioned in note 1, above). He said that the house is not clean (*svacca*) enough for the ritual. I assume that his statement was made to flatter the *amma*, whom he considered to be everpresent and threatening.

33. In ancestor feasts these same 'close exchange relations' are invited guests with a different symbolic role, to express totality.

Chapter 7

PITRA PAKSA FESTIVAL FOR THE APOTHEOSIZED DEAD

The rituals of this chapter emphasise relationships between a family and its ancestors. As with the preceding two studies, ancestor festivals 'present' a complex of varied (required and tabooed) offerings. Like *amma* festivals, those for ancestors make symbolic use of both kinship structures and offerings. Bothering little with symbols of frustration or despair, ancestor festivals are benign occasions for supposedly peaceful spirits—acts intended to make good relationships even better.

The heart of the ancestor festival is a feast which always includes white, boiled rice. This offering is thought to strengthen the future of a family by guaranteeing a stable relationship of interdependence with its predecessors. Other details of the menu and associated rituals expand upon themes of integrity, fertility, spiritual completeness. The spirits of married women appear in this festival as ancestors representing family goals of auspicious activity, movement, and development of human potential. Their 'gold' is mixed with the prevailing 'whiteness' of the occasion.

The ancestor festival is oriented toward life rather than death. Dealing with continuity and with purity or integrity as it does, it is a serious occasion; but it is not necessarily a somber one.

DATES AND TIMES OF ANCESTOR PROPITIATION

Hindu worship of ancestors is known from the *Atharva veda*. The Mahalaya New Moon offering to be discussed here was enjoined as early as the sixth century B.C., according to Ghurye (1962a : 46, 58). The most genealogically

191

specific type of ancient offering is that to three ascending generations of males (the F, FF, and FFF) monthly at the new moon, and is known from the 7th century B.C. *Shrauta Sutra* literature (Ghurye 1962a : 58-59). However, feeding ancestors who spiritually possess guests on the death anniversaries of one's parents, the practice emphasised and prestigious among local Brahmans, is of more 'recent' origin. P. V. Kane has been unable to discover any authority for this death-anniversary practice more ancient than the *Bhavishyapurana* (Kane 1930-62, II : 532-533).

The feast of the ancestors is one of the most important family rituals of the Hindu year. For a period of some twenty days after the full moon of Bhadrapada month (September-October), the time of *pitra paksa* (lit. 'ancestors' fortnight'), the residents of Bandipur and Chinnapura are occupied largely with tending to the needs of their deceased predecessors. The various *jati*-clusters of the region observe the period in different ways, and even at different times, though each group acts largely in unison.

For local Brahmans the full fifteen days of the waning of Bhadrapada is special for ancestors. It is general among Brahmans not to begin any important life's work at this time, although little else distinguishes these ancestral offerings from the others they perform as a matter of monthly routine, they being a generally ritual-conscious group.[1] The Brahmans, and a few of the others, observe the lunar anniversaries of both parents' deaths as a major ritual, rather than attributing any extraordinary importance to the Bhadrapada *pitra paksa* fortnight.

Non-Brahman *jatis* tend to select the new moon (*amavase*) evening or the day following as the time to make their annual offering to ancestors.[2] The new moon at the end of Bhadrapada is for them very much what Yom Kippur is for Jews, All Souls Day for Christians, or Bon for Japanese Buddhists. It is called Mahalaya Amavase; or *maladahabba* 'mahalaya festival', in abbreviated reference. For persons who have lost one or both parents, it is a time of fasting, purification, and a cautious though fervent ritual exchange across the boundary which divides the living and the peaceful dead.

Several A.K.s whom we asked stated that this was their most important festival. Calling it 'Maranami Festival' or 'Mahalaya Feast' (*malada paksa*), they perform the ancestral ritual later than the others do. In 1966, it was five or six days into the period of the waxing moon of Asvija, the next month, when the A.K. Colony houses collectively decided to have their festival.

VIEWS OF THE ANCESTORS

Though there are no ancestral shrines or tablets for specific ancestors in Bandipur or Chinnapura, there is one equivalent in nearly every house that has ever had contact with a photographer. This is the large, unsmiling face of the deceased mother and/or father, displayed prominently in the main room of the house.

In many homes these framed photographs are set together with the colourful figures of gods and goddesses, the 'god-photos' which line the upper portions of the main room walls. In others, the parents' photographs are set apart for frequent garlanding, vermillion application, and incense receipt separately from the gods'. As parents age, many villagers are eager to get their photographs made for the memorial display. The ethnographic photographer was much in demand for this service. In fact, I was surprised to get a request for one old man's photograph which I had taken after his death, his corpse having been bathed and garlanded and seated on his verandah with his son's son-in-law holding up the head and chin as a line of caste-mates made farewell greetings. Although I did present them with an enlargement of their father's corpse's photograph, I refused when their next-door neighbours called me to photograph their dead mother a short time later, since I found the work rather distasteful.

Despite the popularity of these photographs, individualistic memorialism is not performed by local non-Brahmans after the first year of death.

The non-Brahman and A.K. Hindu villager shares with the Japanese the pattern of venerating the collective ancestral spirits in an annual feast. This collectivity of spirits, like the generally deified ancestral spirits called *sorei* in Buddhist Japan, is considered to protect the household once the spirits are out of the transitional, or 'ghostly', state (Smith 1974 : 41). The way that Newell has described the Japanese concept applies in some degree to the general views held by my Hindu informants, though some types of ancestors are still kept distinct in the ways they are ritually treated, as I shall point out below. "There is a parallelism [between ancestors and gods] until the two gradually become identified with each other as time recedes" (Newell 1968 : 300). Both the Japanese and folk-Hindu views are thus distinct from the Confucian-influenced Chinese tradition, which tends to memorialise specific ancestors (or even unrelated predecessors, such as Chinese bureaucratic officials) whose unique identities are preserved over the generations in tombs, shrines, and tablets.

Pitra Paksa is a festival for the collective ancestral spirits, universally referred to by the term *hiriavaru* 'elders'.[3] Although villagers have definite ideas about who is receiving their offerings on these occasions—perhaps a mother, father, or grandparent—they do not address these persons directly in the ritual, since the event is meant to please those whom one does not remember together with family intimates who have died within one's lifetime.[4]

Within the collectivity, however, non-Brahmans and A.K.s do carefully distinguish males and females as two groups. This shows clearly in their ancestral rituals. Every home offering, as far as I could determine, includes a symmetrical arrangement of male and female clothing,[5] jewellery, and other sex-preferred paraphernalia around the central vessel(s) thought to incarcerate the ancestors for the *pitra paksa* offering. Anyone asked would note that the one pile was intended for the women who had died in the family, and the other, for the men. These groups have extensive genealogical knowledge of both male and female ascendants, as I have discussed earlier.

Despite the careful attention they give to female ancestors in household offerings, however, Bandipur villagers' response to a 1966 survey question, 'For which specific ancestors do you perform the ancestor worship?' indicates a clear patrilineal emphasis. Only a few houses mentioned matrilineal predecessors, and none mentioned 'relations of exchange'. (Some houses that mentioned the mother's mother (MM) still have a mother living at home.) This pattern reflects the fact that responsibility for feeding the ancestors generally descends in the patrilineal line, unless there is a special problem such as having no sons. Table 31 presents the findings of this survey.

The two views or approaches to ancestors—one as a collectivity, and one as the founders of a specific patrilineal group—are neither contradictory nor incompatible. They seem to refer to two different levels of caste and family, the broad and inclusive level where relatives and castemates are one; and the narrow and exclusive group of agnates who are interdependent and sharing. By not memorialising specific predecessors in overt ritual acts to any great extent, and especially by not using their names, villagers work at both social levels simultaneously in this feast.

General comments elicited from villagers in 1966 on the needs and feelings of ancestors centered mainly on the *pitra paksa* feast itself, rather than on kin ties, and on the importance of other offerings. The ancestors are hungry, villagers say, and they need clothing. They become angry if not fed (rice and/or meat) on time. And they need the clothing offered annually, so as to either (1) gain admission to the resting place of dead souls, Swaraga; or (2) avoid going to Naraka 'hell'; or (3) to be presentable when they visit the gods' chambers each year.

Abstract discussion about ancestors is vague and often confused. A few non-Brahmans and A.K.s surveyed in 1966 expressed their ideas. Most of them referred to the potential anger of neglected ancestors, elaborating only with terse comments that 'something bad' might happen if this ceremony were not performed. One older man of the Weaver *jati* stated that some 'illness, accident, or other misfortune' surely would come to the family if this offering were neglected. One old woman added that any soothsayer would confirm this—i.e., that if 'something bad' happened, the soothsayer would determine ancestral anger as the cause. Two informants expressed a different view altogether : the ancestors are compassionate and will not harm us if we cannot afford this expensive ceremony. A third man, a Barber, expressed the agnostic/aetheistic view, so to speak : he did not know where the ancestors are. Nor did he think that they do anything at all. (He did however, perform the *pitra paksa* ceremony.) One can only guess at the local views on the power of the normal, peaceful dead in the face of such vague remarks, though the rituals for them do provide some clues.[6]

As in the festivals discussed in the preceding two chapters, ancestral rituals

Table 31—Relationships of Ancestors Propitiated to Heads of Non-Brahman and A.K. Households, Bandipur, 1966

	Households Surveyed									Totals	Percentages
	Farmer	Weaver	Smith	Oil Presser	Toddy Tapper	Fisher-man	Barber	Washer-man	A.K.		
No. General Interviews	44	19	5	11	6	10	5	7	80	187	
No. In-Depth Interviews	12	3	1	3	1	1	2	1	9	33	
Ancestors Propitiated											
Partilineal only (F, FF, M, FM, FFF, etc.)†	43	12	3	10	4	6	2	5	37	122	55.5
Patrilineal and Matrilineal (F, M, FF, MM, etc.)	3	0	2	0	2	0	0	0	3	10	4.5
Lineals and Collaterals (F, FB, B, W, BW)	1	1	0	1	0	0	0	0	4	7	3.2
WM, WF, M, F of Uxorilocal Men	1	0	0	0	0	0	2	0	1	4	1.8
H, HF, HM only, of Female Household Heads	1	0	0	0	1	0	0	1	4	7	3.2
H, HF, HM, M, F of Female Household Heads	1	1	0	0	0	0	0	0	2	4	1.8
No information	3	0	1	1	0	1	1	0	37	44	20.0
Not done	3	8	0	2	0	4	2	2	1	22	10.0
Totals	56	22	6	14	7	11	7	8	89	220	100.0

†Two A.K. houses mentioned deceased sons in in-depth interviews.

pay attention to both restless spirits and contented ones, particularly females, whose feelings might be thought to influence the well-being of the family. One often finds specific, problematic individuals distinguished out of the spiritual collectivity of ancestors. Thus one finds a special Mastiamma vessel set near the usual male-female ancestral offerings, a tribute to some deceased mother-to-be or to a murdered lady, in one Farmer house. The men of a Chinnapura Washerman house repeat their annual ancestral offering a second time at a nearby Mastiamma shrine in the Mahalaya New Moon festival. In another house one finds the *tali* to which a deceased brother has been wed. Still another Farmer family sets out children's clothing—an unusual item in this ritual—in offering to the spirits of two of their children who had been murdered by a mysterious poisoning of the family dinner a few years earlier.[7]

Considered to be as contented and fortunate as any spirits could be, those who died as 'married women'—i.e., those who pre-deceased their husbands—also receive special recognition in home festivals. This is most common when they left sons behind them. In one house, of the Weaver *jati*, a special married woman vessel is adorned with the marital *tali* pendant which their mother had used. This family chants her name as they fill the vessel with water.[8] An old man of the Smith caste describes his father's technique of performing the ancestral ritual: before setting the usual two vessels, one for males and one for females, he used to set up and decorate a 'married woman vessel' (*muttayide kalasa*) in honour of a woman who pre-deceased her husband. Although all three of the Smith family's ancestral vessels used to receive offerings, the full sequence was done for the 'married woman vessel' before the other two. This sequence, the woman first, is parallel to a Brahman custom of making an ancestral offering on auspicious occasions which I shall discuss below. In all of these rituals the honoured married woman is given the greatest deference by this first position in the order of offerings. Whether such actions arise from attitudes of simple respect or from respect mixed with special connotations of power and danger is difficult to determine from the information available at this time.

There is a special ritual for a deceased married woman which is performed annually by some Smartha Brahmans. One old woman described it to me. It is performed during the Dassara festival, which followed Pitra Paksa, in some traditional homes where a 'married woman' has died leaving male descendants. Her daughter-in-law invites five living 'married women' and offers them a set of 'cooling' and pleasing things, in order to 'give peace to her mind'.[9]

Powers of deceased females—i.e., benign or peaceful ones—receive explicit acknowledgement in ancestral rituals of all patrilineal *jatis*. The routine new moon offerings, which are done monthly by some Brahmans at the river's edge[10] acknowledge three ascending generations in both the patrilineal and matrilineal lines according to an old Sanskritic formula. A local Brahman's source book on ancestral rites (Rangaswami Aiyangar 1950 : 47-49) describes the offering that should be made to ancestors in connection with all auspicious family events. This is to get the blessings of all ancestors, male and female, for the newly married couple or other fortunate member of the family. It begins, interestingly enough, with a prefatory *puja* to the 'divine mothers', named as ten goddesses, including Gauri, Savitri, and others. Citing the *Sraddhaprakasa* and *Bhavisya-purana* as authorities, this source explains, ". . . if the [ritual] is begun without first doing the *Matrpuja* [for the 'mothers'], they in their anger will cause harm to the performer of the *Sraddha* [ancestral offering]."

An elderly Smartha Brahman woman also told me that the mother receives first acknowledgement in her daily Sanskrit Prayer. "We say first 'mother is like a god', then 'father . . .', then 'friend . . .', then 'guru . . .', and then 'guest . . .'," she explained. This reverence for mothers carries over to reverence for ancestresses.

In general, definitions of ancestors reflect the structure and ambiguities of definitions of family roles and groupings. These are basically patrilineal, with womens' birth-giving and life-sustaining capacities receiving special symbolic emphasis. But female ancestors who are regarded as sometimes-in/sometimes-out of the 'birth group' get the same ambivalent and minor attention as women themselves do. One notes a vague concern for the welfare of, say, the mother's mother as an example of this pattern.

BEGINNING THE ANCESTOR RITUAL

CLEANING AND DECORATING A SACRED SPACE AND INSTALLING THE ANCESTOR VESSEL

As I mentioned earlier, there are two different styles of propitiating the ancestors—the Brahman, on the one hand, and the non-Brahman and A.K., on the other. Although this study is emphasising the latter, I shall mention some features of the more well-known Brahman ritual in passing, in order to indicate interesting contrasts between the two styles. In general, the non-Brahman and A.K. ritual is performed for a filled vessel in which the ancestors are thought to be incarnated. And the Brahman ritual is performed for two or three living persons in whom the ancestors are thought to be incarnated. The non-Brahman and A.K. ancestor ceremony is done on the Mahalaya new moon day, while the Brahman ritual is done on the death-anniversary of the mother and/or father (whoever is deceased).

Preparations for the ritual begin a day or so before the new moon day, with many whitewashing their houses and purchasing new clothing for the offering. A.K.s wash all their clothing on this day. And most persons bathe. On the day of the festival, one or two senior responsible persons in each house will fast by avoiding all non-liquid foods, while others will fast by eating only 'snacks'. I do not know of a household in which complete fasting was observed by all members.

This lack of complete household fasting suggests that this festival requires a high degree of purity from significant persons, but not total household purity. The various festivals for the cobra spirit and ant hill, which are discussed in the following chapter, have stricter requirements of purity than the ancestor festival does.

The difference does not hold for the way in which the Brahmans celebrate the death-anniversary ritual. As done by Brahmans, the ritual requires strenuous twenty-four-hour food and drink avoidance, but even then it is mainly the responsible persons who fast so completely, and particularly those into whom the ancestors will be temporarily incarnated.

The place for worship is prepared carefully. The location itself varies considerably among those interviewed. Sometimes it is in the 'inside' of the house, near the kitchen and gods' shrine, but in several houses the ritual is conducted in the 'outside' portion of the house, near the front door in the main entry room, more or less at the place where a menstruating woman would sit for a period of isolation.

At the place of the offering, the floor is carefully cleaned with cow dung.

Figure 7. Pitra Paksa *rangolli* on floor around house post, Farmer House, Bandipur 1966

(All those interviewed were careful to point this out to us.) The second stage of the preparation is the drawing of *rangolli* designs in flour on the floor. Two traditional designs used for this occasion in Swamy Gauda's house are copied in Figures 7 and 8. The larger design is the one on which vessels and offerings are set. (Both designs use four parallel lines throughout. The number 4 may or may not be a reference to death.)

Figure 8. Setting for the ancestral vessel : floor design, Farmer House, Bandipur 1966

SETTING UP THE ANCESTRAL VESSEL

On top of the *rangolli* design, in most houses, a low wooden platform (*mane*) is placed, with an end portion of a plantain leaf on it. (In a few houses, the plantain leaf is placed directly on the design on the floor.) The only portion of the plantain leaf which is used on this occasion is the tip—the foremost 18 inches or so—which is called *suli*. On this leaf is poured some raw rice, and on top of that is placed the vessel (or two or three vessels) which incarnates the ancestors. The *kalasa* vessel is a small pot full of water, in which are present 'our people' (*nammavaru*), in the words of one Farmer informant. There are also two lamps, one on each side of the setting; a Farmer informant stated that these should burn butter.

I have discussed the *kalasa* type of vessel earlier as a structure which presents oppositions between mortality and eternity—apt connotations for ancestral rituals or any other utilising (or contemplating) the temporary nature of life forms. There is considerable attention paid to the vessel itself before it is set down in the second space. I shall review the information available on it.

A.K.s, who use a clay pot for the *kalasa*, agree that it is necessary to use a new pot (*kamba*) for this purpose. This is a guarantee of its purity. Informants of other castes, however, did not state a requirement for a new pot, but only stated that the (presumably metal) vessel to be used must be cleaned before being filled.

The act of filling the one or more *kalasas* is described in detail by a few informants. There is no fixed pattern in who fills the *kalasa*: among the A.K.s it is the one in the family who is fasting who does it; but in other families various persons are mentioned, including the unmarried daughter (four cases), the son's wife (one case), the wife's younger sister (one case), and the household head (two cases). The water is drawn from either the nearby river, the irrigation channel, or a well; none mention irrigation tanks, but a more complete survey might have included these also.

The procedure for filling the vessel varies, but each group seems to have a special method. A member of a Farmer family mentions that A.K.s must not see their vessel, lest the ancestors become 'unhappy' (*trpti agilla*).[11]

A Barber informant says that there must be no speech or song while filling the vessel. But the opposite is required in a Weaver family's method, which requires that at the time of taking the water for the vessel they chant the name of the 'eldest female predecessor' (in this case the mother of the household head), putting a special *tali* pendant around the vessel while saying the name.[12] Some betel leaves (three; or five for A.K.s) and a whole coconut are placed in the open top of the filled vessel; *arati* (incense stick/camphor) is done for it; and it is brought back to the house. In Swamy Gauda's house, as soon as the daughter brings the two vessels into the house, her father does *arati* for them and says a prayer about the ancestors.

Once set into the sacred space, the ancestor-vessel(s) receives further decoration. Though some details vary according to sect affiliation of the family or according to varying family customs, the non-Brahman pattern (observed in Farmer houses) seems to be to dot the vessel with vermillion, to hang a small garland of yellow chrysanthemums around the vessel, often together with other necklaces, and to wrap a sari around it. When there are two vessels, one is wrapped with the sari, and the other is set on top of a folded male skirt (*pance*) (Plates 14, 15).

Whether they contain one, two, or three *kalasas*, most of the shrines divide male and female non-food offerings set before the vessel(s). The male items, such as *pance* (waist-cloth/*dhoti*) and towel, and toddy, and liquor, and tobacco, are placed on the right side, facing outward from the shrine (i.e., the stage-right); and female items, palm-leaf earrings, other jewellery, comb, sari and blouse, on the left. In one Weaver house, of fervent Saivite persuasion, the offer-

Plate 14. Male and female ancestor vessels, with offerings (Farmer house, Bandipur 1966)

ed saris "are twisted and stood up like the hood of a cobra." In many houses the clothing is piled over and around the garlanded *kalasa* itself,[13] as in Figure 9.

The arrangement is completed with a laying-out of some fresh bananas, betel-areca sets, some broken coconuts, and a row of longitudinally sliced, peeled cucumber, set upright and spear-like in a row behind the vessel(s).

In brief interviews, I pursued the fact that the vessel itself, the temporary embodiment of the ancestors, is adorned with feminine ornaments, sometimes including a *tali*. The feminine emphasis is especially clear, a feminine garment being wrapped around the vessel, or otherwise set directly near it. The image suggests in its symbolism, at least, that ancestral power or nature is in some sense largely feminine. Nonetheless, Swamy Gauda, for one, explicitly denies that the vessel in the ancestor ceremony is feminine or female, even though it is adorned with feminine ornaments and is called *muttayide kalasa*. His elderly mother-in-law agrees: "No, the vessel is not a female," they both say. "Those ornaments are the things we need for what we call a *kalasa* [vessel] *puja*."

These responses failing to confirm my hypothesis, I must relinquish it (tempo-

Plate 15. Farmer house ancestral offering to one vessel, Chinnapura 1967 (S. Regelson photograph)

rarily, perhaps) for some other. A second possible cultural logic in using femi-nine ornamentation on the ancestral vessel could be in the equation:

married woman decorations = auspiciousness.

This equation has the advantage that it conforms to some other cheerful details of the household ancestral set-up. For instance, the appearance of elaborate white *rangolli* line designs on the floors of Pitra Paksa houses could be seen as a reflection of the presumed lively and benign nature of (most of) the spirits being woshipped. This is an 'auspicious' occasion, in large part. Such line

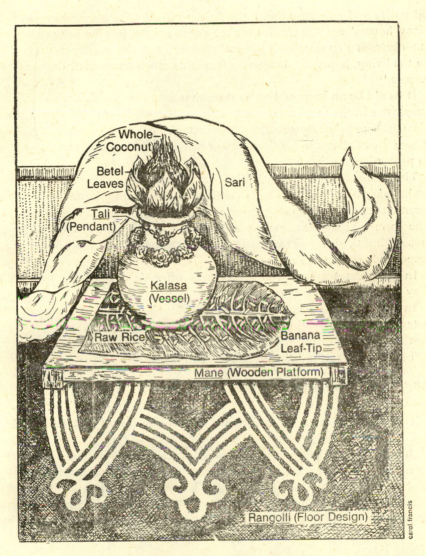

Figure 9. Married woman vessel in ancestor ritual.

designs are absent, creating a stark and barren effect, in the homes mourning souls who have not yet finished their funerary transition into peaceful death.

The typical floral offering also repeats a structural emphasis on auspiciousness. The red oleander, so frequent in rituals for the restless *amma* spirits as to be nearly universal, is conspicuous by its absence in ancestral rites. One finds in its stead the simple, single-stranded garland of yellow chrysanthemums, the favoured flower of the ancestors according to all non-Brahmans whom we interviewed. If the ritual for ancestors were simply and solely concerned with spiritual purity and the eternal soul, the flower should have been white (as it is in many houses' ant hill festival for the cobra spirit). But the yellow chrysanthemum betrays a concern with life and prosperity in the ancestral rites, a focus on the living, hopefully flourishing family as much as on their deceased predecessors.[14]

It would be an exaggeration to state that ancestor rituals are either joyful or auspicious in the same sense that namings or weddings are. They are not. 'Semiauspicious' or some such phrase, might be a preferable designation for these serious efforts of communication with the dead—efforts made with an eye to protecting the living.

The *kalasa* having been installed, decorated, clothed, and welcomed with preliminary offerings, the family continues with worship by means of rotating incense-sticks (*dupa*), bowing (*namaskara*), and burning camphor (*mangalarati*). The former acts (*dupa* and *namaskara*) are done by all or most of the adults present, but the last (*mangalarati*), only by the household head or other senior responsible person in the family.

In some cases affines who are present offer *dupa/arati*; but in other cases they do not.

In a couple of houses where there are widows present, the widows participate fully in the devotion. In Swamy Gauda's house, however, the widowed mother-in-law stops short of offering the final *mangalarati*, and leaves it rather to her adopted son-in-law and daughter to do it.

OFFERING FOOD TO ANCESTORS AND TO ANIMALS

The climactic event of the festival is the offering of the meal. There are numerous rules and prohibitions associated with this meal, each group (even each household) displaying variations in practice. One culinary rule followed by all those interviewed might be called a 'rule of elaborateness'. This is most evident in the multiplicity of offerings. There are often two kinds of meat preparations; 'no less than three different vegetables'; several varieties of 'snacks'; and always an offering of three or more (an odd number) separate banana leaves full of food. I shall review details of the menu itself shortly.

The meals are offered as (*y*)*ede*, i.e., a meal that is offered to a spiritual being and subsequently ingested by a group of worshippers. The meal itself has certain similarities to the *titi* offerings to the recently dead (at the eleventh day after death, and then again on the first anniversary of the death). In using (*y*)*ede* both the Mahalaya New Moon festival and the *titi* in their practice reveal a conceptual merging of the ancestors with the rest of the spiritual beings thought to inhabit the world. (*Y*)*ede* is not offered to living persons, only to spirits.

Each house offers three or more meals. One of these is placed outside the house on the roof, supposedly to be eaten by crows or sparrows, while the remainder are eaten by human participants. One Smith family states that instead of putting the meal on the roof, they give it to a cow that has been cleaned, decorated [with turmeric and vermillion, sandalwood paste, flowers and turmeric-coloured raw rice (*aksate*)], and worshipped. Whether crows, sparrows, or cows are thought to eat this remaining meal, all non-Brahman and A.K. houses do put one of the offered meals to be physically eaten by some animal.

Especially in the case of crows, it is common for an animal to represent a spiritual being and eat a food offering. In Bandipur even dogs can eat offered food that is set out for the major Vedic gods during the Narasimha *jatra* festival. But Pitra Paksa is one of the very few cases I know of where a portion of offered food is physically ingested by an animal before the worshippers eat. This implicitly suggests that crows and other animals are connected with either the ancestors themselves, or with other possibly envious spirits often said to roam about in the darkness of new moon nights. (On the eleventh day after death non-Brahmans set a plate of food on the grave before eating at home.)

Another distinctive quality of this food offering is the requirement that the food be eaten. Unlike other *pujas*, in which it is enough to set a plate before an icon and to assume that it is being absorbed without one's having to see it disappear, the worship of ancestors requires that it physically disappear. In both the non-Brahman/A.K. ritual and the Brahman one, this is the pattern.

THE MENU

The menu itself is the most organised feature of the non-Brahman or A.K. ancestor ritual and presents most of the symbolic material of the festival. It is the main point of the ritual from the participants' point of view (Plate 16).

In addition to the rule of elaborateness, there are a few rules which provide guidelines for an analysis of the meal's symbolism; but in a population the size of Bandipur and Chinnapura there is considerable variation in practice. Rather than detail all of my information on food offerings, I will attempt a summary of some of the major principles, rules, and prohibitions which seem to structure the culinary elements of this ritual: cooked vs. raw; and the four types of food included in the meal namely, rice, meat, vegetables, and snacks.

The Cooked and The Raw : Ancestors and Ghosts

Villagers say that raw rice is 'hot', but cooked rice is 'cool'. And appropriately enough, the rituals in which one finds plain cooked white rice as the basic preparation are funerary rituals for adults.[15] In the funerary period, the first ten days followed by a one-year's observance, the deceased person's soul makes a conceptual transition from ghostly to ancestral status. All funerary rites for adults have this transition as a primary and conscious goal.

Cooked rice appears in rituals of the initial mourning period, and it is con-

Plate 16. The ancestor meals in a Farmer home : On banana leaf are white rice, two *palyas*, dark red millet ball, yoghurt rice ball, *dose* pancake with sweet liquid (*payasa*) on it. Set nearby are *cigani* sesame ball, in leaf cup; and bananas and broken coconuts used as offerings in *puja*. One 'snack' in leaf cup not identified (S. Regelson Photograph, Chinnapura).

stantly associated with departed spirits after that. To cite one example of the uses of raw and cooked rice in funerary ritual, all castes (Brahman, non-Brahman, and A.K.) put a small amount of raw rice ('hot' and uncooked) into the mouth of corpse before it is cremated or buried. All cooking—rice and other—is taboo in the home of the deceased person on the day of the death itself, though it may begin (for consumption by household members only) again on subsequent days. But from third day after death, Brahman mourners, as a case in point, conduct ritual rice cooking at the river's edge. Continuing this through the ninth day, they offer balls of this cooked rice to a ritual fire after doing the cooking.[16] (Some of this rice is also offered as 'demon sacrifice' (*bhutabali*) on each occasion.) On the tenth day the ritual cooking is preceded by some male agnates having their heads shaved. On the eleventh day, outdoor cooking becomes elaborate, including vegetable preparations as well as rice. The specific preparations of vegetables customary for this day are considered 'inauspicious' ones on other occasions.

Non-Brahmans' and A.K.s' funerary rituals are different from those of Brahmans. It is customary among the former to pour a mixture of milk and clarified butter onto the grave three days after burial. A single betel leaf with four holes punched into it and a piece of areca nut on it also is set out at the grave at that time. On the eleventh day, when the deceased is presumed to have been transformed into a peaceful state, a meal of cooked rice and cooked meat is left for him or her.

After the conclusion of the initial mourning period, Brahman families generally perform a twelfth-day ritual. On this day there is a Brahman custom of preparing three *pinda* 'rice balls for ancestors'. Actually a mixture of rice, honey, yoghurt, and white sesame seeds, these balls are named 'father', 'grandfather', and 'great-grandfather'. The 'father' ball is broken into two parts, which are each pressed together with one of the other two, as the deceased parent symbolically joins his own predecessors as one of the 'great predecessors' (*pitamaha*). In this ritual, then, the ancestors not only take rice, but they *are* cooked rice.

Khare presents a similar view, related by a Brahman priest who has presided over many death ceremonies according to the *Garudapurana*. The rice balls which are given to the *preta* (newly departed spirit) for ten days are to make up his "subtle body," quotes Khare, ". . . The first rice ball forms his head, the second—neck and shoulders;" and so on down to the feet. The fifth rice ball makes his navel. (Khare 1976b : 177-78.)

By the end of the initial funerary period, the deceased Hindu soul is as 'cool' and peaceful, and as completely processed as the cooked rice with which it becomes associated. Non-Brahmans and A.K.s, though they perform a different set of funerary rites, also strive to reach the goal of 'coolness' and peace for their recently dead. Like the Brahmans, they associate their peaceful dead with cooked rice, and all subsequent rituals for the now-ancestors are held inside the home, not outdoors.

The distinction between the concept of such rested souls and that of restless, ghostly ones can be summarised in the cooked/raw nature of certain of their respective food offerings. The recently dead corpse takes raw rice into its mouth; the ancestor takes cooked rice and *is* metaphorically associated with cooked rice. They both require meat, in the prevalent non-Brahman and A.K. concept. But where the ghost takes a fresh blood sacrifice, the ancestor takes only cooked meats. In fact, the A.K. ancestors are offered a blood preparation[17]—but even that is *cooked* blood, not raw blood as is found with rice in the *kulu* preparation for restless spirits.

Indeed, insofar as they have presumably lived a full life span and died naturally with adequate funerary arrangements, the ancestors are themselves metaphorically 'cooked'. They have been totally absorbed by the cultural system, processed and transformed to the maximum extent which it is possible for that system to process any soul. They are also seen as controllable, so long as their presumed needs are met. In short, they are fixed, permanent members of the line in a far more secure sense than its currently living members—they encountering various tempting and socially dangerous possibilities—can be. Dumont's and Pocock's general observations on the Indian (and universal) significance of cooking sum up this view quite well:

> Food passes from the non-human to the human world as does man in birth, and initiation. Cooking may be taken to imply a complete appropriation of the food [in this case, ancestors and their food] by the household. It is almost, as if, before being "internally absorbed" (eaten) by the individual, food was, by cooking, collectively predigested . . . [As in Polynesia,] it would appear that cooking means not only appropriating, but also depriving the food of its own life or essence, that is, making it at the same time human, and defenceless. (Dumont and Pocock 1959: 37.)

Rice Preparations

Though the parallel is strongest between the dead and plain cooked rice, some seasoned rice dishes may find their way into the ancestral meal as accompaniment to the basic plain rice which is always present. These supplementary preparations are few and relatively simple. That is, they are not as elaborately 'coloured' as other festival dishes tend to be.

Insofar as red millet is also a staple food of many non-Brahman and A.K. families, millet balls also appear in many families' ancestral meals. But they differ from cooked rice in that they are not omnipresent as rice is, and in that some houses prefer not to offer them as part of the feast meal. Two Farmer informants state that the ancestors do not like to receive millet balls as offerings.

Most of the supplementary rice preparations—yoghurt rice, sour-flavoured rice (*hulianna*), and lemon-flavoured rice (*citranna*)—are sour in flavour. The most important one is yoghurt rice, which is shaped into balls for the occasion and called '*kalasa* ball'.[18]

Rice flour is a required ingredient of other preparations. It appears in such 'snacks' as the *dose* pancake or the oil-fried tangle of crispy threads called *cakli*. Several informants have mentioned that the sweet, watery dessert called *payasa* should only be made with rice for the ancestral feast. (One A.K. house requires that a spoonful of *payasa* be put on top of the plain cooked rice; and other, Farmer houses splash a bit of it onto their pancakes.)

Meat

With very few exceptions the ancestors of non-Brahman and A.K. alike are thought to require meat. A variety of meats is offered by some houses. There is a tendency to emphasise chicken in non-Brahman meals, with one Weaver informant stating that only chicken curry (*koli saru*) is offered to the *kalasa*. But other meats are offered, these including goat, sheep, and fish for non-Brahmans. (The sex of the animal offered is mentioned by only two informants, one of the Washerman caste and one Toddy-Tapper, both of whom offer the meat of a male goat killed for the occasion.) The Fishermen require both chicken and fish in the offered meal.

The emphasis on meat offerings is carried to an extreme among the A.K.s, as far as I can see; meat is clearly the central feature of the meal for them; in fact, rice, *ragi* [millet] ball and meats are the only ingredients of the meal in the one case for which I have detailed menu information. Several A.K. informants stated that the ancestors like meat, 'all kinds of meat'. They were vague on this subject during initial interviews because they preferred not to mention that they offer 'ox meat' (beef). [19] But this practice is generally known, and one Farmer girl told me that they were quite open about this practice until some of their fellow Hindu villagers forced them to be more discrete about it. Although beef seems to be required by their ancestors, the A.K.s seem to want to offer a variety of meats, as Figure 10 shows.

One of our most reliable A.K. informants described an ox-blood preparation which is customary for the Mahalaya New Moon offering. Called *kari* 'black', it is made of ox-blood and unripe plantain. The plantain is boiled first. And then a piece of dried blood is added to it. This is cooked until it is black, and is then seasoned with clarified butter and the pungent *vograne* mixture of fried mustard seeds, garlic, and onion. (S. Regelson notes, 1967.) It is relevant to the structure of the ancestor festival as a whole that this blood preparation is made from blood that is blackened and cooked, not red liquid or fresh. It is symbolically transformed and 'ancestral', rather than crude, wasted, and 'ghostly'.

All of the non-vegetarian families questioned include a single egg, centrally positioned on the eating leaf, as part of the offered meal. One Farmer informant stated that the egg could substitute for meat, but in the meals for which I have information it only accompanies the meat offering.

Despite the proclaimed need for 'all kinds' of meat which ancestors are thought to have, one kind of meat, at least, is taboo. This is pork. Otherwise eaten by many non-vegetarian villagers, pork is an interesting omission from the ancestors' feast. I assume that this has something to do with the distinction between ancestor and ghost. Villagers generally believe that ghosts love pork. They also offer pig sacrifice and pork (*y*)*ede* to *amma* deities thought to be responsible for cattle disease. Pork is considered to soothe and 'cool' the restless spirit, but is (therefore ?) considered an inappropriate offering to the peacefully dead by members of all castes.

Vegetables

Vegetables take on an unusually high degree of symbolic value in non-Brahman

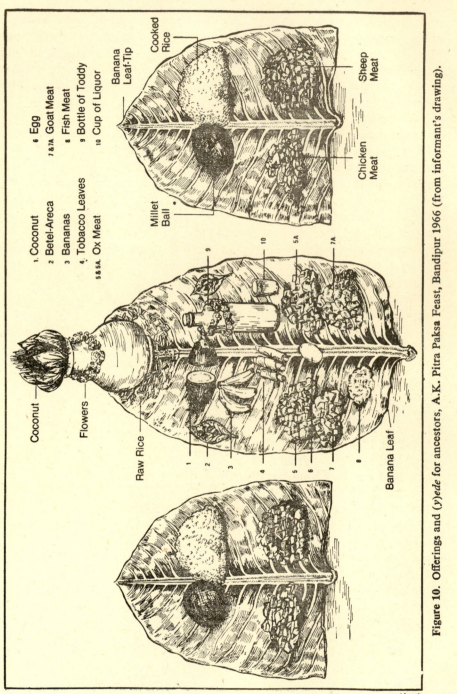

Figure 10. Offerings and (y)ede for ancestors, A.K. Pitra Paksa Feast, Bandipur 1966 (from informant's drawing).

1. Coconut
2 Betel-Areca
3 Bananas
4. Tobacco Leaves
5 & 5A. Ox Meat
6 Egg
7 & 7A Goat Meat
8 Fish Meat
9 Bottle of Toddy
10 Cup of Liquor

Coconut
Flowers
Raw Rice
Banana Leaf

Banana Leaf-Tip
Cooked Rice
Sheep Meat
Chicken Meat
Millet Ball

carol francis

and A.K. ancestral meals. This is the only festival I know of in which specific vegetables are required and others are taboo. (On some other occasions vegetables are given as gifts, but any harvested vegetable will do at such times.) Though developed mutely in festival menus, i.e., without exegetical comment, the symbolic potential of vegetables develops and expands in the ancestor festival.

This fact became evident in detailed interviews about the festival in village houses. One question was, "Are there any foods that the ancestors do not like ?" Villagers surprised us with lists of vegetables in response to this query. They also produced vegetable requirements, along with rice and meat recipes, when we asked about foods preferred by ancestors. Brahmans also utilise vegetables as a basic part of their ancestor-feast menu, preparing a mixture called *saubhagya sunti* 'fortune-bestowing ginger' (also 'married woman/auspiciousness ginger'). This, they say, has the qualities of 1,000 vegetables and can be used in the ancestors' meal to replace all of the vegetables required for that meal.

Vegetables for ancestors, in non-Brahman or A.K. homes, are prepared in a similar style, as boiled and seasoned *palya*, according to all persons interviewed. In making *palya*, villagers cut up vegetables, boil them in water, drain them, and season them with oil-fried spices. *Palya* is a dish in which the vegetable chunks retain their solid shape, unlike an oily and rather liquid preparation called *gojju*, which is not served on this occasion, whether by custom or by preference. Different houses elaborate on the *palya* theme by detailing requirements, such as: No less than three vegetables in a mixed *palya* (one Oil-Presser); Offer five separate *palyas*, one for each of five required vegetables (Farmer house); Offer two *palyas* of three vegetables each (plus *Vigna catjang* beans); and so on. The reader will note the local use of odd numbers 3 and 5, which appear with auspicious connotations in other village festivals.

Some vegetable combinations in specific households' *palyas*, are listed below to give the reader an idea of the uses of these vegetables:

(1) Farmer house: two *palyas*,

    (a) bottle gourd (*sorekayi*) + white radish + *Momordica* + *Vigna catjang* beans;

    (b) Potato + snake gourd + unripe plantain + *Vigna catjang* beans;

(2) Farmer house: two *palyas*,

    (a) bottle gourd + eggplant + stringbeans;

    (b) *Momordica* + potato + stringbeans;

(3) Barber house: one *palya*, of bottle gourd + white radish + *Momordica* + potato + *Vigna catjang* beans;

(4) A.K. house: one *palya*, of unripe plantain + eggplant + potato [potato is the most important ingredient] + ripe tomato.

A few other boiled vegetable combinations appear in ancestor feast menus as well. One A.K. family, for example, prepares a stew (*tallu* or *kayitallu*) of bottle gourd + eggplant + common gourd + *Momordica* + three types of beans. Other families mix in boiled vegetables with the cooked pulses (*saru*) commonly accompanying rice in daily meals.

Vegetables which are required for ancestral feasts are listed in Table 32; and those tabooed, in Table 33. Each house has its distinctive list of requirements and taboos. The set is rarely the same from one house to another, even within the same caste. Sorting vegetables into two groups disregards the specific household sets but enables us to study the patterns of use and non-use of specific vegetables. I hypothesise that these cultural patterns are based on the characteristics of the vegetables themselves as much as on the habits and customs of the families.

Table 32—Vegetables Required for Ancestor Meals of Non-Brahmans and A.K.s

Informants Requiring Each Vegetable (N = 15)	Required Vegetables	
	Kannada Names	English/Other Identifications
3	kumbalakayi†	Common gourd
11	sorekayi	Bottle gourd
4	pada[va]lakayi†	Snake gourd, *Trichosanthes dioica*
2	bendekayi†	Okra, *Hibiscus esculentus*
3	nuggekayi or nugalakayi	Moringa oleifera
6	tadagunikalu	*Vigna catjang*, beans (ripe stage)
10	hagalakayi†	*Momordica charantia*
1	capradavarekayi	Beans?
1	illatikalu	Stringbeans/Green beans
1	kadalekayi	Peanut/Groundnut
1	kosambri	Mixture of soaked pulses
1	avarekalu	Cow gram, *Lablab purpureus*
3	tameta hannu	Ripe tomato
9	alugadde	Potato
11	badaneyikayi or mulagay	Eggplant/Brinjal
3	balekayi	Plantain/Banana, unripe

†These vegetables are tabooed by other families. See Table 33.

Table 33—Vegetables Tabooed for Ancestor Meals of Non-Brahmans and A.K.s

Informants by Jati (No.)					Taboo Vegetables	
Farmer (5)	Weaver (2)	Oil Presser (1)	Barber (1)	A.K. (2)	Kannada Names	English/Other Identifications
1	1		1	1	hirekayi	A gourd, Luffa acutangula
3			1		kumbalakayi†	Common gourd
				1	budkumbalakayi	Ash gourd
3					halusorekayi	Bottle gourd, at dried-up stage
			1	1	pala[va] lakayi†	Snake gourd, Trichosanthes dioica
		1	1		bendekayi†	Okra, Hibiscus esculentus
		1	1		gorikayi	Cyamopsis psoralioides ?
1	1				tadagunikayi	Beans, Vigna cajang (unripe stage)
	1				mulangi	White radish, Raphanus sativus
				1	hagalakayi†	Momordica charantia

†These vegetables are included in meals of other families, which do not taboo them. See Table 32.

Probably for both historical and structural reasons, there is a tendency to emphasise varieties of gourds and squashes both as offerings and as tabooed items. Classical Hindu texts provide some interesting information on gourds and squashes in connection with both fertility and ancestors. In the *Ramayana* (Wilkins 1975 : 463), for example, Sumati wishes for 60,000 sons, and receives as a boon the birth of "a gourd . . . whose rind, when burst and cleft in two, gave sixty thousand babes to view." Since gourds are filled with many seeds, a gourd is a most logical candidate for this high-fertility poetic image.

A long list of tabooed offerings from the *Mahabharata* also includes mention of some gourds and squashes, specifically *Cucurbita pepo* (pumpkin) and *Cucurbita lagenaria* :

> After informing Yudhisthira, what objects should be offered to the Pitris at *Sraddha* ceremonies, Bhisma enlightened him about the objects that should not be offered and said: The species of paddy which should not be offered at *sraddhas* are those called *Kodrava* and *Pulaka*. Among articles used in cooking, Asofoetida (*sic.*), onion, garlic and the produce of *Moringa ptery-gosperma*, *Bauhinia variegata*, the meat of animals slain with poisoned shafts; all varieties of *Cucurbita pepo*, *Cucurbita lagenaria*, black salt, flesh of domestic animals, meat of the animals not slaughtered at sacrifices, *Nigella sativum*, salt called Vid, potherb *Sitapaki* (white *Durva* [grass]), all sprouts like Bamboo, *Trapa bispinosa*, fruits of *Jamvu* (Syzgium cumini syn. Eugenia jambolena), *Sudarsana* (Menisperma tomentosum). (Gupta 1971 : 98.)

In most cases it is easier to see why gourds or squashes might be required for structural features than why they might be tabooed. Not only are they filled with seeds, but also they grow on tendril-bearing vines. Eligible as both body and family metaphors, these fleshy vegetables seem to be the best possible fertility and lineal-continuity symbols that could ever appear in the plant kingdom. (A particularly puzzling taboo in the classical literature is the pumpkin. Being gold in colour, it would seem to be a good representative of the auspiciousness principle.) Data from Bandipur and Chinnapura neither confirm nor reject the pumpkin taboo, though fully ripened bottle gourd is rejected by a few houses. A possible explanation for this taboo might be found in colour symbolism: perhaps the pumpkin is considered to be red, rather than yellow.

The vine pattern of growth is also characteristic of another favourite *palya* ingredient of village ancestor menus: the *Momordica*. It is a member of the same Cucurbitaceae plant family, as are gourds.

Both the eggplant and the potato appear as requirements in a large number of village ancestor feasts. Both the eggplant (an 'unripe fruit' or *kayi*) and the potato (locally classed as a 'root', or *gedde*, rather than a 'vegetable') are white and pulpy. Both the eggplant and potato may therefore be considered as echoes (or redundant elements) of the 'whiteness' principle of the festival.[20]

At least one locally tabooed vegetable presents a clear structural feature which is unambiguously ominous: a transformation from white to black as the seeds mature. The vegetable is *Luffa acutangula*, which is enjoyed as a part of daily meals in the villages. However, it is one of the few tabooed vegetables on which those interviewed agree—that is, it is tabooed by five houses but required by no others, unlike most other vegetables which may be either tabooed or required by different houses.

Also a member of the vine-bearing Cucurbitaceae, with gourds and *Momordica*, this vegetable is contrasted with required others by its ominous transformation. Like the others, its seeds are white when immature. But distinctly unlike the others, its seeds become black when they are ready for planting. This close relatedness-plus-contrast makes it particularly useful for structural opposition. *Luffa acutangula*, therefore, is the structural representative of the physical death, turpitude, static condition (of both ancestors and families) which ancestor ceremonies—like all festivals—seem designed to transform into life and movement. As a negative metaphor in its very form, it is also logical as a tabooed item. The presence of a taboo on this item highlights both the positive and the negative which interact to give this festival its meaning.

Data on other required and tabooed vegetables seems illogical at first, with some of the same items being both required and tabooed by different families. But the interpreter should not be too bewildered by these differences. Some of these customs are based on different features of the plants in question.

An overall system becomes evident in all of this variety if there is a consistency at the level of principles. That is, if there is agreement on the connotations of the colour black, or on the flavour bitter, or on the fertility value of seeds, there can be consistency in folk-classification of certain items. But this does not mean that every household must handle the items in the same way. In fact, they do not. Separate families exercise creative effort in manipulating these principles, one apparently deciding that bitterness does not suit the ancestors, and another deciding that it is suitable to them, and so on. Viewed in this way, the variation in practice becomes a sort of debate. But the parties to this debate are not speaking different languages; in many ways their practices indicate that they agree on many basic questions or issues which give structure to the vegetal items they require or taboo.

For example, in the case of the vegetable okra, certain families may seize on some characteristics of it and use it; while others may focus on others and reject it. The vegetable is not a gourd, but it is well-filled with good, white seeds. Less in its favour as a candidate for this feast, it does not have the pulpy white flesh that some other vegetables have; and its skin is quite rough. The families which utilise the okra may be attracted by the white seeds, but those who taboo it may reject the roughness of the skin and the lack of white flesh in it. There is no contradiction at the level of principles between the two choices—only a difference in which features are noticed as relevant and therefore used by one or another family.

The *Momordica* presents a parallel case of surface confusion and systemic agreement. This vegetable is offered in most homes but tabooed by one other in our sample. Its suitability, as suggested above, may be in its vine pattern of growth as a member of the Cucurbitaceae family. It may also be in its bitter flavour. If its bitter flavour is its distinctive characteristic in the structure of the festival menu, it is clear why at least one family might wish to avoid the unhappy connotations it conveys. But it is also possible to see that it could provide symbolic balance without being overwhelmingly ominous in the symbolic structures of other families' menus. All of the festival rituals studied in preceding chapters introduce an element of balance, a touch of negativity which provides tension and contrast without dominating the meaning of the ritual. There is an exact parallel usage of bitterness in the local celebration of the Lunar New Year, when villagers eat a mixture of bitter margosa and sweet brown sugar in expression of a wish for a proper balance of good and bad luck in the year to come.

Comparing the potato and the white radish, one can see that the same feature may have either positive or negative values in the minds of different ancestor-worshippers. The potato, which is a generally preferred item, is white and solid; and it grows underground. It may therefore be an eligible metaphor-candidate for the peaceful soul of a dead person. But the white radish, which is also white and growing underground, may seem inappropriate to another family for the same reason—that it is too much of a reminder of the actual grave itself. The physiologically 'heating' quality attributed to the radish also contributes to its restlessness image. (The potato is considered 'heating' by some informants, but 'cooling' by others.)[21]

Another sometime-taboo is the snake gourd, *pada(va)lakayi*. One family tells me that some do not wish to cut up this vegetable because it resembles a serpent. In the next chapter we will review the feared results of injuring serpents in some detail. In this context, however, such a taboo is very interesting. For it is a vague hint of a Hindu belief that is more explicit in other regions, namely, a close identity between serpents and ancestors.

One vegetable, the bean *Vigna catjang*, Kannada *tadani*, is required by six families at its mature stage of development (*kalu* 'bean') but tabooed by two families at its unripe (*kayi*) stage. I suspect that folk etymology may be the basis of this range of practices. The Kannada name includes the root *tada*, which means 'obstacle'. Once at the fully ripe, plantable stage, the plant may have overcome whatever 'obstacles' there were to its growth, and may therefore be eligible. In fact, the bean is a constant feature of vegetable menus which otherwise vary in their composition. Could this be the symbol of a hoped-for overcoming of 'obstacles' to family prosperity or growth?

'Snacks'

An assortment of tasty snacks decorates the ancestors' meal, giving it a festive quality. In the eighteen non-Brahman homes for which we have detailed lists, the snacks served are of many flavours and shapes. They are salty, pungent, and sweet. They are balls, flattened-out pancakes, stuffed and unstuffed pastries, or bangles and swirled crispy delights. In short, they are of all sorts, and no strong taboos prevail. Customary snack offerings are listed in Table 34.

Closer inspection of the list does, however, reveal slight differences from the assortments of snacks served at other events. Certain snacks are notable by their absence. For example, of the *cigani-tambittu* pair—ball-shaped sweets always served together at non-Brahman 'auspicious' rites of passage, only *cigani* plays a role here. The absence of the sweet, rice-flour companion (*tambittu*) shows that the Pitra Paksa feast is not quite the same as fully auspicious family rites of passage. Rolled out of a pounded mash of sesame seeds and brown sugar, these barely-digestible balls bear an interesting resemblance to the classical *pindas*. They are not compulsory, however, being served in only half of our sample homes.

Another festive pair, however, is found on the ancestors' banana leaves in many homes This is a combination of fried snacks called *cakkali* and *kodubale*. The former is made from black gram, raw rice, and sesame seeds; and the latter from rice flour. Both are spicy and salty, and both have curvy, linear shapes. *Kodubale* is always in the shape of a few connected circles. Thus its name, 'bangle' (*bale*). *Cakkali*, the one made of black gram and sesame seeds, is crispy and takes as many linear forms as the cook's imagination can produce. It is served in sixteen of the eighteen non-Brahman sample households, while *kodubale* is only in ten.

Also made with black gram is the donut-shaped snack called *vade*. A popular South Indian treat, this fried snack is served in sixteen non-Brahman ancestor feasts. It is considered to be an appropriate food for ancestors in Brahman and non-Brahman neighbourhoods alike. This is so much so that some housewives will not prepare blackgram *vade* in their kitchens on other, non-ancestor days. A brief look at the pulse itself suggests a metaphorical connection between it and the ancestors. It is called black gram because the skin of the bean is black. The skin, however, is usually removed by the time the pulse reaches the kitchen. The inside, the bean itself, is pure white. This combination of black outside and white inside would make it an eligible candidate to represent a dead person whose soul has been released from his or her physical body even to the most elementary folk-symbolism student.

Like *vade*, the large *dose* pancake which covers the ancestors' meat and rice in nine non-Brahman homes is also made with black gram as a major ingredient. In this case, however, the batter is not purely black gram and spices. Soaked black gram and soaked raw rice are mixed together in a ratio of 1 : 2.

Table 34—'Snack' Foods Offered to Ancestors in Non-Brahman and A.K. Homes

Informants by Jati (No.)							Total Houses Offering Each 'Snack'	'Snacks' : Kannada Names
Farmer (10)	Weaver (3)	Smith (1)	Oil Presser (2)	Toddy Tapper (1)	Barber (1)	A.K. (3)		
1	1	0	1	0	0	0	3	karajikayi
5	1	1	1	1	1	0	10	kodubale
4	2	0	1	0	0	1	8	(v)obbattu
4	2	0	2	0	1	0	9	cigani/puttelluvunde
1	1	0	0	0	0	0	2	reve (v)unde
6	1	0	1	1	0	1	10	kajayya/(y)eriappa
9	2	1	2	1	1	1	17	cakkali
9	2	1	2	1	1	1	17	vade
4	2	0	1	1	1	3	12	dose
0	1	0	0	0	0	0	1	ciroti
1	0	0	0	0	0	1	2	puri
0	0	1	0	0	0	0	1	hapla

A little fenugreek and salt flavour the batter.

One auspicious preparation, also made with black gram, is missing from this feast altogether. It is called *kadabu*. The steamed mixture of rice and black gram pastes is a culinary cousin of the more widely-known *iddali*. Though not a favourite of the coffee-house set, *kadabu* has a long and honourable history in Karnataka. It is traditionally required in festivals and rites of passage alike. In the olden days, one Brahman lady tells me, it was unthinkable that anyone could be born or married, or begin her second menstruation, without a distribution of *kadabu* taking place. Now, however, it is mainly required for rituals around the time of the Festival of Lights. We find it in two auspicious events discussed elsewhere in this book—namely, Gauri Festival and serpent worship (Sibling Group Festival) of Brahmans. That *kadabu* is missing from the ancestors' plates at the Mahalaya New Moon Festival is a further testimony to the semi-auspicious atmosphere that prevails.

Sweets, and their benign connotations, are appropriate in this feast nonetheless. Two of the most popular ones, in addition to the *cigani* sesame ball, are flat fried cakes. They are called (*v*)*obbattu* and (*y*)*eriappa*. One is stuffed and the other is not, but they both have a lot of grated coconut and sweet (brown) sugar as ingredients. Made with either light wheat flour or with rice flour, they do not carry a heavy symbolic responsibility in the seven ((*v*)*obbattu*) and ten ((*y*)*eriappa*) homes that offer them to ancestors. Their sweetness is their message: "All should go well for you and for us." Figures 11 and 12 present the arrangement of foods in two homes.

AN UNCEREMONIOUS DEPARTURE

The non-Brahman or A.K. festival concludes the morning after the feast, when someone carries the *kalasa* to a body of water and empties it. Informants state that any member of the household can do this, and I have the impression that little boys often do it. Unlike the bringing, it is an uncermonious occasion. The only rule I have heard stated about this act was by an A.K. who said the *kalasa* should be carried to the river in a banana leaf.

THE COMMENSAL GROUP

Many people share food during the evening of the Mahalaya New Moon Festival. Viewing the event from Swamy Gauda's front room in 1966, I was amazed to see repeated shifts of neighbours come and go. At least three groups of men sat down quietly on the floor of Swamy Gauda's dark village house (the 'outside' portion, near the cattle) and gulped down meals from leaf plates. Once they had eaten, they left quickly for the next houses on their routes. Swamy Gauda himself soon joined the circulating commensal group. It seems that this group saw to it that all members of the same *jati* (actually the mostly endogamous Das sub-group of the Farmer *jati*) shared food that night.

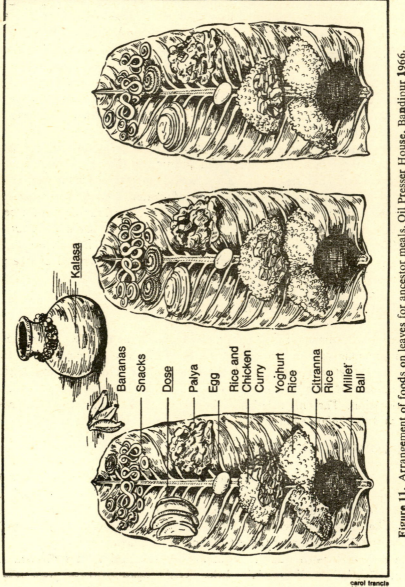

Bananas
Snacks
Dose
Palya
Egg
Rice and
Chicken
Curry
Yoghurt
Rice
Citranna
Rice
Millet'
Ball

Kalasa

Figure 11. Arrangement of foods on leaves for ancestor meals, Oil Presser House, Bandipur 1966.

carol francis

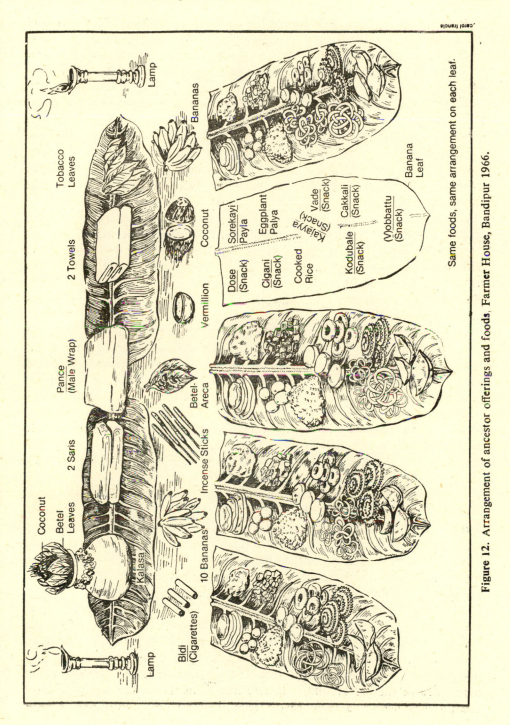

Figure 12. Arrangement of ancestor offerings and foods. Farmer House, Bandipur 1966.

A month or so later, still wondering at the extent and nature of ancestor-meal sharing, I included some questions about it on the villages census questionnaire. 185 non-Brahman and A.K. households volunteered information on who had been invited to their Mahalaya New Moon feasts, at least the most important guests.[22]

The resulting guest lists were short ones, averaging about two identified guests per house. (246 guests were mentioned in 143 non-Brahman or A.K. household interviews, producing an average of 1.72 guests per house. Another 42 houses either did not do the festival or did not invite guests at all.) My experience at Swamy Gauda's house had convinced me that villagers were probably not mentioning everyone who had eaten in their homes on that occasion.

Further interviews revealed that there are two different commensal circles, at least in some village *jatis*. The crowd that I had seen come and go on that night is the general public, so to speak—i.e., whole village *jati*-community. This group receives a portion of the food which has been cooked, but it does not receive the portion (*(y)ede*) actually having been offered to the ancestors. That portion is served to the other, more intimate group, the few relatives mentioned as guests in the survey responses.

These two commensal circles correspond to the two local views of the ancestors themselves. On the one hand, the ancestors are revered as a general, vaguely defined, apotheosized group. They are the collective responsibility of the largest possible group of 'relatives', which, as we know, blends indistinguishably into the *jati* itself. Thus it is appropriate to be as inclusive as possible, inviting all actual or potential relatives to one's feast. In Bandipur it has been customary for houses of at least three *jatis* to feast a wide circle of village caste-mates in recent history. These are the Farmers, the more elitist Weavers, and the A.K.s. I do not have data on whether other groups do this.

On the other hand, villagers identify a specific, mostly partrilineal, group of deceased relatives when asked, "For which 'elders' do you do the ancestor feast?" They hold a specific group of ancestors closely to their hearts. Accordingly, they share the meals offered to them only with a close group of relatives. Though they realise that all of the ancestors come to receive offerings on the night of the feast, they themselves remember their own mothers, fathers, and grandparents with poignant feelings on that night.

A further paradox presents itself, however. They think about their direct, mostly patrilineal ascendants, but the ancestor feast is not a time of lineage unification for most families. Each household tends to do the feast separately, and even true brothers may or may not join together for the occasion. This point is especially clear when the numbers are mentioned: out of 246 guests mentioned in the survey, only 41 were lineage-mates (brothers or patrilineal cousins of a male household head). That is about 17% of the total village guest-list. Even after deducting miscellaneous unidentified caste-mates and some (5.2%) friends, we still find that nearly 60% of invited, special guests— all sharing offered meals—are not members of the lineage whose founders are being worshipped.[23] Table 35 summarises information on invited guests.

Two opposed kin units make up the intimate offering group at the non-Brahman and A.K. ancestor feast. They are (1) the household that is sponsoring the feast, i.e. the 'birth group' whose immediate fortune depends on patrilineal ancestors' good will; and (2) their 'close exchange relations'. These are called *kutumba* and *nentru*, respectively, as I have mentioned. Although *nentru* are often the guests of choice at intimate family festivals, what can their role in patrilineal ancestor worship be?

One possible answer could refer to a system of long-range reciprocity as discussed by Dumont (1957a). This is unlikely, for if the mother's brother or some other 'wife-giver' to the lineage in question were receiving a feast as part of a long-term scheme of ritual exchanges at births, weddings, and so on, then one would expect a structural asymmetry in the types of relatives invited to share. That is, there would be either more 'wife-givers' or 'wife-takers' among the closely related guests, depending on the point at which ancestor feasts fit into the cycle of ritual exchanges. Such asymmetry is not found. In 1966 *nentru* guests are about equally divided among 'wife-givers' and 'wife-takers'.[24] (The ladies in question, daughters or sisters themselves, appear infrequently.)

A symbolic explanation seems more apt. *Kutumba* and *nentru* are perfectly opposite 'relatives'. One is in, and one is out, but they are as closely linked as any non-lineal relatives can be. As such, they are a perfect symbol for the whole group of 'relatives'. Their opposition is the best possible shorthand for totality in a culture-area where many opposites are paired with exactly that meaning. (Cf. Eichinger Ferro-Luzzi 1977, for example, for further discussion of this point.) Better than the miscellaneous assortment of caste-mates who may or may not represent a whole 'relatives'-*jati* group depending on the demography of the situation, the *kutumba-nentru* pair says, We are *all* here for *all* of you.

Once again, then, the focus shifts away from the patrilineal ancestors to the larger collectivity of which they are a part. The composition of the worshipping group provides a symbolic insurance that all will make ritual offerings, and that all will receive them. The purity or perfection of this ideal of wholeness is appropriately symbolised by the colour white, which dominates in the structure of Pitra Paksa.

DISCUSSION

In conclusion, ancestor propitiation—the most important annual ritual performed by a Hindu family—pays tribute to the spirits of the peaceful dead. The

Table 35—Guests Invited to Pitra Paksa Feasts in Non-Brahman and A.K. Homes, Bandipur 1966

Types of Guests Mentioned, by Relationship to House-hold Heads	Houses Interviewed									Totals
	Farmer (44)	Weaver (19)	Smith (3)	Oil Presser (11)	Toddy Tapper (6)	Fisher-man (11)	Barber (5)	Washer-man (7)	A.K. (80)	
	No. Mentioning Each Type of Guest									
Patrilineage Mates (B, S, FB, FBS, etc.)	5	0	0	4	0	1	1	0	30	41
'Daughters' (D, BD)	7	2	0	3	1	2	0	0	3	18
'Sisters'	2	3	0	1	0	1	1	0	6	14
Wife's Sister. WiSiHu, MoSi	4	1	0	3	1	1	1	0	2	13
Sister's Husband, FaSi, Sister's Children	6	1	0	2	1	0	2	1	11	24
DaHu, DaHuFa/Mo, BaDaHu and Children	7	2	0	2	0	1	0	1	11	24
MoBr, MoBrWi, FaMoBr	2	1	0	0	0	0	0	0	2	5
Wives' Relatives (WiFa/Mo, BrWiFa/Mo, SoWiBr, BrSoWiBr, SoWiFa/Mo, BrWiBr, WiBr)	16	4	3	3	2	1	2	3	15	49
'Caste Mates' (includes some relatives)	3	1	2	1	2	0	0	0	23	32

Friends	6	2	0	1	4	0	0	0	0	13
Other (M, Si, of Female Head, WMSiSo, WiMoSiDaHu, SiDaHu, Fa, WiBrWiFa/Mo, BrDaHuFaSi)	5	0	0	3	0	0	4	0	2	14
No Guests	7	1	0	1	0	3	0	2	7	21
Do Not Perform Ceremony	3	9	0	2	0	4	2	2	1	23
										291

ancestors represent completeness and satisfaction, and they are thought to remain involved with the family as protective spirits after death. To remain on good terms with their descendants, they are said to require only this annual offering. Plain boiled rice, the main offering, is a condensed symbol representing their state of final, peaceful repose after having passed through all stages of life. Cooked, white rice is also a metaphor for their having given life to those who follow them, and for the general purity or integrity of the family.

Concepts of the ancestors as a group of benign spirits are related to concepts of the wider family as described earlier. For instance, ancestors are represented as either male or female, and families are careful to attend to the needs of both sexes. This practice reinforces our finding in studying local genealogies that, although inheritance is patrilineal, women are considered by most families to be nearly equal to men as both founders and perpetuators of a family, and also as links to affines.

Among *puja* offerings presentational symbolism in Pitra Paksa uses colours, numbers, and other objects such as the *kalasa* in ways that are familiar from preceding festival studies. Ancestor propitiation rituals, however, make more use of vegetables as elements of symbolism than other festivals do. Seen as plants, the vegetables used as offerings have qualities which illuminate concepts of the role of ancestors and the festival in family life. For instance, many of them grow on vines, emphasising the image of a family (past, present, and future members included) as a continuing, growing entity.

Unlike other family festivals, Pitra Paksa includes little or no verbal material, such as myths, to supplement ritual symbolism. The only verbal material we could elicit was in the form of general comments about how ancestors might get angry if neglected. Nonetheless, the elements and organisation of rituals express clearly the auspicious state of being which the festival is intended to produce, and many of the forces thought to produce that state.

The following chapter repeats the theme of family purity and continuity; and it uses symbolism which is similar in some ways to that of Pitra Paksa. In cobra worship, however, the symbolic emphasis is on the present and future generations of a family rather than on its past.

NOTES

1. The Iyengar men of each village gather for a collective offering to ancestors in front of a sacred fire (*Agni*) after they have performed their annual thread-changing (*upakarma*) ceremony in their homes. This is done at the full moon of Sravana. Like other neighbourhood rituals, this ancestor worship gathering has had a shifting composition of sub-groups over the years. Local politics and friendships influence groupings.

2. A few *jatis* observe the new moon at the end of Asvija, the commencement of the Festival of Lights, as ancestors' time. In addition, some households find it necessary to postpone the ancestor feast to this date for reasons of expense. A distinction in timing of this feast also sometimes reflects dissension within a family or within a *jati*. For instance, one

Weaver household of Bandipur observes the death anniversary of their mother during the Festival of Lights because of a quarrel with their father, who does the ritual for her on the Mahalaya Amavase with others of the family.

3. This term is also used for living elders.

4. "We don't mention the dead people for whom we do the *puja*; but we know who they are," said one A.K. informant to Regelson in 1966.

5. The female items are on the left of the male, facing outward from the temporary shrine. Brahmans also talk of 'mothers' along with 'fathers' in accordance with Sanskritic traditions.

6. When I asked what this has to do with reincarnation, there was no response. In fact, common non-Brahman or A.K. notions of reincarnation seem to be rather limited : either (a) one can be re-born as a Brahman if one leads an exemplary life, or (b) murder or some other terrible crime will result in *karma*, i.e., being re-born as an A.K. or an animal (cf. Klass 1978 and Freed and Freed 1964b).

7. Steed (1955 : 140-41) mentions a Gujerati cult for the propitiation of restless ancestors, though she does not indicate whether these are seen as direct lineal ascendants, or males, or females. Involving expensive ceremonies, this cult was formed in anxiety over not having children.

Gough (1958) mentions that Nayars believe affines give the most trouble after death.

8. Of the two *talis* a woman receives at the time of her marriage, it is the husband's family pendant that is used on this occasion rather than the one from the 'mother's house'.

9. This offering is called *huvilya* in Kannada. It includes: betel-areca, turmeric, vermillion, flowers, perfume, milk, yoghurt, tender coconut, lime juice flavoured with sugar and cardamom, and three snacks—*cigali, tambittu,* and *kosambari*.

The ritual is also performed before auspicious events, such as marriages or boys' sacred thread investiture.

10. Even those Brahmans who neglect the monthly ritual often make a point of doing it at the Mahalaya New Moon.

11. The same family restricts the women to the house when they are preparing rice flour snacks for the Cobra Festival, so that they should not look at an A.K. and become polluted.

12. The woman named here is not in fact the eldest female predecessor known to this family, but her name may summon the others.

13. For the death-anniversary ritual of the Brahmans, the temporary container for ancestor spirits is not a *kalasa*; it is a human male—two or three men, in fact—one(s) of a different agnatic group than the family (and ancestors) involved. These men are summoned formally by the household head sponsoring the ritual. They come to the house in a state of strict, twenty-four-hour food and water fasting. With the recitation of appropriate verbal formulae, ancestors are thought to enter each of their seated bodies. Ancestors are fed by feeding these guests. According to custom, food should be forced on them until the guests, now seen as the hungry ancestors incarnate, say they have had enough.

Srinivas (1965 : 163-65) describes a parallel, though different, Coorg practice of communicating with ancestors through oracles or mediums. These oracles, whose performances are dramatic, come from non-Coorg groups, Banna or Panika.

14. This same type of single-stranded garland of yellow chrysanthemums is found a few days later, used in a Dassara Festival sacrifice to mechanical objects, the *ayudu puja*. In this sacrifice, mechanical objects are annointed with blood and then garlanded with chrysanthemum strands.

15. Some groups, especially Brahmans, observe another transitional ritual requiring plain cooked rice. This is called *anna-prasana*. It is the first feeding of cooked rice to a baby. This has in common with funerary ritual the association with the boundary between society (family) and extra-social existence: the baby enters society, and the deceased person departs.

The baby's rice is different from the ancestors in that it has some brown sugar and clarified butter in it.

16. On the second day after death, when the burnt bones are gathered, there is some rice cooking also; but this is only as a demon sacrifice offering, and apparently not intended to benefit the deceased person's soul.

17. The Farmers of the Das subcaste prepare a similar dish, though without the ox-blood ingredient, as an offering to a minor spirit (*harigedevaru*) before each wedding. The recipe is rather different, but it is called 'blood sauce'.

18. Yoghurt is considered to be physiologically 'cooling'; but tamarind, a major ingredient of sour-flavoured rice, is said to be 'heating' (Regelson 1972 : 83 ff.).

19. Both chicken and beef are considered to be 'heating' (Regelson 1972).

20. Eggplant is considered to be 'heating' by most villagers, though some disagree. Of Regelson's nine informants commenting on its qualities, six said it was 'heating', one 'cooling' and two, 'neutral' (Regelson 1972 : 87-88).

21. Regelson (1972 : 87-88) lists eight informants' classifications of potato as either 'heating' (four), 'cooling' (two), or 'neutral' (two).

22. Even 21 Muslim households responded with ancestor feast guest lists, though for a different, Muslim festival.

23. In a couple of houses for which I have information, 'close exchange relations' did *puja* for the ancestors, but in most houses they did not. In all of the 19 houses asked, however, they did share offered meals.

24. ' Wife-givers' to the agnatic group include such relatives as MB, WB, FMB, BSWB, SWB, BWB, WF/M, BWF, SWF/M. 'Wife-takers' include FZH, ZH, DHF/M, DH, BDH.

Chapter 8

WHITE FLOWER OFFERINGS : ANT HILL FESTIVALS FOR PURITY AND THE COBRA DEITY

This chapter will deal with two local festivals for a cobra deity which is thought to have power over the physical well-being of a family and its children. This deity is worshipped either as Nagappa (male cobra) or as Nagappa-Nagamma (male-female cobra pair). The symbolism of these festivals is parallel to that of the non-Brahman or A.K. ancestor festival insofar as both are oriented toward the development and purity of the family line. In the festivals for the cobra spirit, however, children and the future of the physical family are primary issues, and concern for the integrity of the home, marriage and sexuality, and relations between siblings becomes visible. The responsibilities of women are central in cobra worship as in other family festivals; but some women who perform these rituals do so in stark white clothing rather than in their usual varied colours.

Emphasis on white is appropriate to the meanings of cobra festivals. Struggling with questions of both spiritual and bodily purity, villagers pour a white liquid, cook with white rice flour, dress in white, and/or offer a white cow gram flower in honour of the cobra deity.[1]

Like ancestor rituals, cobra festivals highlight purity concerns. In fact, the requirements of purification by bathing or fasting are even more stringent for cobra worship than for ancestor ritual, whole families having to observe purification regimens in the former. Unlike the ancestor festival of non-Brahmans or A. K.s, the cobra festival requires a strictly vegetarian feast. Vegetarian fare is considered to be more pure than non-vegetarian.

229

Although purity is the main semantic focus here, the most immediate and explicit purpose of the festivals discussed is to avoid wounds and skin diseases. This is not the only part of India where serpent-spirits are connected with skin disorders in folk tradition, but in Bandipur and Chinnapura's cobra festivals this connection is discussed almost to the exclusion of other problems. Villagers state that an angry cobra spirit shows its wrath to a family by afflicting its members, usually its children, with rashes (*kajji*), boils (*kura*), wounds (*gaya*), or festering sores and swellings on the skin (*hunnu*).

The concern with skin disorders itself probably has at least as much metaphorical value as physical importance. Observing a symbolic equivalence or analogy between the serpent's body (mutilated in several myths), the human body (afflicted with wounds or skin diseases), and the family 'body' (pure or impure), one finds the preoccupation with skin disorders appearing as a concern for all sorts of destruction of physical integrity, i.e., with impurity in the sense of disintegration or surface mutilation. A family's decision to perform a festival ritual for the cobra deity thus appears as a culturally based recognition that something is wrong with the family's physical state, and that special action to restore purity (integrity) is necessary to rectify the disorder beneath their physical disease. The several village families who are expiating a collective guilt in a cobra festival for having injured a serpent at some time in their history seem to believe that their own integrity was also disrupted in committing that offense.[2]

Although these festivals are dedicated to the cobra deity, one sees few icons of the deity in the course of rituals and no actual snakes. The physical center of offerings is, rather, a large ant hill of the sort in which serpents are said to live. This jagged mound dotted with large holes is the work of termite ants. Like the boils which its rituals are said to cure, it erupts out of the red earth of a village field to a height of 3-10 feet or so.

Some cultural background on notions of purity and pollution may assist the reader in interpreting basic principles of cobra festivals' symbolism. The Hindu vocabulary relating to these concepts is elaborate in all Indian languages, and Kannada is no exception. At least one basic rule applies to all: 'purity' always is separate from 'impurity'. The two ideological constructs go together in the sense that they define each other in their contrast. Thus we find that in these purity-enhancing, regularity-glorifying festivals, impurity is also a recurrent symbolic element.

Rituals and myths of cobra festivals create pure and impure by employing symbolic forms that heighten their contrastive values and strengthen their dramatic powers. This accenting effect is a result of the 'marking' function of festival symbolism. In general, it is useful to view such extremes of either purity or pollution as 'marked' conditions, in the sense that they are unusual and non-ordinary conditions created by special devices producing states which contrast with ordinary states of being (cf. Greenberg 1969).[3]

Harper's (1964) article on personal purity and pollution concepts of Havik Brahmans in a neighbouring district of Karnataka also applies to the cultural views of Bandipur and Chinnapura villagers. In that article, Harper describes three named (culturally marked) states: *madi* 'purity', *mailige* 'regular, daily pollution', and *muttu* 'extreme pollution'. For instance, just after a bath a person is *madi*; after sexual intercourse one is *mailige*; and during menstruation women are *muttu*. All of these are special states which contrast with an unnamed (unmarked), ordinary condition which is generally neutral as to purity or pollution. Srinivas's (1965) study on the Coorgs also includes much on these concepts.

As a group, a family shares what Mandelbaum (1970) would call 'corporate pollution' on some occasions. Named states of pollution apply to the patrilineage (*dayadi*) as a group. These are called *sutaka* by most villagers, and are associated with three major transitions of a lineage. The transitions are (1) the first menstruation of a daughter; (2) the birth of a lineage-member's child; and (3) the death of any member.[4] On such occasions, as Harper's (1964) article discusses, patrilineage members isolate themselves. They do not give food to outsiders for at least ten days at such times. When the lineage is polluted by *sutaka*, its members' bodies are considered to be *mailige*, or personally 'polluted'.

There is, however, no exact, named opposite of collective 'pollution'—i.e., family purity. The explanation for this lack may be that the ordinary state of a lineage (*dayadi*), i.e., the state of not being in a life-crisis transition, is an unmarked condition. The closest term for family purity that I have been able to elicit refers, interestingly enough, to the 'birth group' (*kutumba*) and not to the patrilineal group. As I said in Chapter 2 above, the family (as 'birth group') strives to be 'good' in the sense of genuine and flawless. This is the state of pearl-like purity, wholeness, and integrity that the 'white' cobra festivals seem to celebrate.

Like the people and families which live in it, a home is also subject to a sort of purity-pollution. It is said to be either 'clean' (*svacca/socca*), as when newly whitewashed and having its floors wiped with cow dung paste; or 'dirty' (*kolaku*). This distinction appears in details of festival rituals also, emphasising by repetition the general principle of deep concern to villagers here and drawing a parallel between cleanliness and ritual purity.

THE MEANINGS OF SERPENTS IN LITERARY AND ORAL TRADITIONS

In one myth benign, in another malevolent—sometimes facilitating, sometimes obstructing—the serpent is a many-faceted symbol in this culture area and has been so for at least two millenia. Playing more religious mythological roles than most other animals, serpents appear as powerful animal spirits in several guises. Among them are the immortal cobra, called Naga; the devouring and polluting python, called Rahu; and the long serpent rope used to rotate the mountain-churn in the creation myth, 'Churning of the Ocean of Milk'. The infinite cosmic ocean itself, as the bed on which Visnu reclines, is represented iconographically as a cobra called Sesa or Ananta. The cobra is always represented as a decorative garland around the neck of the powerful ascetic god Siva.

Nagas or cobra spirits, are traditionally associated with bodies of water and subterranean zones, and correspondingly with rains, ponds, oceans, the roots of trees and holes in the earth (such as in ant hill mounds). In fact, the myth of the subterranean serpent or dragon is widespread in south, east, and southeast Asian cultures alike.[5] The extent of its distribution indicates that this figure in one form or another is probably quite old in the eastern part of the Eurasian continent. The tradition of the Chinese dragon—benign symbol of imperial domain—may well be historically related to that of the Hindu serpent spirits. Like the serpent, the Chinese dragon has been depicted as living underground. And also like the serpent, the dragon has been represented as a benign though powerful spiritual figure.

While the cobra is a poisonous snake, it is important for this study to recognise that its other characteristics receive more cultural recognition than its poison does. It fact, its length, its coils, and its spreading hood are the assets emphasised in most myths and works of art. It is actually the sheltering hood and the fat coils of the sacred cobra which dominate its iconographic representation and not its fangs.

Some serpent figures of literary and iconographic renown are depicted as females. There is, for example, the myth of the 'Poisonous Damsel', Visakannike, which is still current in Kannada Brahman oral traditions. This figure is a type of female who is partly serpent and partly human, who uses her venomous power to destroy a mortal male attracted to her. The immortal *nagas* also have their female counterparts in *naginis*. According to Zimmer (1946 : 63), "serpent princesses, celebrated for their cleverness and charm, figure among the ancestresses of many a South Indian dynasty: a *nagini* or *naga* in the family tree gives one a background."

But unlike the Western Biblical tradition connecting the sin of Eve with the satanic serpent-tempter, these female serpents are not totally evil. They serve, rather, as the partners of *nagas*, and, like them, are said to be powerful, immortal, and capable of using their powers for either constructive or destructive ends.

This is significant as a point of connection between literary and oral traditions, since the serpent spirit is often worshipped as a male-female pair in Karnataka.[6] The pair is called *nagappa-nagamma*, 'Sir Naga'-'Lady Naga' in the Kannada usage of Hassan District. And though the male spirit is important, in the festival rituals described below offerings are generally made to the pair rather than to a single spirit.

Pearls and other jewels are associated with the serpent in Hindu traditions. Generalising about *naga* spirits, Zimmer (1946 : 63) points out that they "inhabit subaquatic paradises, dwelling . . . in resplendent palaces studded with gems and pearls," and that, "they are supposed to carry a precious jewel in their heads. The treasure of their immortality is [said to be] concentrated" in this gem, the proverbial *naga-rattinam*. (See also Buck 1974.)[7]

The folklore of India is replete with serpent spirits—even more so than are literary and iconographic traditions. There is a sizable amount of descriptive material in English on this subject by Bhattacharyya (1960, 1961, 1965) and others. One of the most interesting series of studies deals with Bengali myths of Manasa, goddess of snakes, by Dimock, and by Dimock and Ramanujan (Dimock 1962, Dimock 1969, Dimock and Ramanujan 1964).

Most villagers in Bandipur and Chinnapura also draw a general conceptual picture of the cobra deity or deities. Though it is inspired by classical traditions and incorporates some of them into its image of the godling, its rough outlines only hint at the many philosophical possibilities outlined above. The cobra deity is seen as a benign force, despite the fact that a number of villagers die of cobra bite each year. One woman explained to me, for example, that if a polluted person (she used the example of a menstruating woman) should try to enter the village temple compound, a cobra would strike out in protection of the temple.

Another interesting feature of the Karnataka village picture of the cobra deity is the emphasis on its eyes. As with the violent *amma* spirits discussed earlier, villagers speak of the eyes as if they were the most sensitive and powerful bodily organs, especially when it comes to doing harm by discharging anger. (Physically it should be fangs, but symbolically it is eyes.) Thus villagers use a phrase, 'cooling the eyes' of the cobra deity, in describing the festival ritual's magical effects. In the case of the cobra spirit, villagers try to soothe and 'cool' the eyes; in the case of the *amma*, they try to avoid the deity's stare altogether.

This detail also recalls the 'Mangala Gauri' myth, in which the visual capacity is significant as the sensor of pleasurable images. The mythological serpent's association with gold and jewels, the most beautiful and colourful of all objects, may be a further emphasis on visual pleasure, as it is in 'Mangla Gauri'.

The concept of 'cooling' or 'heating' the eyes in cobra festivals may have some connection with the purity-pollution theme. If Babb (1975) is correct in his observation that 'coolness' and purity can be culturally linked, this would support the possibility of a correlation in the Karnataka festivals. (I have not heard statements to this effect in Bandipur or Chinnapura.) The act of 'putting coolness' (*tanni (y)eriyuvudu*) in cobra festival rituals is said by my informants to induce a condition of 'peace' in the cobra deity. They avoid 'heating' items in this festival, they say, since they believe that 'heat' would incite the spirit's anger. For instance, they avoid using chillies in seasoning the food offered in their ritual since, they say, these would 'heat the eyes' of the serpent or serpent pair. Some avoid grinding spices for the same reason.

THE ANT HILL AS A SHRINE

The basic ritual act in local versions of the cobra festival is the same: it consists of pouring a white liquid—a mixture of milk and clarified butter—into a hole (or holes) of an ant hill mound. An alternative to this ritual is to bring home some ant hill mud from the space around a hole and make oblations in the home itself.

Although pan-Asian traditions associate the serpent spirit mainly with water, India's folk traditions often identify the ant hill as the serpent's abode. The association is found in a *Pancatantra* story. The story is of a poor Brahman named Haridatta, a farmer who received gold pieces from a 'hooded snake' who crept daily out of an ant hill in his fields. In exchange for the gold pieces, the farmer and his son fed the serpent with milk, until the son tried to kill the snake one day and was himself killed by it. The farmer continued to make offerings to the serpent after this, but his friendship was rejected by the occupant of the ant hill. The farewell comments of the wounded snake are interesting in that they show him to be somewhat compassionate. The conclusion of the story also introduces the (white) pearl as a gem special to the cobra.

[The serpent speaks to the bereaved father:]

"From this time forward friendship between us is impossible. Your son struck me in youthful ignorance, and I have bitten him to death. How can I forget the blow with the cudgel? And how can you forget the pain and grief at the loss of your son?" So speaking, it gave the Brahman a costly pearl and disappeared. But before it went away it said: "Come back no more." The Brahman took the pearl, and went back home, cursing the folly of his son. (Jacobs 1969 : 112-14, "The Gold-giving Serpent.)"[8]

This ancient figure is still thought to guard buried treasure in all parts of Karnataka. Parvathamma (1971 : 123) mentions that in northern Karnataka "The belief is that ant hills grow to cover hidden wealth and are safeguarded by a cobra." Citing *Panjab Notes and Queries*, Crooke (1896 : II. 145) mentions that in north India the serpent also is thought to live in an ant hill:

[In the Panjab Hills,] no image of a cobra or other venomous snake is ever made for purposes of worship. Ant hills are believed to be the homes of snakes, and there the people offer sugar, rice, and millet for forty days.

In reviewing the folklore literature, I have found some references to ant hill shrines which are not associated with serpents. One with classical overtones is from the Boya and Paidi castes of south India, some of whom have assumed the name of Valmika or Valmiki. Thurston's (1909 : VII. 310-311) report on these peoples associates the growth of an ant hill with the devotional services of the author of the *Ramayana*:

[These peoples] claim to be descended from Valmiki, the author of the Ramayana, who did penance for so long in one spot that a white ant hill (valmikam) grew up round him.

. . . In the North Arcot Manual, Valmikulu, as a synonym of the Vedans, is made to mean those who live on the products of ant hills.

In some tribal groups of central India, the Korwas and the Khariyas, the gods Bhagwan and Parameswar are worshipped at their ant hill shrines (Crooke 1896 : I. 9-10). And Whitehead (1921 : 74-75) describes a shrine in Bellary Town, northern Karnataka (Mysore) which is dedicated to the goddess Durgamma. The shrine consists of an ant hill with a plain stone edifice built over it. The structure is about 30 feet long, 6 feet deep and 8-10 feet high. In this last case, a link was made between the ant hill and a serpent; for a snake who lived in a nearby wall was enticed to come daily to the ant hill to be fed.

Crooke (1896 : II. 256) mentions a ritual offering made by some to the termite ants themselves:

. . . Ants are carefully fed on certain days by Hindus and Jainas and are in some way connected with the souls of the sainted dead.[9]

As to the metaphorical value of the ant hill as a ritual object, its physical features are of symbolic importance. These features give it several bodily characteristics. The features on which ritual attention is focused are (1) its eminence, (2) the earth of which it is built-up, (3) its container-qualities i.e., the fact that it supposedly houses a serpent and/or golden treasure, and (4) its holes, the earth around the holes, or the holes as receptacles of the ritual offerings.

If the ant hill is a metaphorical body, then the serpent is a symbol of several different possible values in relation to it. First, it could represent the soul in the body, as suggested by Buck (1974). Or, it could represent the spiritual responsibility to keep purity, as the guardian of the soul represented by the golden treasure. Secondly, it could represent the sexual agent, the phallic organ which goes in and out of the hole of the ant hill. Thirdly, the poisonous venom of the serpent represents the life-and-death significance of sexual and purity questions to the family and lineage or caste.

The folklore literature suggests that the ant hill may have a history of its own, separate from the serpent-worship tradition. How the two came to be combined is not yet known. But in the rituals to be discussed in this chapter, as in rituals of other parts of India, the two are often combined. And the combination provides a powerful metaphor for several vital issues, centering on purity and the physical body, which are most probably the basis of the meanings of the ant hill rituals.

ANT HILL FESTIVALS FOR THE GOLD-KEEPING SERPENT

Two local cobra festivals are performed at different times of year by different *jati*-clusters but in a similar fashion. They are (1) 'Cobra Festival' (*Nagara Habba* or *Nagarapancami*), performed at the end of the second fortnight of the Hindu month of Margasira or at the beginning of the following month of Pusya (mid–January) by some A.K. and non-Brahman families; and (2) 'Sibling Group Festival' (*Vodahuttidavara Habba*,[10] also called *Siriyalasristi* or *Nagarapancami*), performed at the beginning of the light half of the month of Sravana (mid-August) by Smartha Brahmans.[11]

Since these festivals are mostly associated with long-standing family vows, families perform the rituals separately to a great extent, if they do them at all. But the Sibling Group Festival turns into a neighbourhood event at one phase, in which pairs of Smartha Brahman women exchange gifts.

As with other such obligations, there is considerable anxiety about discontinuing these rituals. This anxiety is further reinforced by local soothsayers, who often instruct families to initiate these rituals to appease an angry serpent spirit who is causing skin diseases in their children.

Despite the separateness of familistic traditions which these festivals represent, they overlap considerably in verbal justifications, mythical structures, and action patterns.

COBRA FESTIVAL RITUALS

The rituals for the Cobra Festival occupy one day early in the first half of the Hindu month of Pusya.[12] In Chinnapura and Bandipur alike the day of the festival is a day of frenzied activity in many non-Brahman and A.K. houses, where an atmosphere of 'purity' (*madi*) must prevail. Everyone in the house may be required to bathe, washing hair and body alike; and a complete fast is observed by all. Although the women are more bound by purity restrictions than are other members of the family, many villagers of both sexes take no food or drink at all until after the ant hill ritual. Even the refreshing betel-areca is forbidden. Babies are indulged to the extent that they need their own mothers' milk; but for families who are strict in their observance, even cow milk is forbidden to the little ones.

Of course the house itself will be cleaned. This generally means washing a mud floor with a soft mixture of cow dung, purchasing new clay pots, or cleaning metal vessels with tamarind. In some A.K. houses the woman of the family will prepare a small hole in a corner of her main room. The purifying cow dung covers this as well.[13] Later on she will be pounding paddy there as she starts her ritual food preparation.

In non-Brahman houses the woman takes over special responsibility for the maintenance of purity. She does not leave the house, for to do so would be to risk the defiling glance or shadow of an A.K., and a subsequent polluting (*mailige*) of the offering which she is to prepare. She is the guardian of the ritual food, secluded with her charge for the time, while others may come and go as they please. Those who have been outside are reminded to avoid touching her rice flour and other cooking ingredients.

In some A.K. houses it is a solitary housewife who fasts, bathes, and prepares the ritual offering according to the instructions handed down from mother-in-law to daughter-in-law. She will have received a special gold 'Cobra-*tali*' from her mother-in-law for use in festival ritual. In other A.K. houses it is a male-female pair which takes charge of the family's offering by observing the strict purity requirements. All participants will have avoided meat for three days in conformity with the A.K. mode of preparation for a pure, vegetarian feast day such as this one.

In one Chinnapura Washerman family an individual man performs the ritual. He begins by taking a cold river bath in solemn recollection of a severe rash caused by a deed of his father's when he himself was one year old. The father had tried to remove an ant hill which was near their house. He had accidentally cut a snake in half as it came out of the ant hill. Although he had intended to offer a silver snake image to the village temple, he soon forgot about the matter. It was many years later that this man and his own children had gotten the rash on their heads; and the local Brahman soothsayer had traced the cause and instructed him to do this ritual at 4 : 00 a.m. once each year. After his bath he dons the required white clothing and performs the ritual offering to an ant hill in perfect silence, avoiding the glance of those he considers lower than himself on the caste ranking scale—Barbers and A.K.s.[14]

Here and there one might also see a solitary Brahman housewife bathing in the river on this morning as she fulfills a vow for the sake of her children's health.

Once having purified herself and her house, the A.K. housewife begins to pound some paddy in the hole she has prepared. After the paddy has been husked, she uses the winnowing basket to remove the husks, and sorts out the broken rice grains with a sieve. She will use this rice (whole grains only) in cooking the meal for the serpent deity who lives in an ant hill. For her, the cooking is to be itself a ritual act, done in white clothing outdoors in the vicinity of the ant hill, which is temporarily transformed into a shrine by this action.

The separation of grain from husk is a frequent occurrence in folk-Hindu rituals. Various utensils associated with this process, especially the winnowing fan, also appear in festivals and rites of passage, as discussed above. In this context the husking of the grain, as an act of separation, is a part of the general purificatory process which is occurring in village homes.

Having prepared the rice grains, the A.K. woman gathers together the things she needs: the rice she has just husked, a special bundle of spices (dill and onion flower, called 'serpent greens'), and two new clay vessels. She brings other seasonings too, but avoids the taboo chillies which would 'heat' the serpent's eyes. She also brings the special cobra *tali* which she keeps just for this purpose; a mixture of milk and clarified butter; and the required bananas, turmeric, vermillion and incense sticks needed for *puja*. These will be given on a winnowing fan in which she has placed the tip-end (*suli*) of a banana leaf.

One item which is virtually omnipresent in other *pujas* is omitted from this list: a coconut. The coconut is taboo as an offering to the ant hill serpent spirit on this occasion for both A.K.s and non-Brahmans. Two possible explanations for this taboo have occurred to me. One is that it would be inappropriate to break a coconut, as is usually done in offering one, in a ritual that is symbolically struggling on behalf of wholeness and purity against bodily injury or mutilation and impurity. The other is based on a bit of comparative data from Sri Lanka, where the two ends of a coconut are said to correspond to male and female (Leach 1970). If this has any relevance to Karnataka folk beliefs (I cannot say whether it does or not), then breaking a coconut would suggest a symbolic rupture in relations between the sexes.

As the A.K. woman, in white clothing, makes her way to the ant hill with uncooked foods and *puja* offerings, the non-Brahman woman is still at home, having pounded and mixed rice flour with sweet flavourings transforming it into *tamta* (*tambittu*). Both will soon begin cooking the seasoned mixture of rice and green gram : *huggianna*, also called *nagarbana* or *huggibana*, which is specially favoured by the serpent spirits and always offered to them on this occasion. An important difference is that the A.K. woman cooks outdoors, and the non-Brahman woman, indoors.

One A.K. woman tells me that she does her outdoor cooking and offering individually while others cook nearby. The scene which I witnessed in 1967 had male-female pairs performing ritual acts separately, although their stoves were lined up in rows with those of other couples (See Plates 17-A and 17-B).

All A.K.s have one common social restriction in performing this ritual—that those who cook and offer together must not be siblings. Neither brothers nor sisters nor a brother-sister pair can do this ritual as a unit. Except for the prohibition on sibling unity, there does not seem to be any further restriction on which opposite-sexed relatives can pair up as partners in this ritual.

In the A.K. ritual which I observed, a group of thirteen couples gathered to cook and offer food together. The few pairs which I was able to identify represent a sufficiently varied assortment of relationships to indicate that it is only

Plate 17-A. A. K. women dressed in white, cooking for cobra spirit (S. Regelson Photograph, Bandipur 1966)

Plate 17-B. A. K. woman cooking for cobra spirit (S. Regelson Photograph, Bandipur 1966)

their maleness and femaleness and their non-sibling relationship which are determinant social criteria for the pairing. The identified pairs included a mother and son, a father and daughter, and two husband-wife couples. The group represented a merging of two subcastes which have intermarried among themselves. And although these people were probably all related to each other, they identified themselves simply as a 'god group', which meant nothing more than that they had gathered to worship the same god.

The act of A.K. outdoor cooking is circumscribed with several other require-ments and taboos. These give a distinct form to the ritual, structuring it largely in terms of the male-female sexual dichotomy, which is correlated with purity-impurity. The sequence begins with the construction of a row of mud stoves (see Plate 18). These stoves are constructed in pairs. The two parts of each pair are strictly separated and distinguished from one another. One is female (for Nagamma) and 'dirty' (*kolaku*); the other, male (for Nagappa) and 'clean' (*socca*). Some keep a smaller pot for the female and a larger one for the male. Others prefer to distinguish the two in the quantity of rice : one contain-er (*seer*) of rice cooked for the female, and two for the male. The female stove is placed on the left, and the male, on the right. Even the firewood piles for the two stoves are separate.[15]

A further requirement in A.K. Cobra Festival cooking relates to the stirring implement. It must be a piece of a coconut tree frond (*gari*, the portion from

Plate 18. A pair of mud stoves built for Cobra Festival ritual cooking (S. Regelson
          Photograph, Bandipur 1966)

which the fronds extend). All informants declare firmly that no other stirring utensil can be used for this purpose.[16] (Separate stirrers for male and female pots are set apart, of course.)

Although the ritual stoves are distinguished in terms of their purity and pollution, they are both protected from the pollution of human saliva : neither fire is fanned by the usual method of blowing on it through a tube.

After the stoves have been constructed, the cooking begins, and the group waits until the meal is ready. The rice will boil with seasonings and pulses, each white-clad woman tending her own pair of stoves, as the members of each A.K. 'god group' sit around their cleared plaza chatting informally.

Meanwhile in non-Brahman homes women continue to work indoors. Their cooking is done inside their kitchens, hidden from the polluting view of strangers.

Once the cooking is finished, the offering to the ant hill will begin. For the A.K. group, as for a few non-Brahman families, this offering will be made at the ant hill itself. But for other non-Brahman families, a portion of ant hill earth, dug from the area around a hole, will be brought back to the house by a child to receive its 'cooling' ritual offering in the very pure, domestic setting.

The form of the ant hill offering varies somewhat from family to family, or 'god-group' to 'god-group'. In its general outline, however, it seems to be the same for all as the offering which I observed : (1) a man smears the ant hill surface (or the pile of earth, in some non-Brahman houses) with purifying cow dung and decorates it with either vermillion or a turmeric-vermillion combination. (2) He takes special care to put vermillion around the two holes which are to receive male or female food offerings. (3) He then pours a white mixture of milk and clarified butter (or plain butter, for one family, also white) into each of the two holes.[17] (4) He concludes this phase of the offering by placing bananas near each hole and solemnly circling incense sticks before the ant hill, turning thrice-round, pausing with his back to the offering, and sticking the burning incense into the edges of the holes. This last series of gestures is called *dupa* 'incense'.[18] (5) He then places the pile of offerings—betel and areca, plantains, flowers, and a golden *tali*—next to the female hole; and a similar set, with or without jewellery (earrings, *kadaka*), next to the male hole.[19]

One further offering which appears in the Cobra Festival *puja* is the (white) flower of a cow gram plant—*avare huvu* in Kannada. Most non-Brahman informants mention customarily offering it, sometimes as a dried flower (*honnavare huvu*), although I have not observed their *pujas*. A few give yellow flowers along with it, or instead of it.

It is common to require a gold ornament, usually a *tali*, rather than a silver ornament, to the cobra deity (see Plate 19). Most families, including all A.K.s, stress this as a necessity in the Cobra Festival, one family supporting their belief with a comment about something bad that happened when an acquaintance mistakenly offered silver. Asking about the gold requirement in an A.K.

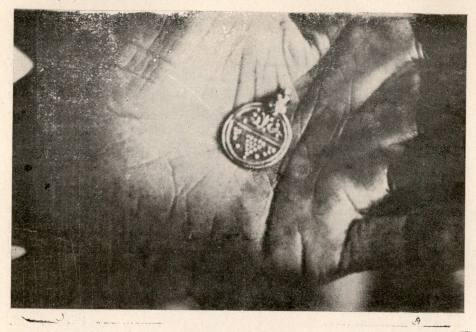

Plate 19. Cobra *Tali*

house in 1976, I tried to elicit information on the possibility of offering silver
(as, for example, when a family could not afford a piece of gold). But the three
middle-aged and older women whom I confronted with this possibility merely
looked incredulously at me and repeated their statement that only gold can
serve as an offering to the cobra deity.[20]

> You should put down gold to Nagappa in this *puja*. About four or five
> years ago one woman in a nearby village put down silver instead. That night
> many festering sores came to her baby. She did the 'asking *sastra*' (as is
> done by the Smith soothsayer of our village), and Nagappa said that he was
> very angry that she put silver to him, and that the sore would go only if she
> put gold to him within eight days. She put gold, and the child became well.
> (S. Hanchett notes, January 10, 1967, Farmer informant.)

The climax of the Cobra Festival *puja* is offering cooked food. This final act
at the ant hill is performed by women, in the case of the A. K.s, at least.
Maintaining the distinction between male and female offerings, each woman
sets two separate meals, one from each stove, side-by-side onto two distinct
banana leaf-tips in her winnowing fan.[21] Each meal consists of three balls of
the special rice-green gram preparation she has cooked: *huggianna*. (Non-Brahmans place a special *tamta* 'snack' cake onto the offering tray as well.) She

carries her winnowing fan over to the ant hill and awaits her turn by standing in a line as others make their offerings. After worshipping her foods with application of turmeric-vermillion and rotation of incense sticks, she places three of the 'male' *huggianna* balls next to the hole designated for Nagappa. After rinsing her hands, she offers the second three balls next to the hole for Nagamma, the female.

After doing this the A.K. woman makes a gesture of blessing by pinching and flipping some raw rice grains onto the ant-hill. She then picks up the golden *tali* which her male partner had left for the snake, and returns to gather together the remainder of the food which she has cooked on her two stoves, wrapping it in banana leaves to carry back to her house.[22] Later on, they say, 'the men' will push the triple-ball offering into each hole.

Once she is back at home, her special actions gradually return the family to a non-ritual, ordinary state.[23] The A.K. woman removes her white clothing, changing into another sari. She purifies a second space on her house floor by washing it with watery cow dung. For this she uses a vessel of water (*bindige*) which she had set there as part of the morning's purification activity. This is the site of an offering of the *huggianna* to her house god. This offering is a small ritual in its own right, the food being set in three plates and garnished with some additional items, one of which is some chopped-up coconut.[24] (Since coconut is taboo for the serpent offerings, this element defines a different event.) Setting an offering of betel-areca next to the plates, she does the 'incense-rotation' *dupa* for this set. A portion of this food is given to members of the household and never to guests, though guests may be invited later.

In this final commensal act the household partakes of the food which has been offered to the cobra pair on its behalf, defining itself as a unit in the process, and concluding the ritual assured that Nagappa and Nagamma will feel pleasure and 'peace' when they think of this family.[25]

The group which shares the offered meal ((*y*)*ede*) is an intimate group. It consists of persons who make up the household (*mane*), including close relatives (*nentru*) who may be temporarily in residence. The one A.K. informant questioned on this point (Smt. Chennamma) describes the party only as 'house people', rather than by any specific kinship term. This, together with the male-female pairing of stoves and some other details of Cobra Festival symbolism, suggests that the festival as a whole is more concerned with the actions and issues relating to kin who share a home than with those of larger kin groups. This is, of course, the 'birth group' (*kutumba*) in most cases the kin unit with direct involvement in marital sexuality, incest taboos, and birth processes; and the unit which upholds the reputation of the larger family group. (It is appropriate that non-lineage-mate residents be included in the home, since their symbolic importance as 'relations of exchange' does not contradict the general theme of exchange which seems to prevail at this occasion.) The ultimate relevance of all of the rituals to the lineage is indicated in the *puja* for the house god, which is common to all of the houses of the same lineage identification (*dayadi* or *kula*). However, while problems at stake matter to the lineage, responsibility for their solution is assigned to those sharing a home.

COBRA FESTIVAL : OPERATIONAL MEANINGS OF ELEMENTS

Though the milk-clarified butter mixture appears in some groups' wedding rituals, this is not its usual cultural connotation.[26] It is more generally associated with funerals.

All *jatis*, whether A.K., non-Brahman, or Brahman, use the milk-clarified butter mixture in funerals for children. 'Pouring-milk-clarified butter' at the head end of a grave is, in fact, one of the main rituals performed when children die. The mixture is considered 'cooling-soothing' (*tampu*) for both body and soul. (Non-clarified butter, which is 'cold' (*sita*), plays a major role in baby-naming rituals; but clarified butter does not.) Villagers have explained to me that there is a conscious message intended: "You should forget your mother's milk now." This ceremony is performed by different groups at different stages of a child's funeral, but all do it within the first eleven days.[27] Though some groups also pour the mixture onto a grave of an adult at the third day of mourning, this is a minor ritual. With whomever I have asked about it, the first conscious associations made to the milk-clarified butter mixture are only two: children's funerals and cobra worship.

This connection suggests a paradox which must be resolved, if one is to interpret any operational meaning to the use of milk-clarified butter in the Cobra Festival. Why is an element from a funeral ritual used in a festival that is supposed to protect living children and help them flourish ? This is even true for the Brahmans, who tend to eliminate all 'inauspicious' ingredients (i.e., elements associated with death ritual in any way) from life-perpetuating rituals even more systematically than others do.

I suspect that there is a missing piece in the puzzle. One interesting possibility occurs to me. That is, that the serpent spirits are (or were once) believed to be reborn souls of dead children. Those child-souls need to be soothed and fed, so that they will not feel envious of the living family's children. One can neither confirm nor disprove this hypothesis without pursuing further field studies; but circumstantial evidence to support it does exist in the folklore of other regions, which connects serpents and the dead.

One of the food requirements of non-Brahmans is that the festival snack food must be made of rice flour and no other. This can be any one of a number of preparations, but the most common offering is the sweet, round cake called *tamta* or *tambittu*. A significant feature of this in the structure of the rituals is no doubt the white colour of the rice flour. In fact, the pounding of rice flour together with brown sugar took up a significant amount of the women's morning in the one non-Brahman house we visited on this occasion in 1967.

As mentioned in preceding chapters this particular 'snack' (*tamta/tambittu*) ball appears at most auspicious family feasts. Non-Brahmans serve it together with a heavier ball made of sesame seeds, called either *cigani* or *cigali*, at nearly all rites of passage. It may be significant that whereas the other member of the auspicious pair, *cigani*, appears alone in the ancestor feast, this member tends to appear alone in the same families' Cobra Festival feast. Is a complementarity defined here?

The chief food element of significance for the Cobra Festival is the type of rice which is cooked, *huggianna*. This mildly flavoured mixture of rice and green gram has an unmistakable association with birth and naming. *Huggianna* is placed, with a clarified-butter lamp on it, at the exact spot where the birth of a baby has taken place in the Iyengar Brahman, llth day naming ceremony. (Gurulingaiah notes, 1967.) And in the feast of the naming ceremony day it is required as part of the menu by most non-Brahman families. So far as we have been able to determine, nearly all the *jatis* of the area serve *huggianna* when a baby is eleven days old.

The appearance of *huggianna* as an offering after the milk-clarified butter mixture has been poured gives the ritual sequence a rhythmic movement from death-association to birth-association. It seems as though villagers are non-consciously enacting a drama in which an angry soul is appeased and 'cooled' so that it will not set up obstacles to the success of family births. At the offering itself, three balls of *huggianna* are set near the two ant hill holes; the appearance of the number 3 here tends to support the view that the phenomenon of birth is the symbolic climax of festival ritual symbolism. (Cf. earlier discussion of the ritual uses of number 3 in connection with Prati and Gauri festivals.)

Both the milk-clarified butter mixture and *huggianna* also function as markers of the removal of pollution. Their appearances in the system of rites of passage, at the third day after the death of a child and on the eleventh day after the birth of a child, respectively, are specifically at points where corporate pollution (*sutaka*) disappears from the lineage. (Children's deaths do not pollute the family for as long as adults' deaths do.) This aspect of their 'operational meanings' serves the purpose of transforming impurity into normality, which is basic to the Cobra Festival as a whole.

One last element of festival symbolism, silver, has a special meaning in the larger ritual system which may shed light on its usage—or rather, its non-usage—in Cobra Festival ritual. At first sight, prohibiting silver offerings appears to be out of keeping with the overall organisation of festival ritual, since silver is considered to be 'white' in colour. Why prohibit a white offering in a festival that otherwise emphasises this colour?

Prohibiting silver offerings, if we consider the role of silver jewellery in non-Brahman and A.K. life, is a structural parallel to prohibiting siblings from performing cobra rituals together. Silver jewellery, mainly as belts, bracelets and ankle bracelets, is customary ornamentation for women of these *jati*-clusters in Bandipur and Chinnapura. They receive this jewellery as dowry from their natal families at the time they are married. (Gold is the metal used for earrings nowadays. But most A.K.s and non-Brahmans cannot afford gold earrings for their daughters; nor is this a traditional necessity, the old-fashioned earrings for married women being *biccole* palm-leaf strips.) From their husbands' families and, less often, from their natal families women receive gold, as a *tali*, at the time of their marriages.

While silver marriage gifts link a woman to her natal family, silver widowhood gifts link her to her male siblings. It is the custom among non-Brahmans and A.K.s that when a woman is widowed her brother presents her with a set of silver bangles. (Mr. G. has mentioned to me that the bangles presented may be of any metal, but I have never seen any but silver ones.)

Thus, both at the beginning and at the end of a woman's married life silver is connected with her natal family, specifically with her brother at widowhood; and gold with her marital family. To taboo a silver offering repeats the taboo on a sibling connection, and orients festival symbolism away from the family of orientation into the family of marital sexuality and births for the husband's patriline.

The theme of marriage vs. sibling ties will become more and more important as we consider the structure of the 'Cobra Festival Myth', which pits incestuous tendencies against exogamous marriage. It is an important theme in the following, Sibling Group, Festival also, especially in one phase of it and in the 'Sister Saves Brother' myth. The detail of tabooing silver in Cobra Festival offerings, if the interpretation offered here is correct, reflects and repeats a profound cultural concern facing the Karnataka Hindu family, namely, the issue of how sibling ties do or do not relate to marital ties. As I shall discuss further below, this is not a simple matter; but a ritual taboo gives family relationships temporary clarity, at least.

COBRA FESTIVAL : OUTLINE OF RITUAL STRUCTURE

Taken as a whole, the combined Cobra Festival ritual practices of non-Brahmans and A.K.s present a clear image of purity superceding impurity. The symbolism of ritual objects and their interrelations directs attention to purity as the heart of a family's integrity or wholeness and its continuity.

Male and female are distinguished and related in these rituals. The sexual distinction is a ritual image of difference between opposites and between pure and impure; it is also, by implication, an image of exchange between different groups. Sexuality is evident in these rituals, but as a means of reproduction rather than a source of physical pleasure. Many features of festival structure emphasise control, discipline, and the limitation of passion as necessary to the purity and general well-being of the family.

Ritual taboos and requirements create a festival emphasis on the birth group and the home. For example, the whole household fasts, and when the festival meal is served, it is shared only among members of the household. The home itself is cleaned, and cooking pots are either purified or replaced with new ones. These and other acts separate the home and those who share it from the rest of society for the time of the festival. In this way they express a concept of the great importance of the birth group in the larger scheme of family continuity.

The overt purpose of festival ritual is to prevent skin diseases from afflicting children, but festival symbolism points to the more serious question of children's lives. The clearest examples of this are in the milk-clarified butter and *huggianna* food offerings discussed above as allusions to children's death or birth. Others are less direct : centrality of the cooking process to festival ritual as a reference to growth and development in general, for instance. The reproductive function of the married couple and the nurturing, sheltering value of the home are also concepts in this festival relating to children's lives.

Table 36 indicates ways in which specific ritual acts and offerings fit into Cobra Festival themes of purity, sexuality, the home, and children as the future of the family.

COBRA FESTIVAL MYTHS

I have mentioned earlier that there are both festival 'legends' and 'myths'. Although they both are often taken as true events by their tellers, they both also have an equal chance of being either true or fictitious. 'Legends' are generally told as accounts of the recent past, and are usually accounts of the immediate first ascending generation. The influence of soothsayers and oracles in inventing (or reviving) these legends is significant: sometimes the oracle will tell someone a story about his own family that he did not previously know, or that he had 'forgotten'. The Bandipur soothsayer tells me that he uses astrological calculations to determine whether a serpent spirit is causing trouble to a family or not, the moment of the consultation with him being the decisive astrological determinant. (He does not, however, instruct families in ritual procedures.)

Legends regarding the Cobra Festival are simple stories, always in the form of an accidental injury or offense to the serpent which is punished by skin disease and which is later remedied by performing this ritual. These are the *vrat* 'vow' type of stories which Wadley (1975) discusses at length. And they vary in form mainly in the ways the serpent is offended—by puncturing with a stick, by being cut up into pieces; and in two cases by being neglected or slighted in ritual (e.g., by having been offered silver rather than gold). These legends constitute affirmation that this spirit is the solution to a family problem and affirmation of the power of the minor deity. Because of their simplicity, they do not demand any detailed attention here, but they repeat familiar symbolic themes of mutilation and purity-impurity.

Table 36—Cobra Festival Ritual Structure

Separation of Purity from Impurity	Elimination or Cooling of Passions	Emphasis on Household and Birth Group	Separation or Distinction Between Male and Female	Mediation : Merging and Exchange Between Sexes	Wholeness and Integrity of the Family : Production of Future Generations
Extreme fasting Bathing Cleaning house Husking rice Purification of cooking vessels	Cooling the serpent's eyes, as object of ritual Taboo on pungently flavoured chillies Use of 'cooling' ingredients in cooking Sweetly and blandly flavoured 'snacks' and other foods	Whole household fasts Whole household bathes Cleaning house Non-Brahman women stay indoors all day to cook Non-cooperation between adult siblings . . . of different sexes	Nagappa (male) and Nagamma (female) each receive offerings		white colour : Non-Brahman white flower offering Requirement of rice flour for making 'snacks' Use of cooked rice in ritual meal Whole spices only (taboo on grinding spices) Coconut frond only stirring implement (tree branch) A. K. women dressed in white to do cooking Ritualised cooking as reference to processing or development of humans as well as food
Separation of A.K. stoves as 'clean' and 'dirty', right vs. left			Separation of A.K. stoves as male vs. female		

Separation of wood piles, pots, other items used in cooking

Use of winnowing fan for making offering

Milk-clarified butter mixture (association with death)

Repeat purification of house floor after ant hill offering

Feast meal shared only by members of one household

Preparation of two separate, male vs. female, meals

Special *tali* kept for this ritual

Identification of two offering holes .... in same ant hill

Huggianna (association with birth)

Male-female pairs make offerings .... jointly

Food presented to cobra deities on a single winnowing fan

Pouring white liquid into reddened hole (sexual image)

Number 3 : *huggianna* offered in sets of three balls to each deity

Members of household share feast meal

Unruptured skin : prevention of skin diseases, goal of festival

The following report is typical of such family legends, which connect a wound inflicted in a serpent, the fear and anger of the snake, and a subsequent danger to children's welfare—especially the condition of a child's skin surface:

When P's younger sister was very young, a cobra wrapped itself around her neck and made a hood over her head as she slept in the house garden. When her mother saw this, she became frightened, and both the mother and child made a lot of noise in their fear.
The snake also became frightened and retreated into a mud pot. A Moslem neighbour poked the snake with a stick, and the snake came out of the pot and quickly disappeared into the garden.
At a later time the child became very ill, and the mother found out [probably through an oracle] that the snake had been pregnant when the neighbour poked it, and that it had died from the pain of the wound. So it was necessary to give the child the name Nagamma (Lady Cobra) and to do this festival rite for the 'peace' of the serpent spirit.
In the succeeding generation P's own daughter developed a big, festering sore (*hunnu*) 'like a snake house [ant hill]' on her head. Consultation with a Brahman oracle produced a message from the snake again: it is important to give the name Naga (Cobra) to a daughter of the family. And after this Naga marries, they should give the name to another of their children or to a brother's child. (Oil-Presser caste informant, male, Bandipur, January 1967, S. Hanchett notes.)

Although this account focuses on the daughter(s) of a patriline—who carries the cobra's name as protection for all against the eternal wrath of the deceased, wounded serpent—most of the other myths focus on sons, as does the *Pancatantra* tale mentioned earlier.

In contrast to these lengends, an A.K. Cobra Festival myth has a complex structure and an involved plot.

'Cobra Festival Myth' (H.S. Malathi and S. Hanchett translation)
Informant: middle-aged A. K. woman, Smt. Chennamma[28]
Date of Interview: July 16, 1977

There were five brothers, four of whom were married. The fifth brother would not accept any girls who were offered to him as brides. So the parents and the other brothers told him to go find himself a bride, that they could not do any more for him. He then made a knife (*katti*) and set off on a horse. He went along for awhile until he got to a banyan tree (Kannada, *paniala-damara*).[29] He tied his horse there to the tree.[29] Then he put a clay vessel beneath the tree, a new clay vessel. Stabbing himself in the chest, he let some of his blood flow into the vessel. Covering the vessel with a pure, white cloth, he removed the dagger from his body and put it down. From the dagger a drop of blood dropped onto the earth. The blood drop turned into a snake (*sarpa*), but he did not notice the snake. He just took away the vessel and left that place.

He then went into a forest and tried to hide the vessel somewhere. As he set it down it turned into a beautiful girl. After twelve years she matured (began to menstruate), and he married her right there in that forest. After the marriage he built a house there. Leaving her there, he told her, "It has been twelve or thirteen years since I saw my people and my country; and I also want to go hunting." He told her that she must not go out of the house until he returned, since no people are there. Even if a holy man or beggar should come, he instructed, she should not go out to give alms. He then left her.

Then the snake started on its way to the house. Everywhere that man went, the snake would be coming toward him, going in the opposite direction. As the snake went to the girl's house, it took the form of a boy. And as it left each time it would take the form of a snake again. So the two began to like each other, the boy and girl.

This had been happening for awhile. As the man went back to his house he would often see a snake leaving the house. He became suspicious, wondering what this was. Thinking that this was possibly an enemy that might harm him, he cut the snake into three pieces. He put the three pieces in a pile, one on top of the other, and went away.

After awhile a holy man (*jogi*) came to the house begging for alms. The girl told him, "I am prepared to give you anything. But please tell me if you saw anything on the way." The holy man said, "I only saw that somebody has killed a snake and cut it into three pieces and kept it there." Then she said, "I'll give you a lot of wealth. Please get that for me." The holy man went and got it for her.

She then took the three pieces and made them into three charms by putting them into tube-shaped cases, which she hung from a single thread around her neck.

Then her husband returned. She was lying on her cot. He asked her what was wrong with her. And she said, "I have a headache. I am going to tell you a riddle. If you solve the riddle, then my headache will go." The riddle went as follows: "Giving one coin (*vara*), I got it. Paying two coins, I got it made; and giving three coins, I have put it to my neck." "If you win and solve the riddle," she said, "I will jump into the fire. If you do not win, you will have to jump into the fire." He could not solve it. The wife made a platform of firewood, and they invited people from villages to attend the cremation.

Now the man had an elder sister who had been given (in marriage) to one of those seven villages. On her way to the cremation she happened to sit beneath the same banyan tree. There on the tree two birds were talking with each other. "It seems," they said, "there was a fellow who felt that if they brought a girl from another family she may have been a cheat or of bad character. So he cut himself . . ." And they related the whole story, concluding with, "Now he has to jump into the fire."

The elder sister got to the place just as the man was about to jump into the fire. She handed over the whole story, which she had written on a sheet, to a village leader (*gaudru*). Then they all read it, and the people there decided that the man had been cheated and made the wife jump into the fire instead of him.

The woman who told me this story concluded with a moral comment of her own: "The very blood from which he hoped to make a trustworthy girl of his own, that blood became his enemy."

This myth is a play on the dilemma of exogamy and incest, the paradoxical need to use outsiders (wives) in order to produce insiders (children). Its elements, viewed in relation to each other, depict a destructive rejection of normal processes of sexual exchange and family birth, marriage with one's own daughter, and withdrawal from human society. The whole body (of the snake) is opposed to its mutilated body, again a re-statement of the normality-perversion dilemma of the myth. The nature of the perversion is summed up in the 'mediating' riddle which the wife poses : the isolated number, one (1) representing the isolated boy; the pair, two (2), his unnatural birth action; and the concluding three (3), the (father's and snake's) incestuous union with one's own blood.

The number three is repeated in the three-pendant necklace which the daughter-wife made of the mutilated snake body, and I see this necklace itself as a further reversal of normality, since it is contrasted implicitly with the normal mark of marriage, which is necklace with a *tali* pendant. Rather than having a *tali* on her throat as a sign of her bond to her husband, she has the cut-up body of her lover as a necklace.

The holy man is culturally defined as celibate and withdrawn for the sake of developing purity and power. This figure contrasts with the man who loses for being withdrawn and incestuously sexual.

The topographical allusions—to home, forest, and banyan tree—also reveal a contrast among themselves. The home is the place of society, exchange, and normality; the forest, the place of isolation from society, incest, and perversion. The role of the banyan tree is paradoxical and 'mediating'. The tree in this myth is the location of the original bleeding into a pot—a vivid parallel to normal sexual exchange, with a sexual reversal. Blood, usually the woman's contribution to conception, substitutes for semen and a vessel substitutes for a womb. But rather than being the site where the girl takes a human form in this image of quasi-normal birth, she is transformed in the further-outside forest environment; it is the site where the snake-son is abnormally produced by a drop of blood falling accidentally on the bare earth. At a later point in the narrative, the married elder sister receives the story from talking birds at the same banyan tree—an event which eventually saves the boy's life. The tree is the scene of three mediating functions of this myth.

The snake plays multiple roles in the structure of this myth. Seen in contrast to the girl, the snake is an unnatural birth. In contrast to the holy man the snake engages in sexual union, is non-celibate. In relation to the man himself leaving his house (a parallel to exogamy), the snake enters simultaneously, transformed into a boy (a parallel to the man's own incest). And later on in the story, the whole body of the snake is mutilated and subsequently made into a non-*tali* of three parts, becoming the subject of the key riddle of numbers one, two, and three.

It is important that the main character of the myth is saved by his elder sister. Indirectly, this is a repetition of the larger theme of exogamy producing life, since the elder sister's daughter is one of the preferred choices for a wife in this kinship system. Knowing this to be true, villagers might see that the marriage to his elder sister's daughter might have saved the man (and his line of descendants), while marriage to his own daughter nearly killed him. The two possibilities are opposed, the former being implied rather than stated. For her to save his life is for the myth to repeat the point that trusting exchange (exogamy) saves, and fearful isolation (incest) kills.

Table 37 outlines relations of motifs in terms of the encompassing themes of the exogamy vs. incest, as social exchange vs. isolation; the choice of one or the other leading to either fertility and growth or mutilation and barrenness.

Ritual symbolism is oriented toward the purity-impurity dichotomy, and toward the phenomenon of birth. In excluding 'heating' and pungent foods, it also conveys a sense of danger in all passion, including but not limited to the supposed anger of the cobra spirit. Approaching the swollen pocked ant hill in a state of heightened purity (and white clothing), participants enact the extremes of both disintegration and impurity (connected with 'heating' things and also with 'dirty' things) and integrity and purity in their rituals for the cobra spirit(s).

The structure of the myth suggests that incest and disorderly sexuality are being singled out as potential disrupters of family integrity—i.e., are being defined as potentially polluting and destructive. The separateness of siblings—all married to outsiders, though all once in the same unit—is important in both ritual and myth. The sibling who did not marry out was the one with the most problems in the myth; and two siblings cannot perform the same offering together in the ritual. Incest is implied by both myth and ritual, though sibling incest is only indirectly suggested (in ritual avoidance of cross-sex sibling unity; and in the snake's incestuous-adulterous affair with his blood sister).

Table 37—'Cobra Festival Myth' : Structural Analysis

Exogamy (relations with community; society; 'outsiders')	Fertility (sexual union; birth creation; continuity)	Incest (anti-social)	Infertility (withdrawal, destruction, no continuity)
[Read lines from left to right across chart.]			
Parents (married) have who are married.	four sons,		
		One son does not trust outsiders	and will not marry.
Boy rides horse into forest.			
	—stops at banyan tree—		
		Stabs himself with knife	and bleeds into clay pot.
Takes clay pot out to forest			
	Covers clay pot with white cloth. Girl born out of blood + vessel.		
		Boy marries his own girl. Live in isolated house ('no people in forest').	Blood + dust = snake born abnormally.
			Man mentions holy men, warning wife/ daughter to avoid them.
Leaves house			
		Snake enters house for adulterous and incestuous affair.	Man kills and mutil- ates body of snake- lover.
	(#3—Snake body cut into three pieces)		Holy man
		gives snake body	
	to unfaith- ful wife.		
		Wife makes necklace (non-tali) of snake.	(Riddle :) One coin (#1) I got it;
	(#2) two coins I got it made;		

Table 37 (contd. on page 255)

Table 37 (contd. from page 254)

Exogamy (relations with community; society; 'outsiders')	Fertility (sexual union; birth creation; continuity)	Incest (anti-social)	Infertility (withdrawal, destruction, no continuity)
		(#3) three coins I have put it to my neck.	Man's cremation planned, near-death.
Married-out elder sister of husband hears	—at banyan tree— (conversation)		
Two (#2) birds tell story. Relates story to gathered group. Daughter dies (removed from group).	Saves life of her brother. Boy survives.		

The ritual emphasis on whiteness and purity, seen in the light of the myth, is not an emphasis on asexuality. Rather it is an emphasis on orderly sexuality (i.e., marital sexuality), and the good consequences of marriage for the lineage (white). Sexual abstinence is probably a part of the inital preparations for the festival (I did not ask about this point), but this does not contradict the significance of purity *per se* as discussed above. Abstinence would be a way of avoiding the mild, personal pollution thought to result from sexual intercourse, rather than any larger message about the ultimate worth of sexuality itself. The home that is set apart and purified for the Cobra Festival ritual is not the isolated, incestuous forest dwelling of the myth. It has normal sexuality in it.

The relation between the sexes in marriage is seen as a difficult and potentially dangerous one. Both ritual and myth make this point with great clarity. In the ritual building of stoves, the A.K.s associate femininity with 'dirt' and masculinity with 'cleanliness'. The myth begins by introducing the main character's fear and mistrust of all prospective wives presented to him by his family. And the treachery of his own daughter-wife repeats the general point, even though in a different way. Perhaps it is a sort of solution for the A.K. woman to dress in white as she cooks for the ritual : is she declaring her unambiguous allegiance to the lineage by this gesture?

It is possible that the strict vegetarianism of the festival has something to do with the male-female purity-pollution issue. If whiteness is patrilineality, and the milk-clarified butter some sort of semen symbol; then meat (blood) would be female, a necessity whose dangerous qualities are symbolically avoided and controlled in rituals, for the sake of family integrity and good births. The vegetarian appears as non-meat-eater and masculinity oriented.

Both myth and ritual use the mutilation motif, either as the cause or consequence of family problems. In the legend of Mr. P's family, a pergnant cobra is wounded by puncturing and demands compensation from the family by having her name passed on to their daughters. In the 'Cobra Festival Myth' the treacherous snake-lover is cut up and made into a necklace, a logical and justifiable result of a perverted arrangement. In the festival ritual, ground spices are taboo; and the coconut, which would have to be offered broken, is also. Ritual taboos eliminate what myths present as the physical danger of the situation.

The Sibling Group Festival develops most of these same cultural themes—purity-impurity, wholeness-mutilation, siblings-marriage, birth, and others—though by means of a slightly different set of ritual and mythic symbolic devices.

SIBLING GROUP FESTIVAL RITUALS

Shortly after the new moon, on the first Saturday of the month of Sravana, the Smarthas of this region celebrate the Sibling Group Festival,[30] (V)odahuttidavara Habba. Like the Cobra Festival, it is done for the sake of avoiding skin diseases and in order to ensure the health and well-being of children.

Also like the Cobra Festival, the Sibling Group Festival is a time dedicated to 'purity' (madi) by those who celebrate it. (Regelson notes, 1967.) This condition is established by cleaning the house and by all members of the house taking oil baths (women on Friday, men on Saturday). The family also fasts, avoiding a rice meal on the Friday evening before the festival, dining only on the steamed kadabu cakes customary for this occasion.

This is also a day of purification of the green tamarind fruit, according to some informants. The tamarind, itself a purifying agent used on vessels, is said to be 'polluting' (mailige) until this time, when, as part of festival ritual, it receives ritual attention. After this day it is said to be 'pure' (madi) for eating.[31]

Like the foods of the Cobra Festival of the non-Brahmans and A.K.s, the Sibling Group Festival foods are prepared with a seasoning taboo. This is a taboo on the pungently-flavoured mixture of deep-fried mustard seeds and red chillies, a common ingredient in south Indian cooking which has a 'pungent' (kara) flavour. This taboo does not generalise to all 'pungent' things, however, as it does in the Cobra Festival, since the steamed kadabu festival cakes are cooked with green chillies. Despite this, the taboo on the fried spices is firm, and it corresponds in principle to the Cobra Festival seasoning taboo as a restriction of a pungently flavoured item.

The ritual is done in three parts: I. An offering to Nagappa at an ant hill followed by puja to a 'snake baby' in the house; this is done by all. II. A celebration of sibling unity, and unity of those in the same generation, done in houses where appropriate. III. A ritual exchange among the mothers of sons, for the welfare of their boys. This last is done on the day after the ant hill and sibling rituals.

PHASE I OF SIBLING GROUP FESTIVAL

Women perform the ant hill offering. First they take a river bath. They pour the milk-clarified butter mixture into a decorated ant hill hole while still in wet clothing.[32] The ornaments and offerings in this ceremony include the pandanus flower (*tale huvu* in Kannada). Mentioned earlier, this flower is a motif in the 'Brother Saves Sister' story, discussed below, and is special for this festival.

A broken coconut appears in this set of ritual offerings. This means, of course, that the coconut offering is not taboo here, as it is in the Cobra Festival. But there is still a cutting-taboo later on in this ritual, when a cut-up plantain leaf is forbidden.

After performing the ritual, the gathered women (and my assistant Mrs. Joyce George, as observer) each take a small amount of the mud from around the ant hill hole and swallow it, applying more mud to their ears and hands, and eating some of the sweet 'snack' called *tambittu*—the same sweet as non-Brahmans prepare for the Cobra Festival and a favourite for many other ritual occasions.

The women bring some of the ant hill hole mud back to each of their houses, together with a twig needed for the *puja* they do for 'snake baby' in the house.[33] The serpent spirit has been formally invited into the house, by means of a powder-line drawing inside the front door (Figure 13, Chinnapura 1967).

In the house, the male household head takes over the remainder of the ritual. The man places a whole banana leaf (one cut across the middle is forbidden) onto a small wooden platform. He mixes some of the ant hill hole mud with 'pure' water, shaping it into a square on the leaf and putting the twig into it, upright. (This platform (*mane*) serves as a seat for all human objects of ritual attention as well, e.g. persons going through auspicious rites of passage.)

He then puts on the large leaf some raw rice and installs the guest of honour: a 'snake baby' which has been molded out of rice-flour or farina dough. The 'snake baby' lies inside of a rice-flour/farina dough cradle. A silver image of a serpent is set nearby. The reader will note the absence of a taboo on silver, which was so important in the Cobra Festival. (In Bandipur, worship was offered to a floor diagram, the large and small serpent pair depicted in Figure 14.)

There is a substantial case for birth-and-naming symbolism here, with the woman bringing pieces of the hole (womb?) into the house, and the man (representative of patriline) worshipping the infant in its cradle, which is a clear baby symbol without any need of further interpretation being imposed on it. As I suggested above, in discussing the 'Cobra Festival Myth', the snake motif can serve as a stand-in for a human. Other items which are arranged around the 'snake baby' reinforce the birth-naming symbolism. For instance,

Figure 13.　Chinnapura design inside threshold, facing into house, 1967.

one of the items is soaked Bangal gram, which is customarily distributed by this caste after the naming ceremony of a baby.

One family keeps two snakes, just as the Bandipur people diagram two. One is called 'Nagappa', and the other, smaller one, 'Nagappa's Baby'. Just as at the naming ceremony the baby becomes a part of human society, so also 'Nagappa's Baby' (the male's rather than the mother's baby) is a reasonable designation for the successor to the patrilineal heritage. This form circumvents the contribution of the mother to the birth process, rather than struggling with it.

Other items arranged around the 'snake baby' include milk (for drinking), castor beans, rice flour, tamarind fruits, coconut, bananas, betel-areca, and the various foods prepared for the occasion. With floral decorations,[34] cotton necklaces, application of vermillion and turmeric, milk-clarified butter anointment, and incense-stick rotation, *puja* is completed. Some perform an additional camphor-burning tribute at the conclusion.

In the course of the *puja*, some of the items set around the 'snake baby'

Figure 14. Design in Gods' Room, Bandipur 1966

receive special gestures of worship and respect on their own. These are the soaked Bengal gram; a cup of the milk-clarified butter mixture used at the ant hill offering; some rice flour; a mixture of rice flour and Bengal gram; and, importantly, the cup of fresh tamarind. The tamarind is said to become 'pure' and edible on this occasion, where it was 'polluted' (*mailige*) until this time. Offering it a special gesture of respect is a celebration, though in a small way, of 'purity' itself as a principle of ritual structure and festival symbolism. If the Bengal gram is a birth symbol by virtue of its association with birth and children's rites of passage; and if the white rice flour is a symbol of family integrity and continuity; then the blessings of these objects amount to a 'marking' or emphasis of birth, lineal continuity, and purity.

PHASE II OF SIBLING GROUP FESTIVAL

In the families which continue from this point, an interesting event follows. Beginning with the eldest boy of the house, each sibling is seated in turn while the others (brothers first, then sisters) place a plate of snacks (including the rice-flour sweet, *tambittu*, together with the pounded sesame seed and jaggery mixture, *cigali*, but not including the steamed *kadabu* cake served before the festival), bananas, and betel-areca in his or her lap. As the honoured sibling holds betel-areca in his or her hands, each of the others in turn dips a flower spike of the fragrant, yellow pandanus flower into some milk-clarified butter and puts the mixture onto his or her umbilicus and onto the back. (Regelson 1967 notes; Joyce George 1967 notes.)

The snack pair used here —*tambittu-cigali*—received some attention in the preceding chapter, in connection with ancestor feasts, where only *cigali* (the same as *cigani*) is served. I used this as evidence of the semi-auspicious nature of the ancestor festival, since the pair of snacks is so important in village rites of passage. In the Cobra Festival as celebrated by non-Brahmans, as in phase I of this festival, the other snack, *tambittu*, appears alone on the offering tray. This birth group ritual, phase II, is the first time the *tambittu-cigali* pair appears as a pair in any of the family festivals. The interrelationship of this event with family rites of passage is, therefore, worth noting.

In 1976 I researched the possible birth symbolism of this Sibling Group ritual, especially the application of clarified butter, asking a local midwife (Washerman caste) if the vernix which covers a newborn baby is ever called 'butter' (*benne*). She said that it is called 'butter-like', and that she did not know any other name for it.[35]

To focus on the umbilicus further accentuates the birth imagery already established in this ritual. In fact, this is a graphic display of Frazer's 'law of similarity', an enactment in sympathetic magic of the birth event which has been performed by the grace of Nagappa. But there is a slight twist in the symbolism of this ritual: the mother herself is not a participant in it. It is focused on the descending generation only.

After performing this ceremony, the whole family eats a rice meal together. Several informants mentioned that they must all share this meal, a self-conscious sign of their unity as a group.[36]

The roles of the Sibling Group Festival have commonality with those of the Cobra Festival. In both festivals we find the woman in a special state of purity, the performing household distinguished from other households, and the (implied) sexuality of parents in the male-female (A.K. or Brahman) ritual-performing pair.[37]

But the Sibling Group Festival roles constitute a further development of the family continuity theme, introducing the descending generation in concrete form, first as 'snake baby', and then in person. I shall return to the matter of siblings *per se* in connection with the 'Sister Saves Brother' myth, below.

PHASE III OF SIBLING GROUP FESTIVAL

The Sibling Group Festival concludes with an emphasis on the hitherto neglected heroine of this family drama: the mother of sons, a woman whose husband is alive. On this occasion, one informant stated, Nagappa becomes the god of the married woman (*muttayide*). Here she is all-powerful in her capacity to maintain male children and, by implication, patrilineages.

This ritual takes place on the day following I and II. The women of the Smartha Brahman community who have sons form pairs. It is necessary only that they be of distinct patrilineal groups (*dayadi*). Women of the same patriline i.e., married into the same patriline—cannot do this ritual for each other. This means that if a daughter is visiting her natal home at this time, her mother can be her partner, and she often is. Each woman does the rite for Nagappa *and* for her (patriline's) house god, appropriately enough.

It is possible for a widow who is a mother of sons to take a blessing as a pair with a married woman, for the sake of her (the widow's) sons, though it is not possible for her to give such a blessing to another mother.

The women of each pair observe a complete fast, taking no food or drink until after their ritual has been completed. They stay inside their houses also, to ensure their full purity (*madi*), as do non-Brahman women in the Cobra Festival. The mothers of sons cook a pair of rice dishes which seem to be the virtual mark of the married-woman ritual in this system: yoghurt rice and sour-flavour rice, one white and the other yellow in colour (cf. Gauri Festival discussion). To these they also may add other dishes, making a tasty meal. Still alone, each mother offers the foods, with banana, coconut, betel-areca, and incense, in a *puja* to her house god and to Nagappa, the serpent deity. The food offerings are now transformed into sanctified *naivedya* or *prasad*, the remains of a deity's meal. And she will call her ritual partner for their ceremonial exchange.

The ritual recipient of food comes to her partner's house in a state of purity, having taken no food or drink. The donor touches the feet of her partner before giving her the offered foods, rice and sour-flavour rice. Although the donor is doing this offering for the sake of her son, it is important that he *not* observe this transaction.

The son of the donor is then summoned. He also touches the feet of the visiting married woman, herself the mother of a boy. She then blesses him by sprinkling him with turmeric-coloured raw rice. (This raw rice, called *aksate*, is a gesture of welcome and blessing, given at weddings and other joyful events, as discussed earlier in connection with Gauri and Prati festivals. For instance, as the snake was being 'welcomed in' by means of the line drawing at the beginning of this festival, *aksate* raw rice had been sprinkled on the threshold of the house.)

Having ensured the well-being of her family line for the year, the mother of sons may return to public life by inviting a friend or two to eat dinner in the evening. She concludes the festival with a second line drawing, a formal sending-off of the serpent spirit, now directed outward from the house as in Figure 15.

Figure 15.   Sending-off drawing, Chinnapura 1967

In phase III of the Sibling Group Festival, it is the woman's motherhood of sons which is her foremost quality. The ritual performance clearly reflects her obligation to protect and nurture her male offspring, a well-known social value in Hindu culture. The appearance of another, reinforcing mother of sons here is hardly surprising.

Beyond this manifest content of the ritual, however, the sociological restrictions on group membership of the two mothers who serve as partners seggest that other meanings may be involved as well. Requiring that the woman who gives a blessing be of a different patriline than the boy's mother, and forbidding the son to watch the initial meeting and exchange between his mother and the guest suggest a parallel with relations between two exogamous lines which exchange marriage partners. The two women who participate in this ritual are potential affines. This ritual thus may represent the social interdependence between affines, and the social power which they have over each other especially over descendants. Seen in this way, it is a continuation of the exogamy and exchange principle of the 'Cobra Festival Myth' of the A.K.s.

If we view the ritual as a drama or metaphor of a relationship between two potentially intermarrying lines, the absence of the boy in the first phase makes sense. For, of course, the alliance between two groups existed prior to his birth. It was from an exogamous alliance, a marriage, that he was born at all. Thus he appears in the second act of the symbolic ritual, so to speak, after his mother's and father's families had gotten together. Festival myths expand on such themes.

FESTIVAL MYTHS : 'SISTER SAVES BROTHER' AND 'SIRI YALA SRISTI'

The two myths associated with the Sibling Group Festival relate to different phases of it. 'Sister Saves Brother' is connected with phase II, in which siblings bless each other reciprocally. 'Siri Yala Sristi', the more generally used myth for all villagers who perform phases I and III, is a widely-known myth among worshippers of Siva such as local Smartha Brahmans are.

"Sister Saves Brother"[38]
Mrs. Joyce George translation

Informant: an old Smartha Brahman woman of Chinnapura, Smt. Subbhamma, August 9, 1967 (a second variant was told to S. Hanchett, Bandipur, August 20, 1966):

Once there was a poor man who had seven sons and one daughter. Six boys were married and had gone away. But there were still a brother and a sister at home. Once when this feast came, the girl's brother at home told his sister to bathe and get ready for *puja*-offering. Meanwhile he would go and bring a pandanus flower for the ritual.
The sister got ready and waited for her brother to return, but he did not return. So she went in search of him. After walking some distance she saw him lying dead beneath a pandanus tree.
The boy had climbed the tree to pluck the flower. But a snake that was lying inside the flower bit the boy. He had come sliding down from the tree and fallen dead.

When the girl saw her brother lying dead, she began to pray to Lord Siva to give back her brother's life. She made *puja* to the god as usual. The Lord Siva was pleased with her faith, and so he appeared to her in the form of an old man. He told her to utter some magical formulas (*mantras*) and sprinkle some water on her brother. She did as he told her, and her brother got up, seeing his sister next to him. [Second variant: the *puja* forced the snake to take back the poison and make the boy live again.] The brother told the sister that somehow he had felt sleepy, and that he had gone to sleep.

Then he gave his sister the flowers, and both of them went home happily. The girl then made *puja* with her brother.

One informant's comment on the story is that this is why the festival is called the festival for those who were born together, that is, because the sister got back her brother on that day. Another said that if a sister does this ritual, her brother will not be bitten by snakes.

A structural analysis suggests that this myth is more similar to the 'Cobra Festival Myth' than might seem at first glance. To my mind this myth is a statement of the same dilemma as the first, though in much abbreviated form: the keeping of lineage/house girls at home as opposed to the separating out from them. It is a myth of separation, the crucial and reviving separation between those relatives who cannot remain joined for too long, namely brothers and sisters. The reference to other, married brothers underscores the dilemma in it contrasts to the one unmarried brother. The initial situation of the 'Cobra Festival Myth' is similarly one of all brothers except one being married.

Although the story ends with the brother and sister cooperating in a ritual, they have gone through a trip outside of the house (parallel to exogamy), death, purification, and rebirth. And they have exchanged gifts, a universal image of separation-cum-relationship (as opposed to simple unity).

The mediating, transformative images in this myth are the cobra inside the pandanus flower; the withdrawal of poison (in second variant); the sister's purification/separation and her speaking words which revive the brother. A third, resolving separation is the gift of the flowers from the brother to the sister.

The first mediator, serpent inside pandanus, is a parallel to the marriageable girl kept too long within the house unmarried. This parallel might be described in a simple set of oppositions such as those in Table 38.

It is the action of this mediator—rather, the combination of these elements in one contradictory unit (the pandanus with snake inside it)—which produces the boy's death (and perhaps by implication the family's death since he is the one son remaining at home).

The second and third transformative images are those of the sister's separation and purification (washing); this is followed by the sibling pair's cooperation as now-separate units. In short, this is the story of a *union* transformed

Table 38—Opposites Combined in Mediator Image, 'Sister Saves Brother'

Structural Dilemma of Myth:	Wealth (Gold) and Exchange (Life of family)	Poverty/Dying-out (Poison of family)
Image of Serpent Inside Flower :	Yellow flower, Strong/Sweet fragrance	Venom of serpent (Red/Black?)
Family Symbolism :	Daughter	Non-separation of daughter

into an *alliance*. The girl saves her brother's life (as does the sister in the 'Cobra Festival Myth') but only after she is symbolically separated from him.

In these myths, as in the rituals, ordinary objects take on abstract values and interact symbolically with each other. The 'chemistry' of this process, in myth and ritual, creates and affirms symbolic dilemmas which are the basis of many patterns of Hindu culture.

The structural summary of this myth is provided in Table 39.

Table 39—Structure of 'Sister Saves Brother'

Those outside the 'house'	—Mediation— (Separation/ Alliance)	Those inside	—Mediation— (Perversion)	Poverty/ Death
				Poor man
	(and wife)	had children.		
Six sons gone.		Son/Daughter at home.		
Brother goes far from house to get flowers.	Sister bathes for ritual.		Snake in flower.	Death of brother (and of 'house').
Sister goes far out of house. (Sister prays and) Siva comes as old man.	Sister purifies brother, [poison back to snake].	Sister brings brother back to life.		
	Brother gives flower gift to sister.			
	Sister and brother cooperate in *puja*.			

The 'Sister Saves Brother' myth differs from the associated ritual, which clearly stresses the common birth and unity of the sibling group without any apparent division beyond the separation implied by their distinct, reciprocated ritual roles in applying the milk-clarified butter mixture to each other's umbilici. The solution to this apparent contradiction may be to accept the contradiction itself as a transformation which replicates acceptable social process—the ritual representing the original unity of the sibling group as children of the same mother and father; and the myth representing the inevitable separation between siblings, at least in its structure, if not in its obvious narrative content.

'SIRI YALA SRISTI'

Sometimes called 'Sirutonda', this myth is found in the Tamil *Periyapuranam* by Sekkilar, in the Telugu *Basava Puranamu* by Palakuriki Somanathudu, and in other sources. (Roghair 1977, I: 171; II: 216 ff.)

According to Fuller (1944) this story is told in Maharashtra in connection with the same festival (Nagpancami, on fifth day of light half of Sravan), the story being called *Chilaya Bal* there.

Since nearly all Smartha Brahmans of Bandipur and Chinnapura are good readers, I assume that some of them have access to written variants. Nonetheless, their 'Siri Yala Sristi' myth differs sufficiently from others of India to indicate that there is a vital oral tradition at work in its perpetuation by village families.

'Siri Yala Sristi' Myth[39] (Translator: Mrs Joyce George)
Date: August 11, 1967

A Brahman who worshipped Lord Eswara (Siva) was a very poor man. He had no children for many years. After some years he got a son.

Siva wanted to test this Brahman. So he came as a holy man (*sannyasi*) to the house and asked for food. He asked the Brahman and his wife to make a perparation from human flesh. The flesh had to be that of a boy, the only son of his parents, and of a holy family. The Brahmans agreed to serve this dish to the holy man, and went in search of such a boy as the holy man wanted. But though the poor Brahman searched all over the place, he could not find such a boy. He came home, and both husband and wife began to cry because they could not get the boy they wanted.

When their son saw them crying, he asked them what was wrong. His parents told him the reason for their despair, and when he heard this, the boy told them not to cry, since he could be the sacrificial victim. Although the parents hesitated to sacrifice their own son, the son told them not to delay, as it was already late and the holy man would get angry and curse them all ('us'). The holy man was very powerful because of his intense spiritual discipline (*tapas*). The holy man had instructed the mother to cut the boy's head off and cook his body.[40] The mother did as the holy man told her to do. She cooked the body and put the head in front of the god. After cooking she served food to the holy man.

The holy man told her to put down three eating leaves for the meal, though the woman wondered, "Why does this holy man ask me to put down three?" After she served the meals, the holy man asked her to call her son. But the mother cried, thinking, "How can my son come when I have cut him up and served him here?" But the holy man insisted on it, saying that she could call the name three times, and the boy came running from outside, as if he had been playing for a long time. As he came, he called out, "Mother" (amma)! When the mother saw the boy she was very happy. She went inside to see what had happened to the head she had kept near the god.

Inside she saw that the head had turned into a coconut; the fingers, into plantains; and the preparation, into vegetarian palya.[41] The other foods she had cooked were transformed into 'sour-flavour rice' (hulianna) and 'yoghurt rice' (mosaranna). She then served the three meals.

After eating the meal, the holy man took the form of Lord Siva and told them that he was pleased with them, and that he had wanted to test them. Then he asked them what blessing they wanted. The mother answered that she did not want anything, that her son coming back to life was enough. "But let us keep the same faith in you." So Siva blessed them and told them to do this ritual every year.

But the mother repeated her request to give them the same faith in Siva. And for that, he said, "You should make a feast like this every year at this time and give all these preparations to any married woman who has given birth to a male child. So saying, he disappeared.

Like the other two festival myths, this one isolates out one son for special treatment, and thus emphasises the phenomenon of patrilineal continuity as the others do. But in this case it focuses on a boy himself cooked (and possibly eaten, or at least almost eaten), rather than on a girl taken in incestuous union or kept too long in her natal home. And it is the boy whose body is mutilated, not a serpent. Unlike the other two myths, which deal concretely with the social and physical outside-world, this myth includes outsiders only if we consider the (married-in) mother to be an outsider, and if we see the visiting holy man as such. Still, insofar as the patrilineage is an element in the structure of the other myths, this myth can easily be seen as a variation on a similar theme.

In this myth the mother herself appears as the agent of the boy's mutilation. I think that this portion of the narrative reflects a belief in her life/death power over her son, a belief repeated in the associated ritual. In fact this power is not unrelated to the 'outsider' aspect of mother's role, since the outsider as an ambiguous figure—necessary though of questionable loyalty—has received explicit recognition more than once in this review of ant hill festival symbolism.

The holy man can be contrasted with the old Brahman father as celibate ascetic vs. family man, and an a-sexual/sexual dichotomy is thus established through their opposition. Though sexuality is far less overt in this myth than in the 'Cobra Festival Myth', this a-sexual/sexual pair also echoes a theme of the latter.

The most prominent opposition in this myth distinguishes purity, pollution, and the mid-state between the two. This is summarised in the distinction between three types of food, one extremely pure and raw (coconut and plantain); another ordinary, cooked vegetarian (boiled and spiced vegetables and the pair of rice dishes); and a third, polluting to the highest degree (human flesh, boiled and spiced, red in colour). The division of the boy's body into head vs. the rest also echoes this dichotomy, though in a two-part distinction which is analogous to the mind-body distinction in general, and the holy man (spiritual)-family man (corporeal) distinction in particular. Such a three-part scheme is analogous to that described by Harper in his (1964) study on the Havik Brahmans, discussed earlier: *madi, mailige,* and *muttu,* 'purity', 'regular pollution', and 'extreme pollution'.

Table 40 presents a structural analysis summarising the dilemmas at the heart of the 'Siri Yala Sristi' myth.

DISCUSSION

Folk myths and rituals complement each other in ant hill festivals for the cobra deity; the pattern of their complementarity is similar to that observed in other festival studies. Rituals tend to emphasise the auspicious possibilities for human life, neglecting (or only hinting at) the macabre and inauspicious possibilities well-developed in myths. For instance, while ant hill festivals require extreme purity of the families observing them, myths depict states and acts of extreme pollution, such as cannibalism and incest. While bland and sweet festival foods avert the venomous anger of the cobra spirit, the stories of Mr. P. and 'Sister Saves Brother' give full expression to the danger it presents. In the Sibling Group Festival real siblings perform ritual acts of birth-group unity, although the mythic sister and brother go through separation and purification ordeals. While a married woman who is a mother ritually blesses her neighbour's son, a companion myth, 'Siri Yala', dwells on the details of a mythic mother killing, dismembering, and cooking her own boy. Rituals control and defy mythically defined danger.

This chapter, like some others in this book, indicates that local Hindu culture utilises the concept of a family as a body. As a corporeal entity, however, a family is seen as vulnerable to physical dangers such as pollution and mutilation. Festival symbols express a varied range of possibilities. (Cf. Marriott and Inden 1974 and Marriott 1976a,b for further discussion of family or caste as a corporeal entity from a different theoretical viewpoint.)

Whereas ancestor festivals stress the vine-like continuity of a family in their

Table 40—'Siri Yala Sristi' : Structural Analysis

Absolute purity, celibacy	—mediation— (positive)	Ordinary life processes	—mediation— (negative)	Absolute pollution, no life, self-destruction
				Poor Brahman, no children
	—Prayed—			
to Eswara—	—god creator— —mother creator—	Got one son		
Holy man visits			—God destroyer orders cannibal feast—	
		Boy's WHOLE body	—Mother-des-troyer—	Kills; Dismembered body
			cooks	
Boy's head and fingers :		Boy's body (Other body parts :)		
	—god revivor—			
Coconut and plantain (raw, white)		Vegetable *palya* (boiled, spiced) *Hulianna* (sour, yellow) + *Mosaranna* (white, sour)		Human meat ⎰ cooked, spiced, red ⎱
# 1 Plantain leaf, for holy man		# 2 Plantain leaf for father		
		# 3 Plantain leaf, for boy (link between ascending and descending generations).		

symbolism, an image similar to that of the serpent, the festivals discussed in this chapter express concern about the future of the family's physical growth, i.e., the production of future generations, and about the dangers of that future being cut off. Festival foods, especially *huggianna*, the customary food associated with birth, further highlight the ant hill festival's focus on the family's future.

In both festivals, however, the pre-eminent colour is white and the pre-eminent concept is purity or integrity of the family as a whole entity.

Like the Gauri and Prati festivals, festivals for the cobra deity relate to marriage, though stressing sexuality somewhat more than Brahman women's festivals did. Like the 'Mangala Gauri' Myth, the 'Cobra Festival Myth' dwells on the problem of having to incorporate outsiders into a patrilineal family (exogamous marriage) in order to have it grow. In the 'Cobra Festival Myth' incest is the course chosen, but both of these myths address the same social dilemma.

The many points of similarity among the preceding four festival studies show that, in the culture of this region at least, Hindu concepts of the past, present, and future of a family are closely interconnected.

NOTES

1. Kannada *avare*, cow gram; its bean is a popular food.

2. Fertility problems inspire much cobra worship. Local rituals for this purpose, however, more often consist of dedicating stone tablets set at the bases of sacred fig trees than of making offerings to ant hills.

3. This view of purity and impurity was developed through a series of personal conversations with Susan Bean in 1977.

4. Brahmans have an additional term for birth pollution, *purudu*, which distinguishes it from death pollution.

5. Serpent venom is one expression of a strong, non-personalised power according to beliefs of the Ho tribe. They call this power *bonga* (Majumdar 1950, quoted in Sarana n.d., page 9).

Beliefs in serpent spirits associated with water and with subterranean zones is common throughout Asian lore. Eberhard (1968) reports on such beliefs among tribes of southeastern China. Dentan (1968 : 21) mentions that the Semai, a horticultural tribe of the Malay Peninsula, associate rainbows with "huge horned subterranean dragons" called *naga* or *dangga*. Ainu peoples of Japan also believe in a 'dragon serpent', which they consider to possess shamanesses (Kitagawa 1969 : 318-19).

Basic references on serpent beliefs in south Asian folklore are Vogel (1926), Fergusson (1873), and Evans-Wentz (1958).

6. In 1976 two informants of Bandipur told me that although Nagappa, the male, is a cobra, Nagamma, the female, is not. They both claimed that they had observed this pair of serpents engaging in coitus with intense passion.

7. Buck discusses serpent imagery in the Sittar songs, a combination of *bhakti* and yogic philosophical patterns. The songs use a number of folk motifs in their composition. They were written down sometime between the 15th and the 17th centuries.

8. The source of this story is given as Pantschatantra (*sic*.), III.V., tr. Benfey, ii.244-47. Jacobs (1969 : 246-47) also presents Latin and Greek tales similar to this one, arguing that the Indian version is, "the original of both."

9. Serpents are associated with ancestors in some folk traditions. I have heard in Hassan District that serpents in cremation grounds are deceased spirits. Crooke (1896 : II. 45 *et passim*) also mentions this type of belief in north Indian lore.

10. (*V*) *odahuttidavaru* 'those born close together' is a term for the group of persons of the same generation, either siblings or cousins.

11. Gnanambal (n.d., page 8) mentions this festival under another name, Garuda Pancami, stating that it is performed by "certain sections of Brahmans in South India."

A third local cobra festival, Subramanya-Sresti, also called Sresti or Sasti, is celebrated on the sixth day of the light half of Margasira (mid-December) by a few Brahman and non-Brahman families. This festival's rituals repeat those of the other two in large part.

This list does not exhaust all the possibilities of serpent worship. Other rituals should be considered separately, since they do not have distinctive customs, such as ant hill offerings, associated with the festivals discussed here.

12. In 1967 the festival was observed on January 14 in Chinnapura. It should not be celebrated on the new moon day; but that same year the residents of Bandipur celebrated it early, on January 10, because of a scheduling conflict with January 14 festival (Sankranti) in which meat is served.

This report is a composite of data from several sources. Regelson and I conducted interviews of 6 non-Brahmans in Bandipur and some residents of Chinnapura. We also observed ritual cooking and offering of food by a group of 26 A.K.s in Bandipur. In 1976 I supplemented these observations and interviews with further interviews of some Bandipur non-Brahmans and A.K.s.

13. One A.K. woman tells me that she sweeps the whole floor with a twig of a special plant after purifying the house with cow dung. The plant is *Vitex negundo* L. (Kannada, *lakke soppu*). It has a three-leaved pattern similar to *bel*, or wood apple (*Aegle marmelos* (L.) Correa), which is sacred to Siva throughout India.

14. Our assistant, Mr. George, asked Gidda, "If you meet a Brahman, can you speak ?" His answer was, "No, When I started this *puja* my rash was cured."

15. One non-Brahman offers two meals at the ant hill. Otherwise, we do not have detailed information on non-Brahman cooking arrangements. We have three verbal descriptions of the non-Brahman offering—from a Washerman, a Fisherman, and a Farmer—which form the basis of our information on it.

16. The requirement of a coconut frond ladle has a basis in ethnobotany of the region. The taxonomy distinguishes palm trees, such as the coconut, from other types of trees. In local terminology a frond is distinguished from a branch. Its different growth pattern, remaining green for about three years before it drops, presents different symbolic-interpretive possibilities than does the growth pattern of a branch on another type of tree. Like children of a family, the palm frond makes the tree taller, but it does not live forever to become part of the tree. I have discussed this matter in an unpublished paper, "Plant Symbolism and India's Folk Traditions."

17. On the occasion when I observed the A.K. offering, a mixture of crushed raw rice, water, and brown sugar was called *hal-tuppa* 'milk-clarified butter' and substituted.

18. In the A.K. ritual observed one man did (1) — (4) on behalf of the group. The following actions were performed by separate worshipping pairs. The male member of each pair did (5), after which each woman came forward with food offerings.

19. Some non-Brahman houses also use a special thread, called *hanginula*, in this offering. I heard about this from a Fisherman woman. The offered *tali* has turmeric and vermillion put on it.

20. As with most other folk Hindu practices, this rule also has its exceptions. Once in a while one finds a family offering silver, but the requirement of gold definitely prevails in village Cobra Festival customs.

21. The banana leaf-tip (*suli*) is required for occasions when respect is being given. Thus, honoured guests at a wedding will be served meals only on a leaf-tip, not on the mid-section of the leaf. Ancestors also receive food only on the leaf-tip, as discussed in Chapter 7.

22. My notes do not indicate whether she carries the male and female foods home separately.

23. All of the descriptions of A.K. festival actions done at home are based on a 1976 verbal report.

24. Cooking oil, clarified butter, yoghurt made from cow milk, coconut, bananas, and brown sugar.

25. As one A.K. woman put it in 1976, "The outdoor *puja* is for Nagappa, so that, eating with pleasure, he will keep our house prosperous."

26. In our interviews of three groups—A.K., Smiths, and Barbers—we were told that the joined hands of a bride and groom are anointed with the mixture before the *tali* is tied. Others, however, prefer to use milk alone for this purpose, and Brahmans use water.

Barbers use the mixture in a pre-wedding ritual called *kalina sastra*. In this ritual, the groom is ritually shaved and has his fingernails and toenails cut. When shaving him, they use the milk-clarified butter mixture to moisten his beard. Before cutting his nails, they dab them with a piece of *garike* grass (*Cynodon dactylon*) that has been dipped in the same mixture.

During agricultural rituals associated with the Festival of Lights, most non-Brahmans bathe and decorate their cattle and worship them. As a sort of blessing after doing worship, Farmers sprinkle them with the milk-clarified butter mixture (Regelson notes, November 1967).

27. The 'pouring' may be done on the first, third, fifth, tenth, or eleventh day after a child's death depending on *jati* custom. Among Brahmans, Smarthas do it for little children, under age five, whom they bury rather than cremate. Iyengars do it on the day after the cremation of an unmarried son or daughter, pouring the mixture over the burnt bones before gathering them together for the final immersion in a body of water.

The same Barber informants who mentioned using milk-clarified butter in pre-wedding rituals (see footnote 26) deny using it in children's funerals but I feel that this *jati's* customs require further study.

28. It is not clear how or when the myth is told as part of the ritual. My informant, however, did indicate that it is special to the Cobra Festival.

A. K. Ramanujan has collected a variant of this myth in another region of Karnataka for a forthcoming book of Kannada folktales (Ramanujan n.d.). He gives his translation the title, "The Prince Who Married His Left Half." The story does not appear as a type in the lists of either Thompson and Roberts (1960) or Bødker (1957). (See Thompson and Balys 1958, D191 : 101.)

29. *Ficus indica* L., also called *Ficus benghalensis,* is called *aladamara* in Kannada, and here, *panialadamara*.

30. The celebration is held on the first Saturday after the first Friday in Sravana. It is called *madulane Sravana Senevara* 'first Sravana Saturday'. We studied the festival in 1966 and 1967, the principal observer being Mrs. Joyce George.

31. Others disagreed, stating that the tamarind was polluting until the forthcoming Varamahalaksmi Festival.

32. Some women take their children with them to bathe and do *puja*. Local Brahmans believe that to perform a ritual in wet clothing ensures one's purity as completely as possible.

33. The twig is from *Securinela leucopyrus*. Its Kannada name is *hulikaddi* or *sulikaddi*.

34. Pandanus flower is customary. One family also offers lotus. The pandanus received discussion earlier, with the Prati Festival.

35. A second old woman informant concurred in this, but only to a limited extent. She said that there is a special word for vernix (unknown to the midwife), and that vernix is only buttery if the pregnant woman has eaten curds and other dairy foods.

36. Discussing this festival as Garuda Pancami, Gnanambal (n.d., p. 8) points out that, "The essential aim of the rite is said to be the conferring of [longevity] to the brothers of the performers. Accordingly, the felicitation of brothers with blessings and a feast is an important element of the festival." In our study, of course, the group consists of brothers and sisters making a reciprocal exchange. It is functionally equivalent to the popular Rakhi

Bandan Festival of northern and central India, when brothers and sisters express their mutual commitment by tying threads to each others' wrists.

37. The act of pouring milk-clarified butter into reddened holes indicates a sexual metaphor. This interpretation, in order to be substantiated, however, would require research on personal associations, a different field method than the one we used.

38. Joyce George heard this myth from an old Smartha woman in 1967.

39. Joyce George heard this myth from a middle-aged Smartha woman in 1967.

40. In the version which Fuller (1944 : 76) collected in Maharashtra, Siva demanded that the parents prepare a special dish of the boy's brains, "and that they do it all smiling and share the terrible meal."

41. Kannada *sappen palya*, 'bland' *palya*. The *palya* preparation is discussed in Chapter 7.

Chapter 9

CONCLUSION

Indian folklore is a key to Hindu culture and Indian social life as culturally
defined. In this study certain features of a tradition-bound Karnataka Hindu
world-view have manifested themselves. These are deep cultural concerns of
a philosophical nature. Though they are rarely expressed in words by the
villagers with whom I have worked, these ideas permeate their symbolic activities with metaphorical value. These implicit cultural concerns lead many
Hindus to ply individuals and families alike with elaborate ritual attentions of
the sort presented above.

The over-arching philosophical issue at stake in family festivals (and rites
of passage) may be called 'process' vs. 'stasis'. As the auspicious growth and
movement of people/families through correct phases of development, 'process'
is seen as inherently good. It is affirmed in a variety of homespun folk metaphors. 'Stasis', on the other hand, is a danger which people/families must
confront and control. It is represented in obstacles such as physical death itself.
It is all stagnation, ending, solitude, even numbers that do not 'grow'—in
general, the inauspicious lack of movement or development. Ritual preoccupation with proper beginnings, the overcoming of obstacles, and uninterrupted
progress to satisfactory conclusions expresses this cultural concern. Its anti-
quity and importance are attested to in a custom of the distant Brahui, a
nomadic Dravidian tribe of Baluchistan and Iran. Having begun the movement
of a caravan with great fanfare and ritual care, the Brahui consider it highly
unlucky (inauspicious) to have to stop, and apparently will not do so for any
reason until they reach their destination.[1]

Another example, geographically closer to Karnataka than the Brahui, is in
the myth of the stalled temple cart, found scattered through the ethnographic

274

literature. A legendary instance of this event was the subject of my previous work (1971), in which I discussed the Bandipur belief that unresolved factional conflict could magically interfere with the free movement of the cart during a procession. The Brahui's uninterrupted travel, however, is not so far from everyday religious processions of south India as it might seem at first. Both are endowed with a clear metaphorical value as movement or process *par excellence*.

Though a journey may or may not be considered to be a ritual, most Hindu rituals have the nature of journeys. Therefore it is necessary to have at least one performer committed to complete a ritual event, regardless of what interruptions might face the group during it. Such a commitment is indicated in such acts as tying a thread around the wrist of crucial performers of a ritual. Each of the festivals studied above has its committed performer or performers. In the case of some serpent festivals a whole household carries the responsibility. Such requirements indicate that an unfinished ritual 'journey' is considered to be as dangerous as the completed event would be spiritually helpful.

Like movement in space or time, the growth of plants offers rich metaphorical material for Hindu folk ritual. 'Process' images play in the use of newly sprouted leaf tips (e.g., in the Prati Festival offering), the newly unfurled banana leaf (for ancestors' meals), and other vigorous beginnings of vegetal life. The germination of seedlings, a widespread ritual practice in both temples and homes, is another popular 'good-beginnings' Hindu symbol. A local custom of Chinnapura Farmers links vegetal growth with human birth. The mother's brother of a newborn baby sows a combination of three grains[2] as he walks to a special upright stone and back home again. The uncle holds a piece of sweet jaggery in his mouth as he performs this rite, further emphasising the benign and joyful spirit that should prevail. As I have discussed in connection with ancestor meals, the total growth pattern may be a culturally significant factor in ritual use of a plant, such as a vine.

In at least one local tradition of north India there is a proverbial simile established between a large, growing family and a banyan tree. The aerial roots of the tree drop down in a pattern which has at times produced whole forests out of a single tree, just as a large lineage has expanded from an ancestor.

Plants are also available to serve as stasis victims, sometimes cut down in hopes of removing the fate from humans. There is a Chinnapura custom of setting a whole banana plant (earlier cut off at its base) before a Maramma goddess in procession, so that it, instead of humans, would receive her furious stare. Other customs reported throughout the ethnographic literature show that a tree or sapling may be cut down as a substitute for a human victim.

While not all ritual plants are edible, staple grains offer themselves for a special type of symbolic treatment: cooking. This can be an intricately structured matter, given the nature of Indian cuisine. It is in itself worthy of several monographs along the lines suggested by Khare (1976b). Though few of the customary festival (or rite of passage) dishes are prepared with conscious symbolic intent, they do lend themselves to study along these lines. Several folk distinctions are available to lead the student. Is a pulse split (Kannada *bele*) or left whole (*kalu*), for instance? Is it soaked in water (*nene*—) and served in a salad such as *kosambari* (cf. Gauri Festival, above), or is it boiled in water? The distinctions proliferate as we add in soaking + dry-frying, oil-frying, and so on. In the discussion of ancestors, I referred to the conscious cultural signification of boiling rice as the perfect cooking-transformation act.

There are other cases of cooking which are more abrupt than ordinary boiling or frying. These too could offer folk metaphors for extraordinary cases. One such case may be the favourite food of baby Krishna, popped rice (Kannada, *aralu*). Linked with the playful god in *puranic* tales of his worshipper bringing it to him, popped rice, which is served on the occasion of his birthday (Krishna Jayanti), has an interesting similarity to the god himself. Just as the soaked grain, still in its husk, explodes into its edible form on a pan of heated sand, so also the naughty baby god instantly showed his full divinity to his foster mother by merely opening his little mouth, in which she saw the whole universe. This brings to mind a north Indian practice of not cremating holy men (*sannyasis*). In an area where cremation is universally practised, holy men are considered to have passed the need for such ordinary transformations within their life spans. I have been told that no funerary ritual is performed for holy men at all. They are no longer formally attached to a human social group; nor do they need the rituals of common people. In the metaphor established above, enlightened people are already 'cooked'. More generally, process may be differently organised for varying status-groups; but gradual swelling and explosion are both movement.

In the process of harvesting and cooking food another symbolic concern emerges, namely, purity vs. pollution. Both of these states are necessary to the auspicious development of life; but the former is oriented metaphorically toward refinement, permanence, and integrity, while the latter is a normal part of day-to-day physical change and contamination from processes such as reproduction. In order to be useful in most cooking, rice paddy must be husked by pounding. The useless chaff must then be separated from the grain by a winnowing process. These activities refine the staple to a point where it can be of use in a household diet. Like rice grains, human infants are contaminated with physical irrelevancies at birth. And like rice, they must be refined before they are suitable for human society. The parallel is established in a local folk custom associated with birth. Not only are home-born infants restricted from contact with others (except for mothers and midwives) for ten days of 'pollution', but also they are each set into a winnowing fan for a few days after their first washing, as I have mentioned earlier.

Though Hindu concepts of personal birth or death pollution have received much scholarly attention by now, the cultural focus in this book is on purity as separateness, wholeness, and refinement to be restored after experiences of contamination or injury. Serpent festivals, for example, express this concept of danger to family integrity when describing the anger of a wounded serpent.

Unlike 'process' vs. 'stasis', purity vs. pollution is not always a question of good vs. bad. As several writers on the subject of purity and impurity have pointed out (e.g., Dumont 1970 and Babb 1975), living in this world can distract us from questions of the eternal future of our souls. In the case of a family, this means that in the normal course of its growth and development, it will have to deal with contamination associated with physical change. However, these changes relate to a fixed family core as a bloom opens out from a lotus root. For example, normal menstrual and birth periods of women produce a sort of auspicious impurity for a family. The common Hindu concern with women's menstruation and birthing activity places them in a position of alternating back and forth, in and out of states of purity or refinement. Despite fears of pollution, there is a general awareness that if they did not alternate in this way, the family would not endure.

In this study a parallel has developed between rice 'white'/'coloured' and the family eternal/changing. In other words, each family seems to arrange its ritual foods with some plain 'white' and some seasoned ('coloured') rice dishes. And in the assortment of preparations, a semi-conscious metaphor is at play. I say semi-conscious because there are occasions, even proverbs, which parallel life and character with food flavours. In the Ugadi Lunar New Year Festival, for instance, a combination of bitter and sweet flavours is ingested to ensure a normal balance of fortune. There are also proverbs and customs throughout India which assert that women love sour-flavoured things such as lemon pickles or mangoes. Such customs express a cultural distinction between serious, long-term matters and the (literally and figuratively) colourful, tasty delights of ordinary family life. This is no doubt Khare's (1976b) meaning when he states briefly, that men are concerned with purity, and women with auspiciousness—i.e., the balanced family has some persons more associated with eternal, spiritual identities and others, with changeability and normal biological processes.

In the festivals described in this book the colour white, as the colour of eternity and continuity, is opposed to all other colours. The variety and movement implied in reds, golds, or greens, is philosophically antithetical to whiteness's fixity. Translating to family processes, the family's future is a question of both eternity (whiteness, ancestors, separateness from others, flowing water) and involvement in worldly distractions (greeness and birth, women's bleeding, golden reciprocity and exchange for the sake of maintaining family prestige). Decoration energises the otherwise inert, though constant, family core.

Several myths associated with family festivals, however, indicate that this distinction is as problematic as it is necessary. The purity-pollution dichotomy is cacophony as often as harmony. The best illustration of this point is in the Bandipur A.K. 'Cobra Festival Myth' of the young man who would not marry anyone who was not of his own flesh. In this and other folklore, wives are presented as dangers to a patrilineal family. The key paradox is that in order to remain whole and continuous, a family has to allow women outsiders to invade (and injure?) it. Like that myth, this book has not proposed any workable solutions to Hindu cultural paradoxes of this type; but it has, I hope, demonstrated their symbolic complexity, and the subtle power they wield in the lives of men and women—especially women—of traditional families.

FESTIVALS AND FAMILY STRUCTURE

Family structure is the presumed social basis of the festivals considered in this book. Each myth and ritual highlights a slightly different aspect of that structure; and the group of festivals together express a relatively coherent (though not uniform for all groups) cultural view of it.

What, then, is 'the family' as portrayed in these Karnataka folk festivals? Though the festivals assume patrilineality and virilocality as a backdrop, they parade so many females and cross-sex ties across the stage that a strong bilateral emphasis is impossible to ignore. In one myth an only son is in danger of his (and the patrilineage's) life. But in several others a daughter seeks the protection of her mother, or a brother depends on his sister to save his life. In balancing patrilineal and other types of kinship links, these festivals repeat and reinforce the importance attributed to women in local genealogies themselves. Like genealogies, family festivals counteract, and perhaps compensate for, a tendency toward the male-centered view natural in patrilineal and virilocal systems. As wives, daughters, ghosts, and ancestors, women are key creative and destructive figures in nearly all of these festivals. Their relationships, furthermore, are also central to the concept of family that emerges in the festivals.

As home-centered festivals, this set emphasises the 'birth group', or *kutumba*, more often than any other kin unit. This is both physically and culturally significant, for the *kutumba* is the most intimate and active segment. Together with 'close relations of exchange', or *nentru*, this locus of birth, cooking (real or symbolic), and marriage is most vital to the survival of the larger collectivity of kinsfolk. It is therefore natural that the *kutumba-nentru* pair, or the *kutumba* alone, should play a major role in rituals to stimulate family 'process'.

In one festival, for the restless Mastiamma, a local patrilineage (*dayadi*) group is the main unit of action and cooperation. This event demonstrates that the patrilineage is thought to share and transmit curses as much as it shares and transmits birth/death pollution or property. Other festivals (Piriyapattanad-amma or Cobra Festival) indicate a similar belief even though they do not happen to be occasions for patrilineage gatherings in this corpus of observations.

Whichever relationships or segments are highlighted by specific festivals, 'the family' comes through as a quasi-corporeal unit. Like actual persons, it grows or does not. It is vulnerable to the 'process-stasis' alternation. It bleeds or blooms in festival symbolism. It is whole or mutilated. By their symbolic manipulations, festivals transform an abstract collection of social roles into a sort of concrete being. Festivals then ply it with rituals derived not only from cosmically-oriented theology, but also with rituals derived from person-oriented rites of passage.

The kinship system functions symbolically in two different ways—as chief object, or referent, of symbolic attention, and as a symbol itself in one or two instances. In its role as symbolic object, the kinship system receives much symbolic attention in these festivals, sometimes from a perspective that is rarely verbalised. These rituals and myths present what might be called a Hindu family drama. That is, the object of symbolic attention is presented as a rather turbulent and exciting process of encounter and moral contrast. Prominent symbolic 'issues' comprise a familiar list of socio-cultural distinctions : sexuality vs. celibacy, destruction vs. growth, purity vs. pollution, the home vs. the outside, satisfaction vs. frustration, and so on. The list itself is less surprising than the vigour and complexity of ritual practices which articulate the dramatic tensions involved even in the humblest of peasant homes.

As a symbol itself, the kinship system is mobilised to produce specific effects in some of the festivals studied here. In the festival for Mastiamma a local patrilineal group gathers outdoors but disperses indoors to avert the danger of focussing her curse on the line. In ancestor worship a pattern of organisation of kin expresess a concept of wholeness or completeness.

IMAGES OF PROCESS : THE HINDU FAMILY DRAMA

Festival myths and rituals demonstrate that every phase of family development is plagued by at least one culturally defined danger, and often more than one. For every image of auspicious increase there is a corollary disaster. The imagery of both fortune and misfortune is more and more vivid as we observe them in symbolic tandem through our materials on folk practice. For every satisfaction, there is a frustrating deprival image, whether the hunger be for food, sexual love, or wealth and children. For every vision of the whole, growing family body, there is a mutilation image. And along with the strongly defined value of exchange with other families, there is a persistent theme of withdrawal and incest. These images go far beyond a simple life-death dichotomy to embellish every possible pl asure or virtue with the grace note of an attendant painful alternative.

But this is not a gloomy perspective on family life. On the contrary, I have the impression that these images enhance cultural ideals. As many students of cultural symbolism have pointed out by now, such conceptual struggles provide guiding, and perhaps strengthening, views of an otherwise muddled universe.

Such images invest the Hindu family, its subdivisions, and its ritual-performing members with powers that are difficult to apprehend from the outside. The misfortune and pain inherent in the imagery of folk symbolism often over-shadow simple and pleasant ideals. Cannibalistic ghosts, angry ancestors, and other demons provide a grand opponent to overcome in the struggle for a sense of competence and clarity in the village family's world.

THE END

Whatever had happened had happened, and . . . the crowds of Hindus began a desultory move back into the town. The image went back too, and on the following day underwent a private death of its own, when some curtains of magenta and green were lowered in front of the dynastic shrine. The singing went on even longer . . . ragged edges of religion . . . unsatisfactory and undramatic tangles . . . "God is love."
Looking back at the great blur of the last twenty-four hours, no man could say where was the emotional centre of it, any more than he could locate the heart of a cloud. (E. M. Forster 1924/1952.)

NOTES

1. Warren Swidler, personal communication.
2. Called *accande*, the seed mixture consists of red millet, paddy, and horse gram (Kannada, *ragi, batta,* and *hurali kalu*).

APPENDICES

Appendix A

CONVENTIONAL MEANINGS OF SPECIFIC COLOURS IN HINDU FOLK CULTURE

In the course of studying colour symbolism in Karnataka family festivals, I gathered some general information, presented here, about specific colours and their meanings in this region and elsewhere in India. In 1976 I was able to conduct a few interviews on individuals' associations between colour and emotion. These were open-ended interviews which began with a question such as, "What emotion do you associate with the colour———?" I held these interviews with some four or five people, all of whom found it easy to make the associations requested. Their responses were similar enough to indicate that there are cultural patterns of symbolic uses of colours. The most detailed interview was kindly provided by my research assistant, Miss H. Malathi, a young woman of the Smartha Brahman caste of Mysore City. In the following pages I shall present the results of this interview and others, together with folkloric information from other parts of India.

YELLOW

Yellow is an important colour for auspicious occasions. As the colour of 'human auspicious increase' (Beck 1969 : 559), it has connotations of good fortune and associations with a special type of beauty called *laksana* in Kannada.

In flowers, in turmeric, and in gold itself—one finds yellow associated with the good times of a well-ordered Hindu life. My assistant, H. Malathi explained it to me this way in 1976 :

When you do a *puja* [ritual offering] you put out the turmeric-vermillion,

flowers, coconut, betel, camphor, incense sticks, lamps. These are all a must.
When you get these all arranged, then only will you have that satisfaction,
that you are doing a good auspicious thing. That has *laksana*.

I pursued the question in terms of colour-symbolism :

Q—Is there any feeling associated with yellow colour ?
A—No, no feeling.
Q—How about *santosa* ['pleasure'] ?
A—[In Kannada :] "If one sees *laksana*, one feels *santosa*." They will say like
   that.

Translating *santosa* as 'happiness', she explained that this was the joy in
worldly successes, such as, "your son passing an exam, or winning a lottery,
like that. You will show it by hugging someone or laughing." (S. Hanchett
notes, Bandipur, July 16, 1976).

This person's thoughtful comments summarise much of the meaning of
yellow as a ritual symbol—its pleasant associations, its connotations of general
well-being in life, its expression in turmeric and its special relation to the
married woman as the good status *par excellence*.

A comment from the neighbouring state of Kerala emphasises the association
between yellow, women, marriage and good appearance—in this case in a
vegetal idiom. Nair (1965 : 95) speaks of the "golden, sparkling yellow flowers"
of the East Indian Kino tree (*Kannikona* or *Vengai*). He states that, "the
flowering season of this tree is an auspicious period for marriages." Among
Nayars, he claims, "The wearing of this flower shows that a girl is recently
married." "Lord Muruga, son of Siva, is the patron deity of this tree," and the
tree "is worshipped on the occasion of the Vishu . . . festival . . . (April-May).
It forms one of the essential elements of the seven sacred objects that are used
for the Kani (auspicious sight) which is taken from house to house on this
occasion." (Cf. Abbott 1974 : 397.)

Throughout south India, and perhaps south Asia as a whole, the colour
yellow is most prominent in the ritual use of turmeric.

In fact, the privileged daily toilet of south Indian married women involves
application of turmeric to the tops of the feet and to the sides of the face as
well as to the spot on the forehead. One also occasionally sees a woman who
has rubbed her whole face with a light cover of the yellow powder, in the
hopes that she will appear fair-complexioned. (Correspondingly, widows rarely
if ever have turmeric applied to their bodies; nor do menstruating women use
the powder as ornament, according to custom.) These observations are corro-
borated in the work of Dr. Beck (1969 : 559) on Tamilnadu, and in that of
Dr. Jacobson and Dr. Luschinsky, respectively, for central and northern
India.[1] Turmeric yellow is not, however, limited to women. As a prelude to
the marriage ceremony, brides and grooms of all castes are anointed with the

yellow powder.[2] The announcement of any good event, including the first-thread ceremony for a teenage boy, is made on a card marked with turmeric. Dr. Doranne Jacobson states that in Madhya Pradesh one finds upright turmeric hand-prints in some shrines as a sign that a request for a baby son was granted.[3]

As the colour of gold, yellow also can have a specific association with wealth and prestige. According to Regelson's notes on the flowers used in the agricultural fertility ritual for goddess Tipamma (Laksmi) during the Dipavali festival, in the compost pile—the flowers "should be yellow because of the association with gold." (Regelson notes, July 1966.) Other devotees of Laksmi, the goddess of wealth, also recognise several yellow flowers as her favourites, in addition of course to the lotus from which she was born.

The *tali* pendant worn by the married woman of the south is also gold, as are the *talis* which we find in festival and other rituals. Although the widow may wear other gold jewellery, she does not wear her *tali* after the death of her husband.

The subject of gold as a literary and ritual image is vast. A few literary and ethnographic cases will demonstrate the power of gold as a symbol of wealth, life, and possibly also chastity and purity in Hindu culture. In the origin myth of the "Churning of the Ocean of Milk," we find that the devas achieved immortality from the milk of juices having the power of elixir, "together with the residue of molten gold" (Long 1976). The legendary *parijata* flower of the *Bhagavata* was capable of satisfying any wish of its owner, even to the extent of giving four maunds of gold on demand. This flower, however, was possessed only by the dutiful Rukmini, and never by her independent and spirited co-wife Satyabamma, who went so far as to battle with Indra for the right to grow the plant in her own garden.[4]

The theme of buried gold treasure is a prominent one in south Indian oral traditions. And in these myths the gold often takes on a magical significance. One informant (a resident of Mysore City) told me in 1976 that gold that has been long buried requires human sacrifice before it can be used, because of the malevolent spirits which come to occupy it over the years.

One of the chief guardians of hidden treasure is the serpent deity, Nagappa. In this context it is interesting to note that the serpent of Hindu lore guards *purity* as carefully as he guards his gold.

Among the Smith peoples of Hassan District there is a game which is played at weddings in which a bride and groom compete by fishing around in a vessel for a gold ring. The vessel is filled with a mixture of 'five grains', areca nut, and some water.[5] One of many wedding games symbolising affinal rivalry, the object of this game is to grasp a piece of gold—possibly a symbol of the wealth and prestige competition which is such a prominent aspect of the affinal relationship in south India. (Cf. Hanchett 1975.)

I should add that, in Karnataka at least, gold is a preoccupation of many women. They measure the regard of both their natal and conjugal families precisely in the numbers of grams which each side presents to them in marriage and over the years. By this means the colour yellow, as a quality of gold, again is related to the married woman.

There is some use of turmeric in death-related rituals; but I agree with Dr. Jacobson, who points out that the use of yellow (turmeric) in death probably has more to do with a transition to a normal, ancestral status than with the act of dying. In Madhya Pradesh, for instance, "When taking bones to the Ganges, the bits are put into a small bag coloured with [turmeric] to be carried by the pilgrim around his neck."[6] As it is the final and perfect home of the deceased body, the return to the Ganges is an auspicious transition, not an inauspicious one.

RED

Throughout India red is a colour of energy or power. This concept is evident in texts and folk practices alike. It can be the vitality of a north Indian bride, in her bright red sari threaded with gold. It can be the ornamental vermillion dot on the forehead of one who is in a good state of life or of one who has partaken of a worship experience. And, as the colour of blood, it is considered to be one of the bases of physical strength and stamina.[7] As the colour of blood, it is also the colour naturally associated with the meat-eating Ksatriya (warrior varna). And, as the colour of blood, it also can attract the attention of malevolent ghosts and spirits, conceived as the most blood-lusting of all creatures.

The individual colour red seems to have a different significance in north and south India. In the north, the colour red is generally auspicious :

Red is an auspicious colour they say—the very essence of energy, of joy, of life itself. It is the colour for festive occasions. Wedding invitations are written with red ink; the bride wears a red sari, red sandals and many red bangles of glass or lacquer. (Erikson 19: 8 : 13.)

In Karnataka, the colour red is good in the vermillion-mark; but otherwise used it is a wild and difficult colour, sometimes good but often dangerous.

My Mysore Brahman friend, H. Malathi, states, "Red we call apaya, the dangerous colour, a danger signal." She associates the colour with blood, as do many others of south India. In fact, she points out, many fastidious vegetarians of southern Brahman communities avoid tomatoes and beets because these are the colour of blood. I have heard similar statements from many others during my visits to south India.

This association with blood and danger may derive from the emphasis on sacrificial ritual in the south. Sacrifice of animals (and even of persons, on rare occasions) is basic to much southern Hindu folk ritual and is especially evident in the rituals performed by non-Brahman and A.K. specialists for the restless female deities. H. Malathi expands on the association between red and blood : "Red is associated with blood, like in non-Brahman sacrifices."

In sacrificial ritual, the offering of blood is graphic and direct. Blood may be squirted out of the throat of the sacrificial victim directly onto the image of a deity, or it may be collected in a special vessel for later application. Some rituals require special foods prepared with blood as a main ingredient. One Farmer-caste informant tells us that blood has 'strength' (*miridu*), and this is the basis of its appeal to energetic spirits.

Although Brahmans generally remain aloof from sacrifices of animals, some of my Brahman acquaintances seem to accept blood-offering as a necessary procedure. The Brahman temple priest of Chinnapura once explained to me that his Sanskritic, vegetarian charge, Laksminarasimha (the god and his consort in a pair), was far less powerful than the local goddess Maramma. This was, he claimed, because of the differences in diet. Maramma had the strength to protect the village to a radius of two miles because of her blood diet, while Laksminarasimha was barely strong enough to reach to the village boundaries because he subsisted on rice, yoghurt, and other vegetarian fare.[8]

The Brahmans of Bandipur are frequently shocked at the compliant attitude of the Chinnapura Brahmans in the face of animal sacrifice. In 1966, one Brahman of Bandipur related to me the way in which the Chinnapura Brahmans formerly shared in the annual sacrifice of a male buffalo to Maramma. Not only did they contribute money to the maintenance of the future victim, he explained, but they also remained nearby while the cooked meat was eaten by others, this being an unthinkable transgression of vegetarianism in his view. Brahmans, however, also offer sacrifice, in a vegetarian form. On some occasions, however, an ash gourd is sprinkled with vermillion powder [a conscious blood substitute in this context] and cloven with the swift strike of a knife.

Red is the colour associated with the Brahman widow, most inauspicious of all statuses in Karnataka. The shaven-headed Brahman widow traditionally wears a plain red sari in Karnataka. A custom which is rapidly disappearing in all parts of the south, it deserves mention in this context. To don the colour red is probably to indicate to the community her dangerously strong connection with her dead husband, and also the witch-like tendencies she is assumed to have (cf. Harper 1969).

Widows in many other regions of India customarily wear plain white saris. This transformation may have a scholarly basis as well as a structural one. Beck (1969 : 571), referring to some unpublished material of Van Buitenen's on this subject, states that there has been an inversion of red and white in Hindu religious history, red taking primacy in the earliest literature.

Whatever the basis of the variation in widows' sari colours, both the red and the white are supposed to be plain and undecorated saris. In both cases the

widow image is a static, single-faceted one. There is a connotation of barrenness in the solitude of the sari colour, as in her lack of the combined colours
of floral ornamentation and in other details of her grooming. Widows of
different ages may dress very differently nowadays. It is mainly the very old,
more orthodox Brahman widows who keep up the extremely simple form of
dress that tradition dictates.

One can speculate on red and its possible connection with turmeric or yellow.
There is some circumstantial folkloric evidence that turmeric may in some way
be connected with blood or red colour. Perhaps it was once considered red,
although now 'turmeric-colour' is the very name of yellow in most Indian
languages. I shall present the evidence for the reader's consideration. As Regelson (1972 : 286) points out, there is no indigenous morpho-phonemic way of
referring to the yellow colour in Kannada. Thus there may have been no colour
yellow recognised separately from green in the early history of the Dravidian
languages. Regelson (1972 : 200) suggests that turmeric may be historically
'red' on three other grounds as well—(1) its presumed 'heating' nature; (2) its
capacity to turn bright red when combined with water and lime (sunna)—a
mixture often used to remove the evil eye. In the words of one informant,
"Even blood itself is not so red" as this mixture. (3) The offering to bhuta
demons at the end of the Bandipur Narasimha festival (jatra) is plain cooked
rice coloured with turmeric. Given the thirst for blood of these spirits, this
may be a structural substitute for blood-rice.

The connection of turmeric, blood, and demons is supported by two other
ethnographic items. First, for Coimbatore District, Tamilnadu, Beck (1969 :
559) describes an adoption ceremony in which the blood of a nursing mother
is drunk. This blood is called 'turmeric water'. Secondly, Jacobson reports
from Bhopal District, Madhya Pradesh :

"Wet haldi [turmeric] is not put on a pregnant woman, nor is . . . red foot
paint. . . . or . . . henna . . . There are things that might attract . . . evil
spirits . . . Haldi is that sort of thing that might attract a bhuta [ghost or
evil spirit] with its nice scent." (Doranne Jacobson, unpublished field notes
on "Turmeric," Madhya Pradesh, October 4, 1974).

In this statement red foot paint, henna, and turmeric are grouped together as
things that might attract malevolent spirits. Although it is specifically the scent
of turmeric, and not its colour, that is mentioned, its grouping in this way with
red things is worth noting.

Furthermore, Dr. Jacobson's notes mention a red coloured type of turmeric
used for medicinal purposes. In Hindi this is called ami hardi [haldi,] or bari
hardi [haldi]. She distinguishes the ordinary yellow turmeric by the Hindi term
chhoti haldi.

Although these materials are inconclusive, they are suggestive. They also emphasise the need to determine just how a local person would name the colour of a given item. As the anthropological literature on colour has amply suggested, the outside observer cannot rely on his or her own colour terms in interpreting those of a foreign culture.[9]

BLACK

As an isolated colour, black has several unfortunate and unhappy connotations. My Mysore Brahman informant associated black colour with dying (a death announcement being marked in black), failure, grief and depression ("no work, morose"). A young Brahman man of Bandipur explained to me that if someone appears at an auspicious event wearing black clothing, "People will think about grief (*duka*)."[10]

Majumdar (1969 : 152) calls the black colour "ominous." He (1969 : 155) attributes the role of the buffalo as Yama's vehicle partly to its black colour:

The buffalo, due to its black colour, brutish appearance and dangerous temper, naturally typifies death, and is the vehicle of Yama god of death.

Probably because of its black colour, iron also has some ominous connotations:

Iron is used in many forms as an amulet. [But] it is said that stools required in religious ceremonies must have no nail or other iron in them; for, iron [frightens] away not only bad but even good spirits. (Majumdar 1969 : 151.)

As an ominous colour, black is thought to have the power to protect one against that which it represents. First, it is believed to have the power to repel the evil eye. Thus it is used as a mark on the faces of children, and even occasionally beautiful women. The black glass bangles customarily given to a bride or married woman are not to indicate an inauspicious condition, but rather to prevent misfortune from coming to her. Mahapatra (1969 : 39) discusses this idea as part of Jain folklore as well: since black or bitter materials may counteract the evil eye, " . . . the women use black thread, when using a new jewellery." In Karnataka it is customary for women to wear their marital *tali* pendant on a string of black beads (or alternating black and gold beads) for the same reason.

Thus one will find black playing a role in auspicious events, although it is not a dominant colour there. Some Farmer caste groups require that a black blanket be the seat of a bride and groom during the wedding rites (Gurulingaiah notes, 30 October, 1967). In discussing festival foods, a Brahman lady told me that the preparation called *cigali* can be made with either white or black sesame seeds as a main ingredient, but "for festivals, [for] distribution with betel and areca nut, [the] black [type] is *auspicious*." (S. Hanchett notes, 14 July, 1976, Bandipur.) Brown sugar, or jaggery, is another food used (in large cubes) in many auspicious rituals. Although the lighter and darker types are labelled 'white jaggery' and 'black jaggery' respectively, I have found no restriction on the use of the black type.

Secondly, in reference to the powers of black, it has a special relation to destructive spirits. It can repel the evil eye (a relatively impersonal force), but it can both represent and recruit the more anthropomorphic spiritual beings. In the Maramma *jatra* festival as traditionally performed in Bandipur, certain A.K. men smear their faces with black colour, in order to appear as 'malevolent ghosts' (*dayyas*) in the service of the goddess.

Abbott (1974 : 279) has observed that while white threads are used to invoke the power of beneficent spirits, black ones are used to invoke the power of [malevolent] spirits.

Thirdly, black is the colour of night-time and darkness. And, in the words of Majumdar (1969 : 150), "Night is the time when demons come out to do evil." It is especially so during the nights of the new moon, an important period for the casting and lifting of spells by *mantravadis*.

In spite of its deathly associations, black plays a minor role in funerary rituals. The A.K.s of Chinnapura smear black on the forehead of a dead child or adult. And a Brahman of Bandipur once told me that only a widow ought to wear a black sari, though others do like to wear black because it makes the fair complexion seem bright. It is, however, most important in the propiation or repulsion of destructive spirits.

WHITE

In the words of H. Malathi, white is associated with "purity of heart." This type of 'purity' (*pavitra* 'holy' or *suddhavada* 'pure/clean') is the sincerity of an honest person, the devotion of a serious worshipper, and the calm (*santi*) of a peaceful mind. In itself the colour has benign connotations.

A white cloth covers many ritual offerings (e.g., foods) in Karnataka, the whiteness of the cloth being in itself a sign of ritual purity (*madi*) according to one A.K. informant. In the Cobra Festival feast the A.K. women must wear white clothing as they prepare the very pure food for offering to the serpent deity.

The typical daily clothing of a Bandipur or Chinnapura man is the pure white *pance* wrap. This length of cloth is wrapped around the waist and left to hang gracefully around the legs. The *dhotis* (wrapped in a more elaborate fashion around the legs and hips) which Brahman men put on for ritual occasions are also white, sometimes with a narrow gold border. These occasions of course require ritual purity (*madi*), but men are considered to be generally more ritually pure than women, since they do not menstruate.

White is also the colour of (husked) raw and cooked rice; the colour of milk; and of the cooling, 'milky sap' (*sone*) of certain sacred trees. Rice being the basis of food and 'meals' (*uta*) in this region, its whiteness may also be associated with nourishment and (in exchanges) the continuity of caste and familial ties.

White also is associated with death and mourning, especially with the death of men or patrilineal relatives. Several castes prefer to clothe male corpses in white cloth (females in colours). At a Brahman funeral, plain white rice is cooked and eaten by close mourners at the cremation site. Abbott (1974 : 280) states that " . . . in severe mourning white is used and the winding sheet of the dead is white."

The auspicious and inauspicious associations of white are not mutually exclusive. Just as the pure mind is steady and devoted, so also the pure body is integrated within a caste and family line. The semen of this line is white, as is the cooked rice exchanged among its members—the living and the dead alike. The line moves through males. The white-garbed males are the basis of family continuity.

GREEN

Although one of the basic named Kannada colours, green plays a minor role in the popular rituals I have observed. "Green is the colour of growing things," as a young Brahman man explained to me, but, he continued, "it is not significant in any wider sense."

There are two major ritual occasions, nonetheless, when one finds the colour green prominent. First, it is a widely preferred colour for the bride's sari at the time her *tali* marriage pendant is tied. This preference is found among Brahmans and non Brahmans alike. Secondly, it is the colour of glass bangles customarily fitted on a woman in her seventh month of pregnancy. Both of these are times of a beginning, the *tali*-tying being the confirmation of the marital union; and the seventh month being the time when a woman customarily goes to her natal home to await the birth of her child. In signifying a beginning, the green colour echoes the theme inherent in the ritual use of germination of grains. The metaphor is established between new vegetal growth and human beginnings. Beck (1969) also refers to green as a colour of "vegetal abundance" in Tamilnadu.[11]

I have seen two references to green colour being used in the construction of a *mandala* design. One is from Hassan District, in a non-Brahman report of an exorcism ritual which requires a *mandala* design so brightly coloured that, 'one should feel fear when looking at it'. Green is one of the many colours used in such a *mandala*, according to my information.[12] The second reference is in an article by Ashton (1976), who mentions "green powder" forming part of a "Nagamandalam" she observed in South Kanara District, Karnataka.

Regarding the other named colours, I have found no value attached (consciously or non-consciously) to their use in my Karnataka studies. It is probable that blue and brown, and perhaps some other colours, will be significant in practices of other regions. But it seems unlikely that the white, red, yellow, black, and green group would anywhere fade into insignificance, because of the heavy symbolic load borne by each of these colours in popular Hindu culture of many regions.

NOTES

1. Dr. Doranne Jacobson has extensive comments on the subject of use of turmeric in Madhya Pradesh in an unpublished October 1974 field report. Turmeric is, she states, a generally purifying agent and "an auspicious medium of transition" in many rites of passage. It also has medicinal uses. In a note to the same report, Dr. Jerome Jacobson adds that turmeric "seems to be also a symbol of generation, perhaps the female's generative powers." The comments of my Mysore Brahman informant and the material presented in Chapter 5 do not, however, give much emphasis to fertility as a cultural theme related to turmeric use by married women.

2. Dr. Jacobson points out that the bride keeps a sharp object with her during this ceremony to ward off evil spirits.

3. In the aforementioned October 1974 field report.

4. Cf. *Sri Krishna Parijata*, published in Kannada by Mysore University Press.

5. This information was gathered by K. Gurulingaiah in 1967, on the *todkin akki* game. Dr. Jacobson (October 1974 report) mentions a similar game played among a Brahman group of Madhya Pradesh. In this game, however, the object of value is silver, not gold : "[The] bride and groom have a ritual power struggle, trying to grasp a bit of silver or silver jewellry in a platter of [turmeric-] water."

6. October 1974 report, *op. cit.*

7. Kannada, *miridu* 'strength', which is in blood (Regelson notes, 1967).

8. In fact, yoghurt-rice (*mosaranna*) is considered to be a special favourite of Maramma in Hassan District. This, however, is because of its 'cooling' and soothing effect on her angry temperament, not because it is the mainstay of her diet.

9. Sahlins (1977 : 196) argues that as a result of the perceptual nature of redness, "Where the complete triad of red-white-black is in use, then, one can expect—as in all such cases of mediation—that certain meaningful values of red will themselves be opposed in moral sign, positive and negative. Furthermore, two additional dyads will be included in the structural set, red vs. white and red vs. black, the latter because of the low brightness value of saturated red, probably the stronger or more marked opposition."

10. I have, nonetheless, seen an A. K. woman guest at a wedding dressed in black.

11. In spite of these vegetal metaphors, the colour green is insignificant in agricultural rituals.

12. 1976 notes on an interview with a Smith soothsayer, a relative of a Bandipur resident. This soothsayer lives elsewhere in Hassan District.

Appendix B

LOCAL MYTHS OF *AMMA* GODDESSES

MARAMMA

An A.K. boy learned all the customs of the Brahmans, and, pretending to be a Brahman, he married a Brahman girl. When their child learned to talk, it asked its mother, "Please get me a water buffalo's leg to eat." The mother was surprised. She investigated and found out the truth by asking her husband why their son was asking for this. Her husband told her the truth.

The wife got angry, had a fire built, and immolated herself. Before jumping, she gave a curse: "You must be born as a buffalo, and your people must bring you before me, and sacrifice you."

She became Mari, and her husband became a male buffalo.

(Stanley Regelson notes, 2 March 1967)

PIRIYAPATTANADAMMA AND KANNAMBADIAMMA

Piriyapattanadamma and Kannambadiamma lived on the same street in the town of Piriyapattana. Piriyapattanadamma ate meat, but Kannambadiamma was a vegetarian. They had been friends but had a fight. In that town there was a custom of having a temple cart festival for each goddess on the same day each year. Two carts were used, one for each goddess. Because of their fight, Kannambadiamma was about to leave town. Piriyapattanadamma went to her as she was leaving and asked her not to go. She said, "First I'll have your cart

293

festival, and one month later, I'll have my own." At the moment when Piriyapattanadamma was pleading with her, Kannambadiamma turned into a statue on the spot.

(Weaver woman story teller, Bandipur, 15 August 1977)

GLOSSARY

GLOSSARY

Term	Transliteration	Meaning
Acari	*Ācāri*	Smith caste, Visvakarma
accande	*accande*	a mixture of seeds
adhika	*adhika*	redundant
Adidravida (*A.D.*)	*Ādidrāviḍa*	a Harijan caste, Māḍiga
Adikarnataka (*A.K.*)	*Ādikarṇāṭaka*	a Harijan caste, Holeya
Agasa	*Agasa*	Washerman caste
ainoru	*ainōru*	a type of non-Brahman ritual specialist
akki	*akki*	raw rice
aksate	*akṣate, akṣata*	turmeric-coloured raw rice
ala	*āla*	banyan tree, *Ficus indica L.* or *F. benghalensis*
aladamara	*āladamara*	banyan tree (see *ala*)
alugedde	*ālūgeḍḍe, ālūgaḍḍe*	potato
amanta	*amānta*	lunisolar calendar
amavase	*āmavādase* (colloq. *amāvāsye/amāvāse*)	new moon day
amma	*amma*	mother, lady, goddess
ammanavara (*y*)*ecca*	*ammanāvara ecca*	offerings to *amma* type of goddess
anna	*anna*	boiled rice
annadaa	*annadāa*	the giving of food
anna-prasana	*anna-prāśana*	ritual first feeding of cooked rice to a baby
anna-tammandiru	*anna-tammandiru*	brothers, lineage-mates
apaya	*apāya*	danger

297

Term	Transliteration	Meaning
arali	*araḷi*	pipal or sacred fig tree, *Ficus religiosa* L.
aralu	*araḷu*	popped rice
arasina	*araśina*	turmeric, *Curcuma longa* L. (Family, Zingiberaceae), yellow colour
arasinada kulu	*araśinada kūḷu*	turmeric-coloured cooked rice
arati	*ārati*	ceremony in which a lamp is waved before object of worship
atman	*atman*	universal soul
atti	*atti*	country fig tree, *Ficus glomerata* Roxb.
avalakki	*avalakki*	dried pressed rice
avare	*avare*	a pulse, cow gram, *Lablab purpureus* (L.) Sweet (*Dolichos lablab* L.)
avarekalu	*avarekāḷu*	cow gram, whole bean not split (see *avare*)
ayudhu puja	*ayūdhu* (or *ayudha*) *pūjā*	ritual honouring instruments of productive work
badanekayi	*badanekāyi*	eggplant, brinjal
bagina	*bāgina*	fortunate state, gift
baginamara	*bāginamara*	auspicious gifts presented in winnowing fan
balaga	*baḷaga*	close affines : same as *nentru* (local term)
balehannu	*bāḷehaṇṇu*	plantains/bananas, ripe
balekayi	*bāḷekāyi*	plantains/bananas, unripe
bali	*bali*	sacrifice
bandavaru	*bandāvaru*	distant affines, relations of exchange
bandugalu	*bandugaḷu*	distant affines, relations of exchange
banna	*baṇṇa*	colour
bannagur	*baṇṇaguṛ/baṇṇaguḷ*	lit. 'coloured cooked rice', used for oblations (old term)
basavi	*basavi*	a female who has undergone marriage to Siva, or God

Term	Transliteration	Meaning
batta	batta	rice in the husk
bele	bēḷe	split pulse
bendekayi	benḍēkāyi	okra, *Hibiscus esculentus*
besa	besa	odd (number)
Besta	Bēsta/Bēstāru	Fisherman caste
bettadavare	beṭṭadavare (hūvu)	dahlia (flower)
bhava, bava	bhāva, bāva	brother-in-law, WiBr, SiHu
bhuta	bhūta	a malignant spirit
bhuta bali	bhūtā baḷi	sacrificial offering to malignant spirit
biccole	biccōle	rolled palmyra leaf earlobe ornaments
bigaru	bīgāru	parents of individuals who are married (SoWiMo/Fa, DaHuMo/Fa)
bili	biḷi	white colour
bindige	bindige	a type of water vessel
brahmacarya	brahmacarya	religious student, celibate
buda	buḍa, buḍḍe	base, stock (e.g., of a tree or family)
budkumbalakayi	buḍkumbaḷakāyi	ash gourd
buvve sastra	buvve śāstra	a commensal ceremony during wedding rituals
cakkali	cakkali	a salted, fried snack
cakra	cakra	a wheel, circle
capradavarekayi	capradāvarekāyi	beans
caudi	cauḍi	female spirit with violent temperament
cigali	cigaḷi	a fried, sweet sesame seed cake
cigani	cigaṇi	a fried sweet, same as *putelluvunde*
cigaru	cigaru	a sprout or new leaf
cikka	cikka	small, younger
ciroti	cirōti	a fried, sweet pastry
citranna	citranna	a lemon flavoured boiled rice preparation
daksinayana	dakṣiṇāyana	half year period following summer solstice
danyadavsa	dānyadavsa	grams, grains, and pulses

Term	Transliteration	Meaning
daridra	daridra	impoverished
dayadi	dāyādi	minimal agnatic lineage segment
dayya	dayya	malevolent spirit
Devanga	Dēvanga	Weaver caste
devaru	dēvaru	god or gods
devastana	dēvastāna	temple
dharbe	dharbe	a grass
dhare	dhāre	'pouring', a central part of wedding ritual
divasa	divasa	the day, the solar day
dodda	doḍḍa	big, elder
dose	dōse	rice flour pancakes
dupa	dūpa, dhūpa	incense, *puja*
(y)ecca	ecca	ritual gift for girl at menarche
(y)ede	eḍe	a religious offering of a cooked meal
(y)ele	ele	leaf; eating leaf
(y)ele-adike	ele-aḍike	betel leaf and areca nut
(y)ellu	elḷu	mixture of grams, dried coconut, and white sesame seeds
(y)eriappa	eriappa	a fried pastry
gadde	gadde	cultivated wet land, paddy field
gaddige	gaḍḍige	mud platform prepared for use in worship
gali	gāḷi	ghost, malignant spirit
Ganiga	Gāṇiga	Oil Presser caste
gari	gari	palm frond or branch
garike	gārike	a grass, *Cynodon dactylon* Pers.
gauda, gaudru	gauḍa, gauḍru	village headman, farmer
gaya	gāya	a bruise or wound
gejjestra	gejjestra	ceremonial cotton necklace
godibanna	gōdibaṇṇa	wheat colour
godinaga	gōdināga	a type of brown coloured snake

Term	Transliteration	Meaning
gojju	gojju	fried vegetable preparation
gorikayi	gorikāyi	a vegetable, possibly : *Cyamopsis psoralioides* (Family, Fabaceae)
gudi	guḍi	small temple
gumpu	gumpu	group
habba	habba	festival, cyclical rite
hagalakayi	hāgalakāyi	*Momordica charantia* (Family, Cucurbitaceae)
Hajama	Hajāma	Barber caste
halnentru	haḷeneṇṭru, colloq. haḷneṇṭru	'old relatives', linked by previous marriage
halu	hālu	milk
hal-tuppa	hāl-tuppa	milk-clarified butter mixture used in rituals
halsorekayi	hālsōrēkāyi	bottle gourd (*sorekayi*), dessicated
hanginula	hanginula	a special thread used in ritual
hannu	haṇṇu	fruit
hannu-vilada (y)ele	haṇṇu-vīḷadēle	fruit and betel-areca, for offering
hapla	hapla	a fried snack, *papadam*
harabali	harabaḷi	a form of chicken sacrifice
harake	harake	short-term vow
harigedevaru	harigedēvaru	a type of minor spirit
hase mane	hāse maṇe	small, wooden platform used in ritual, also *maṇe*
hasiru	hasiru, hasaru	green colour
hesaru	hesaru	green gram, *Phaseolus aureus*
hirekayi	hīrekāyi	a vegetable, *Luffa acutangula* (L.) Roxb. (Family, Cucurbitaceae)
hiriavaru	hiriāvaru, hiriāru	elders, ancestors
hosnentru	hosneṇṭru	'new relatives', linked by recent marriage
huggianna	huggiyanna, huggibāna	a cooked rice preparation
huli	hūḷi	sour flavour
hulianna	hūḷianna	a cooked rice preparation, sour flavoured

Term	Transliteration	Meaning
hulikaddi	hulikaḍḍi, or sulikaḍḍi	a twig of *Securinela leucopyrus* (Wild.) Mueller
hunnu	huṇṇu	a swelling on skin
hurali	huraḷi	horse gram
hurikadale	huri kaḍaḷe	roasted Bengal gram
huttidabannagalu	huṭṭidabaṇṇagaḷu	natural colours, not artificial produced
huttidamane	huṭṭidamane	house of birth
huttu	huttu, or hutta	ant hill
huvilya	huviḷya	offering given to five married women in honour of a deceased married woman
hwala	hwāla, hōla	land, unirrigated field
hwate-punya	hwate-punya	birth fortune (lit. 'stomach fortune')
idakayi	ɪdakāyi	coconut-breaking, a type of ritual act
iddali	iḍḍali	a steamed dumpling
Idiga	īḍiga	Toddy Tapper caste
illatikalu	illatikāḷu	string beans, green beans
jagarne	jāgarṇe	a vigil, or 'sleep-fast'
jajman	jajmān, yejemān	boss, landowner, head of household
jati	jāti	caste
jatra	jātra	festival, all-village festival
jilebi	jilēbi	a sweet pastry
jodidari	jōḍidāri	referring to a tax-farming system of land-holding
jogi	jōgi	a wise man, a yogi
jyoti	jyōti	a burning lamp
kacu	kācu	a gum derived from *Acacia catechu*, chewed with betel
kadabu	kaḍabu	steamed dumplings
kadaka	kaḍaka, kaḍaku	jewellery, earring
kadale	kaḍaḷe	Bengal gram, *Cicer arietinum*
kadalekayi	kaḍalekāyi	peanuts, groundnuts
kadamba	kadamba	a seasoned boiled rice preparation

Term	Transliteration	Meaning
kajji	*kajji*	scabs, itchy skin condition
kalasa	*kaḷasa*	a water-filled vessel used in ritual
kalina sastra	*kālina śāstra*	ritual shaving, part of a wedding
kalsha	(?)	variant of *kaḷasa*
kalu	*kāḷu*	whole gram, bean, seed
kamba	*kamba*	a pillar or mast
kamma	*kamma*	fragrance
kanda, kandu	*kanda, kandu, kanddu*	broun colour
kanigal	*kaṇigaḷ, kaṇigaḷu*	oleander, *Nerium indicum* Miller (syn. *N. odorum*) (Family, Apocynaceae)
Kannambadiamma	*Kannambāḍiamma*	name of a goddess
kannubannugalu	*kaṇṇubaṇṇagaḷu*	artificial colours
karajikayi	*karajikāyi*	a snack food
kappu	*kappu*	black colour (see also *kari*)
kara	*kāra*	pungent, hot flavour
kari	*kari*	black (see also *kappu*)
kate	*kate*	story or myth
katti	*katti*	knife or sword
kay	*kay, kahi*	bitter flavour
kayi	*kāyi*	vegetable, unripe fruit
kempkanigal	*kempkaṇigaḷ (hūvu)*	red oleander (flower)
kempu	*kempu*	red colour
kenda	*keṇḍa*	red hot, or colour of burning coals
kodubale	*kōḍubaḷe*	a salted, fried cake in ring shape
kolkatte	*kolkaṭṭe, kolakaṭṭe*	(Tamil word) a steamed pastry
kolaku	*kolaku*	dirty or impure
koli	*kōḷi*	chicken, male or female fowl
kopa	*kōpa*	anger, wrath
kosambari, kosambri	*kōsambari, kōsambri*	a salad made of soaked grams, spiced
krattike	*krattike*	the Pleiades
ksudradevaru	*kśudradēvaru*	malevolent spirit type
kudlu	*kudlu*	sickle, scythe
kula	*kūḷa*	agnatic unit, clan
kulu	*kūḷu*	cooked rice (old word); mixture of cooked rice and blood

Term	Transliteration	Meaning
kumbalakayi	kumbaḷakāyi	common gourd
kumkum	kumkum	vermillion, a brightly red coloured powder
kura	kura	boils on the skin
Kuruba	Kuruba	Shepherd caste
kuta	kūṭa	meeting, gathering
kutumba	kuṭumba	birth group, intimate relatives
ladduge	laḍḍuge	a sweet, ball-shaped pastry
lakke	lakke	a plant that grows in a three-leaved pattern, *Vitex negundo* L. (Family, Verbenaceae)
lakke soppu	lakke soppu	leaves of *Vitex negundo*
laksana	lakṣaṇa	good appearance
madi	maḍi	the state of ritual purity
madilakki	maḍilakki	food gifts placed in *maḍilu* (q.v.)
madilu	maḍilu	lap pocket formed in sari when a woman sits
madulane Sravana Senevara	madulane Śrāvana Senevāra	first Saturday in lunar month of Sravana
mahalaya amavase	mahālaya amāvase	new moon day in lunar month of Bhadrapada, or Asvija; occasion of ancestor worship
maidan	maidān	plains of eastern Karnataka
mailige	mailige	state of ordinary impurity
makara	makara	zodiacal sign of Capricorn
maladahabba	māḷadahabba, māḷyadahabba	ancestor worship occasion
malnad	malnāḍu	rainy land, the Mysore plateau
mandala	maṇḍāla	a disk, a circular array, ritual design
mane	mane	house
mane	maṇe	low bench or platform, used in ritual, also *hase maṇe*
mangalarati	mangaḷārati	*ārati* (q.v.) performed with burning camphor
mantapa	maṇṭapa	shrine, often small or temporary

Term	Transliteration	Meaning
mantra	*mantra*	a holy verse, a spell
mantravadi	*mantravāḍi*	a specialist in the use of **spells**
mara	*mara*	winnowing fan
Mari, **Maramma**	*Māri*, *Māramma*	name of a goddess
masala banna	*masālā baṇṇa*	lit. 'spice colour', a yellowish white
masi	*masi*	soot-black; impure
mava	*māva*	father-in-law, uncle (MoBr, FaSiHu)
miridu	*miridu*	energy (for ghosts)
mohini	*mōhini*	a beguiling female ghost
mosaranna	*mosaranna*	a boiled rice preparation, with yoghurt
motuli	*motūḷi* (also, *hambukaḷḷi*)	a plant, *Sarcostemma brevistigma* [now] *acidum* (Roxb.) Voigt; or *Cryptolepis buchanani* Roem. & Schult. (Family, Asclepiadaceae)
mulagayi	*mulagāyi*	eggplant, brinjal (local term)
mulangi	*mūlangi*	white radish, *Raphanus sativus*
munji	*munji*	the twice-born initiation ceremony, *upanayana*
muttayide	*muṭṭāyide*	a state of well-being, specifically that of being a married woman whose husband is alive
muttu	*muṭṭu*	a state of strong ritual impurity
nadani	*nādani*	female cross-cousin, (MoBrDa, FaSiDa); sister-in-law (YoBrWi, HuYoSi)
naga	*nāga*	a serpent, especially **cobra**
nagarbana	*nāgarbāna*	food offered to a serpent
naksatra	*nakṣatra*	sidereal, relating to **lunar** mansions
naivedya	*naivēdya*	food offered to a deity
namaskara	*namaskāra*	greeting
nammavaru	*nammāvaru*	our people, ancestors
nene	*nene*	soak, moisten
nentru	*neṇru*	affines, close relations of exchange

Term	Transliteration	Meaning
nesada banna	nesada baṇṇa	lit. 'snuff colour', a purple
nili	nīli	blue colour
nuggekayi	nuggekāyi, also, nugalakāyi	a vegetable, *Moringa oleifera* Lamk. (Family, Moringaceae)
(v)obbattu	obbaṭṭu	a sweet, fried pastry
(v)odahuttidavaru	odahuṭṭidāvaru	those born closely together, siblings or cousins
(v)ogaru	ogaru	astringent flavour
Okkaliga	Okkaliga	Farmer caste
(v)olle	oḷḷe	good, high quality
padavalakayi, padalakayi	paḍavalakāyi, also, paḍalakāyi	snake gourd, *Trichosanthes dioica* Roxb. (Family, Cucurbitaceae)
paksa	pakśa	the side of anything; half of a lunar month
palegar	pālegār	minor feudal lord
palya	palya	a preparation of seasoned, boiled vegetable
pancamrita	pancamṛita	ritual beverage
pancanga	pancanga	almanac
parijata	pārijāta	mythical flower
pavitra	pavītra	holy, purification
payasa	pāyasa	a sweet, liquid preparation
phala-tambula	phala-tambūlā	ritual payment of fruits and betel-areca to a priest
pinda	piṇḍa	sesame and rice ball, offered to ancestors
Piriyapattanadamma	Piriyapaṭṭaṇadamma	name of a goddess
pitamaha	pitāmahā	paternal ancestors, male; grandfather
pitri	pitṛi	ancestor, lit. 'father'
pongal	pongaḷ	a boiled rice preparation
pradaksana	pradakśana	ritual prostration
prasad	prasād	food consecrated by service to a deity
prasta	prasta	a ritual preceding the consummation of a marriage

Term	Transliteration	Meaning
Prati	*Prāṭi*	name of a goddess (Laksmi)
preta	*prēta*	a corpse, the spirit of the recently deceased
puja	*pūja or pūjā*	worship or ritual involving an offering
puliyogare	*puḷiyōgare*	a rice preparation with tamarind and spices
punya	*puṇya*	good fortune
purana	*purāṇa*	established Hindu mythological text
puri	*puri*	puffed rice
purnakumbha	*pūrṇakumbha*	a vessel filled with sanctified water
purnima	*pūrṇima*	full moon
purohit	*purōhit*	priest
purta/pura	*purta/pura*	pure, true (colour)
puttellu	*puṭṭeḷḷu*	sesame seed
puttellu vunde	*pūṭṭeḷḷuvunde*	a sweet, same as *cigaṇi*
pyun	*pyūn*	bearer (from Eng. peon)
ragi	*rāgi*	finger millet
rangolli	*rangōlli or rangōle*	ornamental line drawings on floors or thresholds
rasayana	*rasāyana*	very sweet fruit mixture
risi	*riṣi*	a sage (Skt. *rsi*)
ratha	*ratha*	a chariot; temple cart (*teru*)
rayatwari	*rāyatwāri*	referring to cultivator-owned land holding system
roja	*rōja*	rose (flower); pink colour
sajjappa	*sajjappa*	a sweet snack food
sama	*sama*	even (number)
samaja	*samāja*	a gathering
sambandigalu	*sambandigaḷu*	relatives
sampige	*sampige*	champak, *Michelia champaca* Lamarck
sampigehuvu	*sampigehūvu*	champak flower
samsara	*samsāra*	marital couple, nuclear family
sankranti	*śankrantī*	solar transition to new zodiacal sign

Term	Transliteration	Meaning
santi	śānti	peace
santosa	santōśa	happiness, satisfaction
sannyasi	sannyāsi	sage, holy man, hermit
sappe	sappe	bland flavour
saru	sāru	sauce poured over rice
sastra	śāstra	a ritually required behaviour
sastra-helavaru	śāstra-hēḷāvaru	a type of soothsayer
saubhagya	saubhāgya	extreme good fortune
seve	sēve	service
sihi	sihi	sweet flavour
sire	sīre	sari
sita	sīta	cold
socca	socca	colloq. form of svacca
sogilakki	sōgilakki	same as maḍilakki (q.v.), Smartha Brahman term
sone	sōne	milky sap of a tree or other plant
sorekayi	sōrēkāyi	bottle gourd (see halsorekayi)
sose	sōse	daughter-in-law, niece (a man's SiDa, or woman's BrDa)
suddhavada	śuddhavāda	pure
suli	suḷi	tip of banana leaf
sunna	suṇṇa	chemical lime
sunti	śuṇṭi	ginger
sutaka	sūtaka	birth or death pollution
svacca	svacca	clean, also socca
tada	taḍa	obstacle
tadaguni, tadani	taḍaguṇi taḍaṇi	a pulse, Vigna catjang Walp. (syn : Alsande)
tadaguni kalu	taḍaguṇi kāḷu	whole bean of V. catjang
tadaguni kayi	taḍaguṇi kāyi	unripe fruit of V. catjang
tale	tāḷe, tāḷa	pandanus, screw pine or calders bush, Pandanus fascicularis Lamarck (Family, Pandanaceae)
talehuvu	tāḷehūvu	pandanus flower
tali	tāḷi	wedding pendant
tallu	taḷḷu	a stewed preparation
taluk	tāluk	a subdistrict

Term	Transliteration	Meaning
tambittu	tambiṭṭu	a fried pastry
tameta	ṭamēṭa, ṭamēṭa haṇṇu	tomato, ripe tomato fruit
tampu	tampu	coolness
tamta	tamta	a fried cake
tani (y)eriyuvudu	tani eriyuvudu	a ritual for 'cooling' purposes
tapas	tapas	austerity, penance, heat
tende	teṇḍe	branch; branch of a clan
tera	tera	bridewealth
teru	tēru	temple cart; ratha
tindi	tiṇḍi	snack food
tirta	tīrta	sanctified water
tithi	tīthi	lunar day
todkin akki	toḍkin akki	a wedding game
togari	togari	red gram, Cajanus cajan
tota	tōṭa	garden land, cultivated enclosure
trpti agilla	trpti āgilla	expression meaning, 'misfortune will not come'
tuppa	tuppa	clarified butter
uddu	uddu	black gram, Phaseolus mungo
ugra	ugra	fierce, cruel, angry
upakarana upakarma	upakārma	annual ceremony of changing the sacred thread
upanayana	upanāyana	the ceremony at which a male first puts on the sacred thread (also, munji)
upayadana	upāyadāna	ritual gifts presented at initiation
uta	ūṭa	a meal
uttarayana	uttarāyaṇa	half year period following the winter solstice
vade	vaḍe	a snack food
vamsa	vamśa	total agnatic family
vara puja	vāra pūja	a wedding ritual for groom
volemasni	volemasni	stove soot
vilya	vīlya	areca nut served with betel leaf
vrata	vrata	a vow
vara	vāra	a week
varsa	varśa	a year

BIBLIOGRAPHY

Abbott, J. (1974). *The Keys of Power; A Study of Indian Ritual and Belief.* Seacaucus, New Jersey : University Books. (Originally published 1932.)

Aiyangar, K. V. Rangaswami (Ed.) (1950). *Kṛtyakalpataru of Bhaṭṭa Lakṣhmīdhara.* Volume IV : *Srāddhakāṇḍa.* Baroda : Oriental Institute.

Arensberg, Conrad M., and Solon T. Kimball (1965). *Culture and Community.* New York: Harcourt, Brace and World.

Ashton, Martha B. (1976). Night Life in South Kanara. In : *Mangalapex-76 Souvenir; South Kanara District Philatelic Exhibition, 1976; at Catholic Club, Mangalore, from 12th March to 14th March, 1976,* pp. 49-51 + 2 pages of plates. Indian Posts and Telegraphs Department, Mangalore Postal Division.

Babb, Lawrence A. (1970a). The Food of the Gods in Chhattisgarh : Some Structural Features of Hindu Ritual. *Southwestern Journal of Anthropology* 26 : 287-304.

_____ (1970b). Marriage and Malevolence : the Uses of Sexual Opposition in a Hindu Pantheon. *Ethnology* 9(2) : 137-148.

_____ (1975). *The Divine Hierarchy : Popular Hinduism in Central India.* New York and London : Columbia University Press.

Bailey, H. W. (1961). Cognates of Pūjā. *The Adyar Library Bulletin* (Jubilee Volume) 25(1-4): 1-12.

Banerjee, Bhavani (1966). *Marriage and Kinship of the Gangadikara Vokkaligas of Mysore.* Poona : Deccan College Dissertation Series, No. 27.

Bangalore Press (1967). *Calendar.* Bangalore City.

Bean, Susan S. (1975). Referential and Indexical Meanings of *amma* in Kannada : Mother, Woman, Goddess, Pox, and Help ! *Journal of Anthropological Research* (formerly *Southwestern Journal of Anthropology*) 31(4) : 313-330.

_____ (1978). *Symbolic and Pragmatic Semantics.* Chicago and London : The University of Chicago Press.

Beck, Brenda E. F. (1969). Colour and Heat in South Indian Ritual. *Man* (n.s.); *The Journal of the Royal Anthropological Institute* 4(4) : 553-572.

_____ (1972). *Peasant Society in Koṅku; A Study of Right and Left Subcastes in South India.* Vancouver : University of British Columbia Press.

_____ (1974). The Kin Nucleus in Tamil Folklore. In : Thomas R. Trautmann (ed.), *Kinship and History in South Asia.* Michigan Papers on South and Southeast Asia (The University of Michigan), No. 7, pp. 1-27.

Bennett, Lynn (1983). *Dangerous Wives and Sacred Sisters; Social and Symbolic Roles of High-Caste Women in Nepal.* New York : Columbia University Press.

Berlin, Brent, and Paul Kay (1969). *Basic Colour Terms: Their Universality and Evolution.* Berkeley and Los Angeles : University of California Press.

Bhat, M. Mariappa (1968-1970). *Kittel's Kannada-English Dictionary,* 4 volumes. Madras : University of Madras.

Bhattacharyya, Asutosh (1960). Serpent Lore of Bengal: Introduction. *Folklore* (Calcutta) 1(2) : 105-112.

    (1961). The Serpent in Bengali Proverbs. *Folklore* (Calcutta) 2 : 329-342.

_____ (1965). The Serpent as a Folk-Deity in Bengal. *Asian Folklore Studies* 24(1) : 1-10.

Bødker, Laurits (1957). *Indian Animal Tales* : *A Preliminary Survey.* FF Communications No. 170. Helsinki : Suomalainen Tiedeakatemia, Academia Scientiarum Fennica.

Brubaker, Richard L. (1977). Lustful Woman, Chaste Wife, Ambivalent Goddess; A South Indian Myth. *Anima* 3(2) : 60-62.

Buck, David (1974). The Snake in the Song of a Sittar. In : Harry M. Buck and Glenn E. Yocum (eds.), *Structural Approaches to South India Studies,* pp. 162-183. Chambersburg, Pennsylvania : Wilson Books.

_____ (1976). *Dance, Snake! Dance! A Translation with Comments of the Song of Pāmpāṭṭi-Cittar.* Calcutta : P. Lal, A Writers Workshop Saffronbird Book.

Burrow, T. and M. B. Emeneau (1960). *A Dravidian Etymological Dictionary.* Oxford : Clarendon Press.

Carter, A. T. (1974). A Comparative Analysis of Systems of Kinship and Marriage in South India (Curl Prize Essay for 1973). *Proceedings of the Royal Anthropological Institute for 1973,* pp. 29-54.

Chatterji, Mohini M. (1960). *The Bhagavad Gita.* New York : Julian Press.

Chaudhary, G. V. (1968). *Vedic Numerology.* Bombay : Bharatiya Vidya Bhavan.

Claus, Peter J. (1975). The Siri Myth and Ritual: A Mass Possession Cult of South India. *Ethnology* 14 : 47-58.

Clothey, Fred (1969). Skanda-Saṣṭi : A Festival in Tamil India. *History of Religions* 8(3) : 236-259.

Contributions to Indian Sociology, No. III. July 1959 issue, edited by Louis Dumont and D. Pocock. Paris and The Hague : Mouton & Co.

Cook, Stanley Arthur (1911). Serpent-Worship. In : *The Encyclopaedia Britannica,* eleventh edition. Volume XXIII, pp. 676-682.

Crooke, W. (1896). *The Popular Religion and Folk-Lore of Northern India,* revised edition, 2 volumes (reprinted 1968). Delhi : Munshiram Manoharlal.

Daniélou, Alain (1964). *Hindu Polytheism.* Bollingen Series LXXIII. New York : Pantheon Books.

Das, Veena (1977a). On the Categorization of Space in Hindu Ritual. In : Ravindra K. Jain (ed.), *Text and Context; The Social Anthropology of Tradition.* A.S.A. Essays in Social Anthropology, Vol. 2, pp. 9-27. Philadelphia : Institute for the Study of Human Issues.

_____ (1977b). *Structure and Cognition; Aspects of Hindu Caste and Ritual.* Delhi : Oxford University Press.

David, Kenneth (1973). Until Marriage Do Us Part : A Cultural Account of Jaffna Tamil Categories for Kinsman. *Man; Journal of the Royal Anthropological Institute* 8(4) : 521-535.

Dell, David, Thomas Hopkins, Suzanne Hanchett, *et al.* (1981). *Guide to Hindu Religion.* Boston : G. K. Hall & Co.

Dentan, Robert Knox (1968). *The Semai; A Nonviolent People of Malaya.* New York : Holt, Rinehart & Winston.

Diehl, Carl Gustav (1956). *Instrument and Purpose*; *Studies on Rites and Rituals in South India*. Lund : CWK Gleerup.

Dimock, Edward C., Jr. (1962). The Goddess of Snakes in Medieval Bengali Literature. *History of Religions* 1 : 307-321.

———— (1969). Manasa, Goddess of Snakes : The Sasthi Myth. In : Joseph M. Kitagawa and Charles H. Long (eds.), *Myths and Symbols* : *Studies in Honor of Mircea Eliade*, pp. 217-222. Chicago : University of Chicago Press.

Dimock, Edward C., Jr., and A. K. Ramanujan (1964). The Goddess of Snakes in Medieval Bengali Literature, Part 2. *History of Religions* 3 : 300-322.

Douglas, Mary (1966). *Purity and Danger*; *An Analysis of Concepts of Pollution and Taboo*. London; Routledge and Kegan Paul, Ltd.

Dube, S. C. (1955). *Indian Village*. London : Routledge and Kegan Paul, Ltd.

———— (1963). Men's and Women's Roles in India ; A Sociological Review. *In* : Barbara E. Ward [Barbara Jackson] (ed.), *Women in the New Asia*, pp. 174-228. Paris : United Nations Educational, Scientific and Cultural Organization.

Dubois, Abbe J. A. (Henry K. Beauchamp, trans. and editor) (1906). *Hindu Manners, Customs and Ceremonies*. Oxford : Clarendon Press, third edition.

Dumont, Louis (1957a). *Hierarchy and Marriage Alliance in South Indian Kinship*. Occasional Papers of the Royal Anthropological Institute, No. 12.

———— (1957b). *Une sous-caste de l'Inde du sud*; *Organisation sociale et religion des Pramalai Kallar*. Etudes No. 1, Première Série, Le Monde d'Ôutre-mer Passé et Présent, École Pratique des Hautes Études, VIᵉ Section. Paris and The Hague : Mouton.

———— (1959). A Structural Definition of a Folk Deity of Tamil Nad : Aiyanar the Lord. *Contributions to Indian Sociology* III : 75-87.

———— (1970). *Homo Hierarchicus*. Chicago : University of Chicago Press. (Mark Sainsbury, translator)

———— (1975). Terminology and Prestations Revisited. *Contributions to Indian Sociology* (*n.s.*) 9(2) : 197-215.

Dumont, Louis, and D. Pocock (1959). Pure and Impure. *Contributions to Indian Sociology* III : 9-39.

Durkheim, Emile (Joseph Ward Swain, translator) (1915). *The Elementary Forms of the Religious Life*. London : George Allen and Unwin, Ltd.

Durkheim, Emile (D. F. Pocock, translator) (1953). *Sociology and Philosophy*. Glencoe, Illinois : The Free Press.

Eberhard, Wolfram (1968). *The Local Cultures of South and East China*. Leiden: E. J. Brill.

Eichinger Ferro-Luzzi, Gabriella (1974). Women's Pollution Periods in Tamilnadu (India). *Anthropos* 69 : 113-161.

———— (1977). Ritual as Language : The Case of South Indian Food Offerings. *Current Anthropology* 18(3) : 507-514.

Epstein, T. Scarlett (1960). Economic Development and Peasant Marriage in South India. *Man in India* 40 : 192-232.

———— (1962). *Economic Development and Social Change in South India*. Manchester University Press.

Erikson, Joan (1968). *Māta nī Pachedi*; *A Book on the Temple Cloth of the Mother Goddess*. Ahmedabad : National Institute of Design.

Evans-Wentz, W. Y. (1958). *Tibetan Yoga and Secret Doctrines*. New York : Oxford University Press.

Felton, Monica (1966). *A Child Widow's Story*. New York : Harcourt, Brace and World.

Femina Magazine (1973). Bengal; India's Chief Worshipper of Durga. *Femina*, October 12, 1973: 40-43, 55.

Fergusson, James (1873). *Tree and Serpent Worship*; *or Illustrations of Mythology and Art in*

India. London, Second edition.

Forster, E. M. (1952). *A Passage to India*. New York : Harcourt, Brace and World. (Originally published 1924.)

Freed, Ruth S., and Stanley A. Freed (1962). Two Mother Goddess Ceremonies of Delhi State in the Great and Little Traditions. *Southwestern Journal of Anthropology* **18** : 246-277.

_____(1964a). Calendars, Ceremonies, and Festivals in a North Indian Village : Necessary Calendrical Information for Fieldwork. *Southwestern Journal of Anthropology* **20**: 67-90.

_____(1964b). Spirit Possession as Illness in a Northern Indian Village. *Ethnology* **3** : 152-171.

_____(1980). Rites of Passage in Shanti Nagar. *Anthropological Papers of the American Museum of Natural History* (New York), **56**(3) : 323-554.

Freud, Sigmund (James Strachey, translator) (1961). *The Interpretation of Dreams*. New York : Science Editions, Inc.

Fuller, Mary (1944). Nag-Panchami. *Man in India* **24** : 75-81.

Geertz, Clifford (1973). The Impact of the Concept of Culture on the Concept of Man. In : *The Interpretation of Cultures; Selected Essays*, pp. 33-54. New York : Basic Books.

Ghosh, Manomohan, translator (1950). *Natyasastra*. Calcutta : Royal Society of Bengal.

Ghurye, G. S. (1962a). *Family and Kin in Indo-European Culture*, second edition. University of Bombay, Sociology Series; No. 4. London : Oxford University Press.

_____(1962b). *Gods and Men*. Bombay : Popular Book Depot.

Gluckman, Max (1962). Les Rites de Passage. In : Max Gluckman (ed.), *Essays on the Ritual of Social Relations*, pp. 1-52. New York : Humanities Press.

_____(1965). *Politics, Law and Ritual in Tribal Society*. Chicago : Aldine Publishing Company.

Gnanambal, K. (n.d.). *Festivals of India*. Calcutta : Anthropological Survey of India, Memoir No. 19 (ca. 1969).

Goodman, John Stuart (1963). Malayalam Color Categories. *Anthropological Linguistics* **5**(4) : 1-12.

Gough, E. Kathleen (1955). Female Initiation Rites on the Malabar Coast. *The Journal of the Royal Anthropological Institute* **85** : 45-80.

_____(1956). Brahman Kinship in a Tamil Village. *American Anthropologist* **58**(5) : 826-853.

_____(1958). Cults of the Dead Among the Nāyars. *Journal of American Folklore* **71**(281) : 446-478. (Traditional India : Structure and Change. Milton Singer, ed.).

Greenberg, Joseph H. (1969). Language Universals : A Research Frontier. *Science* **166**(3904): 473-478. (24 October 1969).

Gupta, Shakti M. (1971). *Plant Myths and Traditions in India*. Leiden : E. J. Brill.

Hallpike, C. R. (1969). Social Hair. *Man* (*n.s.*) **4**(2) : 256-264.

Hanchett, Suzanne L. (1971). *Changing Economic, Social, and Ritual Relationships in a Modern South Indian Village*. New York : Columbia University, Ph. D. dissertation.

_____(1972). Festivals and Social Relations in a Mysore Village : Mechanics of Two Processions. *Economic and Political Weekly* (Bombay) **VII**(31-33) : 1517-1522.

_____(1974). Reflections and Oppositions : On Structuralism. In : Harry M. Buck and Glenn E. Yocum (eds.), *Structural Approaches to South Indian Studies*, pp. 5-16. Chambersburg, Pennsylvania : Wilson Books.

_____(1975). Hindu Potlatches : Ceremonial Reciprocity and Prestige in South India. In : Helen E. Ullrich (ed.), *Competition and Modernization in South Asia*, pp. 27-59. Delhi : Abhinav.

_____(1976). Land Tenure and Social Change in a Mysore Village. In : S. Devadas Pillai (ed.), *Changing India : Studies in Honour of Professor G. S. Ghurye*, pp. 181-188. Bombay : Popular Prakashan.

Hanchett, Suzanne L. (1978a). Five Books in Symbolic Anthropology. *American Anthropologist* 80(3) : 613-621.

_____ (1978b). Recent Trends in the Study of Folk Hinduism and India's Folklore. *Journal of Indian Folkloristics* (Mysore) 1(1) : 40-54.

Hanchett, Suzanne, and Leslie Casale (1976). The Theory of Transitional Phenomena and Cultural Symbols. *Contemporary Psychoanalysis* (New York) 12(4) : 496-507.

Handoo, Jawaharlal (1977) : *A Bibliography of Indian Folk Literature.* Mysore : Central Institute of Indian Languages, CIIL Folklore Series, No. 2.

Harper, Edward B. (1959). A Hindu Village Pantheon. *Southwestern Journal of Anthropology* 15 : 227-234.

_____ (1964). Ritual Pollution as an Integrator of Caste and Religion. In : Edward B. Harper (ed.), *Religion in South Asia,* pp. 151-196. Seattle : University of Washington Press.

_____ (1969). Fear and the Status of Women. *Southwestern Journal of Anthropology* 25 : 81-95.

Harper, Edward B. (ed.) (1964a). *Religion in South Asia.* Seattle : University of Washington Press.

Hart, George L., III (1973a). *The Poems of Ancient Tamil; Their Milieu and Their Sanskrit Counterparts.* Berkeley, Los Angeles, and London : University of California Press.

_____ (1973b). Woman and the Sacred in Ancient Tamilnadu. *Journal of Asian Studies* 32(2) : 233-250.

Hayavadana Rao, C. (ed.) (1930). *Mysore Gazetteer,* Volume V. Bangalore : Government Press, new edition.

Hershman, P. (1974). Hair, Sex and Dirt. *Man* (n.s.); *Journal of the Royal Anthropological Institute* 9(2) : 274-298.

Hopkins, Thomas J. (1971). *The Hindu Religious Tradition.* Encino, California : Dickenson Publishing Co.

Inden, Ronald B., and Ralph W. Nicholas (1977). *Kinship in Bengali Culture.* Chicago and London : University of Chicago Press.

Irschick, Eugene F. (1969). *Politics and Social Conflict in South India; The Non-Brahmin Movement and Tamil Separatism, 1916-1929.* Berkeley : University of California Press.

Iyengar, Masti Venkatesa (1943). Masumatti. In : *Short Stories,* Four Volumes, Volume I, pp. 164-184. Bangalore.

Jacobs, Joseph (1969). *Indian Fairy Tales.* New York : Dover Publications. (Originally published in 1892 by David Nutt, London).

Jacobson, Doranne (1976). Women and Jewelry in Rural India. In : Giri Raj Gupta (ed.), *Main Currents in Indian Sociology,* Vol. II : *Family and Social Change in India,* pp. 135-183. New Delhi : Vikas Publishing House Pvt Ltd.

_____ (1977). The Women of North and Central India : Goddesses and Wives. In : *Women in India; Two Perspectives,* by Doranne Jacobson and Susan S. Wadley, pp. 17-111. Delhi : Manohar.

_____ (1978). The Chaste Wife : Cultural Norm and Individual Experience. In : Sylvia Vatuk (ed.), *American Studies in the Anthropology of India,* pp. 95-138. New Delhi : Manohar, and the American Institute of Indian Studies.

Kakar, Sudhir (1978). *The Inner World : A Psycho-Analytic Study of Childhood and Society in India.* Delhi, Oxford, and New York : Oxford University Press.

Kane, Pandurang Vaman (1930-1962). *History of Dharma Sastra;* Five Volumes in Seven. Poona [Poone] : Bhandarkar Oriental Research.

Kapadia, K. M. (1966). *Marriage and Family in India,* third edition. London : Oxford University Press.

Karve, Irawati (1965). *Kinship Organization in India,* second revised edition. Bombay : Asia

Publishing House.

Khare, R. S. (1976a). *Culture and Reality*; *Essays on the Hindu System of Managing Food*. Simla : Indian Institute of Advanced Study.

_____(1976b). *The Hindu Hearth and Home*. New Delhi : Vikas Publishing House Pvt Ltd.

Kirfel, W. (1961). Zahlen— und Farbensymbole (Numerical and Colour Symbols). *Saeculum* **12**(3) : 237-247.

Kitagawa, Joseph M. (1969). Ainu Myth. In : Joseph M. Kitagawa and Charles H. Long (eds.), *Myths and Symbols*; *Studies in Honor of Mircea Eliade*, pp. 309-323. Chicago : University of Chicago Press.

Klass, Morton (1966). Marriage Rules in Bengal. *American Anthropologist* **68**(4) : 951-970.

_____(1978). *From Field to Factory*; *Community Structure and Industrialization in West Bengal*. Philadelphia : Institute for the Study of Human Issues.

Kolenda, Pauline M. (1967). Regional Differences in Indian Family Structure. In : Robert I. Crane (ed.), *Regions ana Regionalism in South Asian Studies* : *an Explanatory Study*, pp. 147-226. Duke University Monograph and Occasional Papers Series, Monograph No. 5.

_____(1968). Region, Caste, and Family Structure : A Comparative Study of the Indian "Joint" Family. In : Milton Singer and Bernard S. Cohn (eds.), *Structure and Change in Indian Society*, pp. 339-396. Viking Fund Publications in Anthropology, No. 47.

Köngäs-Maranda, Elli (1971). The Logic of Riddles. In : Pierre Maranda and Elli Köngäs-Maranda (eds.), *Structural Analysis of Oral Tradition*, pp. 189-232. Philadelphia : University of Pennsylvania Press.

Lane, Michael (ed.) (1970). *Structuralism : a Reader*. London : Jonathan Cape. (Also available as *Introduction to Structuralism*. New York : Basic Books.)

Langer, Susanne K. (1953). *Feeling and Form*. New York : Charles Scribner's Sons, paperback edition.

_____(1957). *Philosophy in a New Key*. Cambridge, Massachusetts : Harvard University Press, paperback edition.

Lannoy, Richard (1971). *The Speaking Tree*; *A Study of Indian Culture and Society*. London: Oxford University Press.

Laplanche, J., and J.—B. Pontalis (Donald Nicholson-Smith, trans.) (1973). *The Language of Psycho-Analysis*. New York : W. W. Norton and Co., Inc.

Leach, Edmund R. (1958). Magical Hair (Curl Bequest Prize Essay for 1957). *Journal of the Royal Anthropological Institute* **88**(II) : 147-164.

_____(1970). A Critique of Yalman's Interpretation of Sinhalese Girl's Puberty Ceremonial. In : Jean Pouillon and Pierre Maranda eds.), *Échanges et communications* : *Mélanges offerts a Claude Lévi-Strauss a l'occasion de son 60éme anniversaire*, pp. 819-828. The Hague and Paris : Mouton.

Leach, Edmund R. (ed.) (1967). *The Structural Study of Myth and Totemism*. London : Tavistock Publications.

Lévi-Strauss, Claude (1955). The Structural Study of Myth. In : Thomas A. Sebeok (ed.), *Myth*; *A Symposium*, pp. 81-106. Bloomington and London : Indiana University Press.

_____(1963). *Structural Anthropology* (Claire Jacobson and Brooke Grundfest Schoepf, translators). New York : Basic Books, Inc.

_____(1966). The Culinary Triangle (translated by Peter Brooks). *Partisan Review* **33**(4) : 586-595.

_____(1969a). *The Elementary Structures of Kinship* (*Les Structures élémentaires de la parenté*) (translated by James Harle Bell, John Richard von Sturmer, and Rodney Needham, editor), revised edition. London : Eyre and Spottiswoode.

_____(1969b). *The Raw and the Cooked*; *Introduction to a Science of Mythology* : I. (John and Doreen Weightman, translators). New York : Harper and Row.

Lévi-Strauss, Claude (1976a). The Scope of Anthropology (translated by Monique Layton). In : *Structural Anthropology*, Volume II, pp. 3-32. New York : Basic Books.

_____ (1976b). Structure and Form : Reflections on a Work by Vladimir Propp (translated by Monique Layton). In : *Structural Anrhropology*, Volume II, pp. 115-145. New York : Basic Books.

Lewis, I. M. (1971) . *Ecstatic Religion; An Anthropological Study of Spirit Possession an Shamanism.* Middlesex, England ; Penguin Books.

Lewis, Oscar (1956). The Festival in a North Indian Jat Village. *Proceedings of the American Philosophical Society* 100(3) : 168-196.

_____ (ed.) (1958). *Village Life in Northern India; Studies in a Delhi Village.* Urbana : University of Illinois Press.

Long, J. Bruce (1976). Life Out of Death : A Structural Analysis of the Myth of the 'Churning of the Ocean of Milk'. In : Bardwell L. Smith (ed.), *Hinduism; New Essays in the History of Religions,* pp. 171-207. Leiden ; E. J. Brill.

Luschinsky, Mildred Stroop (1969). *The Life of Women in a Village of North India; A Study of Role and Status.* Ithaca,. New York : Cornell University; Ph.D. dissertation.

Lynch, Owen (1962). Dr. Ambedkar—Myth and Charisma. In : J. Michael Mahar (ed.), *The Untouchables in Contemporary India,* pp. 97-112. Tucson : University of Arizona Press.

Madan, T. N. (1980). Concerning the Categories *Shubha* and *Shuddha* in Hindu Culture; Some Notes and Queries. Washington, D.C. : Paper presented at annual meetings of Conference on Religion in South India. Draft, 31 pp.

Mahapatra, Piyushkanti (1969). Ancient Jaina Women and Their Folk-Life. In : Sankar Sen Gupta (ed.), *Women in Indian Folklore,* pp. 33-40. Calcutta : Indian Publications.

Majumdar, D. N. (1950) *Affairs of a Tribe.* Lucknow : The Universal Publishers, Ltd.

Majumdar, M. R. (1969). Women in Gujarati Folklore. In : Sankar Sen Gupta (ed.), *Women in Indian Folklore,* pp. 138-156. Calcutta : Indian Publications.

Mandelbaum, David G. (1970). *Society in India,* 2 volumes. Berkeley : University of California Press.

Marglin, Frédérique (1980). *Wives of the God-King : The Rituals of Hindu Temple Courtesans.* Waltham, Massachusetts : Brandeis University, Ph.D. dissertation.

Marriott, McKim (1976a). Hindu Transactions : Diversity Without Dualism. In : Bruce Kapferer (ed.), *Transaction and Meaning,* pp. 109-142. Philadelphia : Institute for the Study of Human Issues.

_____ (1976b). Interpreting Indian Society : A Monistic Alternative to Dumont's Dualism. *The Journal of Asian Studies* 36(1) : 189-195.

Marriott, McKim, and Ronald B. Inden (1974). Caste Systems. In : *Encyclopaedia Britannica,* 15th edition. *Macropaedia,* Volume 3, pp. 982-991. Chicago : Encyclopaedia Britannica, Inc.

Mauss, Marcel (Ian Cunnison, translator) (1954). *The Gift : Forms and Functions of Exchange in Archaic Societies.* Glencoe, Illinois : The Free Press.

Meenakshi Ammal, S. (A. V. Padma, translator) (1968). *Cook and See* ("Samaithu par"), Part 1. (*The Book on South India Vegetarian Recipes.*) Madras : S. Meenakshi Ammal Publications, "Samaithu Par" House.

Murphy, Robert F. (1971). *The Dialectics of Social Life : Alarms and Excursions in Anthropological Theory.* New York : Basic Books, Inc.

Mysore Government Press (1965). *Calendar for 1966 (Rashtriya Panchanga—Saka Era 1887-88, Salivahana Saka 1888-89, Sri Visvavasu, and Sri Parabhava, Hijri 1385-86, Fasli Year 1375-76).* Bangalore.

Nagendra, S. P. (1971). *The Concept of Ritual in Modern Sociological Theory.* New Delhi Academic Journals of India.

Nair, P. Thankappan (1965). Tree-symbol Worship Among the Nairs of Kerala. In : Sankar Sen Gupta (ed.), *Tree Symbol Worship*, pp. 93-103. Calcutta : Indian Publications.

Newell, William H. (1968). Some Comparative Features of Chinese and Japanese Ancestor Worship. *Proceedings VIIIth International Congress of Anthropological and Enthnological Sciences, 1968, Tokyo and Kyoto*, Volume III; *Ethnology and Archaeology*, pp. 300-301. Tokyo ; Science Council of Japan.

Newell, William H. (Ed.) (1976). *Ancestors*. Chicago, Illinois : Aldine.

Nichter, Mark (1977). *Health Ideologies and Medical Culture in the South Kanara Areca-Nut Belt*. Edinburgh : University of Edinburgh, Ph.D. dissertation, 2 vols.

Nilakanta Sastri, K. A. (1966). *A History of South India from Prehistoric Times to the Fall of Vijayanagar*. London : Oxford University Press.

O'Flaherty, Wendy Doniger (1973). *Asceticism and Eroticism in the Mythology of Siva*. London : Oxford University Press, (Reprinted in 1981 as Śiva; the *Erotic Ascetic*.)

_____(1978). Sexual Fluids in the Vedas and Purāṇas. Unpublished manuscript, 45 pp. Chicago : The University of Chicago, Divinity School.

Omvedt, Gail, and Eleanor Zelliot (1978). Introduction to Dalit Poems. *Bulletin of Concerned Asian Scholars* 10(3) : 2-11.

Opler, Morris E. (1959). Family, Anxiety, and Religion in a Community of North India. In: Marvin K. Opler (ed.), *Culture and Mental Health; Cross Cultural Studies*, pp. 273-289. New York : The MacMillan Company.

Orenstein, Henry (1970). Death and Kinship in Hinduism : Structural and Functional Interpretations. *American Anthropologist* 72(6) : 1357-1377.

Ortner, Sherry (1973). On Key Symbols. *American Anthropologist* 75 : 1338-1346.

Parvathamma, C. (1971). *Politics and Religion (A Study of Historial Interaction between Socio-political Relationships in a Mysore Village)*. New Delhi : Sterling Publishers (P) Ltd.

Piaget, Jean (Chaninah Maschler, translator and editor) (1971). *Structuralism*. New York : Harper and Row, Publishers.

Propp, V. (1968). *Morphology of the Folktale* (translated by Laurence Scott, second English language edition, revised and edited by Louis A. Wagner). Austin and London: University of Texas Press.

Ramanujan, A. K. (1967). *The Interior Landscape; Love Poems from a Classical Tamil Anthology*, translated by A. K. Ramanujan. Bloomington and London : Indiana University Press.

_____(1973). *Speaking of Śiva*, translated with an introduction by A. K. Ramanujan. Baltimore, Maryland : Penguin Books.

_____(n.d.). Kannada Folktales. Manuscript in preparation.

Regelson, Stanley (1972). *Some Aspects of Food Behaviour in a South Indian Village*. New York : Columbia University, Ph.D. dissertation.

Robinson, Marguerite S. (1968). 'The House of the Mighty Hero' or 'The House of Enough Paddy'? Some Implications of a Sinhalese Myth. In. E. R. Leach (ed.), *Dialectic in Practical Religion*, pp. 122-152. Cambridge Papers in Social Anthropology, No. 5. (Reprinted in Lane 1970 : 293-329.)

Roghair, Gene H. (1977). *The Epic of Palnāḍu : A Study and Translation of Palnāṭi Virula Katha, A Telugu Oral Tradition as Sung by Āliśeṭṭi Galeyya*. Madison, Wisconsin : University of Wisconsin, Ph.D. dissertation, 2 vols.

Rosman, Abraham, and Paula G. Rubel (1971). *Feasting with Mine Enemy : Rank and Exchange Among Northwest Coast Societies*. New York : Columbia University Press.

Sahlins, Marshall (1977). Colors and Cultures. In : Janet L. Dolgin, David S. Kemnitzer, and David M. Schneider (eds.), *Symbolic Anthropology; A Reader in the Study of Symbols and Meanings*, pp. 165-180. New York : Columbia University Press. (Reprinted from *Semiotica* 16 : 1-22, 1976).

Sakala, Carol (1980). *Women of South Asia*; *A Guide to Resources*. Millwood, New York : Kraus International Publications.

Saldanha, Cecil J., and Dan H. Nicolson (Eds.) (1976). *Flora of Hassan District Karnataka, India*. New Delhi, New York, etc. : Amerind Publishing Co. Pvt. Ltd.

Sampath Iyengar, G. S. (compiler) (1977). *Calendar*. Madras : Professor K. Srinivasa Raghavan (Principal, Bharath Chronological Institute), Publisher.

Sarana, Gopala (n. d.). Professor Majumdar and Anthropology of Indian Religion. In : L.P. Vidyarthi (ed.), *Aspects of Religion in Indian Society*, pp. 1-12. Meerut : Kedar Nath Ram Nath (1961 or 1962).

Sastri, Laksminarasimha (compiler) (1961). *Satīka Vrataratnam*. Bangalore : T.N. Krishnaiah Setty and Sons.

Selwyn, Tom (1979). Images of Reproduction : An Analysis of a Hindu Marriage Ceremony. *Man* (n. s.); *Journal of the Royal Anthropological Institute* 14(4) : 684-698.

Sen Gupta, Sankar (ed.) (1965). *Tree Symbol Worship in India*; *A New Survey of a Pattern of Folk-Religion*. Calcutta : Indian Publications.

_____(1967). *A Bibliography of Indian Folklore and Related Subjects*. Calcutta : Indian Publications.

_____(1969). *Women in Indian Folklore . . . .* Calcutta : Indian Publications.

Sharma, Ursula M. (1970). The Problem of Village Hinduism : 'Fragmentation' and 'Integration'. *Contributions to Indian Sociology* (n. s.) 4 : 1-22.

Shastri, J. L. (ed.) (1970). *The Śiva-Purāna*, translated by a board of scholars. 4 vols. Delhi : Motilal Banarsidass.

Simmel, Georg (Kurt H. Wolff and Reinhard Bendix, translators). (1955). *Conflict*; *The Web of Group Affiliations*. New York : The Free Press.

Smith, Robert John (1974). *Ancestor Worship in Contemporary Japan*. Stanford, California : Standford University Press.

Sperber, Dan (Alice L. Morton, translator) (1975). *Rethinking Symbolism*. Cambridge : Cambridge Universtiy Press.

Sreenivasa Murthy, H. V., and R. Ramakrishnan (1977). *A History of Karnataka* (*From the Earliest Times to the Present Day*). New Delhi : S. Chand and Company, Ltd.

Srinivas, M. N. (1965). *Religion and Society Among the Coorgs of South India*. Bombay : Asia Publishing House. (Reprint of 1952 edition.)

_____(1977). The Changing Position of Indian Women. *Man* (n.s.); *Journal of the Royal Anthropological Institute* 12(2) : 221-238.

Steed, Gitel P. (1955). Notes on an Approach to a Study of Personality Formation in a Hindu Village in Gujarat. In : McKim Marriott (ed.), *Village India*; *Studies in the Little Community*, pp. 102-144. Chicago and London : University of Chicago Press.

Tambaiah, S. J. (1973a). Dowry and Bridewealth, and the Property Rights of Women in South Asia. In : *Bridewealth and Dowry*, by Jack Goody and S. J. Tambaiah, pp. 59-169. Cambridge Papers in Social Anthropology, No. 7.

_____(1973b). Form and Meaning in Magical Acts : A Point of View. In : Robin Horton and Ruth Finnegan (eds.), *Modes of Thought*. London : Faber and Faber.

Thapar, Romila (1966). *A History of India*, Volume I. Middlesex, England : Penguin Books.

Thompson, Stith (1946). *The Folktale*. New York : Holt, Rinehart and Winston.

Thompson, Stith, and Jonas Balys (1958). *The Oral Tales of India*. Indiana University Publications, Folklore Series, No. 10. Bloomington : Indiana University Press.

Thompson, Stith, and Warren E. Roberts (1960). *Types of Indic Oral Tales*; *India, Pakistan, and Ceylon*. FF Communications, No. 180. Helsinki : Suomalainen Tiedeakatemia, Academia Scientiarum Fennica.

Thurston, Edgar (assisted by K. Rangachari) (1909). *Castes and Tribes of Southern India*, 7 volumes. Madras : Government Press.

Turner, Victor W. (1966). Colour Classification in Ndembu Ritual; A Problem in Primitive Classification. In : Michael Banton (ed.), *Anthropological Approaches to the Study of Religion*. A.S.A. Monographs, No. 3 (London : Tavistock Publications), pp. 47-84. (Reprinted as Chapter III of *The Forest of Symbols*, by Victor Turner. Ithaca : Cornell University Press, 1967.)

_____(1969). *The Ritual Process : Structure and Anti-Structure*. Chicago : Aldine Publishing Company.

_____(1974). *Dramas, Fields, and Metaphors*. Ithaca : Cornell University Press.

Tyler, Stephen A. (1973). *India : An Anthropological Perspective*. Pacific Palisades, California : Goodyear Publishing Co.

Ullman, Stephen (1962). *The Principles of Semantics*. Oxford : Basil Blackwell.

Ullrich, Helen E. (1975)· Women in Selected Kannada Folktales. In: Giri Raj Gupta (ed.), *Main Currents in Indian Sociology*, Volume II. New Delhi : Vikas Publishing House.

_____(1977). Caste Differences and Female Roles in a South Indian Village. In : Alice Schlegel (ed.), *Sexual Stratification : A Cross Cultural View*. New York : Columbia University Press.

_____(1980). Changing Attitudes Towards Marriage Among Havik Brahmins. *Social Action* 30.

Underhill, M. M. (1921). *The Hindu Religious Year*. London : Oxford University Press.

Vanamalai, N. (1969). Women in Tamil Folklore. In : Sankar Sen Gupta (ed.), *Women in Indian Folklore*, pp. 1-19. Calcutta : Indian Publications.

Vatuk, Sylvia (1975). Gifts and Affines in North India. *Contributions to Indian Sociology* (n. s.) 9(2) : 155-196.

Veeraswamy, E. P. (1936). *Indian Cookery for Use in All Countries*. (Reprinted, 1953) London : Arco Publishers Limited.

Vidyarthi, L. P. (ed.) (n. d.). *Aspects of Religion in Indian Society*. Meerut : Kedar Nath Ram Nath. (Foreword dated 1961.)

Vogel, J. Ph. (1926). *Indian Serpent Lore*. London : A. Probsthain. (Reprinted in 1972, Varanasi : Prithivi Prakashan)

Wadley, Susan Snow (1975). *Shakti; Power in the Conceptual Structure of Karimpur Religion*. Chicago : Department of Anthropology, University of Chicago.

_____(ed.) (1975a). Folk Literature of South Asia. *Journal of South Asian Literature* 11(1, 2).

_____(ed.) (1980). *The Powers of Tamil Women*. Syracuse, New York : Syracuse University, Maxwell School of Citizenship and Public Affairs; Foreign and Comparative Studies/ South Asian Series, No. 6.

Whitehead, Henry (1921). *The Village Gods of South India*, second edition. Calcutta : Association Press, and London : Oxford University Press.

Wilkins, W. J. (1975). *Hindu Mythology, Vedic and Purānic*, second edition. Delhi etc. : Rupa and Co.

Williams, C. A. S. (1941). *Outlines of Chinese Symbolism and Art Motives*, third revised edition. Shanghai : Kelly and Walsh, Ltd.

Wilson, H. H. (translator) (1961). *The Vishnu Purāna; A System of Hindu Mythology and Tradition*, third edition. Calcutta : Punthi Pustak.

Witkowski, Stanley R., and Cecil H. Brown (1977). An Explanation of Color Nomenclature Universals. *American Anthropologist* 79(1) : 50-57.

Yalman, Nur (1962). The Structure of the Sinhalese Kindred : a Re-examination of the Dravidian Terminology. *American Anthropologist* 64(3) : 548-575.

_____(1963). On the Purity of Women in the Castes of Ceylon and Malabar; The Curl Bequest Prize Essay, 1961. *Journal of the Royal Anthropological Institute* 93(I) : 25-58.

Yalman, Nur (1969a). On the Meaning of Food Offerings in Ceylon. In : *Forms of Symbolic Action; Proceedings of the 1969 Annual Spring Meeting of the American Ethnological Society*, pp. 81-96. Seattle : University of Washington Press.

_____(1969b). The Semantics of Kinship in South India and Ceylon. In : Thomas A. Sebeok, (ed.), *Current Trends in Linguistics*, Volume 5 : *Linguistics in South Asia*. The Hague : Mouton and Co.

Zimmer, F. A. (1971). Green is for Coolness, Yellow for Good Auspices. *Natural History* **80**(1) : 54-59. New York : American Museum of Natural History.

Zimmer, Heinrich (1946). *Myths and Symbols in Indian Art and Civilization*, edited by Joseph Campbell. Princeton, New Jersey : Princeton University Press.

INDEX

A. K. (Adikarnataka) jati, ancestor worship customs of, 209; Bandipur jatis of, 9-10; Cobra Festival rituals of, 236; Colony, Maramma Festival of, 157; local sacrifice of, 10; replicate ritual service division of labour, 41

Affines. *See* Relations of exchange

Agriculture, 10-11, 14; and fertility, themes in myth, 172; harvesting symbolism, 276; processes of, as metaphors, 58, 170; references to, in goddess names, 167; rituals, 180; seasons, cycle of, 43. *See also* Grain; Land; Plants

Aksate. *See* Rice

Amma deities. *See* Deities and spirits

Ancestors, 37, 161, 277; anger of, 194; associated with serpents, 216; bowing to, 204; food for, 245; housed in shrines or not, 38-39; hunger of, 194; impersonated, 37; individual memorialism of, 193; known founders of local families. 16, 26; male and female, 194, 197, 200, 201; meals for, 180; meat offerings to, 209; photographs of, 192-93; pinda balls for, 207; shrine for, in house, 198; similar to gods, 193; status of, transition to, 27, 148. *See also* Festivals, Pitra Paksa; Foods

Ancestors, propitiation of, 180, 214; Brahman compared to oth rs, 197; caste variation in, 192; Japanese compared with Hindu, 193; at Mahalaya New Moon, 191

Anger, 286; of ancestors, 194; of goddess, 160, 169, 172, 275; of holy man, 267; of serpent spirit, 160, 230, 233, 245, 277

Animals, birds, 205; buffalo, 289-290; dogs, 205; male and female, for ancestors, 209;

talking, in myth 252. *See also* Cattle; Sacrifice

Ant-hill, 230; as metaphor for human body, 235; earth from, for puja, 234, 241; in Sibling Group Festival, 257; inhabited by serpents, 234; mud, eating of, 257; shrine, 234. *See also* Festivals; Cobra Festival; Serpent

Arati, 140, 200; gatherings, Brahman, 35-36, 138; rotation of incense, 137; rotation of lamps, 35, 117, 118; with red liquid, 62, 123-124; with turmeric water, 139

Ashton, Martha, 291-292

Astronomy and astrology, 40, 90, 191, 232. *See also* Calendar; Stars

Atharva Veda, 191, 232

Atman, 57

Auspicious, impurity, 277; state, as family well-being, 188; state, goal of family festivals, 153-154; symbols and gestures, for married daughter, 123. *See also* Auspiciousness; Inauspicious

Auspicious and inauspicious, numbers, 105; offerings, 163; symbols, 59; times of year, 40-41

Auspicious and semi-auspicious occasions 204, 219

Auspiciousness, 78, 202, 268, 277; as 'process', 274; of married woman, 73-74; of winnowing fan, 142

Babb, Lawrence A., 57, 187, 233

Banana. *See* Fruits

Bandipur Village, general description, 8. *See also* Community